Step Across This Line

SALMAN RUSHDIE

Step Across This Line

Collected Nonfiction 1992–2002

ALFRED A. KNOPF CANADA

PUBLISHED BY ALFRED A. KNOPF CANADA

Copyright © 2002 Salman Rushdie

National Library of Canada Cataloguing in Publication
Rushdie, Salman
Step across this line : essays, 1991–2002 / Salman Rushdie.
ISBN 0-676-97543-7
I. Title.
PR6068.U757A16   2002   824'.914   C2002-902855-8

First Edition

www.randomhouse.ca

Printed and bound in the United States of America on acid-free paper

246897531

TO CHRISTOPHER HITCHENS

Contents

PART I

Essays

Out of Kansas

I wrote my first short story in Bombay at the age of ten. Its title was "Over the Rainbow." It amounted to a dozen or so pages, was dutifully typed up by my father's secretary on flimsy paper, and was eventually lost somewhere along my family's mazy journeyings between India, England, and Pakistan. Shortly before my father's death in 1987, he claimed to have found a copy moldering in an old file, but despite my pleadings he never produced it. I've often wondered about this incident. Maybe he never really found the story, in which case he had succumbed to the lure of fantasy, and this was the last of the many fairy tales he told me. Or else he did find it, and hugged it to himself as a talisman and a reminder of simpler times, thinking of it as his treasure, not mine—his pot of nostalgic, parental gold.

I don't remember much about the story. It was about a ten-year-old Bombay boy who one day happens upon the beginning of a rainbow, a place as elusive as any pot-of-gold end zone, and as rich in promise. The rainbow is broad, as wide as the sidewalk, and constructed like a grand staircase. Naturally, the boy begins to climb. I have forgotten almost everything about his adventures, except for an encounter with a talking pianola whose personality is an improbable hybrid of Judy Garland, Elvis Presley, and the "playback singers" of the Hindi movies, many of which made *The Wizard of Oz* look like kitchen-sink realism.

My bad memory—what my mother would call a "forgettery"—is

probably a blessing. Anyway, I remember what matters. I remember that *The Wizard of Oz* (the film, not the book, which I didn't read as a child) was my very first literary influence. More than that: I remember that when the possibility of my going to school in England was mentioned, it felt as exciting as any voyage over rainbows. England felt as wonderful a prospect as Oz.

The wizard, however, was right there in Bombay. My father, Anis Ahmed Rushdie, was a magical parent of young children, but he was also prone to explosions, thunderous rages, bolts of emotional lightning, puffs of dragon smoke, and other menaces of the type also practiced by Oz, the great and terrible, the first Wizard Deluxe. And when the curtain fell away and we, his growing offspring, discovered (like Dorothy) the truth about adult humbug, it was easy for us to think, as she did, that our wizard must be a very bad man indeed. It took me half a lifetime to discover that the Great Oz's *apologia pro vita sua* fitted my father equally well; that he too was a good man but a very bad wizard.

I have begun with these personal reminiscences because *The Wizard of Oz* is a film whose driving force is the inadequacy of adults, even of good adults. At its beginning, the weaknesses of grown-ups force a child to take control of her own destiny (and her dog's). Thus, ironically, she begins the process of becoming a grown-up herself. The journey from Kansas to Oz is a rite of passage from a world in which Dorothy's parent-substitutes, Auntie Em and Uncle Henry, are powerless to help her save her dog, Toto, from the marauding Miss Gulch, into a world where the people are her own size, and in which she is never treated as a child but always treated as a heroine. She gains this status by accident, it's true, having played no part in her house's decision to squash the Wicked Witch of the East; but by the end of her adventure she has certainly grown to fill those shoes—or, rather, those famous ruby slippers. "Who'd have thought a girl like you could destroy my beautiful wickedness?" laments the Wicked Witch of the West as she melts—an adult becoming smaller than, and giving way to, a child. As the Wicked Witch of the West "grows down," so Dorothy is seen to have grown up. In my view, this is a much more satisfactory explanation for Dorothy's newfound power over the ruby slippers than the sentimental reasons offered by the ineffably soppy Good Witch Glinda, and then by Dorothy herself, in a cloying ending that I find untrue to the film's anarchic spirit. (More about this later.)

The helplessness of Auntie Em and Uncle Henry in the face of Miss

Gulch's desire to annihilate Toto the dog leads Dorothy to think, child-ishly, of running away from home—of escape. And that's why, when the tornado hits, she isn't with the others in the storm shelter, and as a result is whirled away to an escape beyond her wildest dreams. Later, however, when she is confronted by the weakness of the Wizard of Oz, she doesn't run away but goes into battle—first against the Witch and then against the Wizard himself. The Wizard's ineffectuality is one of the film's many symmetries, rhyming with the feebleness of Dorothy's folks; but the difference in the way Dorothy reacts is the point.

The ten-year-old boy who watched *The Wizard of Oz* in Bombay's Metro cinema knew very little about foreign parts and even less about growing up. He did, however, know a great deal more about the cinema of the fantastic than any Western child of the same age. In the West, *The Wizard of Oz* was an oddball, an attempt to make a live-action version of a Disney cartoon feature despite the industry's received wisdom (how times change!) that fantasy movies usually flopped. There's little doubt that the excitement engendered by *Snow White and the Seven Dwarfs* ac-counts for MGM's decision to give the full, all-stops-out treatment to a thirty-nine-year-old book. This was not, however, the first screen version. I haven't seen the silent film of 1925, but its reputation is poor. It did, however, star Oliver Hardy as the Tin Man.

The Wizard of Oz never really made money until it became a televi-sion standard years after its original theatrical release, though it should be said in mitigation that coming out two weeks before the start of World War II can't have helped its chances. In India, however, it fitted into what was then, and remains today, one of the mainstreams of "Bollywood" film production.

It's easy to satirize the Indian commercial cinema industry. In James Ivory's film *Bombay Talkie,* a journalist (the touching Jennifer Kendal, who died in 1984) visits a studio soundstage and watches an amazing dance number featuring scantily clad nautch girls prancing on the keys of a giant typewriter. The director explains that this is no less than the Typewriter of Life, and we are all dancing out "the story of our Fate" upon that mighty machine. "It's very symbolic," the journalist suggests. The director, simpering, replies: "Thank you."

Typewriters of Life, sex goddesses in wet saris (the Indian equivalent of wet T-shirts), gods descending from the heavens to meddle in human affairs, magic potions, superheroes, demonic villains, and so on have always been the staple diet of the Indian filmgoer. Blond Glinda arriving in Munchkinland in her magic bubble might cause Dorothy to comment on the high speed and oddity of local transport operating in Oz, but to an Indian audience Glinda was arriving exactly as a god should arrive: *ex machina,* out of her divine machine. The Wicked Witch of the West's orange puffs of smoke were equally appropriate to her super-bad status. But in spite of all the similarities, there are important differences between the Bombay cinema and a film like *The Wizard of Oz.* Good fairies and bad witches might superficially resemble the deities and demons of the Hindu pantheon, but in reality one of the most striking aspects of the worldview of *The Wizard of Oz* is its joyful and almost complete secularism. Religion is mentioned only once in the film. Auntie Em, sputtering with anger at the gruesome Miss Gulch, reveals that she's waited years to tell her what she thinks of her, "and now, because I'm a good Christian woman, I can't do so." Apart from this moment, in which Christian charity prevents some old-fashioned plain speaking, the film is breezily godless. There's not a trace of religion in Oz itself. Bad witches are feared, good ones liked, but none are sanctified; and while the Wizard of Oz is thought to be something very close to all-powerful, nobody thinks to worship him. This absence of higher values greatly increases the film's charm and is an important aspect of its success in creating a world in which nothing is deemed more important than the loves, cares, and needs of human beings (and, of course, tin beings, straw beings, lions, and dogs).

The other major difference is harder to define, because it is, finally, a matter of quality. Most Hindi movies were then and are now what can only be called trashy. The pleasure to be had from such films (and some of them are extremely enjoyable) is something like the fun of eating junk food. The classic Bombay talkie uses scripts of dreadful corniness, looks tawdry and garish, and relies on the mass appeal of its star performers and musical numbers to provide a little zing. *The Wizard of Oz* also has movie stars and musical numbers, but it is also very definitely a Good Film. It takes the fantasy of Bombay and adds high production values and something more. Call it imaginative truth. Call it (reach for your revolvers now) art.

But if *The Wizard of Oz* is a work of art, it's extremely difficult to say who the artist was. The birth of Oz itself has already passed into legend: the author, L. Frank Baum, named his magic world after the letters O–Z on the bottom drawer of his filing cabinet. Baum had an odd, roller-coaster life. Born rich, he inherited a string of little theaters from his father and lost them all through mismanagement. He wrote one successful play and several flops. The Oz books made him one of the leading children's writers of his day, but all his other fantasy novels bombed. *The Wonderful Wizard of Oz,* and a musical adaptation of it for the stage, restored Baum's finances, but a financially disastrous attempt to tour America promoting his books with a "fairylogue" of slides and films led him to file for bankruptcy in 1911. He became a slightly shabby, if still frock-coated, figure, living on his wife's money at "Ozcot" in Hollywood, where he raised chickens and won prizes at flower shows. The small success of another musical, *The Tik-Tok Man of Oz,* improved his finances, but he ruined them again by setting up his own movie company, the Oz Film Company, and trying unsuccessfully to film and distribute the Oz books. After two bedridden years, and still, we are told, optimistic, he died in May 1919. However, as we shall see, his frock coat lived on into a strange immortality.

The Wonderful Wizard of Oz, published in 1900, contains many of the ingredients of the magic potion—all the major characters and events are here, as well as the most important locations, the Yellow Brick Road, the Deadly Poppy Field, the Emerald City. But *The Wizard of Oz* is that great rarity, a film that improves on the good book from which it came. One of the changes is the expansion of the Kansas section, which in the novel takes up precisely two pages before the tornado arrives, and just nine lines at the end. The story line in the Oz section is also simplified, by jettisoning several sub-plots, such as the visits to the Fighting Trees, the Dainty China Country, and the Quadlings that come, in the novel, just after the dramatic high point of the Witch's destruction and fritter away the story's narrative drive. And there are two even more important alterations: to the colors of the Wizard's city and of Dorothy's shoes.

Frank Baum's Emerald City was green only because everyone in it had to wear emerald-tinted glasses, whereas in the movie it really is a futuristic, chlorophyll green—except, that is, for the Horse of a Different Color You've Heard Tell Of. The Horse changes color in each successive shot, a change brought about by covering it in a variety of shades of powdered Jell-O.*

Frank Baum did not make up the ruby slippers. He called them

---

* See Aljean Harmetz's definitive *The Making of the Wizard of Oz* (Pavilion Books, 1989).

Silver Shoes. Baum believed that America's stability required a switch from the gold to the silver standard, and the Shoes were a metaphor of the magical advantages of Silver. Noel Langley, the first of the film's three credited screenwriters, originally went along with Baum's idea. But in his fourth script, the script of May 14, 1938, known as the DO NOT MAKE CHANGES script, the clunky, metallic, and non-mythic footwear is jettisoned and the immortal jewel shoes are introduced for the first time, probably in response to the demand for color. (In Shot 114, "the ruby shoes appear on Dorothy's feet, glittering and sparkling in the sun.")

Other writers contributed important details to the finished screenplay. Florence Ryerson and Edgar Allan Woolf were probably responsible for "There's no place like home," which, to me, is the least convincing idea in the film (it's one thing for Dorothy to want to get home, quite another that she can do so only by eulogizing the ideal state, which Kansas so obviously is not).★ But there's some dispute about this, too. A studio memo implies that it could have been the associate producer Arthur Freed who came up with the cutesy slogan. And, after much quarreling between Langley and Ryerson–Woolf, it was the film's lyricist, Yip Harburg, who pulled the final script together and added the crucial scene in which the Wizard, unable to give the companions what they demand, hands out emblems instead, and to our satisfaction these symbols do the job. The name of the rose turns out to be the rose, after all.

Who, then, was the auteur of *The Wizard of Oz*? No single writer can claim that honor, not even the author of the original book. The producers, Mervyn LeRoy and Arthur Freed, both have their champions. At least four directors worked on the picture, most notably Victor Fleming; but he left before shooting ended (King Vidor was his uncredited replacement) to make *Gone With the Wind*, ironically enough the movie that dominated the Oscars while *The Wizard of Oz* won just three: Best Song ("Over the Rainbow"), Best Musical Score, and a Special Award for Judy Garland. The truth is that this great movie, in which the quarrels, sackings, and bungles of all concerned produced what seems like pure, effortless, and somehow inevitable felicity, is as

★ When I first published this essay in 1992, the idea of "home" had become problematic for me, for reasons I have little interest in rehearsing here. (But see Part II, "Messages from the Plague Years.") I won't deny that I did a great deal of thinking, in those days, about the advantages of a good pair of ruby shoes.

near as dammit to that will-o'-the-wisp of modern critical theory: the authorless text.

———

Kansas as described by L. Frank Baum is a depressing place, in which everything is gray as far as the eye can see—the prairie is gray and so is the house in which Dorothy lives. As for Auntie Em, "The sun and wind . . . had taken the sparkle from her eyes and left them a sober gray; they had taken the red from her cheeks and lips, and they were gray also. She was thin and gaunt, and never smiled now." Whereas: "Uncle Henry never laughed. He was gray also, from his long beard to his rough boots." And the sky? "It was even grayer than usual." Toto, though, was spared grayness. He "saved Dorothy from growing as gray as her surroundings." He was not exactly colorful, though his eyes twinkled and his hair was silky. Toto was black.

It is out of this grayness—the gathering, cumulative grayness of that bleak world—that calamity comes. The tornado is the grayness gathered together and whirled about and unleashed, so to speak, against itself. And to all this the film is astonishingly faithful, shooting the Kansas scenes in what we call black-and-white but what is in reality a multiplicity of shades of gray, and darkening its images until the whirlwind sucks them up and rips them into pieces.

———

There is, however, another way of understanding the tornado. Dorothy has a surname: Gale. And in many ways Dorothy is the gale blowing through this little corner of nowhere. She demands justice for her little dog while the adults give in meekly to the powerful Miss Gulch. She is prepared to interrupt the gray inevitability of her life by running away but is so tenderhearted that she runs back again when Professor Marvel tells her that Auntie Em is distraught that she has fled. Dorothy is the life-force of this Kansas, just as Miss Gulch is the force of death; and perhaps it is Dorothy's turmoil, the cyclone of feeling unleashed by the conflict between Dorothy and Miss Gulch, that is made actual in the great dark snake of cloud that wriggles across the prairie, eating the world.

The Kansas of the film is a little less unremittingly bleak than that of the book, if only because of the introduction of the three farmhands and of Professor Marvel, four characters who will find their rhymes, their counterparts, in the Three Companions of Oz and the Wizard himself. Then again, the movie Kansas is also more terrifying, because it adds a presence of real evil: the angular Miss Gulch, with a profile that could carve a turkey, riding stiffly on her bicycle with a hat on her head like a plum pudding or a bomb, and claiming the protection of the Law for her campaign against Toto. Thanks to Miss Gulch, this cinematic Kansas is informed not only by the sadness of dirt-poverty but also by the badness of would-be dog murderers.

And *this* is the home that there's no place like? This is the lost Eden that we are asked to prefer (as Dorothy does) to Oz?

I remember (or I imagine I remember) that when I first saw this film, Dorothy's place struck me as being pretty much a dump. I was lucky, and had a good, comfortable home, and so, I reasoned to myself, if *I'd* been whisked off to Oz, I'd naturally want to get home again. But Dorothy? Maybe we should invite her over to stay. Anywhere looks better than *that*.

I thought one further thought, which I had better confess now, as it gave me a sneaking regard for Miss Gulch and her fantasy counterpart, the Wicked Witch, and, some might say, a secret sympathy for all persons of her witchy disposition, which has remained with me ever since: I couldn't stand Toto. I still can't. As Gollum says of the hobbit Bilbo Baggins in another great fantasy: "*Baggins:* we hates it to pieces."

Toto, that little yapping hairpiece of a creature, that meddlesome rug! L. Frank Baum, excellent fellow, gave the dog a distinctly minor role: it kept Dorothy happy, and when she was not, it had a tendency to "whine dismally"—not an endearing trait. Its only significant contribution to Baum's story came when it accidentally knocked over the screen behind which the Wizard of Oz was concealed. The film-Toto rather more deliberately pulls aside a curtain to reveal the Great Humbug, and in spite of everything I found this an irritating piece of mischief-making. I was not surprised to learn that the pooch playing Toto was possessed of a star's temperament, and even brought the shoot to a standstill at one point by staging a nervous breakdown. That Toto should be the film's one true object of love has always rankled. But such protest is useless, if satisfying. Nobody, now, can rid me of this turbulent toupee.

———

When I first saw *The Wizard of Oz* it made a writer of me. Many years later, I began to devise the yarn that eventually became *Haroun and the*

Sea of Stories. I felt strongly that—if I could only strike the right note—it must be possible to write the tale in such a way as to make it of interest to adults as well as children. The world of books has become a severely categorized and demarcated place, in which children's fiction is not only a kind of ghetto but one subdivided into writing for a number of different age-groups. The movies, however, have regularly risen above such categorizing. From Spielberg to Schwarzenegger, from Disney to Gilliam, the cinema has often come up with offerings before which kids and adults sit happily side by side. I watched *Who Framed Roger Rabbit* in an afternoon movie theater full of excited, rowdy children and went back to see it the next evening, at an hour too late for the kids, so that I could hear all the gags properly, enjoy the movie in-jokes, and marvel at the brilliance of the Toontown concept. But of all movies, the one that helped me most as I tried to find the right voice for *Haroun* was *The Wizard of Oz*. The film's influence is there in the text, plain to see. In Haroun's companions there are clear echoes of the friends who danced with Dorothy down the Yellow Brick Road.

———

And now I'm doing something strange, something that ought to destroy my love for the movie but doesn't: I'm watching a videotape with a notebook on my lap, a pen in one hand and a remote-control zapper in the other, subjecting *The Wizard of Oz* to the indignities of slow-motion, fast-forward, and freeze-frame, trying to learn the secret of the magic trick; and, yes, seeing things I'd never noticed before . . .

The film begins. We are in the monochrome "real" world of Kansas. A girl and her dog run down a country lane. *She isn't coming yet, Toto. Did she hurt you? She tried to, didn't she?* A real girl, a real dog, and the beginning, with the very first line of dialogue, of real drama. Kansas, however, is not real, no more real than Oz. Kansas is a painting. Dorothy and Toto have been running down a short stretch of "road" in the MGM studios, and this shot has been matted into a picture of emptiness. "Real" emptiness would probably not look empty enough. It's as close as makes no difference to the universal gray of Frank Baum's story, the void broken only by a couple of fences and the vertical lines of telegraph poles. If Oz is *nowhere,* then the studio setting of the Kansas scenes suggests that *so is Kansas.* This is necessary. A realistic depiction of the extreme poverty of Dorothy Gale's circumstances would have created a burden, a heaviness, that would have rendered impossible the imaginative leap into Storyland, the soaring flight into Oz. The

Grimms' fairy tales, it's true, were often realistic. In "The Fisherman and His Wife," the eponymous couple live, until they meet the magic flounder, in what is tersely described as "a pisspot." But in many children's versions of the Grimms, the pisspot is bowdlerized into a "hovel" or some even gentler word. Hollywood's vision has always been of this soft-focus variety. Dorothy looks extremely well fed, and she is not really, but *unreally,* poor.

She arrives at the farmyard, and here (freezing the frame) we see the beginning of what will be a recurring visual motif. In the scene we have frozen, Dorothy and Toto are in the background, heading for a gate. To the left of the screen is a tree trunk, a vertical line echoing the telegraph poles of the scene before. Hanging from an approximately horizontal branch are a triangle (for calling farmhands to dinner) and a circle (actually a rubber tire). In mid-shot are further geometric elements: the parallel lines of the wooden fence, the bisecting diagonal wooden bar at the gate. Later, when we see the house, the theme of simple geometry is present once again; it is all right angles and triangles. The world of Kansas, that great void, is shaped into "home" by the use of simple, uncomplicated shapes; none of your citified complexity here. Throughout *The Wizard of Oz,* home and safety are represented by such geometrical simplicity, whereas danger and evil are invariably twisty, irregular, and misshapen.

The tornado is just such an untrustworthy, sinuous, shifting shape. Random, unfixed, it wrecks the plain shapes of that no-frills life.

The Kansas sequence invokes not only geometry but mathematics too. When Dorothy, like the chaotic force she is, bursts upon Auntie Em and Uncle Henry with her fears about Toto, what are they doing? Why do they shoo her away? "We're trying to count," they admonish her, as they take a census of the eggs, counting their metaphorical chickens, their small hopes of income, which the tornado will shortly blow away. So, with simple shapes and numbers, Dorothy's family erects its defenses against the immense, maddening emptiness; and these defenses are useless, of course.

Leap ahead to Oz and it becomes obvious that this opposition between the geometric and the twisty is no accident. Look at the beginning of the Yellow Brick Road: it's a perfect spiral. Look again at Glinda's carriage, that perfect, luminous sphere. Look at the regimented routines of the Munchkins as they greet Dorothy and thank her for squashing the Wicked Witch of the East. Move on to the Emerald

City: see it in the distance, its straight lines soaring into the sky! And now, by contrast, observe the Wicked Witch of the West: her bent figure, her misshapen hat. How does she depart? In a puff of shapeless smoke . . . "Only bad witches are ugly," Glinda tells Dorothy, a remark of high political incorrectness that emphasizes the film's animosity toward whatever is tangled, claw-crooked, and weird. Woods are invariably frightening—the gnarled branches of trees are capable of coming to life—and the one moment when the Yellow Brick Road itself bewilders Dorothy is the moment when it ceases to be geometric (first spiral, then rectilinear) and splits and forks every which way.

—

Back in Kansas, Auntie Em is delivering the scolding that is the prelude to one of the cinema's immortal moments. *You always get yourself into a fret about nothing . . . find yourself a place where you won't get into any trouble!*

Some place where there isn't any trouble. Do you suppose there is such a place, Toto? There must be. Anybody who has swallowed the scriptwriters' notion that this is a film about the superiority of "home" over "away," that the "moral" of *The Wizard of Oz* is as sickly-sweet as an embroidered sampler—"East, West, home's best"—would do well to listen to the yearning in Judy Garland's voice as her face tilts up toward the skies. What she expresses here, what she embodies with the purity of an archetype, is the human dream of *leaving,* a dream at least as powerful as its countervailing dream of roots. At the heart of *The Wizard of Oz* is the tension between these two dreams; but as the music swells and that big, clean voice flies into the anguished longings of the song, can anyone doubt which message is the stronger? In its most potent emotional moment, this is unarguably a film about the joys of going away, of leaving the grayness and entering the color, of making a new life in the "place where there isn't any trouble." "Over the Rainbow" is, or ought to be, the anthem of all the world's migrants, all those who go in search of the place where "the dreams that you dare to dream really do come true." It is a celebration of Escape, a grand paean to the uprooted self, a hymn—*the* hymn—to Elsewhere.

E. Y. Harburg, the lyricist of "Brother, Can You Spare a Dime?" and Harold Arlen, who had written "It's Only a Paper Moon" with Harburg, made the songs for *The Wizard of Oz,* and Arlen actually did think of the melody line outside Schwab's drugstore in Hollywood. Aljean Harmetz records Harburg's disappointment with the music: too complex for a sixteen-year-old to sing, too advanced by comparison with Disney hits like "Heigh Ho! Heigh Ho! It's Off to Work We Go." Harmetz adds: "To please Harburg, Arlen wrote the melody for the tinkling middle section of the song." *Where troubles melt like lemon drops / Away above the chimney tops / That's where you'll find me . . .* A little higher up, in short, than the protagonist of that other great ode to flight, "Up on the Roof."

That "Over the Rainbow" came close to being cut out of the movie is well known, and proof that Hollywood makes its masterpieces by accident, because it doesn't really know what it is doing. Other songs were dropped: "The Jitter Bug," after five weeks' filming, and almost all of "Lions and Tigers and Bears," which survives only as the chant of the Companions as they pass through the forest along the Yellow Brick Road: *Lions and Tigers and Bears—oh, my!* It's impossible to say if the film would have been improved or damaged by the addition of these songs; would *Catch-22* be *Catch-22* if it had been published under its original title of *Catch-18*? What we can say, however, is that Yip Harburg (no admirer of Judy) was wrong about Garland's voice.

The principal actors in the cast complained that there was "no acting" in the movie, and in the conventional sense they were right. But Garland singing "Over the Rainbow" did something extraordinary. In that moment she gave the film its heart. The force of her rendition is strong and sweet and deep enough to carry us through all the tomfoolery that follows, even to bestow a touching quality upon it, a vulnerable charm that is matched only by Bert Lahr's equally extraordinary interpretation of the role of the Cowardly Lion.

What is left to say about Garland's Dorothy? The conventional wisdom is that the performance gains in ironic force because its innocence contrasts so starkly with what we know of the actress's difficult later life. I'm not sure this is right, though it's the kind of remark movie buffs like making. It seems to me that Garland's performance succeeds on its own terms, and on the film's. She is required to pull off what sounds like an impossible trick. On the one hand she is to be the film's tabula rasa, the blank slate upon which the action of the story gradually writes itself—or rather, because this is a movie, after all, the blank screen upon which the action plays. Armed only with her look of wide-eyed innocence, she must be the object of the film as well as its subject, must allow herself to be the empty vessel that the movie slowly fills. And yet, on the other hand, she must—with a little help from the

Cowardly Lion—carry the entire emotional weight, the whole cyclonic force of the film. That she achieves this is due not only to the mature depths of her singing voice but also to the odd stockiness, the physical gaucherie that endears us precisely because it is half unbeautiful, *jolie-laide,* instead of the posturing prettiness Shirley Temple would have brought to the role—and Temple was seriously considered for the part. The scrubbed, ever so slightly lumpy unsexiness of Garland's playing is what makes the movie work. One can only imagine the catastrophic flirtatiousness young Shirley would have insisted on employing, and be grateful that the MGM executives were persuaded to go with Judy.

The tornado that I've suggested is the product of the Gale in Dorothy's name was actually made of muslin stiffened with wire. A props man had to lower himself into the muslin tunnel to help pull the needles through and push them out again. "It was pretty uncomfortable when we reached the narrow end," he confessed. The discomfort was worth it, because that tornado, swooping down on Dorothy's home, creates the second genuinely mythic image of *The Wizard of Oz*: the archetypal myth, one might say, of moving house.

In this, the transitional sequence of the movie, when the unreal reality of Kansas gives way to the realistic surreality of the world of wizardry, there is, as befits a threshold moment, much business involving windows and doors. First, the farmhands open up the doors of the storm shelter, and Uncle Henry, heroic as ever, persuades Auntie Em that they can't afford to wait for Dorothy. Second, Dorothy, returning with Toto from her attempt at running away, struggles against the wind to open the screen door of the main house; this outer door is instantly ripped from its hinges and blows away. Third, we see the others closing the doors of the storm shelter. Fourth, Dorothy, inside the house, opens and shuts the doors of various rooms, calling out frantically for Auntie Em. Fifth, Dorothy goes to the storm shelter, but its doors are locked against her. Sixth, Dorothy retreats back inside the main house, her cries for Auntie Em now weak and fearful; whereupon a window, echoing the screen door, blows off its hinges and knocks her cold. She falls upon the bed, and from now on magic reigns. We have passed through the film's most important gateway.

This device—the knocking out of Dorothy—is the most radical and in some ways the worst of all the changes wrought to Frank Baum's original conception. For in the book there is no question that Oz is real, that it is a place of the same order, though not of the same type, as

Kansas. The film, like the TV soap opera *Dallas,* introduces an element of bad faith when it permits the possibility that everything that follows is a dream. This type of bad faith cost *Dallas* its audience and eventually killed it off. That *The Wizard of Oz* avoided the soap opera's fate is a testament to the general integrity of the film, which enabled it to transcend this hoary cliché.

While the house flies through the air, looking in longshot like a tiny toy, Dorothy "awakes." What she sees through the window is a sort of movie—the window acts as a cinema screen, a frame within the frame—which prepares her for the new sort of movie she is about to step into. The effect shots, sophisticated for their time, include a lady knitting in her rocking chair as the tornado whirls her by, a cow standing placidly in the eye of the storm, two men rowing a boat through the twisting air, and, most important of all, the figure of Miss Gulch on her bicycle, which transforms, as we watch it, into the figure of the Wicked Witch of the West on her broomstick, her cape flying out behind her, and her huge cackling laugh rising above the noise of the storm.

——

The house lands. Dorothy emerges from her bedroom with Toto in her arms. We have reached the moment of color.

The first color shot, in which Dorothy walks away from the camera toward the front door, is deliberately dull, to match the preceding monochrome. But once the door is open, color floods the screen. In these color-glutted days it's hard to imagine a time when color films were still relatively new. Thinking back once again to my Bombay childhood in the 1950s, when Hindi movies were all in black-and-white, I can recall the excitement of the advent of color. In an epic about the Grand Mughal, the emperor Akbar, entitled *Mughal-e-Azam,* there was only one reel of color cinematography, featuring a dance at court by the fabled Anarkali. Yet this reel alone guaranteed the film's success, drawing in the crowds by the million.

The makers of *The Wizard of Oz* clearly decided they were going to make their color as colorful as possible, much as Michelangelo Antonioni, a very different sort of filmmaker, did years later in his first color feature, *Red Desert.* In the Antonioni film, color is used to create heightened, often surrealistic effects. *The Wizard of Oz* likewise goes for bold, expressionist splashes—the yellow of the Brick Road, the red of the Poppy Field, the green of the Emerald City and of the witch's skin. So striking were these colors that, soon after seeing the film as a child, I began to dream of green-skinned witches. Years afterward, I gave these dreams to the narrator of *Midnight's Children,* having completely forgotten their source: "No colors except green and black the walls are green the sky is black . . . the Widow is green but her hair is black as black." In this stream-of-consciousness dream sequence a nightmare of Indira Gandhi is fused with the equally nightmarish figure of Margaret Hamilton: a coming together of the Wicked Witches of the East and West.

Dorothy, stepping into color, framed by exotic foliage with a cluster of dwarfy cottages behind her and looking like a blue-smocked Snow White, no princess but a good demotic American gal, is clearly struck by the absence of her familiar homey gray. *Toto, I have a feeling we're not in Kansas anymore.* That camp classic of a line has detached itself from the movie to become a great American catchphrase, endlessly recycled, even turning up as an epigraph to Thomas Pynchon's mammoth paranoid fantasy of World War II, *Gravity's Rainbow,* whose characters' destiny lies not "behind the moon, beyond the rain" but "beyond the zero" of consciousness, where lies a land at least as odd as Oz.

Dorothy has done more than step out of grayness into Technicolor. She has been *unhoused,* and her homelessness is underlined by the fact that, after all the door-play of the transitional sequence, she will not enter any interior at all until she reaches the Emerald City. From tornado to Oz, Dorothy never has a roof over her head.

Out there amid the giant hollyhocks, whose blooms look like old His-Master's-Voice gramophone trumpets; out there in the vulnerability of open space, albeit open space that isn't at all like the prairie, Dorothy is about to outdo Snow White by a factor of nearly fifty. You can almost hear the MGM studio chiefs plotting to put the Disney hit in the shade, not just by providing in live action almost as many miraculous effects as the Disney cartoonists created, but also in the matter of little people. If Snow White had seven dwarfs, then Dorothy Gale, from the star called Kansas, would have three hundred and fifty. There's some disagreement about how this many Munchkins were brought to Hollywood and signed up. The official version is that they were provided by an impresario named Leo Singer. John Lahr's biography of his father, Bert, tells a different tale, which I prefer for reasons Roger Rabbit would understand—i.e., because it is funny. Lahr quotes the film's casting director, Bill Grady:

Leo [Singer] could only give me 150. I went to a midget monologist called Major Doyle. . . . I said I had 150 from Singer. "I'll not give you one if you do business with that son-of-a-bitch." "What am I gonna do?" I said. "I'll get you the 350." . . . So I called up Leo and explained the situation. . . . When I told the Major that I'd called off Singer, he danced a jig right on the street in front of Dinty Moore's.

The Major gets these midgets for me. . . . I bring them out West in buses. . . . Major Doyle took the [first three] buses and arrived at Singer's house. The Major went to the doorman. "Phone upstairs and tell Leo Singer to look out the window." It took about ten minutes. Then Singer looked from his fifth-floor window. And there were all those midgets in those buses in front of his house with their bare behinds sticking out the window.

This incident became known as Major Doyle's Revenge.*

What began with a strip continued cartoonishly. The Munchkins were made up and costumed exactly like 3-D cartoon figures. The Mayor of Munchkinland is quite implausibly rotund, the Coroner (*and she's not only merely dead / She's really most sincerely dead*) reads the Witch of the East's death notice from a scroll while wearing a hat with an absurdly scroll-like brim;† the quiffs of the Lollipop Kids, who appear to have arrived in Oz by way of Bash Street and Dead End, stand up more stiffly than Tintin's. But what might have been a grotesque and unappetizing sequence—it is, after all, a celebration of death—instead becomes the scene in which *The Wizard of Oz* captures its audience once and for all, allying the natural charm of the story to brilliant MGM choreography, which punctuates large-scale routines with neat little set-pieces like the dance of the Lullaby League, or the Sleepy Heads awaking mobcapped and benightied out of cracked blue eggshells set in a giant nest. And of course there's also the infectious gaiety of Arlen

---

* According to some contemporary revisionists, Major Doyle never got the 350 Munchkins, and the filmmakers had to settle for 124.

† After the publication of an earlier version of this essay in *The New Yorker*, I received an appreciative letter from the Munchkin Coroner, Manfred Raabe, now living in a Penney Retirement Community in Fort Lauderdale, Florida. He liked what I had to say so much that he sent me a gift: a color photocopy of a picture of his big moment on the steps of the Town Hall, holding up that big scroll with its Gothic lettering reading "Certificate of Death." Under this lettering he had painstakingly filled out my name. I don't know what it means to have a Munchkin death certificate, but I've got one.

and Harburg's exceptionally witty ensemble number, "Ding, Dong, the Witch Is Dead."

Arlen was a little contemptuous of this song and the equally memorable "We're Off to See the Wizard," calling them his "lemon-drop songs"—perhaps because in both cases the real inventiveness lies in Harburg's lyrics. In Dorothy's intro to "Ding, Dong," Harburg embarks on a pyrotechnic display of A-A-A rhyming (*the wind began to switch / the house to pitch;* until at length we meet the *witch, to satisfy an itch / Went flying on her broomstick thumbing for a hitch;* and *what happened then was rich* . . .). As with a vaudeville barker's alliterations, we cheer each new rhyme as a sort of gymnastic triumph. Verbal play continues to characterize both songs. In "Ding, Dong," Harburg invents punning word-concertinas:

> Ding, Dong, the witch is dead!
> —*Whicholwitch?*
> —The wicked witch!

This technique found much fuller expression in "We're Off to See the Wizard," becoming the real "hook" of the song:

> We're off to see the Wizard,
> The wonderful *Wizzardavoz,*
> We hear he is a *Whizzavawiz,*
> If ever a *whizztherwoz.*
> If *everoever a whizztherwoz*
> The *Wizzardavoz* is one because . . .

Is it too fanciful to suggest that Harburg's use throughout the film of internal rhymes and assonances is a conscious echo of the "rhyming" of the plot itself, the paralleling of characters in Kansas with those in Oz, the echoes of themes bouncing back and forth between the monochrome and Technicolor worlds?

Few of the Munchkins could actually sing their lines, as they mostly didn't speak English. They weren't required to do much in the movie, but they made up for this by their activities off-camera. Some film historians try to play down the stories of sexual shenanigans, knife-play, and general mayhem, but the legend of the Munchkin hordes cutting a swathe through Hollywood is not easily dispelled. In Angela Carter's novel *Wise Children* there is an account of a fictitious version of *A Midsummer Night's Dream* that owes much to the Munchkins' antics and, indeed, to Munchkinland:

> The concept of this wood was scaled to the size of fairy folk, so all was twice as large as life. Larger. Daisies big as your head and white as spooks, foxgloves as tall as the tower of Pisa that chimed like bells if shook. . . . Even the wee folk were real; the studio scoured the country for dwarfs. Soon, true or not, wild tales began to circulate—how one poor chap fell into the toilet and splashed around for half an hour before someone dashed in for a piss and fished him out of the bowl; another one got offered a high chair in the Brown Derby when he went out for a hamburger.

Amidst all this Munchkining we are given two very different portraits of grown-ups. The Good Witch Glinda is pretty in pink (well, prettyish, even if Dorothy is moved to call her "beautiful"). She has a high, cooing voice, and a smile that seems to have jammed. She has one excellent gag-line. After Dorothy disclaims witchy status, Glinda inquires, pointing at Toto: *Well, then, is* that *the witch?* This joke apart, she spends the scene simpering and looking vaguely benevolent and loving and rather too heavily powdered. It is interesting that though she is the Good Witch, the goodness of Oz does not inhere in her. The people of Oz are naturally good, unless they are under the power of the Wicked Witch (as is shown by the improved behavior of her soldiers after she melts). In the moral universe of the film, only evil is external, dwelling solely in the dual devil-figure of Miss Gulch / Wicked Witch.

(A parenthetical worry about Munchkinland: is it not altogether too pretty, too kempt, too sweetly sweet for a place that was, until Dorothy's arrival, under the absolute power of the Wicked Witch of the East? How is it that this squashed Witch had no castle? How could her despotism have left so little mark upon the land? Why are the Munchkins so relatively unafraid, hiding only briefly before they emerge, and giggling while they hide? The heretical thought occurs: maybe the Witch of the East *wasn't as bad as all that*—she certainly kept the streets clean, the houses painted and in good repair, and, no doubt, such trains as there might have been running on time. Moreover, and again unlike her sister, she seems to have ruled without the aid of soldiers, policemen, or other regiments of oppression. Why, then, was she so hated? I only ask.)

Glinda and the Witch of the West are the only two symbols of power in a film which is largely about the powerless, and it's instructive to "unpack" them. They are both women, and a striking aspect of *The Wizard of Oz* is its lack of a male hero—because for all their brains, heart, and courage, it's impossible to see the Scarecrow, the Tin Man, and the Cowardly Lion as classic Hollywood leading men. The power center of the film is a triangle at whose corners are Dorothy, Glinda, and the Witch. The fourth point, at which the Wizard is thought for most of the film to stand, turns out to be an illusion. The power of men is illusory, the film suggests. The power of women is real.

Of the two witches, good and bad, can there be anyone who'd choose to spend five minutes with Glinda? The actress who played her, Billie Burke, the ex-wife of Flo Ziegfeld, sounds every bit as wimpy as her role (she was prone to react to criticism with a trembling lip and a faltering cry of "Oh, you're *browbeating* me!"). By contrast, Margaret Hamilton's Wicked Witch of the West seizes hold of the movie from her very first green-faced snarl. Of course Glinda is "good" and the Wicked Witch "bad," but Glinda is a trilling pain in the neck, while the Wicked Witch is lean and mean. Check out their clothes: frilly pink versus slimline black. *No contest.* Consider their attitudes to their fellow-women: Glinda simpers upon being called beautiful, and denigrates her unbeautiful sisters; whereas the Wicked Witch is in a rage because of her sister's death, demonstrating, one might say, a commendable sense of solidarity. We may hiss at her, and she may terrify us as children, but at least she doesn't embarrass us the way Glinda does. True, Glinda exudes a sort of raddled motherly safeness, while the Witch of the West looks, in this scene anyhow, curiously frail and impotent, obliged to mouth empty-sounding threats—*I'll bide my time. But you just try and keep out of my way*—but just as feminism has sought to rehabilitate old pejorative words such as "hag," "crone," "witch," so the Wicked Witch of the West could be said to represent the more positive of the two images of powerful womanhood on offer here.

Glinda and the Witch clash most fiercely over the ruby slippers, which Glinda magics off the feet of the late Witch of the East and onto Dorothy's feet, and which the Wicked Witch of the West is apparently unable to remove. But Glinda's instructions to Dorothy are oddly enigmatic, even contradictory. She tells Dorothy (1) "Their magic must be very powerful or she wouldn't want them so badly," and, later, (2) "Never let those ruby slippers off your feet for a moment or you will be at the mercy of the Wicked Witch of the West." Statement One implies that Glinda is unclear about the nature of the ruby slippers' capabilities, whereas Statement Two suggests that she knows all about their protective powers. Nor does either statement hint at the slippers' later role in helping to get Dorothy back to Kansas. It seems probable that these confusions are hangovers from the long, dissension-riddled scripting process, during which the function of the slippers was the subject of considerable disagreement. But one can also see Glinda's obliqueness as proof that a good fairy or witch, when she sets out to be of assistance, never gives you everything. Glinda is not so unlike her own description of the Wizard of Oz: *oh, he's very good, but very mysterious.*

———

Just follow the Yellow Brick Road, says Glinda, and bubbles off into the blue hills in the distance, and Dorothy, geometrically influenced, as who would not be after a childhood among triangles, circles, and squares, begins her journey at the very point from which the Road spirals outward. And as she and the Munchkins echo Glinda's instructions in tones both raucously high and gutturally low, something begins to happen to Dorothy's feet. Their motion acquires a syncopation, which in beautifully slow stages grows more noticeable. By the time the ensemble breaks into the film's theme song—*You're off to see the Wizard*—we see, fully developed, the clever, shuffling little skip that will be the journey's leitmotiv:

> *You're off to see the Wizard*
> (s-skip)
> *The wonderful Wizzardavoz*
> (s-skip)

In this way, s-skipping along, Dorothy Gale, already a National Hero of Munchkinland, already (as the Munchkins have assured her) History, a girl destined to be *a Bust in the Hall of Fame,* steps out along the road of destiny and heads, as Americans must, into the West.

Off-camera anecdotes about a film's production can be simultaneously delicious and disappointing. On the one hand there's an undeniable Trivial Pursuit–ish pleasure to be had: did you know that Buddy Ebsen, later the patriarch of the Beverly Hillbillies, was the original Scarecrow, then switched roles with Ray Bolger, who didn't want to play the Tin Man? And did you know that Ebsen had to leave the film after his "tin" costume gave him aluminum poisoning? And did you know that Margaret Hamilton's hand was badly burned during the filming of the scene in which the Witch writes SURRENDER DOROTHY in smoke in the sky over Emerald City, and that her stunt double Betty Danko was even more badly burned during the scene's reshoot? Did you know that Jack Haley (the third and final choice for the Tin Man) couldn't sit down in his costume and could only rest against a specially devised "leaning board"? Or that the three leading men weren't allowed to eat their meals in the MGM refectory because their makeup was thought too revolting? Or that Margaret Hamilton was given a coarse tent instead of a proper dressing-room, as if she really was a witch? Or that Toto was a female and her name was Terry? Above all, did you know that the frock coat worn by Frank Morgan, playing Professor Marvel / the Wizard of Oz, was bought from a secondhand store, and had L. Frank Baum's name stitched inside? It turned out that the coat had indeed been made for the author; thus, in the movie, the Wizard actually wears his creator's clothes.

Many of these behind-the-scenes tales show us, sadly, that a film that has made so many audiences so happy was not a happy film to make. It is almost certainly untrue that Haley, Bolger, and Lahr were unkind to Judy Garland, as some have said, but Margaret Hamilton definitely felt excluded by the boys. She was lonely on set, her studio days barely coinciding with those of the one actor she already knew, Frank Morgan, and she couldn't even take a leak without assistance. In fact, hardly anyone—certainly not Lahr, Haley, and Bolger in their elaborate makeup, which they dreaded putting on every day—seems to have had any fun making one of the most enjoyable pictures in movie history. We do not really want to know this; and yet, so fatally willing are we to do what may destroy our illusions that we also do want to know, we do, we do.

As I delved into the secrets of the Wizard of Oz's drinking problem, and learned that Morgan was only third choice for the part, behind W. C. Fields and Ed Wynn, and as I wondered what contemptuous wildness Fields might have brought to the role, and how it might have been if his female opposite number, the Witch, had been played by the first choice, Gale Sondergaard, not only a great beauty but also another Gale to set alongside Dorothy and the tornado, I found myself staring at an old color photograph of the Scarecrow, the Tin Man, and Dorothy posing in a forest set, surrounded by autumn leaves; and realized that I was looking not at the stars at all but at their stunt doubles, their stand-ins. It was an unremarkable studio still, but it took my breath away; for it, too, was both mesmerizing and sad. It felt like a perfect metaphor for the doubleness of my own responses.

There they stand, Nathanael West's locusts, the ultimate wanna-bes. Garland's shadow, Bobbie Koshay, with her hands clasped behind her back and a white bow in her hair, is doing her brave best to smile, but she knows she's a counterfeit, all right; there are no ruby slippers on her feet. The mock-Scarecrow looks glum, too, even though he has avoided the full-scale burlap-sack makeup that was Bolger's daily fate. If it weren't for the clump of straw poking out of his right sleeve, you'd think he was some kind of hobo. Between them, in full metallic drag, stands the Tin Man's tinnier echo, looking miserable. Stand-ins know their fate: they know we don't want to admit their existence. Even when reason tells us that in this or that difficult shot—when the Witch flies, or the Cowardly Lion dives through a glass window—we aren't really watching the stars, still the part of us that has suspended disbelief insists on seeing the stars and not their doubles. Thus the stand-ins become invisible even when they are in full view. They remain off-camera even when they are on-screen.

This is not the only reason for the curious fascination of the stand-ins' photograph. It's so haunting because, in the case of a beloved film, *we are all the stars' doubles.* Imagination puts us in the Lion's skin, places the sparkling slippers on our feet, sends us cackling through the air on a broomstick. To look at this photograph is to look into a mirror. In it we see ourselves. The world of *The Wizard of Oz* has possessed us. We have become the stand-ins.

A pair of ruby slippers, found in a bin in the MGM basement, was sold at auction in May 1970 for the amazing sum of $15,000. The purchaser was, and has remained, anonymous. Who was it who wished so profoundly to possess, perhaps even to wear, Dorothy's magic shoes? Was it, dear reader, you? Was it I?

At the same auction the second highest price was paid for the Cowardly Lion's costume ($2,400). This was twice as much as the third largest bid, $1,200 for Clark Gable's trench coat. The high prices commanded by *Wizard of Oz* memorabilia testify to the power of the film over its admirers—to our desire, quite literally, to clothe ourselves in its raiment. (It turned out, incidentally, that the $15,000 slippers were too large to have fitted Judy Garland's feet. They had in all probability been made for her double, Bobbie Koshay, whose feet were two sizes larger. Is it not fitting that the shoes made for the stand-in to stand in should have passed into the possession of another kind of surrogate: a film fan?)

———

If asked to pick a single defining image of *The Wizard of Oz,* most of us would, I suspect, come up with the Scarecrow, the Tin Man, the Cowardly Lion, and Dorothy s-skipping down the Yellow Brick Road (actually, the skip grows more pronounced during the journey, becoming an exaggerated h-hop). How strange that the most famous passage of this very filmic film, a film packed with technical wizardry and effects, should be the least cinematic, the most "stagy" part of the whole! Or perhaps not so strange, for this is primarily a passage of surreal comedy, and we recall that the equally inspired clowning of the Marx Brothers was no less stagily filmed. The zany mayhem of the playing rendered all but the simplest camera techniques unusable.

"Where is Vaudeville?" Somewhere on the way to the Wizard, apparently. The Scarecrow and the Tin Man are both pure products of the burlesque theater, specializing in pantomime exaggerations of voice and movements, pratfalls (the Scarecrow descending from his post), improbable leanings beyond the center of gravity (the Tin Man during his little dance) and, of course, the smart-ass backchat of the cross-talk act:

> TIN MAN, *rusted solid:* (Squawks)
> DOROTHY: He said "oil can"!
> SCARECROW: Oil can what?

At the pinnacle of all this clowning is that comic masterpiece, Bert Lahr's Cowardly Lion, all elongated vowel sounds (*Put 'em uuuuuuup*), ridiculous rhymes (*rhinoceros / imposserous*), transparent bravado, and operatic, tail-tugging, blubbing terror. All three, Scarecrow, Tin Man, and Lion, are, in Eliot's phrase, hollow men. The Scarecrow actually does have a "headpiece filled with straw, alas"; but the Tin Man is no less empty—he even bangs on his chest to prove that his innards are missing, because "the Tinsmith," his shadowy maker, forgot to provide a heart. The Lion lacks the most leonine of qualities, lamenting:

> What makes the Hottentot so hot,
> What puts the ape in apricot,
> What have they got that I ain't got?
> Courage!

Perhaps it's because they are hollow that our imaginations can occupy them so easily. That is to say, it is their anti-heroism, their apparent lack of Great Qualities, that makes them our size, or even smaller, so that we can stand among them as equals, like Dorothy among the Munchkins. Gradually, however, we discover that along with their "straight man," Dorothy (who plays, in this part of the film, the part of the unfunny Marx Brother, the one who could sing and look hunky and do little else), they embody one of the film's "messages"—that we already possess what we seek most fervently. The Scarecrow regularly comes up with bright ideas, which he offers with self-deprecating disclaimers. The Tin Man can weep with grief long before the Wizard gives him a heart. And Dorothy's capture by the Witch brings out the Lion's courage, though he pleads with his friends to "talk me out of it."

For this message to have its full impact, however, we must learn the futility of looking for solutions outside ourselves. We must learn about one more hollow man: the Wizard of Oz himself. Just as the Tinsmith was a flawed maker of Tin Men—just as, in this secular movie, the Tin Man's god is dead—so too must our belief in Wizards perish, so that we may believe in ourselves. We must survive the Deadly Poppy Field, helped by a mysterious snowfall (why *does* snow overcome the poppies' poison?), and so arrive, accompanied by heavenly choirs, at the city gates.

Here the film changes convention once again. Now it's about hicks from the sticks arriving at the metropolis, one of the classic themes of American cinema, with echoes in *Mr. Deeds Goes to Town,* or even in Clark Kent from Smallville's arrival at the *Daily Planet* in *Superman.* Dorothy is a country bumpkin, "Dorothy the small and meek"; her companions are backwoods buffoons. Yet—this too is a familiar Hollywood trope—it is the out-of-towners, the country mice, who will save the day.

There never was a metropolis quite like the Emerald City. It looks from the outside like a fairy tale of New York, a thicket of skyscraping green towers. Inside its walls, though, it's the very essence of quaintness. It is startling that the citizens—many of them played by Frank

Morgan, who adds the parts of the gatekeeper, the driver of the horse-drawn buggy, and the palace guard to those of Professor Marvel and the Wizard—speak with English accents that rival Dick Van Dyke's immortal cockney in *Mary Poppins. Tyke yer anyplace in the city, we does,* says the coachman, adding, *I'll tyke yer to a place where you can tidy up a bit, what?* Other members of the citizenry are dressed like Grand Hotel bellhops and glitzy nuns, and they say, or rather sing, things like *Jolly good fun!* Dorothy catches on quickly. At the Wash and Brush Up, a tribute to urban technological genius that has none of the dark doubts of a *Modern Times* or *City Lights,* our heroine even gets a little English herself:

> DOROTHY (*sings*): Can you even dye my
>   eyes to match my gown?
> ATTENDANTS (*in unison*): Uh-huh!
> DOROTHY: Jolly old town!

Most of the citizens are cheerful and friendly, and those that appear not to be—the gatekeeper, the palace guard—are quickly won over. (In this respect, once again, they are untypical city folk.) Our four friends gain entry to the Wizard's palace because Dorothy's tears of frustration un-dam a quite alarming reservoir of liquid in the guard, whose face is soon sodden with tears, and as you watch this Niagara you are struck by the number of occasions on which people cry in this film. Apart from Dorothy and the guard, there is the Cowardly Lion, who cries when Dorothy bops him on the nose; the Tin Man, who almost rusts up again from weeping; and Dorothy again, captured by the Witch. (If the Witch had been closer at hand on one of these occasions and gotten herself wet, the movie might have been much shorter.)

So: into the palace we go, down an arched corridor that looks like an elongated version of the Looney Tunes logo, and at last we confront a Wizard whose illusions—giant heads, flashes of fire—conceal, but only for a while, his essential kinship with Dorothy. He, too, is an immigrant in Oz; indeed, as he will later reveal, he is a Kansas man himself. (In the novel, he came from Omaha.) These two immigrants, Dorothy and the Wizard, have adopted opposite strategies of survival in the new, strange land. Dorothy has been unfailingly polite, careful, courteously "small and meek," whereas the Wizard has been fire and smoke, bravado and bombast, and has hustled his way to the top—floated there, so to speak, on a current of his own hot air. But Dorothy learns that meekness isn't enough, and the Wizard—as his balloon gets the better of him for a second time—that his command of hot air isn't all it should be. It's hard for a migrant like myself not to see in these shifting destinies a parable of the migrant condition.

The Wizard's stipulation, that he will grant no wishes until the four friends have brought him the Witch's broomstick, ushers in the penultimate and least challenging (though most action-packed and "exciting") movement of the film, which is, in this phase, at once a buddy movie, a straightforward adventure yarn, and, after Dorothy's capture, a more or less conventional princess rescue story. After the great dramatic climax of the confrontation with the Wizard of Oz, the film sags for a while and doesn't really regain momentum until the equally climactic final struggle with the Wicked Witch of the West, ending with her melting, her "growing down" into nothingness. The relative dullness of this sequence has something to do with the script's inability to make much of the Winged Monkeys, who remain ciphers throughout, whereas they could have been used (for example) to show us what the oppressed Munchkins might have been like under the power of the Witch of the East, before their liberation by Dorothy's falling house.

(One interesting detail. When the Witch dispatches the Winged Monkeys to capture Dorothy, she speaks a line that makes no sense at all. Assuring the chief Monkey that his prey will give him no trouble, the Witch explains, *I've sent a little insect on ahead to take the fight out of them.* But, as we cut down to the forest, we learn nothing further about this insect. It's simply not in the film. It was, though. The line of dialogue is left over from an earlier version of the film, and it refers to a ghost of the discarded musical sequence I mentioned earlier. The "little insect" was once a fully fledged song that took over a month to film. He is the Jitter Bug.)

Fast-forward. The Witch is gone. The Wizard has been unmasked and, in the moment after his unveiling, has succeeded in a spot of true magic, giving Dorothy's companions the gifts they did not believe they possessed until that instant. The Wizard has gone, too, and without Dorothy, their plans having been fouled up by (who else but) Toto. And here's Glinda, telling Dorothy she has to learn the meaning of the ruby slippers for herself . . .

> GLINDA: What have you learned?
> DOROTHY: If I ever go looking for my

> heart's desire again, I won't look further
> than my own back yard. And if it isn't
> there, I never really lost it to begin with.
> Is that right?
> GLINDA: That's all it is. And now those
> magic slippers will take you home in
> two seconds. Close your eyes . . . click
> your heels together three times . . . and
> think to yourself . . . there's no place
> like . . .

Hold it. Hold *it*.

How does it come about, at the close of this radical and enabling film, which teaches us in the least didactic way possible to build on what we have, to make the best of ourselves, that we are given this conservative little homily? Are we to believe that Dorothy has learned no more on her journey than that she didn't need to make such a journey in the first place? Must we accept that she now accepts the limitations of her home life, and agrees that the things she doesn't have there are no loss to her? *"Is that right?"* Well, excuse *me*, Glinda, but it isn't.

Home again in black-and-white, with Auntie Em and Uncle Henry and the rude mechanicals clustered round her bed, Dorothy begins her second revolt, fighting not only against the patronizing dismissals of her own folk but also against the scriptwriters, and the sentimental moralizing of the entire Hollywood studio system. *It wasn't a dream, it was a place,* she cries piteously. *A real, truly live place! Doesn't anyone believe me?*

Many, many people did believe her. Frank Baum's readers believed her, and their interest in Oz led him to write thirteen further Oz books, admittedly of diminishing quality; the series was continued, even more feebly, by other hands after his death. Dorothy, ignoring the "lessons" of the ruby slippers, went back to Oz, in spite of the efforts of Kansas folk, including Auntie Em and Uncle Henry, to have her dreams brainwashed out of her (see the terrifying electroconvulsive therapy sequence in the Disney film *Return to Oz*); and, in the sixth book of the series, she took Auntie Em and Uncle Henry with her, and they all settled down in Oz, where Dorothy became a princess.

So Oz finally *became* home; the imagined world became the actual world, as it does for us all, because the truth is that once we have left our childhood places and started out to make up our own lives, armed only with what we have and are, we understand that the real secret of the ruby slippers is not that "there's no place like home" but rather that there is no longer any such place *as* home: except, of course, for the home we make, or the homes that are made for us, in Oz, which is anywhere, and everywhere, except the place from which we began.

In the place from which I began, after all, I watched the film from the child's—Dorothy's—point of view. I experienced, with her, the frustration of being brushed aside by Uncle Henry and Auntie Em, busy with their dull grown-up counting. Like all adults, they couldn't focus on what was really important to Dorothy: namely, the threat to Toto. I ran away with Dorothy and then ran back. Even the shock of discovering that the Wizard was a humbug was a shock I felt as a child, a shock to the child's faith in adults. Perhaps, too, I felt something deeper, something I couldn't articulate; perhaps some half-formed suspicion about grown-ups was being confirmed.

Now, as I look at the movie again, I have become the fallible adult. Now I am a member of the tribe of imperfect parents who cannot listen to their children's voices. I, who no longer have a father, have become a father instead, and now it is my fate to be unable to satisfy the longings of a child. This is the last and most terrible lesson of the film: that there is one final, unexpected rite of passage. In the end, ceasing to be children, we all become magicians without magic, exposed conjurers, with only our simple humanity to get us through.

We are the humbugs now.

April 1992

The Best of Young
British Novelists

[*In 1983, the following twenty writers were chosen as the "Best of Young British Novelists": Martin Amis, Pat Barker, Julian Barnes, Ursula Bentley, William Boyd, Buchi Emecheta, Maggie Gee, Kazuo Ishiguro, Alan Judd, Ian McEwan, Adam Mars-Jones, Shiva Naipaul, Philip Norman, Christopher Priest, Salman Rushdie, Clive Sinclair, Lisa St. Aubin de Teran, Graham Swift, Rose Tremain, and A. N. Wilson. Notable omissions included Bruce Chatwin and Timothy Mo.*

Ten years later, I helped make the second such selection. Our final list was as follows: Iain Banks, Louis de Bernières, Anne Billson, Tibor Fischer, Esther Freud, Alan Hollinghurst, Kazuo Ishiguro, A. L. Kennedy, Philip Kerr, Hanif Kureishi, Adam Lively, Candia McWilliam, Adam Mars-Jones, Lawrence Norfolk, Ben Okri, Caryl Phillips, Will Self, Nicholas Shakespeare, Helen Simpson, and Jeanette Winterson.]

On Friday, January 8, 1993, Bill Buford, the editor of *Granta*, rang the *Sunday Times* to announce the names of the twenty writers selected for the second Best of Young British Novelists promotion. Like the other judges—the novelist and critic A. S. Byatt, John Mitchinson of Waterstone's, and myself—he was in a state of some excitement. We were all proud of the list, and felt sure that readers would be as delighted as we had been to discover so many vivid, confident, and ambitious new writers. The smart book-world chatter about this "generation" says that it's no good. How pleasant, we thought, to be able to disprove that proposition.

On Sunday, January 10, the *Sunday Times*—which had assured us of its support for the promotion, and had therefore been given the exclusive right to publish the list—ran a piece by its acting literary editor, Harry Ritchie, which was about as supportive as a fatwa.★ It compared the list unfavorably to the first Best of Young British list in 1983. It suggested that the publicity "may backfire by revealing the absence of literary talent." It quoted such reliable sneerers as Julie Burchill and Kingsley Amis saying that the list was "crap," and it tried to twist Martin Amis's neutral remarks into another attack. It was a poisonously ungenerous article from someone whose very job ought to depend on his love of writing and his willingness to champion the best of the new. Ritchie, when confronted, admitted to me that he had no knowledge of the work of half the writers on the list.

The comparison with 1983 isn't fair unless one is reminded of the point those writers had reached at that time. In the summer of 1983, Martin Amis hadn't published *Money, London Fields,* or *Time's Arrow.* Ian McEwan hadn't published *The Child in Time, The Innocent,* or *Black Dogs.* Julian Barnes hadn't published *Flaubert's Parrot, A History of the World in 10½ Chapters,* or *The Porcupine.* William Boyd hadn't published his "breakthrough novel," *The New Confessions;* Rose Tremain hadn't published *Restoration;* Graham Swift hadn't published *Waterland;* Adam Mars-Jones had written just one collection of short stories; Kazuo Ishiguro had not yet published either *An Artist of the Floating World* or the Booker-winning *The Remains of the Day.* Pat Barker's best work was still to come, as were the novels of Clive Sinclair.

These were, in short, highly promising writers with some achievements and a great future ahead of them—exactly like the 1993 group. The earlier group contained one Booker winner; the new one contains two, as well as numerous winners of Somerset Maugham, John Llewellyn Rhys, Trask, and Whitbread prizes. Virtually none of the

---

★ There were those who criticized me for making this comparison. Apparently I am the only person not allowed to make fatwa cracks. My job, no doubt, is to be the butt of them.

1983 group had built up a large, loyal readership, though some were beginning to do so; of the 1993 group, Iain Banks, Kazuo Ishiguro, Ben Okri, Jeanette Winterson, Philip Kerr—an innovative thriller writer I'd never previously read—and Hanif Kureishi have legions of fans.

It is true that some of the names on our list will be unknown to most readers. These include some of the best and most exciting writers on the list. It seems to me astonishing that a writer with the narrative drive and comic brio of Louis de Bernières is so little known, especially as he has won a Commonwealth literature prize. Another surprise package is Tibor Fischer, whose Trask-winning first novel, *Under the Frog,* is a delicate seriocomic treasure, a novel about Hungary in 1956—Fischer is of Hungarian parentage—seen through the eyes of a basketball team traveling the country in the nude. Esther Freud's much-praised first novel, *Hideous Kinky,* also earned her a well-deserved place on this list.

Two writers I hadn't read before amazed me with their ambition, erudition, and skill. Lawrence Norfolk's *Lemprière's Dictionary* is a dazzling linguistic and formal achievement that takes on a rich and under-explored subject: the East India Company. (There are countless Raj fictions but few imaginings of the earlier period of Company rule.) It reminded me at times of the Dutch masterpiece of colonial trade, Multatuli's *Max Havelaar.* And Adam Lively's monster-novel of a dystopic future, *Sing the Body Electric,* is as rich and complex a novel of ideas as one could wish for.

To see so diverse a list dumped on by people who simply haven't read the books is to feel a kind of despair about the culture of denigration in which we live. Can't we be fair-minded enough to give these books, these writers, a chance? Can't we even let them have their fifteen minutes in the spotlight before we start trashing them?

The list's critics say that by forty, writers should have some solid triumphs under their belts. How about *The Remains of the Day, The Wasp Factory, The Swimming-Pool Library, The Buddha of Suburbia, The Famished Road, The Passion*? They say the young writers on the list don't merit attention. But Fischer, Freud, and Nicholas Shakespeare have been acclaimed and won prizes; Will Self is already a cult figure.

True, some of these twenty writers are only just arriving at publication: for example, A. L. Kennedy, a writer rich in the humanity and warmth that seems at a premium in these bleak times, and well able to handle a layered narrative and build to a shocking climax that is fully earned and not a bit gratuitous.

It is a tribute to the strength of the list that so many highly rated writers—Adam Thorpe, Robert McLiam Wilson, Rose Boyt, Lesley Glaister, Robert Harris, Alexander Stuart, D. J. Taylor, Richard Rayner, David Profumo, Sean French, Jonathan Coe, Mark Lawson, Glenn Patterson, Deborah Levy—didn't make it. I personally regret not having been able to find room for such talented first-time writers as Tim Pears, whose beautiful first novel, *In the Place of Fallen Leaves,* brings just a touch of Macondo to rural Devon in the heat wave of 1984; Nadeem Aslam, whose novel of modern Karachi, *Season of the Rainbirds,* is much better than its title; and Romesh Gunesekera, whose first story-collection, *Monkfish Moon,* gives notice of a fine writer in the making.

Twenty young writers did make the list because in our opinion they were the best we have. We can argue about the names—who should have been in, who should have been out—but for Pete's sake, guys, let's give them a break.

—

If you read two hundred or so novels, you do begin to notice certain general trends and themes. There was a point at which I said that if I read another novel about a young girl beginning to menstruate, I'd scream. (A. S. Byatt pointed out that the best of these novels had in fact been written by a man, Tim Pears, whose point-of-view character is female.) There was a lot of violence about, a lot of writers who wanted to write about pornography, a lot of violence to women—novels that would begin, as it were, "She sat down opposite me on the tube and I wondered what she'd look like with an axe in her face"; and there was Helen Zahavi's hideous, kinky little revenge-novel of violence done to men.

There were a number of wimp-novels: "I had this really boring job as a clerk in a small provincial town," they would begin, "when I met this really wonderful gay cripple and entered a whole new world." (I am lampooning, but only a little.) There was a whole group of son-of-Kelman Scottish novels in which people said "fuck" and "cunt" and recited the names of minor punk bands. There was, too, the Incredibly Badly Sub-Edited Novel. I remember one set in the sixties in which a Communist character couldn't spell "Baader" or "Meinhof" ("Bader," "Meinhoff"). Many of the entries read as if no editor had ever looked at them.

More seriously—and this is probably why there has been a lot of garbage talked about a lost generation—it was easy to see, all over the landscape of contemporary fiction, the devastating effect of the Thatcher years. So many of these writers wrote without hope. They had lost all ambition, all desire to wrestle with the world. Their books dealt with tiny patches of the world, tiny pieces of human experience—a council estate, a mother, a father, a lost job. Very few writers had the courage or even the energy to bite off a big chunk of the universe and chew it over. Very few showed any linguistic or formal innovation. Many were dulled, and therefore dull. (And then, even worse, there were the Hooray Henries and Sloanes who evidently thought that the day of the yuppie-novel, the Bellini-drinking, okay-yah fiction, had dawned. Dukedoms and country-house bulimics abounded.) It was plain that too many books were being published; that too many writers had found their way into print without any justification for it at all; that too many publishers had adopted a kind of random, scattergun policy of publishing for turnover and just hoping that something would strike a chord.

When the general picture is so disheartening, it is easy to miss the good stuff. I agreed to be a judge for "Best of Young British Novelists II" because I wanted to find out for myself if the good stuff really was there. In my view, it is. The four of us have worked extremely hard, reading, re-reading, evaluating, debating. It was a marvelously unbitchy experience, and I hope that we will be seen to have performed some service, not only to the chosen writers but also to readers. I hope just a little of the excitement that surrounded fiction a dozen or so years ago might be regenerated by this list.

One of my old schoolmasters was fond of devising English versions of the epigrams of Martial. I remember only one, his version of Martial's message to a particularly backward-looking critic:

> You only praise the good old days
> We young 'uns get no mention.
> I don't see why I have to die
> To gain your kind attention.

January 1993

Angela Carter

————————

[*First published as an introduction to* The Collected Stories of Angela Carter]

The last time I visited Angela Carter, a few weeks before she died, she had insisted on dressing for tea, in spite of being in considerable pain. She sat bright-eyed and erect, head cocked like a parrot's, lips satirically pursed, and got down to the serious teatime business of giving and receiving the latest dirt: sharp, foulmouthed, passionate. That's what she was like: spikily outspoken—once, after I'd come to the end of a relationship of which she had not approved, she telephoned me to say, "*Well.* You're going to be seeing a *lot* more of *me* from now on"— and at the same time courteous enough to defy mortal suffering for the gentility of a formal afternoon tea.

Death genuinely pissed Angela off, but she had one consolation. She had taken out an "immense" life insurance policy shortly before the cancer struck. The prospect of the insurers being obliged, after receiving so few payments, to hand out a fortune to "her boys" (her husband, Mark, and her son, Alexander) delighted her greatly, and inspired a great gloating black-comedy aria at which it was impossible not to laugh.

She planned her funeral carefully. My instructions were to read Marvell's poem "On a Drop of Dew." This was a surprise. The Angela

I knew had always been the most scatologically irreligious, merrily godless of women; yet she wanted Marvell's meditation on the immortal
soul—"that Drop, that Ray / Of the clear Fountain of Eternal Day"—
spoken over her dead body. Was this a last surrealist joke, of the "thank
God, I die an atheist" variety, or an obeisance to the metaphysician
Marvell's high symbolic language from a writer whose own favored
language was also pitched high, and replete with symbols? It should be
noted that no divinity makes an appearance in Marvell's poem, except
for "th' Almighty Sun." Perhaps Angela, always a giver of light, was asking us, at the end, to imagine her dissolving into the "glories" of that
greater light: the artist becoming a part, simply, of art.

She was too individual, too fierce a writer to dissolve easily, however:
by turns formal and outrageous, exotic and demotic, exquisite and
coarse, precious and raunchy, fabulist and socialist, purple and black.
Her novels are like nobody else's, from the transsexual coloratura of
The Passion of New Eve to the music-hall knees-up of *Wise Children;* but
the best of her, I think, is in her stories. Sometimes, at novel length, the
distinctive Carter voice, those smoky opium-eater's cadences inter-
rupted by harsh or comic discords, that moonstone-and-rhinestone
mix of opulence and flimflam, can be wearying. In her stories, she can
dazzle and swoop, and quit while she's ahead.

Carter arrived almost fully formed; her early story "A Very, Very
Great Lady and Her Son at Home" is already replete with Carterian
motifs. Here is the love of the gothic, of lush language and high culture;
but also of low stinks—falling rose-petals that sound like pigeon's farts,
and a father who smells of horse dung, and bowels that are "great level-
ers." Here is the self as performance: perfumed, decadent, languorous,
erotic, perverse; very like the winged woman, Fevvers, heroine of her
penultimate novel, *Nights at the Circus.*

Another early story, "A Victorian Fable," announces her addiction to
all the arcana of language. This extraordinary text, half "Jabberwocky,"
half *Pale Fire,* exhumes the past as never before, by exhuming its
dead words: "In every snickert and ginnel, bone-grubbers, rufflers,
shivering-jemmies, anglers, clapperdogeons, peterers, sneeze-lurkers
and Whip Jacks with their morts, out of the picaroon, fox and flimp and
ogle."

Be advised, these early stories say: this writer is no meat-and-
potatoes hack; she is a rocket, a Catherine wheel. She will call her first
collection *Fireworks.*

—

Several of the *Fireworks* stories deal with Japan, a country whose tea-ceremony formality and dark eroticism bruised and challenged Carter's imagination. In "A Souvenir of Japan" she arranges polished images of that country before us. "The story of Momotaro, who was born from a peach." "Mirrors make a room uncosy." Her narrator presents her Japanese lover to us as a sex object, complete with bee-stung lips. "I should like to have had him embalmed . . . so that I could watch him all the time and he would not have been able to get away from me." The lover is, at least, beautiful; the narrator's view of her big-boned self, as seen in a mirror, is distinctly uncozy. "In the department store there was a rack of dresses labelled: 'For Young and Cute Girls Only.' When I looked at them, I felt as gross as Glumdalclitch."

In "Flesh and the Mirror" the exquisite, erotic atmosphere thickens, approaching pastiche—for Japanese literature has specialized rather in these heated sexual perversities—except when it is cut through sharply by Carter's constant self-awareness. ("Hadn't I gone eight thousand miles to find a climate with enough anguish and hysteria in it to satisfy me?" her narrator asks; as, in "The Smile of Winter," another unnamed narrator admonishes us: "Do not think I do not realize what I am doing," and then analyzes her story with a perspicacity that rescues—brings to life—what might otherwise have been a static piece of mood music. Carter's cold-water douches of intelligence often come to the rescue of her fancy when it runs too wild.)

In the non-Japanese stories Carter enters, for the first time, the fable-world which she will make her own. A brother and sister are lost in a sensual, malevolent forest whose trees have breasts, and bite. Here the apple tree of knowledge teaches not good and evil but incestuous sexuality. Incest—a recurring Carter subject—crops up again in "The Executioner's Beautiful Daughter," a tale set in a bleak upland village, the quintessential Carter location, where, as she says in the *Bloody Chamber* story "The Werewolf," "they have cold weather, they have cold hearts." Wolves howl around these Carter-country villages, and there are many metamorphoses.

Carter's other country is the fairground, the world of the gimcrack showman, the hypnotist, the trickster, the puppeteer. "The Loves of Lady Purple" takes her closed circus-world to yet another mountainous, Middle European village where suicides are treated like vampires

(wreaths of garlic, stakes through the heart) while real warlocks "prac-
tised rites of immemorial beastliness in the forests." As in all Carter's
fairground stories, "the grotesque is the order of the day." Lady Purple,
the dominatrix marionette, is a moralist's warning—beginning as a
whore, she turns into a puppet because she is "pulled only by the
strings of Lust." She is a female, sexy, and lethal rewrite of Pinocchio,
and, along with the metamorphic cat-woman in "Master," one of the
many dark (and fair) ladies with "unappeasable appetites" to whom Angela Carter is so partial.

In her second collection, *The Bloody Chamber,* these riot ladies inherit
her fictional earth. *The Bloody Chamber* is Carter's masterwork: the
book in which her high, perfervid mode is perfectly married to her stories' needs. (For the best of the low, demotic Carter, read *Wise Children;*
but in spite of all the oo-er-guv, brush-up-your-Shakespeare comedy of
that last novel, *The Bloody Chamber* is the likeliest of her works to en-
dure.)

The novella-length title story begins as classic Grand Guignol: an innocent bride, a much-married millionaire husband, a lonely Castle
stood upon a melting shore, a secret room containing horrors. The
helpless girl and the civilized, decadent, murderous man: Carter's first
variation on the theme of Beauty and the Beast. There is a feminist
twist: instead of the weak father to save whom, in the fairy tale, Beauty
agrees to go to the Beast, we are given, here, an indomitable mother
rushing to her daughter's rescue. It is Carter's genius, in this collection,
to make the fable of Beauty and the Beast a metaphor for all the myriad
yearnings and dangers of sexual relations. Now it is the Beauty who is
the stronger, now the Beast. In "The Courtship of Mr. Lyon," it is for
the Beauty to save the Beast's life; while in "The Tiger's Eye," Beauty
will be erotically transformed into an exquisite animal herself: "each
stroke of his tongue ripped off skin after skin, all the skins of a life in the
world, and left behind a nascent patina of hairs. My earrings turned
back to water. . . . I shrugged the drops off my beautiful fur." As though
her whole body were being deflowered and so metamorphosing into a
new instrument of desire, allowing her admission to a new ("animal" in
the sense of *spiritual* as well as *tigerish*) world. In "The Erl-King," however, Beauty and the Beast will not be reconciled. Here there is neither
healing nor submission but revenge.

The collection expands to take in many other fabulous old tales;
blood and love, always proximate, underlie and unify them all. In "The

Lady of the House of Love" love and blood unite in the person of a vampire: Beauty grown monstrous, Beastly. In "The Snow Child" we are in the fairy-tale territory of white snow, red blood, black bird, and a girl, white, red, and black, born of a count's wishes; but Carter's modern imagination knows that for every count there is a countess, who will not tolerate her fantasy-rival. The battle of the sexes is fought between women, too.

The arrival of Red Riding Hood completes Carter's brilliant, reinventing synthesis of *Kinder- und Hausmärchen*. Now we are offered the radical, shocking suggestion that Grandmother might actually be the Wolf ("The Werewolf"); or, equally shocking, the thought that the girl (Red Riding Hood, Beauty) might easily be as amorally savage as the Wolf/Beast; that she might conquer the Wolf by the power of her own predatory sexuality, her erotic wolfishness. This is the theme of "The Company of Wolves," and to watch *The Company of Wolves,* the film Carter made with Neil Jordan, weaving together several of her wolf-narratives, is to long for the full-scale wolf-novel she never wrote.

"Wolf-Alice" offers final metamorphoses. Now there is no Beauty, only two Beasts: a cannibal Duke and a girl reared by wolves, who thinks of herself as a wolf, and who, arriving at womanhood, is drawn toward self-knowledge by the mystery of her own bloody chamber; that is, her menstrual flow. By blood, and by what she sees in mirrors, which make a house uncozy.

———

At length the grandeur of the mountains becomes monotonous. . . . He turned and stared at the mountain for a long time. He had lived in it for fourteen years but he had never seen it before as it might look to someone who had not known it as almost a part of the self. . . . As he said goodbye to it, he saw it turn into so much scenery, into the wonderful backcloth for an old country tale, tale of a child suckled by wolves, perhaps, or of wolves nursed by a woman.

Carter's farewell to her mountain country, at the end of her last wolf-story, "Peter and the Wolf," in *Black Venus,* signals that, like her hero, she has "tramped onwards, into a different story."

There is one other out-and-out fantasy in this third collection, a meditation on *A Midsummer Night's Dream* that prefigures (and is better than) a passage in *Wise Children.* In this story Carter's linguistic exoticism is in full flight—here are "breezes, juicy as mangoes, that mythopoeically caress the Coast of Coromandel far away on the porphyry and lapis lazuli Indian Shore." But, as usual, her sarcastic common sense yanks the story back to earth before it can disappear in an exquisite puff of smoke. This dream-wood—"nowhere near Athens . . . located somewhere in the English Midlands, possibly near Bletchley"—is damp and waterlogged and the fairies all have colds. Also, it has, since the date of the story, been chopped down to make room for a motorway. Carter's elegant fugue on Shakespearean themes is lifted toward brilliance by her exposition of the difference between the *Dream*'s wood and the "dark necromantic forest" of the Grimms. The forest, she finely reminds us, is a scary place; to be lost in it is to fall prey to monsters and witches. But in a wood, "you purposely mislay your way"; there are no wolves, and the wood "is kind to lovers." Here is the difference between the English and the European fairy tale, precisely and unforgettably defined.

Mostly, however, *Black Venus* and its successor, *American Ghosts and Old World Wonders,* eschew fantasy worlds; Carter's revisionist imagination has turned toward the real, her interest toward portraiture rather than narrative. The best pieces in these later books are portraits—of Baudelaire's black mistress, Jeanne Duval, of Edgar Allan Poe, and, in two stories, of Lizzie Borden long before she "took an ax," and the same Lizzie on the day of her crimes, a day described with languorous precision and attention to detail: the consequences of overdressing in a heat wave and of eating twice-cooked fish both play a part. Beneath the hyper-realism, however, there is an echo of *The Bloody Chamber;* Lizzie's is a bloody deed, and she is, in addition, menstruating. Her own lifeblood flows while the angel of death waits in a nearby tree. (Once again, as with the wolf-stories, one hankers for more; for the Lizzie Borden novel we can't have.)

Baudelaire, Poe, *Dream*-Shakespeare, Hollywood, panto, fairy tale: Carter wears her influences openly, for she is their deconstructionist, their saboteur. She takes what we know and, having broken it, puts it together in her own spiky, courteous way. Her worlds are new and not new, like our own. In her hands Cinderella, given back her original name of Ashputtle, is the fire-scarred heroine of a tale of horrid mutilations wrought by mother-love; John Ford's *'Tis Pity She's a Whore* becomes a movie directed by a very different Ford; and the hidden natures of pantomime characters are revealed.

She opens an old story for us, like an egg, and finds the new story, the now-story we want to hear, within.

—

No such thing as a perfect writer. Carter's high-wire act takes place over a swamp of preciousness, over quicksands of the arch and twee; and there's no denying that she sometimes falls off, no getting away from odd outbreaks of folderol, and some of her puddings, her most ardent admirers will concede, are excessively egged. Too much use of words like "eldritch," too many men who are rich "as Croesus," too much porphyry and lapis lazuli to please a certain sort of purist. But the miracle is how often she pulls it off; how often she pirouettes without falling, or juggles without dropping a ball.

Accused by lazy pens of political correctness, she was the most individual, independent, and idiosyncratic of writers; dismissed by many in her lifetime as a marginal, cultish figure, an exotic hothouse flower, she has become the contemporary writer most studied at British universities—a victory over the mainstream she would have enjoyed.

She hadn't finished. Like Italo Calvino, like Bruce Chatwin, like Raymond Carver, she died at the height of her powers. For writers, these are the cruelest deaths: in mid-sentence, so to speak. The stories in this volume are the measure of our loss. But they are also our treasure, to savor and to hoard. Raymond Carver is said to have told his wife before he died (also of lung cancer), "We're out there now. We're out there in Literature." Carver was the most modest of men, but this is the remark of a man who knew, and who had often been told, how much his work was worth. Angela received less confirmation, in her lifetime, of the value of her unique oeuvre; but she, too, is out there now, out there in Literature, a Ray of the clear Fountain of Eternal Day.

April 1995

Beirut Blues

———————

At one point in Hanan al-Shaykh's new novel, *Beirut Blues,* the narrator, Asmahan, learns that her grandfather, a dirty old man who likes to bruise women's breasts, has taken up with a young Lolita. The nymphet, Juhayna, is suspected by various family members of having designs on their inheritance, but Asmahan is moved to a more generous, and stranger, judgment. "In choosing him she was merely choosing the past which had proved its authenticity compared to the bearded leaders, the conflicting voices, the clash of arms."

The past is mourned throughout *Beirut Blues,* mourned without sentimentality. The past is the place in which Asmahan's grandmother had to fight for the right to literacy, but it is also the lost village land, occupied first by Palestinians and then by local thugs; it is Beirut, that once-beautiful, brilliant, cosmopolitan city, transformed now into the barbarity of ruins in which perch snipers picking off women in blue dresses and other fighters who are afraid of the hooting of owls. The young Asmahan grew addicted to the voice of Billie Holiday. Now she writes letters to departed friends, to her lost land, to her lover, to her city, to the war itself, letters with the quality of slow, sensuous, sad music. Now the strange fruit is hanging from the trees outside Asmahan's own windows, and she has become the lady singing the blues.

"In Lebanon," Edward Said has said, "the novel exists largely as a form recording its own impossibility, shading off or breaking into autobiography (as in the remarkable proliferation of Lebanese women's writing), reportage, pastiche." How to create literature—how to preserve its fragilities, and also its tough-minded individuality—in the middle of an explosion? Elias Khoury, in his brilliant short novel *Little Mountain* (1977), created an amalgam of fable, surrealism, reportage, low comedy, and memoir that provided one response to this question. Hanan al-Shaykh, perhaps the finest of the women writers to whom Said referred—author of the acclaimed *The Story of Zahra* and *Women of Sand and Myrrh*—offers a new solution. What unifies her novel's shattered universe is the presence, everywhere in her prose, of the low, unabated fever of human desire. It is the melancholy, luscious portrait of letter-writing Asmahan, a true sensualist of Beirut, a woman given to spending long afternoons oiling her hair, who acts with a sexual freedom and writes with an explicitness of erotic feeling and description that makes this novel pretty daring by the puritanical, censorious standards of the mosque- and militia-ridden present.

Asmahan begins and ends her epistolary narrative with letters to an old friend, Hayat, now living abroad; and the question of exile is one of the book's recurring motifs. (Modern Arabic literature is, more and more, a literature not only of exile but by exiles; the men of violence and God are making sure of that.) Asmahan feels sorry for her old friend, living away from home and missing Lebanese food; she feels almost contemptuous of the returning writer Jawad, with his smart questions, his appointments, his arrival as a voyeur of her lived reality. "Then one day he opened his eyes . . . the newspapers no longer provided him with a hunting-ground for his sarcastic jokes; it almost seemed to cause him physical pain to read of the senselessness of what was happening." At this moment, he and Asmahan begin their affair; and so she must choose between new love and old home, for Jawad will leave Beirut. She, too, must contemplate exile. Perhaps, in the name of love, she must become like Hayat, her friend and mirror-soul, for whom she has felt such pity, even scorn.

It would be wrong to reveal Asmahan's final choice, but it is not easily made. Her attachment to Beirut is very deep, even though, in a letter to Jill Morrell, she compares herself to the hostages. "My mind is no longer my own. . . . I possess my body but not, even temporarily, the ground I walk on. What does it mean to be kidnapped? Being separated forcibly from your environment, family, friends, home, bed. So in some strange way I can persuade myself that I'm worse off than them. . . . For

I'm still in my own place, but separated from it in a painful way: this is my city and I don't recognize it." Al-Shaykh brings to this transformed Beirut a passion of description. Here are cows that have become addicted to cannabis, and Iranian signs on shopfronts, and plastic-bottle trees. Old place-names have lost meaning and new ones have sprung up. There are Palestinians who speak a Beckettian language: "I'll have to kill myself. No, I must keep going," and there are militias and terrorists, and there is the War. "People have a desperate need to enter any conflict which has become familiar . . . to save them searching further afield and investigating the mysteries of life and death," Asmahan writes. "You [the War] give them confidence and a kind of serenity; people make this precious discovery and play your game."

What shall I do with these ideas? agonizes Asmahan, and perhaps the best answer lies in her indomitable grandmother's advice. "Remember who we are. Make sure the larder and the fridge are never empty." In this, her finest novel, fluently translated by Catherine Cobham, Hanan al-Shaykh makes that act of remembrance, joining it to an unforgettable portrait of a broken city. It should be read by everyone who cares about the truths behind the clichéd Beirut of the TV news; and by everyone who cares about the more enduring, and universal, truths of the heart.

March 1995

Arthur Miller at Eighty

———

[*Originally delivered as part of a birthday celebration for and of Arthur Miller at the University of East Anglia*]

Arthur Miller's is not only a great life; it is also a great book, *Time-bends,* an autobiography that reads like a great American novel—as if Bellow's Augie March had grown up to be a tall Jewish playwright and had, in Bellow's famous words, "made the record in his own way: first to knock, first admitted; sometimes an innocent knock, sometimes a not so innocent."

In an age when much literature and even more literary criticism has turned inward, losing itself in halls of mirrors, Arthur Miller's double insistence on the reality of the real, and on the moral function of writing, sounds once again as radical as it did in his youth. "The effort to locate in the human species a counterforce to the randomness of victimization," he calls it, adding, "But, as history has taught, that force can only be moral. Unfortunately."

When a great writer reaches a great age, the temptation to turn him into an institution, into a statue of himself, is easily succumbed to. But to read Miller is to discover, on every page, the enduring relevance of his thought: "The ultimate human mystery," he writes, "may not be anything more than the claims on us of clan and race, which may yet turn out to have the power, because they defy the rational mind, to kill the world." The sharpness of such perceptions makes Miller very much our contemporary, a man for this season as well as all his others. Willy Loman's line "I still feel kind of temporary about myself" is also the way Arthur Miller says he has always felt. "This desire to move on, to metamorphose—or perhaps it is a talent for being contemporary—was given me as life's inevitable condition." In Miller, the temporary and the contemporary are united, and shown to be the same thing.

Miller's genius has always been to reveal what the opening stage directions to *Death of a Salesman* call the "dream rising out of reality." By paying attention, he discovers the miraculous within the real. His is a life dedicated as passionately to the remembrance, and the enlivening through art, of the small and the unconsidered as it is to the articulation of the great moral issues of the day. Here, in his autobiography, is an endless sequence of men and women caught in wonderful cameos: the great-grandfather who was "an orchestra of scents—each of his gestures smelled different"; and the rabbi who stole the dying patriarch's diamonds, and had to be beaten up by the dying man before he returned them; and Mr. Dozick the pharmacist, who sewed up Miller's brother's ear on his drugstore table; and the Polish school bully who taught Miller some early lessons in anti-Semitism; and Lucky Luciano in Palermo, nostalgic for America, and scarily over-generous, so that Miller began to fear being lost in the Bunyanesque "swamp of Something for Nothing, from which there is no return."

Moral stature is a rare quality in these degraded days. Very few writers possess it. Miller's seems innate but was much increased because he was able to learn from his mistakes. Like Günter Grass, who was brought up in a Nazi household and had the dizzying experience, after the war, of learning that everything he had believed to be true was a lie, Arthur Miller has had—more than once—to discard his worldviews. Coming from a family of profit-minded men, and discovering Marxism at sixteen, he learned that "the true condition of men was the complete opposite of the competitive system I had assumed was normal, with all its mutual hatreds and conniving. Life could be a comradely embrace, people helping one another rather than looking for ways to trip each other up." Later, Marxism came to seem less idealistic. "Deep down in the comradely world of the Marxist promise is parricide," he wrote, and, when he and Lillian Hellman were faced with a Yugoslav man's testimony of the horrors of Soviet domination, he says, unsparingly: "We seemed history's fools."

But he has not remained history's fool. Through his stand against McCarthyism, in his presidency of PEN, his fight against censorship, and his defense of persecuted writers around the world, he has grown into the giant figure we are gathered here to honor. When I needed help, I am proud that Arthur Miller's was one of the first and loudest voices raised on my behalf, and it is a privilege to be able to speak here and thank him tonight.

When Arthur Miller says, "We must re-imagine liberty in every generation, especially since a certain number of people are always afraid of it," his words carry the weight of lived experience, of his own profound re-imaginings. Most of all, however, they carry the weight of his genius. Arthur, we celebrate the genius, and the man. Happy birthday.

October 1995

In Defense of the Novel, Yet Again

At the centenary conference of the British Publishers' Association recently, Professor George Steiner said a mouthful:

> We are getting very tired in our novels. . . . Genres rise, genres fall, the epic, the verse epic, the formal verse tragedy. Great moments, then they ebb. Novels will continue to be written for quite a while but, increasingly, the search is on for hybrid forms, what we will call rather crassly fact/fiction. . . . What novel can today quite compete with the best of reportage, with the very best of immediate narrative? . . .
>
> Pindar [was] the first man on record to say, *this poem will be sung when the city which commissioned it has ceased to exist.* Literature's immense boast against death. To say this today even the greatest poet, I dare venture, would be profoundly embarrassed. . . . The great classical vainglory—but what a wonderful vainglory—of literature. *"I am stronger than death. I can speak about death in poetry, drama, the novel, because I have overcome it, because I am more or less permanent."* That is no longer available.

So here it is once more, wrapped up in the finest, shiniest rhetoric: I mean, of course, that tasty old chestnut, the death of the Novel. To which Professor Steiner adds, for good measure, the death (or at least the radical transformation) of the Reader, into some sort of computer whiz-kid, some sort of super-nerd; and the death (or at least the radical transformation, into electronic form) of the Book itself. The death of the Author having been announced several years ago in France—and the death of Tragedy by Professor Steiner himself in an earlier obituary—that leaves the stage strewn with more bodies than the end of *Hamlet.*

Still standing in the midst of the carnage, however, is a lone, commanding figure, a veritable Fortinbras, before whom all of us, writers of authorless texts, post-literate readers, the House of Usher that is the publishing industry—the *Denmark,* with something rotten in it, that is the publishing industry—and indeed books themselves, must bow our heads: viz., naturally, the Critic.

One prominent writer has also in recent weeks announced the demise of the form of which he has been so celebrated a practitioner. Not only has V. S. Naipaul ceased to write novels: the word "novel" itself, he tells us, now makes him feel ill. Like Professor Steiner, the author of *A House for Mr. Biswas* feels that the novel has outlived its historical moment, no longer fulfills any useful role, and will be replaced by factual writing. Mr. Naipaul, it will surprise no one to learn, is presently to be found at the leading edge of history, creating this new post-fictional literature.*

Another major British writer has this to say. "It hardly needs pointing out that at this moment the prestige of the novel is extremely low, so low that the words 'I never read novels,' which even a dozen years ago were generally uttered with a hint of apology, are now *always* uttered in a tone of pride . . . the novel is likely, if the best literary brains cannot be induced to return to it, to survive in some perfunctory, despised, and hopelessly degenerate form, like modern tomb-stones, or the Punch and Judy Show."

That is George Orwell, writing in 1936. It would appear—as Professor Steiner in fact concedes—that literature has never had a future. Even the *Iliad* and *Odyssey* received bad early reviews. Good writing has always been attacked, notably by other good writers. The most cursory glance at literary history reveals that no masterpiece has been safe from assault at the time of its publication, no writer's reputation unassailed by his contemporaries: Aristophanes called Euripides "a cliché antholo-

---

* Mr. Naipaul—now Sir Vidia—published a new novel, *Half a Life,* five years after making this statement. We must thank him for bringing the dead form back to life.

gist . . . and maker of ragamuffin manikins"; Samuel Pepys thought *A Midsummer Night's Dream* "insipid and ridiculous"; Charlotte Brontë dismissed the work of Jane Austen; Zola pooh-poohed *Les Fleurs du Mal;* Henry James trashed *Middlemarch, Wuthering Heights,* and *Our Mutual Friend.* Everybody sneered at *Moby-Dick. Le Figaro* announced, when *Madame Bovary* was published, that "M. Flaubert is not a writer"; Virginia Woolf called *Ulysses* "underbred"; and the *Odessa Courier* wrote of *Anna Karenina,* "Sentimental rubbish. . . . Show me one page that contains an idea."

So, when today's German critics attack Günter Grass, when today's Italian literati are "surprised," as the French novelist and critic Guy Scarpetta tells us, to learn of Italo Calvino's and Leonardo Scascia's high international reputations, when the cannons of American political correctness are turned on Saul Bellow, when Anthony Burgess belittles Graham Greene moments after Greene's death, and when Professor Steiner, ambitious as ever, takes on not just a few individual writers but the whole literary output of post-war Europe, they may all be suffering from culturally endemic golden-ageism: that recurring, bilious nostalgia for a literary past which never, at the time, seemed that much better than the present does now.

Professor Steiner says, "It is almost axiomatic that today the great novels are coming from the far rim, from India, from the Caribbean, from Latin America," and some will find it surprising that I should take issue with this vision of an exhausted center and vital periphery. If I do so, it is in part because it is such a very Eurocentric lament. Only a Western European intellectual would compose a lament for an entire art form on the basis that the literatures of, say, England, France, Germany, Spain, and Italy were no longer the most interesting on earth. (It is unclear whether Professor Steiner considers the United States to be in the center or on the far rim; the geography of this flat-earther vision of literature is a little hard to follow. From where I sit, American literature looks to be in good shape.) What does it matter where the great novels come from, as long as they keep coming? What is this flat earth on which the good professor lives, with jaded Romans at the center and frightfully gifted Hottentots and Anthropophagi lurking at the edges? The map in Professor Steiner's head is an imperial map, and Europe's empires are long gone. The half century whose literary output proves, for Steiner and Naipaul, the novel's decline is also the first half century of the post-colonial period. Might it not simply be that a new novel is emerging, a post-colonial novel, a de-centered, transnational, inter-lingual, cross-cultural novel; and that in this new world order, or disorder, we find a better explanation of the contemporary novel's health than Professor Steiner's somewhat patronizingly Hegelian view that the reason for the creativity of the "far rim" is that these are areas "which are in an earlier stage of the bourgeois culture, which are in an earlier, rougher, more problematic form."

It was, after all, the Franco regime's success in stifling decade after decade of Spanish literature that shifted the spotlight to the fine writers working in Latin America. The so-called Latin American boom was, accordingly, as much the result of the corruption of the old bourgeois world as of the allegedly primitive creativity of the new. And the description of India's ancient, sophisticated culture as existing in an "earlier, rougher" state than the West is bizarre. India, with its great mercantile classes, its sprawling bureaucracies, its exploding economy, possesses one of the largest and most dynamic bourgeoisies in the world, and has done so for at least as long as Europe. Great literature and a class of literate readers are nothing new in India. What is new is the emergence of a gifted generation of Indian writers *working in English*. What is new is that the "center" has deigned to notice the "rim," because the "rim" has begun to speak in its myriad versions of a language the West can more easily understand.

Even Professor Steiner's portrait of an exhausted Europe is, in my view, simply and demonstrably false. The last fifty years have given us the oeuvres of, to name just a few, Albert Camus, Graham Greene, Doris Lessing, Samuel Beckett, Italo Calvino, Elsa Morante, Vladimir Nabokov, Günter Grass, Aleksandr Solzhenitsyn, Milan Kundera, Danilo Kis, Thomas Bernhard, Marguerite Yourcenar. We can all make our own lists. If we include writers from beyond the frontiers of Europe, it becomes clear that the world has rarely seen so rich a crop of great novelists living and working at the same time—that the easy gloom of the Steiner-Naipaul position is not just depressing but unjustified. If V. S. Naipaul no longer wishes, or is no longer able, to write novels, it is our loss. But the art of the novel will undoubtedly survive without him.

There is, in my view, no crisis in the art of the novel. The novel is precisely that "hybrid form" for which Professor Steiner yearns. It is part social inquiry, part fantasy, part confessional. It crosses frontiers of knowledge as well as topographical boundaries. He is right, however, that many good writers have blurred the boundaries between fact and fiction. Ryszard Kapuscinski's magnificent book about Haile Selassie, *The Emperor,* is an example of this creative blurring. The so-called New Journalism developed in America by Tom Wolfe and others was a straightforward attempt to steal the novel's clothes, and in the case of Wolfe's own *Radical Chic & Mau-Mauing the Flak Catchers,* or *The Right Stuff,* the attempt was persuasively successful. The category of "travel writing" has expanded to include works of profound cultural meditation: Claudio Magris's *Danube,* say, or Neal Ascherson's *Black Sea.* And in the face of a brilliant non-fictional tour de force such as Roberto Calasso's *The Marriage of Cadmus and Harmony,* in which a re-examination of the Greek myths achieves all the tension and intellectual excitement of the best fiction, one can only applaud the arrival of a new kind of imaginative essay writing—or, better, the return of the encyclopedic playfulness of Diderot or Montaigne. The novel can welcome these developments without feeling threatened. There's room for all of us in here.

A few years ago the British novelist Will Self published a funny short story called "The Quantity Theory of Insanity," which suggested that the sum total of sanity available to the human race might be fixed, might be a constant; so that the attempt to cure the insane was useless, as the effect of one individual regaining his sanity would inevitably be that someone somewhere else would lose theirs, as if we were all sleeping in a bed covered by a blanket—of sanity—that wasn't quite big enough to cover us all. One of us pulls the blanket toward us; another's toes are instantly exposed. It is a richly comic idea, and it recurs in Professor Steiner's zaniest argument, which he offers with a perfectly straight face—that at any given moment, there exists a total quantum of creative talent, and at present the lure of the cinema, television, and even of advertising is pulling the blanket of genius away from the novel, which consequently lies exposed, shivering in its pajamas in the depths of our cultural winter.

The trouble with the theory is that it supposes all creative talent to be of the same kind. Apply this notion to athletics and its absurdity becomes apparent. The supply of marathon runners is not diminished by the popularity of sprint events. The quality of high jumpers is unrelated to the number of great exponents of the pole vault.

It is more likely that the advent of new art forms allows new groups of people to enter the creative arena. I know of very few great filmmakers who might have been good novelists—Satyajit Ray, Ingmar Bergman, Woody Allen, Jean Renoir, and that's about it. How many pages of Quentin Tarantino's snappy material, his gangsters' riffs about eating Big Macs in Paris, could you read if you didn't have Samuel Jackson or John Travolta speaking them for you? The best screenwriters are the best precisely because they think not novelistically but pictorially.

I am, in short, much less worried than Steiner about the threat posed to the novel by these newer, high-tech forms. It is perhaps the low-tech nature of the act of writing that will save it. Means of artistic expression that require large quantities of finance and sophisticated technology—films, plays, records—become, by virtue of that dependence, easy to censor and to control. But what one writer can make in the solitude of one room is something no power can easily destroy.

I agree with Professor Steiner's celebration of modern science—"today that is where the joy is, that is where the hope is, the energy, the formidable sense of world upon world opening up," but this burst of scientific creativity is, ironically, the best riposte to his "quantity theory of creativity." The idea that potential great novelists have been lost to the study of sub-atomic physics or black holes is as implausible as its opposite: that the great writers of history—Jane Austen, say, or James Joyce—might easily, had they but taken a different turning, have been the Newtons and Einsteins of their day.

In questioning the quality of creativity to be found in the modern novel, Professor Steiner points us in the wrong direction. If there is a crisis in present-day literature, it is of a somewhat different kind.

The novelist Paul Auster recently told me that all American writers had to accept that they were involved in an activity which was, in the United States, no more than a minority interest, like, say, soccer. This observation chimes with Milan Kundera's complaint, in his new volume of essays, *Testaments Betrayed,* of "Europe's incapacity to defend and explain (explain patiently to itself and to others) that most European of arts, the art of the novel; in other words, to explain and defend its own culture. The 'children of the novel,'" Kundera argues, "have abandoned the art that shaped them. Europe, the society of the novel, has abandoned its own self." Auster is talking about the death of the American reader's interest in this kind of reading matter; Kundera, about the death of the European reader's sense of cultural connection with this kind of cultural product. Add these to Steiner's illiterate, computer-obsessed child of tomorrow, and perhaps we are talking about something like the death of reading itself.

Or perhaps not. For literature, good literature, has always been a minority interest. Its cultural importance derives not from its success in some sort of ratings war but from its success in telling us things about ourselves that we hear from no other quarter. And that minority—the minority that is prepared to read and buy good books—has in truth never been larger than it is now. The problem is to interest it. What is happening is not so much the death as the bewilderment of the reader. In America, in 1999, over five thousand new novels were published. Five thousand! It would be a miracle if five hundred publishable novels had been written in a year. It would be extraordinary if fifty of them were good. It would be cause for universal celebration if five of them— if one of them!—were great.

Publishers are over-publishing because, in house after house, good editors have been fired or not replaced, and an obsession with turnover has replaced the ability to distinguish good books from bad. Let the market decide, too many publishers seem to think. Let's just put this stuff out there. Something's bound to click. So out to the stores they go, into the valley of death go the five thousand, with publicity machines providing inadequate covering fire. This approach is fabulously self-destructive. As Orwell said in 1936—you see that there is nothing new under the sun—"the novel is being shouted out of existence." Readers, unable to hack their way through the rain-forest of junk fiction, made cynical by the debased language of hyperbole with which every book is garlanded, give up. They buy a couple of prizewinners a year, perhaps one or two books by writers whose names they recognize, and flee. Over-publishing and over-hyping creates under-reading. It is not just a question of too many novels chasing too few readers but a question of too many novels actually chasing readers away. If publishing a first novel has become, as Professor Steiner suggests, a "gamble against reality," it is in large part because of this non-discriminatory, scatter-gun approach. We hear a lot, these days, about a new, business-like spirit of financial ruthlessness in publishing. What we need, however, is the best kind of editorial ruthlessness. We need a return to judgment.

And there is another great danger facing literature, and of this Professor Steiner makes no mention: that is, the attack on intellectual liberty itself; intellectual liberty, without which there can be no literature.

This is not a new danger, either. Once again, George Orwell, writing in 1945, offers us much remarkably contemporary wisdom, and you will forgive me if I quote him at some length:

> In our age, the idea of intellectual liberty is under attack from two directions. On the one hand are its theoretical enemies, the apologists of totalitarianism [today one might say, fanaticism], and on the other its immediate practical enemies, monopoly and bureaucracy. In the past . . . the idea of rebellion and the idea of intellectual integrity were mixed up. A heretic—political, moral, religious, or aesthetic—was one who refused to outrage his own conscience.
>
> [Nowadays] the dangerous proposition [is] that freedom is *undesirable* and that intellectual honesty is a form of anti-social selfishness.
>
> The enemies of intellectual liberty always try to present their case as a plea for discipline versus individualism. The writer who refuses to sell his opinions is always branded as a mere *egoist.* He is accused, that is, either of wanting to shut himself up in an ivory tower, or of making an exhibitionist display of his own personality, or of resisting the inevitable current of history in an attempt to cling to unjustified privileges. [But] to write in plain language one has to think fearlessly, and if one thinks fearlessly one cannot be politically orthodox.

The pressures of monopoly and bureaucracy, of corporatism and conservatism, limiting and narrowing the range and quality of what gets published, are known to every working writer. Of the pressures of intolerance and censorship, I personally have in these past years gained perhaps too much knowledge. There are many such struggles taking place in the world today: in Algeria, in China, in Iran, in Turkey, in Egypt, in Nigeria, writers are being censored, harassed, jailed, and even murdered. Even in Europe and the United States, the storm troopers of various "sensitivities" seek to limit our freedom of speech. It has never been more important to continue to defend those values that make the art of literature possible. The death of the novel may be far off, but the violent death of many contemporary novelists is, alas, an inescapable fact. In spite of this, I do not believe that writers have given up on posterity. What George Steiner beautifully calls the "wonderful vainglory" of literature still fires us, even if, as he suggests, we are too embarrassed to say so in public. The poet Ovid sets these great, confident lines at the end of his *Metamorphoses*:

But, with the better part of me, I'll gain
a place that's higher than the stars: my name,
indelible, eternal, will remain.*

I am sure the same ambition still resides in every writer's heart: to be thought of, in times to come, as Rilke thought of Orpheus:

He is one of the staying messengers,
who still holds far into the doors of the dead
bowls with fruits worthy of praise.†

May 2000

---

* Allen Mandelbaum's translation of the *Metamorphoses* of Ovid (Harcourt Brace, 1993).

† M.D. Herter Norton's translation, from *Translations from the Poetry of Rainer Maria Rilke* (W. W. Norton, 1993 reissue).

Notes on Writing and the Nation

———

[*For* Index on Censorship]

1

The ousel singing in the woods of Cilgwri,
Tirelessly as a stream over the mossed stones,
Is not so old as the toad of Cors Fochno
Who feels the cold skin sagging round his bones.

Few writers are as profoundly engaged with their native land as R. S. Thomas, a Welsh nationalist, whose poems seek, by noticing, arguing, rhapsodizing, mythologizing, to write the nation into fierce, lyrical being. Yet this same R. S. Thomas also writes:

Hate takes a long time
To grow in, and mine
Has increased from birth;
Not for the brute earth . . .
I find
This hate's for my own kind.

Startling to find an admission of something close to self-hatred in the lines of a national bard. Yet this perhaps is the only kind of nationalist a writer can be. When the imagination is given sight by passion, it sees darkness as well as light. To feel so ferociously is to feel contempt as well as pride, hatred as well as love. These proud contempts, this hating love, often earn the writer a nation's wrath. The nation requires anthems, flags. The poet offers discord. Rags.

2

Connections have been made between the historical development of the twin "narratives" of the novel and the nation-state. The progress of a story through its pages toward its goal is likened to the self-image of the nation, moving through history toward its manifest destiny. Appealing as such a parallel is, I take it, these days, with a pinch of salt. Eleven years ago, at the famous PEN congress in New York City, the world's writers discussed "The Imagination of the Writer and the Imagination of the State," a subject of Maileresque grandeur, dreamed up, of course, by Norman Mailer. Striking how many ways there were to read that little "and." For many of us, it meant "versus." South African writers—Gordimer, Coetzee—in those days of apartheid set themselves against the official definition of the nation. Rescuing, perhaps, the true nation from those who held it captive. Other writers were more in tune with their nations. John Updike sang an unforgettable hymn of praise to the little mailboxes of America, emblems, for him, of the free transmission of ideas. Danilo Kis gave an example of a "joke" by the state: a letter, received by him in Paris, posted in what was then still Yugoslavia. Inside the sealed envelope, stamped on the first page, were the words *This letter has not been censored.*

3

The nation either co-opts its greatest writers (Shakespeare, Goethe, Camoens, Tagore), or else seeks to destroy them (Ovid's exile, Soyinka's exile). Both fates are problematic. The hush of reverence is inappropriate for literature; great writing makes a great noise in the mind, the heart. There are those who believe that persecution is good for writers. This is false.

4

Beware the writer who sets himself or herself up as the voice of a nation. This includes nations of race, gender, sexual orientation, elective affinity. This is the New Behalfism. Beware behalfies!

The New Behalfism demands uplift, accentuates the positive, offers stirring moral instruction. It abhors the tragic sense of life. Seeing literature as inescapably political, it substitutes political values for literary ones. It is the murderer of thought. Beware!

5

Be advised my passport's green.
America I'm putting my queer shoulder to the wheel.
To forge in the smithy of my soul the uncreated conscience of my race.

Kadare's Albania, Ivo Andric's Bosnia, Achebe's Nigeria, García Márquez's Colombia, Jorge Amado's Brazil: writers are unable to deny the lure of the nation, its tides in our blood. Writing as mapping: the cartography of the imagination. (Or, as modern critical theory might spell it, Imagi/Nation.) In the best writing, however, a map of a nation will also turn out to be a map of the world.

6

History has become debatable. In the aftermath of Empire, in the age of super-power, under the "footprint" of the partisan simplifications beamed down to us from satellites, we can no longer easily agree on *what is the case,* let alone what it might mean. Literature steps into this ring. Historians, media moguls, politicians do not care for the intruder, but the intruder is a stubborn sort. In this ambiguous atmosphere, upon this trampled earth, in these muddy waters, there is work for him to do.

_7_

Nationalism corrupts writers, too. Vide Limonov's poisonous interventions in the war in former Yugoslavia. In a time of ever more narrowly defined nationalisms, of walled-in tribalisms, writers will be found uttering the war cries of their tribes. Closed systems have always appealed to writers. This is why so much writing deals with prisons, police forces, hospitals, schools. Is the nation a closed system? In this internationalized moment, can any system remain closed? Nationalism is that "revolt against history" which seeks to close what cannot any longer be closed. To fence in what should be frontierless.

Good writing assumes a frontierless nation. Writers who serve frontiers have become border guards.

_8_

If writing turns repeatedly toward nation, it just as repeatedly turns away. The deliberately uprooted intellectual (Naipaul) views the world as only a free intelligence can, going where the action is and offering reports. The intellectual uprooted against his will (a category that includes, these days, many of the finest Arab writers) rejects the narrow enclosures that have rejected him. There is great loss, and much yearning, in such rootlessness. But there is also gain. The frontierless nation is not a fantasy.

_9_

Much great writing has no need of the public dimension. Its agony comes from within. The public sphere is as nothing to Elizabeth Bishop. Her prison—her freedom—her subject is elsewhere.

> Lullaby.
> Let nations rage,
> Let nations fall.
> The shadow of the crib makes an enormous cage
> upon the wall.

April 1997

Influence

———

[A lecture delivered at the University of Torino]

The Australian novelist and poet David Malouf tells us that "the real enemy of writing is talk." He warns particularly of the dangers of speaking about work in progress. When writing, one is best advised to keep one's mouth shut, so that the words flow out, instead, through one's fingers. One builds a dam across the river of words in order to create the hydroelectricity of literature.

I propose, therefore, to speak not of my writing but rather of my reading, and in particular of the many ways in which my experience of Italian literature (and, I must add, Italian cinema) has shaped my thoughts about how and what to write. That is, I want to talk about influence.

"Influence." The word itself suggests something fluid, something "flowing in." This feels right, if only because I have always envisaged the world of the imagination not so much as a continent as an ocean. Afloat and terrifyingly free upon these boundless seas, the writer attempts, with his bare hands, the magical task of metamorphosis. Like the figure in the fairy tale who must spin straw into gold, the writer must find the trick of weaving the waters together until they become land: until, all of a sudden, there is solidity where once there was only flow, shape where there was formlessness; there is ground beneath his feet. (And if he fails, of course, he drowns. The fable is the most unforgiving of literary forms.)

The young writer, perhaps uncertain, perhaps ambitious, probably both at once, casts around for help; and sees, within the flow of the ocean, certain sinuous thicknesses, like ropes, the work of earlier weavers, of sorcerers who swam this way before him. Yes, he can use these "in-flowings," he can grasp them and wind his own work around them. He knows, now, that he will survive. Eagerly, he begins.

One of the most remarkable characteristics of literary influence, of these useful streams of other people's consciousness, is that they can flow toward the writer from almost anywhere. Often they travel long distances to reach the one who can use them. In South America, I was impressed by the familiarity of Latin American writers with the work of the Bengali Nobel laureate Rabindranath Tagore. The editor Victoria Ocampo, who met and admired Tagore, had arranged for his work to be well translated and widely published throughout her own continent, and as a result the influence of Tagore is perhaps greater there than in his own homeland, where the translations from Bengali into the many other tongues of India are often of poor quality, and the great man's genius must be taken on trust.

Another example is that of William Faulkner. This great American writer is little read in the United States these days; certainly there are few contemporary American writers who claim him as an influence or teacher. I once asked another fine writer of the American South, Eudora Welty, if Faulkner had been a help or a hindrance to her. "Neither one," she replied. "It's like knowing there's a great mountain in the neighborhood. It's good to know it's there, but it doesn't help you to do your work." Outside the United States, however—in India, in Africa, and again in Latin America—Faulkner is the American writer most praised by local writers as an inspiration, an enabler, an opener of doors.

From this transcultural, translingual capacity of influence we can deduce something about the nature of literature: that (if I may briefly abandon my watery metaphor) books can grow as easily from spores borne on the air as from their makers' particular and local roots. That there are international families of words as well as the more familiar clans of earth and blood. Sometimes—as in the case of the influence of James Joyce on the work of Samuel Beckett, and the subsequent and equal influence of Beckett on the work of Harold Pinter—the sense of dynasty, of a torch handed on down the generations, is very clear and very strong. In other cases the familial links are less obvious but no less powerful for that.

When I first read the novels of Jane Austen, books out of a country and a time far removed from my own upbringing in metropolitan, mid-twentieth-century Bombay, the thing that struck me about her heroines was how Indian, how contemporary, they seemed. Those bright, willful, sharp-tongued women, brimming with potential but doomed by the narrow convention to an interminable *Huis-clos* of ball-room dancing and husband hunting, were women whose counterparts could be found throughout the Indian bourgeoisie. The influence of Austen on Anita Desai's *Clear Light of Day* and Vikram Seth's *A Suitable Boy* is plain to see.

Charles Dickens, too, struck me from the first as a quintessentially Indian novelist. Dickensian London, that stenchy, rotting city full of sly, conniving shysters, that city in which goodness was under constant assault by duplicity, malice, and greed, seemed to me to hold up the mirror to the pullulating cities of India, with their preening elites living the high life in gleaming skyscrapers while the great majority of their compatriots battled to survive in the hurly-burly of the streets below. In my earlier novels I tried to draw on the genius of Dickens. I was particularly taken with what struck me as his real innovation: namely, his unique combination of naturalistic backgrounds and surreal foregrounds. In Dickens, the details of place and social mores are skewered by a pitiless realism, a naturalistic exactitude that has never been bettered. Upon this realistic canvas he places his outsize characters, in whom we have no choice but to believe because we cannot fail to believe in the world they live in. So I tried, in my novel *Midnight's Children,* to set against a scrupulously observed social and historical background—against, that is, the canvas of a "real" India—my "unrealist" notion of children born at the midnight moment of India's independence, and endowed with magical powers by the coincidence, children who were in some way the embodiment of both the hopes and the flaws of that revolution.

Within the authoritative framework of his realism, Dickens can also make us believe in the perfectly Surrealist notion of a government department, the Circumlocution Office, dedicated to making nothing happen; or in the perfectly Absurdist, Ionesco-like case of *Jarndyce v. Jarndyce,* a case whose nature it is never to reach a conclusion; or in the "magical realist" image of the dust-heaps in *Our Mutual Friend*—the physical symbols of a society living in the shadow of its own excrement, which must, incidentally, also have been an influence on a recent American masterpiece, which takes the waste products of America as its central metaphor, Don DeLillo's *Underworld.*

If influence is omnipresent in literature, it is also, one should emphasize, always secondary in any work of quality. When it is too crude, too obvious, the results can be risible. I was once sent, by an aspiring writer, a short story that began, "One morning Mrs. K. awoke to find herself metamorphosed into a front-loading washing machine." One can only imagine how Kafka would have reacted to so inept—so detergent—an act of homage.

Perhaps because so much second-rate writing is derivative—and because so much writing is at best second-rate—the idea of influence has become a kind of accusation, a way of denigrating a writer's work. The frontier between influence and imitation, even between influence and plagiarism, has commenced of late to be somewhat blurred. Two years ago, the distinguished British writer Graham Swift was accused by an obscure Australian academic of something odorously close to plagiarism in his Booker Prize–winning novel *Last Orders*: the "substantial borrowing" of the multi-voiced narrative structure of his novel from William Faulkner's *As I Lay Dying.* The British press whipped this accusation up into a sort of scandal, and now Swift was accused of literary "plundering," and those who defended him were sneered at for their "lofty indulgence" toward him. All this in spite of, or perhaps because of, Swift's ready concession that he had been influenced by Faulkner, and in spite, too, of the awkward fact that the structures of the two books aren't really so very alike, although some echoes are apparent. In the end such simple verities ensured that the scandal fizzled out, but not before Swift had been given a media roasting.

Interesting, then, that when Faulkner published *As I Lay Dying,* he himself had been accused of borrowing its structure from an earlier novel, Nathaniel Hawthorne's *The Scarlet Letter.* His retort is the best possible answer that could be given: that when he was in the throes of composing what he modestly called his tour de force, he took whatever he needed from wherever he could find it, and knew of no writer who would not find such borrowing to be completely justified.

In my novel *Haroun and the Sea of Stories,* a young boy actually travels to the ocean of imagination, which is described to him by his guide:

He looked into the water and saw that it was made up of a thousand thousand thousand and one different currents, each one a different color, weaving in and out of one another like a liquid tapestry of breathtaking complexity; and Iff explained that these were the Streams of Story, that each colored strand represented and contained a single tale. Different parts of the Ocean contained different sorts of stories, and as all the stories that had ever been told and many that were still in the process of being invented could be found here, the Ocean of the Streams of Story was in fact the biggest library in the universe. And because the stories were held here in fluid form, they retained the ability to change, to become new versions of themselves, to join up with other stories and so become yet other stories; so that . . . the Ocean of the Streams of Story was much more than a storeroom of yarns. It was not dead but alive.

By using what is old, and adding to it some new thing of our own, we make what is new. In *The Satanic Verses* I tried to answer the question, how does newness enter the world? Influence, the flowing of the old into the new, is one part of the answer.

In *Invisible Cities,* Italo Calvino describes the fabulous city of Octavia, suspended between two mountains in something like a spider's web. If influence is the spider's web in which we hang our work, then the work is like Octavia itself, that glittering jewel of a dream city, hanging in the filaments of the web, for as long as they are able to bear its weight.

—

I first met Calvino when I was asked to introduce a reading he gave at the Riverside Studios in London in the early 1980s. This was the time of the British publication of *If on a Winter's Night a Traveler,* and I had just published a long essay about his work in the *London Review of Books*— disgracefully, this was one of the earliest serious pieces about Calvino to be published in the British press. I knew Calvino had liked the piece, but nevertheless I was nervous about having to speak about his work in his presence. My nervousness increased when he demanded to see my text before we went out to face the audience. What would I do if he disapproved? He read it in silence, frowning a little, then handed it back and nodded. I had evidently passed the examination, and what had particularly pleased him was my comparison of his work with that of the classical writer Lucius Apuleius, author of *The Golden Ass.*

"Give me a penny and I'll tell you a golden story," the old Milesian oral storytellers used to say, and Apuleius's tale of transformation had used the fabulist manner of these ancient tellers of tall stories to great effect. He possessed, too, those virtues that Calvino also embodied and of which he wrote so well in one of his last works, *Six Memos for the Next Millennium*: the virtues of lightness, quickness, exactitude, visibility, and multiplicity. These qualities were much in my mind when I came to write *Haroun and the Sea of Stories*.

Although the form of this novel is that of a child's fantastic adventure, I wanted the work somehow to erase the division between children's literature and adult books. It was in the end a question of finding precisely the right tone of voice, and Apuleius and Calvino were the ones who helped me to find it. I re-read Calvino's great trilogy, *The Baron in the Trees, The Cloven Viscount,* and *The Nonexistent Knight,* and they gave me the clues I needed. The secret was to use the language of the fable while eschewing the easy moral purpose of, for example, Aesop.

Recently, I have again been thinking about Calvino. The sixth of his "memos for the next millennium" was to have been on the subject of consistency. Consistency is the special genius of Melville's "Bartleby the Scrivener," Calvino was planning to suggest—that heroic, inexplicable Bartleby who simply and unshakably "preferred not to." One might add the names of Kleist's Michael Kohlhaas, so inexorable in his search for small but necessary justice, or of Conrad's Nigger of the Narcissus, who insisted that he must live until he died, or of chivalry-maddened Quixote, or of Kafka's Land Surveyor, eternally yearning toward the unattainable Castle.

We are speaking of an epic consistency, a monomania that strives toward the condition of tragedy or myth. But consistency also may be understood in a darker sense, the consistency of Ahab in pursuit of his whale, of Savonarola who burned the books, of Khomeini's definition of his revolution as a revolt against history itself.

More and more I feel drawn toward Calvino's unexplored sixth value. The new millennium that is upon us already shows signs of being dominated by alarming examples of consistency of all types: the great refusers, the wild quixotics, the narrow-minded, the bigoted, and those who are valiant for truth. But now I am coming close to doing what David Malouf warns against—that is, discussing the nature of my own embryonic, and fragile (because as yet uncreated), work. So I must leave it there, and say only that Calvino, whose early support and encouragement I will always remember, continues to murmur in my ear.

I should add that many other artists both of classical Rome and of modern Italy have been, so to speak, present at my shoulder. When I was writing *Shame,* I re-read Suetonius's great study of the twelve Caesars. Here they were in their palaces, these foul dynasts, power-mad, libidinous, deranged, locked in a series of murderous embraces, doing one another terrible harm. Here was a tale of coup and counter-coup; and yet, as far as their subjects beyond the palace gates were concerned, nothing really changed. Power remained within the family. The Palace was still the Palace.

From Suetonius, I learned much about the paradoxical nature of power elites, and so was able to construct an elite of my own in the version of Pakistan that is the setting for *Shame*: an elite riven by hatreds and fights to the death but joined by bonds of blood and marriage and, crucially, in control of all the power in the land. For the masses, deprived of all power, the brutal wars inside the elite change little or nothing. The Palace still rules, and the people still groan under its heel.

If Suetonius influenced *Shame,* then *The Satanic Verses,* a novel whose central theme is that of metamorphosis, evidently learned much from Ovid; and for *The Ground Beneath Her Feet,* which is informed by the myth of Orpheus and Eurydice, Virgil's *Georgics* were essential reading. And, if I may make one more tentative step toward the unwritten future, I have for a long time been engaged and fascinated by the Florence of the High Renaissance in general, and by the character of Niccolò Machiavelli in particular.

The demonization of Machiavelli strikes me as one of the most successful acts of slander in European history. In the English literature of the Elizabethan golden age, there are around four hundred Machiavellian references, none of them favorable. At that time no work of Machiavelli's was available in the English language; the playwrights of England were basing their satanic portraits on a translated French text, the *Anti-Machiavel.* The sinister, amoral persona created for Machiavelli then still cloaks his reputation. As a fellow writer who has also learned a thing or two about demonization, I feel it may soon be time to reevaluate the maligned Florentine.

I have sought to portray a little of the cultural cross-pollination without which literature becomes parochial and marginal. Before concluding, I must pay tribute to the genius of Federico Fellini, from whose films, as a young man, I learned how one might transmute the highly charged material of childhood and private life into the stuff of showmanship and myth; and to those other Italian masters, Pasolini, Visconti, Antonioni, De Sica, and so on, and so on—for of influence and creative stimulation there can really be no end.

March 1999

Adapting *Midnight's Children*

This is the story of a production that never was. In 1998 I wrote the scripts for a five-episode, 290-minute television adaptation of my novel *Midnight's Children,* a project on which two writers, three directors, at least four producers, and a whole passionately dedicated production team worked for over four years, and which foundered for political reasons when everything was in place and the beginning of principal photography was only a few weeks away.

Midnight's Children was first published in 1981, and after it won the Booker Prize that autumn there was some talk of making it into a movie. The director Jon Amiel, who was pretty "hot" at the time because of his television success with Dennis Potter's *The Singing Detective,* was interested, but the project never got off the ground. I was also approached by Rani Dube, one of the producers of Richard Attenborough's multi-Oscared *Gandhi.* She professed herself very keen indeed to make a film of my book, but went on to say that she felt the novel's crucial later chapters—dealing with the excesses of Indira Gandhi's autocratic rule during the so-called Emergency of the mid-seventies—were really unnecessary and could easily be omitted from any film. Unsurprisingly, this approach, of which Mrs. G. would no doubt have heartily approved, failed to find favor with the book's author. Ms. Dube retreated, and after that things went quiet on the movie front. I put all thoughts of a film or television adaptation out of my mind. To tell the truth, I wasn't too bothered. Books and movies are different languages, and attempts at translation often fail. The wonderful reception that had been accorded to the novel itself was more than enough for me.

Twelve years passed. Then in 1993 *Midnight's Children* was named the Booker of Bookers, in the judges' opinion the best book to have won the prize in its first quarter century. This great compliment attracted the attention of not one but two television channels, and within weeks I was in the fortunate position of being wooed by both Channel Four and the BBC. It was a close thing, but in the end I chose to go with the BBC, because, unlike Channel Four, it was able to fund and produce the serial itself; and because of the reassuring presence of my friend Alan Yentob at the corporation's creative helm. I trusted Alan to steer the project safely through whatever troubles might lie ahead.

Not long afterward, Channel Four signed up Vikram Seth's *A Suitable Boy*, and then there were two "India projects" on the go. I was heartened to think that British television was willing to invest so much time, passion, and money in bringing to the screen these two very different contemporary novels from far away. We might offer a welcome change, or so I hoped, from the many costume-drama adaptations of the English literary canon that came out every year.

From the outset I made it clear to Alan Yentob and the original producer, Kevin Loader, that I would prefer not to write the adaptation myself. I had already spent years of my life writing *Midnight's Children*, and the idea of doing it all over again was both daunting and unappealing. It would feel, to borrow Arundhati Roy's memorable condemnation of the act of rewriting, "like breathing the same breath twice." Besides, I had no experience of writing large-scale television drama. What we needed, or so I argued, was a television professional who would be sympathetic to my book but able to reshape it to fit the very different medium it was now preparing to enter. We needed, in short, an expert translator.

We first approached the highly regarded Andrew Davies, who reread *Midnight's Children*, thought about it for a while, but eventually turned us down, saying that while he was an admirer of the novel he didn't have enough of a feel for India to be confident of success. Then Kevin Loader proposed Ken Taylor, the adapter of Granada TV's *The Jewel in the Crown*. I readily agreed to the suggestion. I was not an admirer of Paul Scott's so-called Raj Quartet but had thought the TV adaptation, with its high production values, brilliant acting, and finely crafted scripts, to be a marked improvement on the original. And, of course, as a result of his work on *Jewel,* Ken knew a good deal about India.

At our first meeting, Ken, while evidently attracted to the project, expressed worries about the nature of the text to be adapted. Television drama has long been dominated by naturalism, and Ken's own inclinations and dramatic instincts were strongly naturalistic. How, then, was he to approach a novel with such a high content of surreal and fabulistic material? What was he to make of hypersensitive noses and lethal knees, optimism diseases and decaying ghosts, humming men and levitating soothsayers, telepaths and witches and one thousand and one magic children, indeed of the novel's central conceit, that Saleem Sinai, a boy born at the instant of Indian independence, had been somehow "handcuffed to history" by the coincidence and that as a result the entire history of modern India might somehow be his fault?

I told him that, however highly fabulated parts of the novel were, the whole was deeply rooted in the real life of the characters and the nation. Many of the apparently "magical" moments had naturalistic explanations. The soothsayer who seems to be levitating is in fact sitting cross-legged on a low shelf. Even Saleem's "telepathic" discovery of the other "magic children" can be understood as an extreme instance of the imaginary friends invented by lonely children. Saleem's idea that he is responsible for history is true for him, I said, but it may or may not be true for us. And all around Saleem is the stuff of real Indian history. On the novel's first publication, Western critics tended to focus on its more fantastic elements, while Indian reviewers treated it like a history book. "I could have written your book," a reader flatteringly told me in Bombay. "I know all that stuff."

Somewhat reassured, Ken agreed to undertake the task. It's easy to be wise after the event, but I now think it was quite wrong of me to "sell" Ken this naturalistic version of my book. I suppose I thought it would allow him to pull the dramatic structure of the serial into shape, and if the scripts needed an injection of "unnaturalism," that could be added later. Things turned out to be more complicated.

Who would direct the scripts? Much too early to think about that, I was told; script first, director later. And would there be difficulties in gaining approval to film from the Indian government? I hoped not; after all, the novel itself had always been freely available throughout India, so what logical reason could there be for objecting to a film of it? In those early days, it was easy to shelve such matters until later.

Ken went punctiliously to work on a seven-episode screenplay, and I went back to my own writing. In these years I was finishing *The Moor's Last Sigh,* beginning *The Ground Beneath Her Feet,* and co-editing *Mirrorwork,* an anthology of Indian writing, so most of my attention was elsewhere. There followed a long phase in which Ken beavered away, Kevin Loader left the BBC, producers came and went, an Indian production company was signed up, one of its major tasks being to secure government approval; and concerns grew about how much the project was going to cost. Meanwhile, over at Channel Four, *A Suitable Boy* bit the dust. It's an ill wind and so on, and there was a small ignoble feeling of relief at our end—we would no longer be competing for the same actors, the same sources of co-financing, the same audience—but we were also saddened, and chastened. The Vikram Seth cancellation was a bad omen for us, too.

I was abroad when a director was finally signed up: Richard Spence, a young filmmaker with a reputation for visual flair. At much the same time, it was decided that seven episodes were too many; could we compress the story into five? In the end we agreed to a feature-length opener followed by four fifty-minute episodes. Two hundred ninety minutes instead of 350: a whole hour less.

When I got back to England I met Richard and was impressed by his ideas. We talked for hours, and I began to feel that we had the makings of something exciting. Richard's imagination would build on the solid foundations of Ken's work.

It soon became apparent, however, that the working relationship between Ken and Richard was deteriorating. When I heard that Richard was asking Ken to make further drastic cuts in the story line—in particular to the hero's childhood years—I began to worry. *Midnight's Children* without children? The original impulse for the novel had been to write a story out of my memories of growing up in Bombay; were we really going to make a TV version which cut all that out?

There was a crunch meeting in Alan Yentob's office at the BBC. For a moment it seemed as if the whole project might founder there and then. I tried to mediate between Ken and Richard. Ken was right that the childhood sequence was essential, and was in his serious way acting as the faithful guardian of my book. But Richard was right that Ken's draft scripts needed revision, to inject exactly that quality of imagination and magic which I'd hoped the involvement of a director would add. By the end of the meeting it seemed we might have hammered out a way forward.

But within days it became plain that Ken and Richard couldn't work together. One of them would have to go. In Hollywood the decision would have been simple and ruthless; whoever heard of a director being fired because the writer couldn't work with him? But this was England, and Ken had been working on the project for a long time. The BBC backed him. Richard was disappointed but graceful, and took his leave.

By now, I had begun to worry about the scripts, too. We had lost our director, the money people at the BBC were not "green-lighting" the production, and I heard that the scripts we had were not attracting other directors or inspiring confidence in the BBC's corridors of power. I myself was now sure that the scripts did need a lot of work, I had all sorts of ideas about how they might be revised, and Ken and I had long telephone conversations about what might be done. But the changes made were minimal. We were going nowhere fast.

It was around this time that Alan Yentob asked me if I'd consider taking over as scriptwriter. I had begun to think this might be the only way forward, but my fondness for Ken and respect for his efforts stopped me from agreeing. Also, I would have to set aside work on my new book, and I wasn't at all keen to do that.

Meanwhile, Gavin Millar had expressed an interest in directing, but had radical ideas about script revisions. In a document entitled "A Modest Proposal" he offered up a series of provocative thoughts, the most extreme being his idea that we should change the narrative sequence of the story. Instead of beginning, as the novel does, with the story of the narrator's grandparents and then parents, Gavin suggested that we should plunge into Saleem's own story, and then tell the other tales in a series of flashbacks that went further and further back in time.

Gavin's note provoked in me a sort of "lightbulb moment." I suddenly saw with great clarity how to write the scripts. I saw how to make his "Modest Proposal" work and, beyond that, how to change the architecture of the screenplay into something much freer, more surrealist. (Later, I would decide to abandon Gavin's time-scrambling ideas and go back to the novel's original, simpler time line. I'm sure it was right to do so, but I'm also sure that Gavin's iconoclastic intervention had freed my imagination, and without it I might never have worked out how to proceed.)

I think that Gavin's note caused an equal and opposite reaction in Ken. It made him feel enough was enough; it made him dig in his heels, and stand by his drafts as if they were shooting scripts. At this point I understood that if anything was ever going to happen, I would have to take over, and after the passage of so much time and effort I wasn't prepared to let the project founder. So I agreed to do it. The moment I started work I saw that little or nothing of the existing screenplays could survive. The entire manner of the scripts would be different now, the episodes would start and finish in different places, the selection of material from the novel and the internal arc of each episode would be different. All the two versions had in common was the dialogue taken directly from the book.

I asked the production team to make it plain to Ken that what had started as a rewrite had become an entirely new piece of work. There was no nice way of saying this, but it needed to be said. Unfortunately, the executives concerned delayed telling Ken, which meant that the human mess was eventually much worse than it need have been. Ken was hurt and angry, I was upset, our friendship was damaged, there were accusations and counter-accusations. In the end, Ken withdrew, like the dignified man he is. I only wish it had all been handled better.

For a while I worked with Gavin, but in the end, he backed out, too, on the grounds that he didn't have the "feel" for India that the films required. I had been writing feverishly, convinced that the scripts could be made to work, and Gavin's withdrawal, coming after everything else, felt like a sledgehammer blow.

All this coming and going had delayed us by over a year, but the delay did give us one lucky break. Tristram Powell, who had earlier been unavailable to direct, was now available. In 1981, when *Midnight's Children* was first published, it had been Tristram who made the Arena documentary about it. He professed himself keen to make the films, but only on the basis of my new approach. I began a mad writing burst. In five weeks in November and December 1996, I finished a draft of the entire five-episode screenplay. I gave myself Christmas Day off, but otherwise was hardly ever away from my desk. As I have already mentioned, I had a great time. I was much less respectful of the original text than Ken had been. His fidelity to the novel, his sense of himself as my representative, had constrained him. Perhaps nobody would have felt free to make the kinds of changes I made so guiltlessly. Out went long sequences—the sojourn in the valley of Kif, the war in the Rann of Kutch. Out went some of the novel's more fanciful notions (a politician who literally hummed with energy) and peripheral characters (the snake-poison expert who lives upstairs from the Sinai family). In came new devices, such as the idea of allowing the peep-show man, Lifafa Das, to introduce each episode as if it were a part of his peep show, and occasional "unnaturalist" moments at which the narrator, Saleem, remembering his past life, is able to step into the bygone moments and watch the action unfold.

Story lines were altered to suit the requirements of episode structure and dramatic form. For example, Saleem's visits to Pakistan were reduced and condensed, and indeed now take place at somewhat different points in the story, to avoid the problem of yo-yoing back and forth at high speed between Bombay and Karachi. Also, in the novel, Saleem's uncle General Zulfikar is murdered by his embittered son. In the screenplay, however, it seemed absurd to introduce a different Pakistani general later in the story, at the end of the war in Bangladesh. So I kept Zulfikar alive until then, and arranged for him to be bumped off in quite a different way.

Perhaps the most significant changes in the plot have to do with the central duo of Saleem and Shiva, the two babies who are swapped at birth and thus lead each other's lives. In the book, Shiva never learns the truth about his parentage, and it doesn't matter, because the reader is aware of it throughout. On the screen, however, so large a plot motif simply insists on a climactic confrontation, and so I have provided one. There is a part of me that thinks that the version of events in this screenplay is more satisfactory than the one in the novel. (At the end of the book, Saleem is not certain if Shiva is dead or alive, and continues to fear his return. In the television version, the audience is offered a resolution of greater clarity.)

The new scripts were well received. There followed a period of several months in 1997 during which Tristram Powell and I worked on the text, refining, clarifying, adding, subtracting. Tristram was so sharp, so helpful, so full of suggestions and improvements, and so completely in tune with the novel that I was sure we had found the ideal director for the job. The two of us worked together easily, and the scripts grew tighter by the day. Even when we had to change things purely because we couldn't afford them, we found solutions that didn't compromise the spirit of the work. For example, all the shipboard scenes in the screenplay now take place in dock; we didn't have the cash to go to sea, but didn't need to. More significant, the Amritsar Massacre of 1919 now happens off-camera. To my mind, the horror of this famous atrocity is actually increased by suggesting rather than showing it.

The production's other problems began to surface. The BBC's bizarre bureaucracy—there were no fewer than five layers of "suits" between the producer and the controller of BBC2—made it virtually impossible to get any definite decisions. Also, it became clear, we were competing for our budget with other drama projects, notably *Tom Jones*. And the money the BBC was putting up was simply not going to be enough. We needed outside investors.

We found them, in the form of an American-based ex-banker and a businessman, both of Indian origin, both fired by patriotic pride. And so, finally, the sums added up, and the long sessions in which Tristram and I worried away at the scripts had produced a screenplay which everyone involved was excited by. We did three casting read-throughs in London, and the quality of the British Asian actors we saw impressed me greatly. At the time of the original publication of *Midnight's Children,* there would have been very few such actors to choose from. One generation later, we were able to audition a diverse and multi-talented throng. I was touched and moved by the actors' feelings for my novel, and their professional excitement at reading for roles other than the usual corner-shop Patels or hospital orderlies that came their way. The only snag we encountered was that some of the younger actors, born and raised in Britain, had difficulty pronouncing Indian names and phrases!

Not all the parts were cast in this way. Some of the senior Indian actors—Saeed Jaffrey, Roshan Seth—were approached and offered their choice of roles. There were also casting sessions in Bombay, and it was there that we found our Saleem, a brilliant young actor called Rahul Bose. Other "discoveries" included Nicole Arumugam as Padma, and Ayesha Dharker as Jamila (her sensational voice stunned us all when, in the middle of one read-through, she burst into unaccompanied song), and it is intensely frustrating that we were not able in the end to give them the opportunity they so richly deserved.

For when the "green light" moment was finally upon us, the Indian government simply refused us permission to film, giving no explanation at all, and no hope of appeal. Worse still was the discovery that the BBC's Indian partners had been told months earlier that the application would be refused. They had not informed us, perhaps believing they could get the decision changed. But they couldn't.

I felt as if we'd nose-dived into the ground at the end of the runway. I also felt personally insulted. That *Midnight's Children* should have been rejected so arbitrarily, with such utter indifference, by the land about which it had been written with all my love and skill was a terrible blow, from which, I must say, I have not really recovered. It was like being told that a lifetime of work had been for nothing. I plunged into a deep depression.

But now the new producer, Christopher Hall, and the rest of the team made a heroic effort to save the project by relocating it in Sri Lanka. And Sri Lanka did indeed give us approval to film. (In writing.) President Chandrika Kumaratunga herself said she was strongly behind the project. Because of the Indian refusal, and the continuing controversy surrounding *The Satanic Verses,* she met with Sri Lankan Muslim MPs to reassure them about the content of our screenplay and to tell them that the project was economically important for Sri Lanka.

So it was all on again. The hurt at my treatment by India remained unassuaged, but at least the film would be made. We found locations (in some ways Sri Lanka was actually an improvement on India in this regard), offered work on the crew to many local people, cast a number of Sri Lankan actors in featured roles. The spirit of cooperation we encountered was a delight. (The Sri Lankan army offered to help us stage the war scenes called for by the script.) We set up a Colombo production office and planned to start filming in January 1998.

Then it all went wrong again. An article appeared in *The Guardian,* written by a journalist named Flora Botsford, who was also attached to the BBC in Colombo, and who, in the view of Chris Hall and the production team, used her inside knowledge of the problems we'd had to stir up a controversy. Local Muslim MPs, who had previously made no objection to the filming, now ascended their high horses. It seems too that this article alerted the Iranians, who then brought pressure on the Sri Lankan government to revoke permission. The entente cordiale that we had worked so hard to establish was breaking down.

The Sri Lankan government was busily trying to get sensitive devolution legislation through its national assembly, and needed the support of opposition MPs. This meant that a tiny handful of parliamentarians were able to demand political concessions in return for their votes. And so, although the Sri Lankan media were strongly in favor of our project, and Muslim as well as non-Muslim commentators wrote daily in our support, permission was in fact revoked, abruptly and without warning, just one day after we had been assured by government ministers that there was no problem, and we should just go right ahead and make our film.

All our bright hopes came to nothing. Like Sisyphus, we had to watch the undoing of all our work, as the great rock of our production ran away downhill into a Sri Lankan ditch. There is nothing as painful to a writer as wasted work, unless it be seeing the disappointment on the faces of people who have spent months and years working on your work's behalf. As for me, the rejection of *Midnight's Children* changed something profound in my relationship with the East. Something broke, and I'm not sure it can be mended.

The story of a failure, then. But what has once been thought cannot be unthought, Friedrich Dürrenmatt wrote. Nothing stays the same. Governments change, attitudes change, times change. And a film brought into half-being by the publication of its screenplay may yet manage, someday, somehow, to get itself born.

A POSTSCRIPT

This essay was written at a gloomy moment in the continuing saga of the adaptation of Midnight's Children. *It turns out, however, that the cautious optimism of the last paragraph may have been justified. First, my own relationship with India has happily been renewed (see "A Dream of Glorious Return"). Second, the screenplays I wrote now form the basis of a stage adaptation of the novel for the Royal Shakespeare Company, directed by Tim Supple (who also staged a wonderful adaptation of* Haroun and the Sea of Stories *at the National Theatre a couple of years ago). Third, there is once again much interest in turning* Midnight's Children *into a feature film . . .*

November 1999

Reservoir Frogs

(OR, PLACES CALLED MAMA'S)

For the first time since the decline of Dadaism, we are witnessing a revival in the fine art of meaningless naming. This thought is prompted by the U.S. release of the British film *Trainspotting,* and by the opening of Lanford Wilson's new play *Virgil Is Still the Frogboy.* Mr. Wilson's play is not about Virgil. No frogs feature therein. The title is taken from an East Hampton, L.I., graffito to whose meaning the play offers no clues. This omission has not diminished the show's success.

As Luis Buñuel knew, obscurity is a characteristic of objects of desire. Accordingly, there is no trainspotting in *Trainspotting;* just a predictable, even sentimental movie that thinks it's hip. (Compared to the work of, say, William S. Burroughs, it's positively cutesy.) It has many admirers, perhaps *because* they are unable even to understand its title, let alone the fashionably indecipherable argot of the dialogue. The fact remains: *Trainspotting* contains no mention of persons keeping obsessive notes on the arrival and departure of trains. The only railway engines are to be found on the wallpaper of the central character's bedroom. Whence, therefore, this choo-choo moniker? Some sort of pun on the word "tracks" may be intended.

Irvine Welsh's original novel does offer some help. The section titled "Trainspotting at Leith Central Station" takes the characters to a derelict, train-less station, where one of them attacks a derelict human being who is, in fact, his father, doling out a goodly quantity of what

Anthony Burgess's hoodlum Alex, in *A Clockwork Orange,* would call "the old ultraviolence." Clearly, something metaphorical is being reached for here, though it's not clear exactly what. In addition, Welsh thoughtfully provides a glossary for American readers: "Rat-arsed—drunk; wanker—masturbator; thrush—minor sexually transmitted disease." At least an effort at translation is being made. Out-and-out incomprehensibilists disdain such coziness.

How many readers of Anthony Burgess's novel *A Clockwork Orange,* or viewers of Stanley Kubrick's film, knew that Burgess took his title from an allegedly common, but actually never used, British simile: "queer as a clockwork orange"? Can anyone recall the meaning of the terms "Koyaanisqatsi" and "Powaqqatsi"? And were there any secrets encrypted in "Lucy in the Sky with Diamonds," or was it just a song about a flying girl with a necklace?

Nowadays, dreary old comprehensibility is still very much around. A film about a boy-man called Jack is called *Jack.* A film about a crazed baseball fan is called *The Fan.* The film version of Jane Austen's *Emma* is called *Emma.*

However, titular mystification continues to intensify. When Oasis, the British pop phenoms, sing "(You're My) Wonderwall," what can they mean? "I intend to ride over you on my motorbike, round and round, at very high speed"? Surely not. And *Blade Runner*? Yes, I know that hunters of android "replicants" are called "blade runners": but why? And yes, yes, William S. Burroughs (again!) used the phrase in a 1979 novel; and, to get really arcane, there's a 1974 medical thriller called *The Bladerunner* by the late Dr. Alan E. Nourse. But what does any of this have to do with Ridley Scott's movie? Harrison Ford runs not, neither does he blade. Shouldn't a work of art give us the keys with which to unlock its meanings? But perhaps there aren't any. Perhaps it's just that the phrase sounds cool, thanks to those echoes of Burroughs, Daddy Cool himself.

In 1928, Luis Buñuel and Salvador Dalí co-directed the Surrealist classic *Un Chien Andalou,* a film about many things, but not Andalusian dogs. So it is with Quentin Tarantino's first film, *Reservoir Dogs.* No reservoir, no dogs, no use of the words "reservoir," "dogs," or "reservoir dogs" at any point in the movie. No imagery derived from dogs or reservoirs or dogs in reservoirs or reservoirs of dogs. *Nada,* or, as Mr. Pink and Co. would say, "Fuckin' *nada.*"

The story goes that when the young Tarantino was working in a Los

Angeles video store, his distaste for fancy-pants European auteurs like, for example, Louis Malle manifested itself in an inability to pronounce the titles of their films. Malle's *Au Revoir les Enfants* defeated him completely (oh reservoir les oh fuck) until he began to refer to it contemptuously as—you guessed it—"those, oh, reservoir dogs." Subsequently he made this the title of his own movie, no doubt as a further gesture of anti-European defiance. Alas, the obliqueness of the gibe meant that the Europeans simply did not comprenday. "What we have here," as the guy in *Cool Hand Luke* remarked, "is a failure to communicate."

But these days the thing about incomprehensibility is that people aren't supposed to get it. In accordance with the new zeitgeist, therefore, the title of this piece has in part been selected—"sampled"—from Lou Reed's wise advice: "Don't eat at places called Mama's," in the diary of his recent tour. To forestall any attempts at exegesis ("Author, Citing Dadaism's Erstwhile Esotericism, Opposes Present-Day 'Mamaist' Obfuscations"), I confess that as a title it means nothing at all; but then the very concept of meaning is now outdated, nerdy, pre-ironic. Welcome to the New Incomprehensibility: gibberish with attitude.

August 1996

Heavy Threads

In the summer of 1967, which I do not recall anyone calling the Summer of Love back then, I rented a room in a maisonette directly above a legendary boutique—legendary, I mean, at the time; there was something about it that was instantly recognized as mythic—called Granny Takes a Trip. The maisonette belonged to a woman called Judy Scutt, who made up a lot of the clothes for the boutique, and whose son Paul was a university friend of mine. (They were members of a family famous in medical circles for having six toes on each foot, but in spite of the psychotropic spirit of the age they insisted, disappointingly, that they themselves were not Six-Toed Scutts.)

Granny Takes a Trip was at World's End, at the wrong end of the King's Road in Chelsea, but to the assorted heads and freaks who hung out there, it was the Mecca, the Olympus, the *Kathmandu* of hippie chic. Mick Jagger was rumored to wear the dresses. Every so often John Lennon's white limo would stop outside and a chauffeur would go into the shop, scoop up an armload of gear "for Cynthia," and disappear with it. German photographers with platoons of stone-faced models would arrive once or twice a week to use Granny's windows as backdrops for their spreads. Granny's had famous windows. For a long time there was a Warhol-style Marilyn painted over the glass. For a further long time there was the front end of a real Mack truck bursting out of a painted Lichtenstein-y explosion. Later, every boutique on the planet would boast an imitation-Warhol Monroe or a Mack truck exploding from its shopfront, but Granny's was the first. Like *Gone With the Wind,* it invented the clichés.

Inside Granny's it was pitch dark. You entered through a heavy bead curtain and were instantly blinded. The air was heavy with incense and patchouli oil and also with the aromas of what the police called Certain Substances. Psychedelic music, big on feedback, terrorized your eardrums. After a time you became aware of a low purple glow, in which you could make out a few motionless shapes. These were probably clothes, probably for sale. You didn't like to ask. Granny's was a pretty scary place.

Granny's people were scornful of the brash boutique-land of the "right," Sloane Square end of the King's Road. All those Quant haircuts and thigh-high "snakey boots," all that shiny plastic, Vidal Sassoon, England-swings-like-a-pendulum-do palaver. All that *light.* It was almost as uncool as (ugh) Carnaby Street. Down there people said "fab" and "groovy." At Granny's, you said "beautiful" to express mild approval, and, when you wanted to call something beautiful, you said "really nice."

I started borrowing my friend Paul's bedspread jackets and beads. I started nodding my head a lot, wisely. In the quest for cool, it helped that I was Indian. "*India,* man," people said. "Far out."

"Yeah," I said, nodding. "Yeah."

"The Maharishi, man," people said. "Beautiful."

"Ravi Shankar, man," I said. At this point people usually ran out of Indians to talk about and we all just went on nodding, beatifically. "Right, right," we said. *"Right."*

In spite of coming from India, I was not cool. Paul was cool. Paul was what a girl in a teen movie had called "straight from the fridge." Paul had access to endless long-limbed girls and an equally endless supply of dope. He had a father in the music business. It would have been easy to hate Paul. One day he persuaded me to pay twenty pounds to take part in a photo session for aspiring male models that was being run by a "friend" of his. He said I could wear his clothes. The "friend" took my money and was never seen again. My modeling career failed to take off.

"Wow," said Paul, first shaking, then nodding his head philosophically. "Bad scene."

At the heart of our little world was Sylvia. (I never knew her last name.) Sylvia ran the shop. She made Twiggy look like a teenager with a puppy-fat problem. She was very pale, probably because she spent her life sitting in the dark. Her lips were always black. She wore mini-dresses in black velvet or see-through white muslin: her vampire and dead-baby looks. She stood knock-kneed and pigeon-toed after the fashion of the period, her feet forming a tiny, ferocious T. She wore immense silver knuckle-duster rings and a black flower in her hair. Half Love Child, half zombie, she was an awe-inspiring sign of the times. I had been there for several weeks without exchanging a word with her. One day I plucked up my courage and went into the shop.

Sylvia was a dim purple presence in the bottomless depths of the boutique.

"Hi," I said. "I just thought I'd drop in and introduce myself, since we're all living here, you know? I just thought it was time we got to know each other. I'm Salman," and at this point I kind of ran out of steam.

Sylvia loomed out of the dark, coming up close and staring, so that I could see the contempt on her face. Eventually, she shrugged.

"Conversation's dead, man," she said.

This was bad news. This was like heavy. *Conversation* was *dead?* Why hadn't I heard? When was the funeral? I was and am a talkative sort of fellow, but I stood before Sylvia's scorn, stunned into silence. Like Paul Simon in "The Boxer," I was enthralled by the tribes of "ragged people" of whom Sylvia was clearly a dark princess, I wanted to be among them, I was "looking for the places only they would know." How unfair that I was doomed to be excluded from the inner circles of the counter-culture, to be banned forever from where it was at, on account of my chattiness. Conversation was dead, and I didn't know the new language. I slunk tragically out of Sylvia's presence, and barely spoke to her again.

Some weeks later, however, she taught me a second lesson about those unusual times. One day—I think it was a Saturday or Sunday, and it was only around noon, so naturally nobody was up, and the shop was shut—the doorbell rang for such a long time that I struggled into a pair of red crushed-velvet flares and staggered downstairs to the door. On the doorstep was an alien: a man in business suit and matching mustache, with a briefcase in one hand and, in the other, a copy of a glossy magazine open at the page on which a model was wearing one of Granny's latest offerings.

"Good afternoon," said the alien. "I have a chain of shops in Lancashire . . ."

Sylvia, naked beneath a rather inadequate dressing gown, cigarette dripping from her lips, came down the stairs. The alien turned a deep shade of red and his eyes started sliding around. I retreated.

"Yeah?" said Sylvia.

"Good afternoon," the alien finally managed. "I have a chain of shops in Lancashire selling ladies' fashions and I am most interested in this particular garment as featured here. With whom would I speak with a view to placing a first order for six dozen items, with an option to repeat?" It was the biggest order Granny Takes a Trip had ever had. I was standing a few paces behind Sylvia, and halfway up the stairs, now, was Judy Scutt. There was a tingle of excitement in the air. The alien waited patiently while Sylvia considered matters. Then, in one of the defining moments of the sixties, she nodded a few times, slowly, *fashionably.*

"We're closed, man," she said, and shut the door.

———

Where Granny's stood, opposite the World's End pub, there is now a café called Entre Nous. I have lost touch with Judy Scutt, but I do know that her son Paul, my friend Paul, became a serious casualty of the sixties. His brains fried by acid, he was working, when I last heard of him, at simple manual jobs: picking up leaves in a park, that sort of thing.

Recently, however, I met a man who claimed not only to know Sylvia but to have gone out with her for years. This was genuinely impressive.

"Did she ever speak to you?" I asked him. "Did she actually *have* anything to say about *anything*?"

"No," he said. "Not a bleeding word."

October 1994

In the Voodoo Lounge

Clap your hands, Mick Jagger commands Wembley, and seventy thousand people obey. It looks like one of those mass calisthenics demonstrations the Chinese used to go in for. Yeah yeah yeah WOO, he prompts us in the middle of "Brown Sugar," and yeah yeah yeah WOO we reply. "You're in good voice tonight," he flatters us, and for a moment we feel as if we're all in the band. When I was twenty I was "volunteered" from a student audience to ding a cowbell for Robin Williamson and Mike Heron's Incredible String Band, but on the whole it's better singing back-up vocals for the Rolling Stones. In a successful stadium rock show, the audience becomes the event as much as the performers or the set, and Jagger knows that. So for two and a half hours, while Keith plays his monster riffs and kisses his guitar, and Charlie lays down the law on his drums, Mick plays us.

What's that *like,* facing tens of thousands of people and working them like a small room? A couple of years ago (never too early to begin your research) your correspondent found himself, for a few minutes, up on the Wembley stage with U2, and is accordingly able to offer a brief report.

Light surrounds you like a wall. You can just about see beyond the bouncers to the first rows of upturned faces but, beyond that, zilch. The space feels almost intimate; then the invisible crowd roars like a sci-fi beast and you, well, if you're a novelist who has somehow strayed out here, you panic. What are you supposed to do with an audience this big? *Sing* to it? But—as in all the best nightmares—you can't sing a note. At which point, the authentic Rock Star takes charge. Standing next to the Star, watching him coax, caress, and control the invisible Hydra out there, you feel more than impressed. You feel grateful.

I had met Bono a few times, but when I looked into his face on the Wembley stage I saw a stranger there, and understood that this was the Star-creature that normally lay hidden in him, a creature as powerful as the big beastie it sang to, so overwhelming that it could be let out only in this cage of light. The Star-creature in Mick Jagger was rampant at Wembley on Tuesday night. It had been going a lot longer than U2; it was old and huge and brilliant.

All the old-age jokes have been trotted out this past week: Rock 'n' Wrinkle, Crock 'n' Roll. I sat next to a man who remembered seeing the Stones on their first tour, September 1963. Thirty-two years ago— *thirty-two years!*—I saw that tour, too; as a sixteen-year-old schoolboy I skived off from school on the bus. My neighbor and I couldn't agree on who had topped the bill that autumn: one of those guys who died in a plane crash, he thought, while my vote was for Gene Vincent singing "Be-Bop-a-Lula." But we were both wrong. It was the Everly Brothers and Bo Diddley. The Stones have been going so long that their original audience's memory has started playing tricks; *that's* how long.

On your way to a galaxy-sized rock supershow like *Voodoo Lounge,* you must pass through meteor showers of facts and factoids. As well as all the age stuff—did you know their average age is higher than the cabinet's?—you hear, once again, the old yarn about Keith Richards having all his blood changed; from a disgruntled hatter who failed to gain Jagger's favor you learn that the great man has a "really tiny head"; it is even suggested—is there no respect anymore?—that Mick has a penchant for exaggerating his assets by shoving assorted fruit and vegetables down the front of his leggings. We also know, by now, that even though the tour is sponsored by Volkswagen ("Stones Team Up with Beetles"), Mick drives a Mercedes; and that, in spite of all their rebellious postures, they're just social climbers, really, in it for the money and the swank. We know that the Ramones are retiring and have advised the Stones to do the same, and that they won't, not while the megabucks are pouring in. We have heard that squillions of dollars are raining down upon our heroes. *What can a poor boy do 'cept to sing for a rock 'n' roll band?* Maybe, these days, they should be singing "Diamond Life" instead.

Even a thirty-two-year devotion to the Rolling Stones can fray, under such a bombardment, into irritability, especially when the Canadian mafia in charge of seat allocation bungs you behind a pillar, and it takes a friendly stadium security officer to get you a seat you can actually see the show from. I'll admit to sharpening a few adjectives while waiting for the dinosaurs to appear.

Then came dragon-fire, and all carping became instantly redundant. Mark Fisher's "Cobra" set came to life: the high-tech serpent head in the sky belched flame. Fisher, also responsible for the recent Pink Floyd and Zoo-TV stages, is currently the man to call if you want to spend a fortune turning sports stadia into futureworlds. The show's promoters like to compare the tour to a military operation, but that misses the mark. What's more astonishing is to reflect that all this theatrical gigantism—"250 personnel, four days to construct, three different steel crews leapfrogging around the country, 8 miles of cable, the world's largest mobile Jumbotron video screen, 56 trailers, 9 buses, and a Boeing 727, 3,840,000 watts of power produced by 6,000-horsepower generators," it says here—is being employed in the cause of mere fun. *Only rock 'n' roll, but I like it.* Good to know that pleasure has its armies, too.

And from the moment the Stones launched into "Not Fade Away" to the single encore of "Jumping Jack Flash," there was pleasure, two and a half hours of it. The set was a pyrotechnic marvel, cascading with light, erupting into fireworks, and conjuring up, during "Sympathy for the Devil," those marvelously eerie giant inflatables—Elvis, a snake, a Star Child, a Hindu goddess—who danced like huge voodoo dolls, slaves to the rhythm, above Jagger's Baron Samedi capers. And the sound was good too, every note rich and clear, every word audible and resonant; and the high-definition video screen was the best I've seen. But none of this is the point.

The point is that the Stones were amazing. Their force, their drive, the sheer quality and freshness of Mick's singing and the band's playing (Keith Richards, during "Satisfaction," seemed at one point to be mouthing "I love this song"); Mick's athleticism and grace of movement (once he would Walk the Dog and do the Funky Chicken the way Tina Turner showed him; now there's something almost Oriental in his dancing, like a Bharat Natyam dancer with 3,840,000 watts of power coursing through him); and Keith, planted front and center with his feet wide apart, whanging his guitar in classic rock-god style, Keith with his ruined–Mount Rushmore head, effortlessly dominating the stage while Mick skipped, leapt, and zoomed. Keith does not run. He leaves that to his mate. (He should probably leave the singing to Mick, too. At the very least he should not tempt fate and the critics by singing songs called "The Worst.")

By their second song, "Tumbling Dice," it was clear that the new "engine room," in which Charlie Watts had been joined by the bass guitarist Darryl Jones, was as tight and potent as ever. It was also evident, from her duet with Mick on "Gimme Shelter," that the backup vocalist Lisa Fischer was a bit of a star herself. Not content with having come onstage in what looked like leather underwear, and fuck-me stilettos with bondage straps all the way up her calves,★ she also unfurled a rich, sexy voice with sustained high notes that could spear you in the heart.

The new songs just about held their own against the wonders of the back catalog, but it was the classics that really got us going; inevitably, because this music—the "Satisfaction" riff, the dirty genius of "Honky Tonk Woman"—has sunk so deep into our blood that we may even be able, by now, to pass the knowledge on genetically to our children, who will be born humming "how come you dance so good" and those old satanic verses, "pleased to meet you, hope you guessed my name." And how satisfying that the Stones haven't fallen into the Bob Dylan trap of murdering their old songs. As a result, Wembley was full of kids bopping happily to songs that were older than they were but felt new. This is not a nostalgia show; these songs are not museum pieces. Listen to Keith's guitar playing on "Wild Horses." These songs are alive.

There was a gray-haired geezer in a pink T-shirt and jeans—still crazy after all these years—who got himself frog-marched out by a squad of Meat Loafs. There was a dark-haired girl in an outfit that seemed to have been painted onto her body who stood up in the posh enclosure and danced so voluptuously, during "Sweet Virginia," that people (men) turned away from the stage to watch her. There was some

★ When this piece was first published in *The Observer,* a caustic reader wrote in to say that although he supposed (wrongly) that I probably hadn't had much sex in recent years, he really didn't want to read about my lusts. Well, too bad, pal.

mutual nipple kissing between Mick and Lisa Fischer that got our attention back. There was an ovation for Charlie Watts. You couldn't have wished for more. The Rolling Stones may not be dangerous now, they may no longer be a threat to decent, civilized society, but they still know how to let it bleed. Yeah yeah yeah WOO.

July 1995

Rock Music—A Sleeve Note

———————

Frank Zappa and the Mothers of Invention are playing at the Albert Hall. It's sometime in the early seventies. (As they say, if you can remember the exact date, you weren't there.) Halfway through the gig, an enormous black guy in a shiny purple shirt climbs up onto the stage. (Security was lighter in those innocent days.) He's swaying gently, and insists on playing with the band.

Zappa, unfazed, asks gravely, "Uh-huh, sir, and what is your instrument of choice?"

"Horn," mumbles the Purple Shirt Guy.

"Give this man a horn," Frank Zappa commands. But the moment the Purple Shirt Guy blows his first terrible note, it's clear his horn skills leave much to be desired. Zappa briefly looks lost in contemplation, chin in hand. "Hmm." Then he moves to the mike. "I wonder," he muses, "what we can think of to accompany this man on his horn." He has a flash of mock inspiration. "I know! The mighty Albert Hall pipe organ!"

The mighty Albert Hall pipe organ has in fact been declared strictly off limits to the band, but now one of the Mothers actually climbs up the face of the great beast, scrambles into the organist's cubbyhole, pulls out every single stop, and almost brings the grand old hall crashing down with his deafening rendition of "Louie, Louie."

Va–va–va / va–voom!

Meanwhile, down on the stage, the Purple Shirt Guy tootles away, blissfully happy, totally inaudible, while Frank Zappa looks fondly on like the benevolent, subversive wit he is.

———

Wit is not the quality most often associated with rock music, and when one listens to the Cro-Magnon grunts of most rock stars, one can readily appreciate why. In spite of the Spice Girls, however, rock 'n' roll actually has a long history of verbal, musical, and off-the-cuff felicities and dexterities.

Here is Elvis, claiming to be itchy as a man on a fuzzy tree.

Here's John Lennon's quickness of tongue. ("How do you find America?" "Turn left at Greenland.")

Here's Randy Newman, proving, in "Sail Away," that a song can be simultaneously anthemic and satirical. ("In America, there's plenty food to eat / Don't have to run through the jungle and scuff up your feet.")

Here are Paul Simon's surreal-associative lyrics. ("Why am I soft in the middle / when the rest of my life is so hard?")

And here is the troubadour beyond categories, Tom Waits, telling his raw wanderer's tales of alley cats and raindogs. ("I got the cards but not the luck / I got the wheels but not the truck / but heh I'm big in Japan.")

In all this there is much for literary folk to study and admire. I don't subscribe to the lyrics-are-poetry school of rock aficionado over-claiming. But I know I'd have been ridiculously proud to have written anything as good as this. And I'd have loved to have had the talent, the humor and speed of thought of Frank Zappa in the Albert Hall that night.

May 1999

U2

————

In the summer of 1986 I was traveling in Nicaragua, working on the book of reportage that was published six months later as *The Jaguar Smile*. It was the seventh anniversary of the Sandinista revolution, and the war against the U.S.-backed Contra forces was intensifying almost daily. I was accompanied by my interpreter Margarita, an improbably glamorous and high-spirited blonde with more than a passing resemblance to Jayne Mansfield. Our days were filled with evidence of hardship and struggle: the scarcity of produce in the markets of Managua, the bomb crater on a country road where a school bus had been blown up by a Contra mine. One morning, however, Margarita seemed unusually excited. "Bono's coming!" she cried, bright-eyed as any fan, and then added, without any change in vocal inflection or dulling of ocular glitter, "Tell me: who is Bono?"

In a way, the question was as vivid a demonstration of her country's beleaguered isolation as anything I heard or saw in the front-line villages, the destitute Atlantic Coast bayous, or the quake-ravaged city streets. In July 1986, the release of U2's monster album *The Joshua Tree* was still nine months away, but they were already, after all, the masters of *War*. Who was Bono? He was the fellow who sang "I can't believe the news today, I can't close my eyes and make it go away." And Nicaragua was one of the places where the news had become unbelievable, and you couldn't shut your eyes to it, and so of course he was there.

I didn't meet Bono in Nicaragua, but he did read *The Jaguar Smile*.

Five years later, when I was involved in some difficulties of my own, my friend the composer Michael Berkeley asked if I wanted to go to a U2 *Achtung Baby* gig, with its hanging psychedelic Trabants. In those days it was hard for me to go most places, but I said yes, and was touched by the enthusiasm with which the request was greeted by U2's people. And so there I was at Earl's Court, standing in the shadows, listening. Backstage, after the show, I was shown into a mobile home full of sandwiches and children. There were no groupies at U2 gigs; just a nursery. Bono came in and was instantly festooned with daughters. My memory of that first chat is that I wanted to talk about music and he was keen to talk politics—Nicaragua, an upcoming protest against nuclear waste at Sellafield, his support for me and my work. We didn't spend long together, but we both enjoyed it.

One year later, when the giant *Zooropa* tour arrived at Wembley Stadium, Bono called to ask if I'd like to come out onstage. U2 wanted to make a gesture of solidarity and this was the biggest one they could think of. When I told my then fourteen-year-old son about the plan, he said, "Just don't sing, Dad. If you sing, I'll have to kill myself." There was no question of my being allowed to sing—U2 aren't stupid people—but I did go out there and feel, for a moment, what it's like to have eighty thousand fans cheering you on. The audience at the average book reading is a little smaller. Girls tend not to climb onto their boyfriends' shoulders during them, and stage-diving is discouraged. Even at the very best book readings, there are only one or two supermodels dancing by the mixing desk. Anton Corbijn took a photograph that day for which he persuaded Bono and me to exchange glasses. There I am looking godlike in Bono's Fly shades, while he peers benignly over my uncool literary specs. There could be no more graphic expression of the difference between our worlds.

It's inevitable that both U2 and I should be criticized for bringing these two worlds together. They have been accused of trying to acquire some borrowed intellectual "cred," and I of course am supposedly starstruck. None of this matters very much. I've been crossing frontiers all my life—physical, social, intellectual, artistic borderlines—and I spotted, in Bono and Edge, whom I've so far come to know better than the others, an equal hunger for the new, for whatever nourishes. I think, too, that the band's involvement in religion—as inescapable a subject in Ireland as it is in India—gave us, when we first met, a subject, and an enemy (fanaticism) in common.

An association with U2 is good for one's anecdote stock. Some of these anecdotes are risibly apocryphal. A couple of years ago, for example, a front-page Irish press report confidently announced that I had been living in "the folly"—the guesthouse with a spectacular view of Killiney Bay that stands in the garden of Bono's Dublin home—for four whole years! Apparently I arrived and departed at dead of night in a helicopter that landed on the beach below the house. Other stories that sound apocryphal are unfortunately true. It is true, for example, that I once danced—or, to be precise, pogoed—with Van Morrison in Bono's living room. It is also true that in the small hours of the following morning I was treated to the rough end of the great man's tongue. (Mr. Morrison has been known to get a little grumpy toward the end of a long evening. It's possible that my pogoing wasn't up to his exacting standards.)

Over the years U2 and I discussed collaborating on various projects. Bono mentioned an idea he had for a stage musical, but my imagination failed to spark. There was another long Dublin night (a bottle of Jameson's was involved) during which the film director Neil Jordan, Bono, and I conspired to make a film of my novel *Haroun and the Sea of Stories.* To my great regret, this never came to anything either. Then, in autumn 1999, I published *The Ground Beneath Her Feet,* in which the Orpheus myth winds through a story set in the world of rock music. Orpheus is the defining myth for both singers and writers—for the Greeks, he was the greatest singer as well as the greatest poet—and it was my Orphic tale that finally made a collaboration possible. It happened, like many good things, without being planned. I sent Bono and U2's manager, Paul McGuinness, pre-publication copies of the novel, in typescript, hoping that they would tell me if the thing worked or not. Bono said afterward that he had been very worried on my behalf, believing that I had taken on an impossible task, and that he began reading the book in the spirit of a "policeman"—that is, to save me from my mistakes. Fortunately, the novel passed the test. Deep inside it is the lyric of what Bono called the novel's "title track," a sad elegy written by the main male character about the woman he loved, who has been swallowed up in an earthquake: a contemporary Orpheus's lament for his lost Eurydice.

Bono called me. "I've written this melody for your words, and I think it might be one of the best things I've done." I was astonished. One of the novel's principal images is that of the permeable frontier between the world of the imagination and the one we inhabit, and here was an imaginary song crossing that frontier. I went to Paul McGuinness's place near Dublin to hear it. Bono took me away from everyone else and played the demo CD to me in his car. Only when he was sure that I liked it—and I liked it right away—did we go back indoors and play it for the assembled company.

There wasn't much, after that, that one would properly call collaboration. There was a long afternoon when Daniel Lanois, who was producing the song, brought his guitar and sat down with me to work out the lyrical structure. And there was the Day of the Lost Words, when I was called urgently by a woman from Principle Management, who look after U2. "They're in the studio and they can't find the lyrics. Could you fax them over?" Otherwise, silence, until the song was ready.

I wasn't expecting it to happen, but I'm proud of it. For U2, too, it was a departure. They haven't often used anyone's lyrics but their own, and they don't usually start with the lyrics; typically, the words come at the very end. But somehow it all worked out. I suggested facetiously that they might consider renaming the band U2 + 1, or, even better, Me2, but I think they'd heard all those gags before.

During an alfresco lunch in Killiney, the film director Wim Wenders startlingly announced that artists must no longer use irony. Plain speaking, he argued, was necessary now: communication should be direct, and anything that might create confusion should be eschewed. Irony, in the rock world, has acquired a special meaning. The multi-media self-consciousness of U2's *Achtung Baby/Zooropa* phase, which simultaneously embraced and debunked the mythology and gobbledygook of rock stardom, capitalism, and power, and of which Bono's white-faced, gold-lamé-suited, red-velvet-horned MacPhisto incarnation was the emblem, is what Wenders was criticizing. Characteristically, U2 responded by taking this approach even further, pushing it further than it would bear, in the less well received *PopMart* tour. After that, it seems, they took Wenders's advice. The new album, and the *Elevation* tour, is the spare, impressive result.

There was a lot riding on this album, this tour. If things hadn't gone well it might have been the end of U2. They certainly discussed that possibility, and the album was much delayed as they agonized over it. Extra-curricular activities—mainly Bono's—also slowed them down, but since these included getting David Trimble and John Hume to shake hands on a public stage, and reducing Jesse Helms—Jesse Helms!—to tears, winning his support for the campaign against Third

World debt, it's hard to argue that these were self-indulgent irrele-
vances. At any event, *All That You Can't Leave Behind* turned out to be
a strong album, a renewal of creative force, and, as Bono put it, there's
a lot of goodwill flowing toward the band right now. I've seen them
three times this year: in the "secret" pre-tour gig in London's little As-
toria theater, and then twice in America, in San Diego and Anaheim.
They've come down out of the giant stadia to play arena-sized venues
that seem tiny after the gigantism of their recent past. The act has been
stripped bare; essentially, it's just the four of them out there, playing
their instruments and singing their songs. For a person of my age, who
remembers when rock music was always like this, the show feels simultaneously nostalgic and innovative. In the age of choreographed,
instrument-less little-boy and little-girl bands (yes, I know the Supremes
didn't play guitars, but they were the Supremes!), it's exhilarating to
watch a great, grown-up quartet do the fine, simple things so well.
Direct communication, as Wim Wenders said. It works.

———

And they're playing my song.

May 2001

An Alternative Career

[Michael Ondaatje asked me to contribute a piece to an issue of the Canadian literary magazine Brick *about alternative careers. This was, obviously, many years before my appearance in the film of* Bridget Jones's Diary . . .]

I always wanted to be an actor, in spite of early reverses.

I started out at the age of seven as a pixie in a school play in Bombay. My costume was made of orange crepe paper, and halfway through the little pixie dance I had to do with several other pixies, it fell off.

When I was twelve, I played the Promoter (that is, prosecutor) in Shaw's *Saint Joan.* I had to sit at a table in a grubby white cassock and make copious notes with a quill pen. The only quill pen that could be found in Bombay was actually a ballpoint with a large red feather attached. I scribbled away merrily. After the play someone congratulated me on my performance and said that he had been especially impressed by the fact that I had been able to write for so long without ever needing to dip my quill pen into the ink.

At school in England the difficulties continued. In one production I played a swarthy Latin hound who got poisoned at the end of Act One. I was permitted a wonderfully melodramatic death scene, full of staggers and clutches at the throat, before crashing down behind a sofa.

In Act Two, however, I had to lie behind the sofa for an hour with my legs sticking out. Stagehands climbed up above the stage and dropped peanut shells onto my face, trying to make my legs twitch. They succeeded.

Next I was cast as one of the lunatics in Friedrich Dürrenmatt's *The Physicists,* but then illness struck down the boy actor playing the megalomaniac hunchback woman doctor in charge of the lunatic asylum in which the play is set, and I was told to take over. (It was a single-sex school, so we were obliged to follow the boys-only casting philosophy of the Elizabethan theater.) I wore thick tartan leggings, a tweed skirt, and a Mad Cherman Akzent. The play was not a success.

At Cambridge I built myself a putty nose extension for a part in an Ionesco play, but on the first night, bending over a lady's hand, I squished my fake hooter sideways and looked more like the Elephant Man than I would have liked.

In a badly under-rehearsed production of Ben Jonson's *The Alchemist,* playing to a first-night front row full of English literature professors, I suddenly understood that the line I was speaking was the answer to the question I was about to be asked. The whole cast immediately panicked and began improvising in something like Jonsonian meter, trying to find our way to a bit—any bit—we knew. It took what seemed like hours, but we managed it. Not one of the assembled luminaries of the Cambridge literature faculty noticed a thing.

After graduating I spent a while involved in London fringe productions. In a production of Megan Terry's *Viet Rock* I was required to insult an audience full of people in wheelchairs, attacking them for their apathy about the war. Why were they not marching in protest, why had they not been at the Grosvenor Square demonstration confronting the mounted police, I demanded righteously. The wheelchair people hung their heads, abashed.

In another production I went back into drag, wearing a long black evening gown and a long blond wig to play a sort of Miss Lonelyhearts figure in a play written by a friend who has since become a successful writer. To make the Nathanael West-ish point that such figures are often men, I also sported a prominent black Zapata mustache. My friend the now-successful writer still threatens from time to time to publish photographs of this performance.

After playing the blonde, I understood that I had a limited future in this line of work and ceased to tread the boards. The itch remains, however. A few years ago another frustrated actor, the writer, editor, and publisher Bill Buford, suggested that we should sign up one summer in the most out-of-the-way American summer-stock company we could find and spend a few happy months playing pixies, swarthy Latins, cassocked prosecutors, mad doctors, et cetera. It never happened, but I wish it had.

Maybe next year.

October 1994

On Leavened Bread

There was leavened bread in Bombay, but it was sorry fare: dry, crumbling, tasteless, unleavened bread's paler, unluckier relation. It wasn't "real." "Real" bread was the chapati, or phulka, served piping hot; the tandoori nan, and its sweeter Frontier variant, the Peshawari nan; and for luxury, the reshmi roti, the shirmal, the paratha. Compared to these aristocrats, the leavened white loaves of my childhood seemed to merit the description that Shaw's immortal dustman, Alfred Doolittle, dreamed up for people like himself: they were, in truth, "the undeserving poor."

My first inkling that there might be more to leavened bread than I knew came on a visit to Karachi, Pakistan, where I learned that a hidden order of nuns, in a place known as the Monastery of the Angels, baked a mean loaf. To buy it you had to get up at dawn—that is, a servant had to get up at dawn—and stand in line outside a small hatch in the monastery's wall. The nuns' baking facilities were limited, the daily "run" was small, and this secret bakery's reputation was high. Only the early bird caught the loaf. The hatch would open, and a nun would hand the bread out to the waiting populace. Loaves were strictly rationed. No bulk buying was permitted. And the price, of course, was high. (All this I knew only by hearsay, for I never got up at such an unearthly hour to see for myself.)

The nuns' bread—white, crusty, full of flavor—was a small revelation but also, on account of its unusual provenance, eccentric. It came from beyond the frontiers of the everyday, a mystery trailing an anecdote behind it. It was almost, well, fictional. (Later, it became fictional, when I put the monastery and its secret sisters into *Midnight's Children*.) Now, in the matter of bread, such extraordinariness is not good. You want bread to be a part of daily life. You want it to be ordinary. You want it to be there. You don't want to get up in the middle of the night and wait by a hatch in a wall. So while the Angels' bread was tasty, it felt like an aberration, a break in the natural order. It didn't really change my mind.

Then, aged thirteen and a half, I flew to England. And suddenly there it was, in every shop window. The White Crusty, the Sliced and the Unsliced. The Small Tin, the Large Tin, the Danish Bloomer. The abandoned, plentiful promiscuity of it. The soft pillowy mattressiness of it. The well-sprung bounciness of it between your teeth. Hard crust and soft center: the sensuality of that perfect textural contrast. I was done for. In the whorehouses of the bakeries, I was serially, gluttonously, irredeemably unfaithful to all those chapatis-next-door waiting for me back home. East was East, but yeast was West.*

This, remember, was long before British bread counters were enlivened by the European invasion, long before olive bread and tomato bread, ciabatta and brioche; this was 1961. But the love affair that began then has never lost its intensity; the new exotic breads have served only to renew the excitement.

I should add that there was a second discovery, almost as thrilling: that is, water. Water back home was dangerous, had to be thoroughly boiled. To be able to drink water from the tap was a privilege indeed. In this respect, life in the West has somewhat declined in quality . . . but I have never forgotten that when I first arrived in these immeasurably wealthy and powerful lands, I found the first proofs of my good fortune in loaf and glass. A regime of bread and water has never, since that time, sounded like a hardship to me.

November 1999

---

* Some of these thoughts found their way into the mind of Ormus Cama, the hero of *The Ground Beneath Her Feet.*

On Being Photographed

O utside a photographic studio in South London, the famous Avedon backdrop of bright white paper awaits, looking oddly like an
absence: a blank space in the world. In Avedon's portrait gallery, his
subjects are asked to occupy, and define, a void. Somebody once told
me that a frog on a lily pad keeps its eyes (which see by relative motion)
so still that they see nothing at all, until an insect flies across their field
of vision and becomes literally the only thing there, captured without
escape on the white canvas of the frog's artificial, temporary blindness.
Then snap, and it's gone.

There is something predatory about all photography. The portrait is
the portraitist's food. In a real-life incident I fictionalized in *Midnight's
Children,* my grandmother once brained an acquaintance with his own
camera for daring to point it at her, because she believed that if he could
capture some part of her essence in his box, then she would necessarily
be deprived of it. What the photographer gained, the subject lost; cam-
eras, like fear, ate the soul.

If you believe the language—and the language itself never lies, though
liars often have the sweetest tongues—then the camera is a weapon: a
photograph is a shot, and a session is a shoot, and a portrait may therefore be the trophy the hunter brings home from his shikar. A stuffed
head for his wall.

It may be gathered from the above that I do not much enjoy having my picture taken, do not enjoy becoming, rather than exploring, a subject. These days writers are endlessly photographed, but for the most part these aren't true portraits—they are publicity pix, and every newspaper, every magazine, must have its own. Mostly the photographers who work with writers are kind. They make us look our best, which isn't always easy. They compliment us on being interesting. They ask our opinions. They may even read our books.

Richard Avedon is the author of some of the most striking portrait photographs of our day, but he is not, in the sense I have used the term, kind. He looks like an American eagle, and he sees his subjects, against white, with a bleak unblinking eye, whether they are writers or the mighty of the earth or anonymous folks or his own dying father. Perhaps, for Avedon, the stripped-down, head-on technique of his portraiture is a necessary alternative to the high-gloss fantasy world of his other life as a fashion photographer. In these portraits he is not selling but telling. And perhaps he is excited, too, by the fact that the people he is looking at are not members of that new tribe created by the camera: the tribe of professional subjects.

If the camera is a stealer of souls, is there not something Faustian about the contract between photographer and model, between the Mephistophilis of the camera and the beautiful young men and women who come to life, hoping for eternity (or at least celebrity), before its one-eyed stare? Models know how to look, the good ones know what the camera sees. They are performers of the surface, manipulators and presenters of their own extraordinary outsides. But finally the model's look is an artificiality, it is a look about how to look. Off-duty models photograph one another ceaselessly, defining each passing moment of their lives—a lunch, a stroll, a meeting—by committing it to film. Garry Winogrand, quoted in Susan Sontag's *On Photography,* says that he takes photographs "to find out what something will look like photographed," and these professional subjects are similarly trapped—they can never step outside the frame. They become quotations of themselves. Until the camera loses interest, and they fade away. The story of Faust does not have a happy ending.

Avedon's glamour photography has often touched on the theme of beauty and its passing. In a recent sequence the supermodel Nadja Auermann is seen in a series of surreal high-fashion clinches with an animated skeleton who is, of course, a photographer. Death and the maiden, a spectacular, with costumes by the great designers of the world. Perhaps Avedon is making a joke at his own expense, the skeleton as grand old man; perhaps he is hinting at the passing of the super-model phenomenon. Equally relevant, however, is his wholehearted willingness to enter into the high-budget, high-gloss elaboration of this type of mega-commercial rag trade extravaganza. This is no ivory tower artist.

The contrast with his portraiture could not be greater. The portrait photograph is Avedon's naked stage, his blasted heath. Is it, I wonder, that one has to *do something* to exceptional beauties—cover their faces in icicles, make them dance with skeletons—to make them interesting to photograph; whereas unbeauties, the faces of real life, are rewarding even (only) when unadorned?

A great portrait photograph is about insides. Cartier-Bresson and Elliott Erwitt catch their people on the wing, as it were: often, their work is revealing because the subjects have been caught off guard. Avedon is more formal: the white sheet, the majestic old plate camera on its tripod. In this setup it is the insect that must be perfectly still, not the frog.

I have seen a lot of photographers work. I remember Barry Lategan in a natty beret snapping away during an interview, nodding every time I said something he liked. I began to watch him carefully, becoming dependent on his nods, growing addicted to his approval: performing for him. I remember Sally Soames persuading me to stretch out on a sofa and more or less lying on top of me to get the shot she wanted, a shot in which, unsurprisingly, I have a rather dreamy expression in my eyes. I remember Lord Snowdon rearranging all the furniture in my house, gathering bits of "Indianness" around me: a picture, a hookah. The resulting picture is one I have never cared for: the writer as exotic. Sometimes photographers come to you with a picture already in their heads, and then you're done for.

I have seen a lot of photographers work, but I never saw anyone take as few pictures in a session as Avedon does with his big plate camera. Is it that he knows exactly what he wants, or that he is content to take what he gets, I wondered: for Mr. Avedon is a man on a tight schedule. Some people will give him more than others—so does the onus of becoming a good photograph rest with us, his non-professional subjects, who know rather more about our insides than our outsides? Must we reveal ourselves, or will his sorcery unveil us anyhow?

He positions me just as he wants me. I am not to sway, even by a millimeter, as I may go out of focus: it's that critical. I must hold my ex-

pression for what seems an eternity. I find myself thinking: this is how I look when I am being made to look like this. This will be a photograph of a man doing something awkward to which he is not accustomed. Then, shrugging inwardly, I surrender to the great man. This is *Richard Avedon,* I tell myself. Just let him take the damn picture and don't argue.

Two setups, one indoors in a long black raincoat and one indoors, very close up, in a pin-striped black shirt. I saw the results of the close-up first, and to tell the truth it shocked and depressed me. It looked, well, satanic. A part of me blamed the photographer; another, larger part blamed my face. The next time I met Avedon, his opening words were "So, did you hate it?" I was unable to grin and say, it's great. "It's very dark," I said. "Oh, but the other picture's much friendlier," he comforted me. The other picture is the one accompanying this piece. Fortunately, I really like it. I'm not sure if "friendly" is the word for it (actually, I am sure, and "friendly" is *not* the word for it; I have a cheery, even chirpy way of looking at times, and this is definitely not one of those times), but I am, as they say, "comfortable" with the way it makes me look. The head is a good shape—my head is not always a good shape in photographs—and the beard is tidy and the face has a certain lived-in melancholy that I can't deny I recognize from my mirror. The black Japanese raincoat looks great.

The way the subject of a photograph looks at the photograph is unlike the way anyone else will ever see it. You hope your worst bits haven't been emphasized too much. You hope not to look like a bag person. You hope not to scare people who come across the picture by chance.

Let me try to see this picture as if I were not its subject. Richard Avedon was not interested in making a picture of a cheery novelist without a care in the world. I think he wanted to make a portrait of a writer to whom a number of bad things had happened. I think the picture shows some of that pain, but also, I hope, it shows something of resistance and endurance. It is a strong picture, and I am grateful to Avedon, for his solidarity, for his picture's clarity, and for its strength.

November 1995

Crash

THE DEATH OF PRINCESS DIANA

———

It has all been so disturbingly novelistic, and the novel I'm thinking of isn't a fairy tale, although Diana's story did begin like a fairy tale, nor is it a soap opera, although goodness knows the long saga of the battling Windsors has been sudsy enough. I'm thinking of J. G. Ballard's *Crash,* whose recent film adaptation by David Cronenberg caused howls from the censorship lobby, particularly in Britain. It is one of the darker ironies of a dark event that the themes and ideas explored by Ballard and Cronenberg, themes and ideas which many in Britain have called pornographic, should have been so lethally acted out in the car accident that killed Princess Diana, Dodi al-Fayed, and their drunken driver.

We live in a culture that routinely eroticizes and glamorizes its consumer technology, notably the motorcar. We also live in the Age of Fame, in which the intensity of our gaze upon celebrity turns the famous into commodities, too, a transformation that has often proved powerful enough to destroy them. Ballard's novel, by bringing together these two powerful erotic fetishes—the Automobile and the Star—in an act of sexual violence (a car crash), created an effect so shocking as to be thought obscene.

The death of Princess Diana is just such an obscenity. One of the reasons why it is so very sad is that it seems so senseless. To die because you don't want to have your picture taken! What could be more meaningless, more absurd? But in fact this frightful accident is freighted with meanings. It tells us uncomfortable truths about what we have become.

In our erotic imaginations, perhaps only the camera can rival the automobile. The camera, as a reporter, captures the news and delivers it to our door and, in more adoring mode, often looks upon beautiful women and offers them up for our delight. In Princess Diana's fatal crash, the Camera (as both Reporter and Lover) is joined to the Automobile and the Star, and the cocktail of death and desire becomes even more powerful than the one in Ballard's book.

Think of it this way. The object of desire, the Beauty (Princess Diana), is repeatedly subjected to the unwelcome attentions of a persistent suitor (the Camera) until a dashing, glamorous knight (riding his Automobile) sweeps her away. The Camera, with its unavoidably phallic long-lensed snout, gives pursuit. And the story reaches its tragic climax, for the Automobile is driven not by a hero but by a clumsy drunk. Put not your trust in fairy tales, or chivalrous knights. The object of desire, in the moment of her death, sees the phallic lenses advancing upon her, snapping, snapping. Think of it this way and the pornography of Diana Spencer's death becomes apparent. She died in a sublimated sexual assault.

Sublimated. That's the point. The Camera is not, finally, a suitor in its own right. True, it seeks to possess the Beauty, to capture her on film, for economic gain. But that's a euphemism. The brutal truth is that the camera is acting on our behalf. If the camera acts voyeuristically, it is because our relationship with the Beauty has always been voyeuristic. If blood is on the hands of the photographers and the photo agencies and the news media's photo editors, it is also on ours. What newspaper do you read? When you saw the pictures of Dodi and Diana cavorting together, did you say, that's none of my business, and turn the page?

We are the lethal voyeurs. "Are you satisfied now?" people in Britain have been shouting at photographers. Could we answer the same question? Are we satisfied now? Are we going to stop being fascinated by those illicit images of Diana's kisses, or by the earlier "sensational scoops" of Prince Charles naked in a distant room, of Fergie getting her toes sucked, all those purloined moments, those stolen secrets of public people's private lives that have, for more than a decade now, been the stuff of our most popular newspapers and magazines? Will we no longer want to eavesdrop on the intimacies of those—like the voluptuous Earthling movie star in a Vonnegut novel, imprisoned with a man in a zoo on the planet Tralfamadore, so that the locals could study her mating habits—whom we imprison in fame?

Not a chance.

———

Princess Diana became skillful at constructing the images of herself she wanted people to see. I recall a British newspaper editor telling me how she composed the famous shot in which she sat, alone and lovelorn, in front of the world's greatest monument to love, the Taj Mahal. She knew, he said, exactly how the public would "read" this photograph. It would bring her great sympathy, and make people think (even) less well of the Prince of Wales than before. Princess Diana was not given to using words like "semiotics," but she was a capable semiotician of herself. With increasing confidence, she gave us the signs by which we might know her as she wished to be known.

Some voices have been saying that her "collusion" with the media in general and with photographers in particular must be an important mitigating factor in any discussion of the paparazzi's role in her death. Perhaps so; but one must also consider the importance attached by a woman in her position to controlling her public image. The public figure is happy to be photographed only when she or he is prepared for it, "on guard," one might say. The paparazzo looks only for the unguarded moment. The battle is for control, for a form of power. Diana did not wish to give the photographers power over her, to be merely their (our) Object. In escaping from the pursuing lenses, she was asserting her determination, perhaps her right, to be something altogether more dignified: that is, to be a Subject. Fleeing from Object to Subject, from commodity toward humanity, she met her death. Wanting to be the mistress of her own life, she surrendered herself to a driver who was not even able to control her car. This, too, is a bitter irony.

———

The Windsors and the Fayeds are the archetypal Insiders and Outsiders. Mohammad al-Fayed, the Egyptian who longed to be British, bought Harrods (and Conservative MPs) in his failed quest for British citizenship, and membership of an Establishment that closed its doors against him. Princess Diana's love of Dodi al-Fayed may have felt to Dodi's father like a moment of sweet triumph over that Establishment. Diana alive was the ultimate trophy. In death, she may unmake al-

Fayed. He has lost his eldest son and perhaps also his last, best chance of being accepted by the British.

I described the Windsors as Insiders, but their status is also in doubt. Once beloved of the nation, they are now widely seen as the family that maltreated the far more beloved Diana. If al-Fayed is fated to remain on the outside looking in, then the Royal Family itself may just possibly be on the way out. The nation's love of Diana will undoubtedly transfer itself to her sons. But if our insatiable, voyeuristic appetite for the iconic Diana was ultimately responsible for her death, then we should ask ourselves some sober questions about these boys. Would they be better off away from the crippling burdens of being Royal? How can they go on living in the real world she tried to show them, the world beyond the closed society of the British aristocracy, beyond Eton College? Diana herself seemed far happier once she'd escaped from the Royal Family. Perhaps Britain too would be happier if it made the same escape, and learned to live without kings and queens. Such are the unthinkable thoughts that have become all too thinkable now.

September 1997

The People's Game

---

1. WE ARE THE WORLD

In 1994, when the soccer World Cup was about to be played across the length and breadth of a largely indifferent America, perhaps the main concern of those few U.S. citizens who knew it was happening was that the alien phenomenon of soccer hooliganism might be about to arrive in the States. Fortunately the England team failed to make the finals, and so the feared English hooligans stayed home. Fortunately for the hooligans, I suspect, for, as I heard an American comedian explaining on British television, the World Cup matches were to be played in some of the toughest neighborhoods of some of the toughest cities in the world. "I tell you what," he suggested. "Why don't you bring your hooligans, and we'll bring ours."

Four years later, the 1998 World Cup was staged in and won by France, and as it happened I watched the entire tournament in America, on ESPN and Univision. The dullness of the ESPN coverage, with its commentators desperately misapplying the terminology of America's ball games to soccer, suggested that America's lack of interest in the rest of the world's favorite game was as great as ever. Even when the USA team was defeated by Iran—Iran!—there was no more than a brief blip of attention before the Yankees, McGwire, and Sosa regained center stage.

Over on the Spanish-language Univision channel, however—"G6666666666666l!!!!!!"—things were very different. Here was all the excitement and color missing from the ESPN commentary. And as it was on television, so it was also in real life; for wherever in polyglot America you stumbled over clumps of French men and women, or Brazilians, Colombians, Mexicans, Croatians, Germans, even Brits, for example in the many-nationed bars of Queens, the tournament and its passions were to be found there also, blazing as fiercely as anywhere else on earth.

The poor performances of the USA team were no doubt due, in part, to the crushing uninterest of the American mainstream but could also, I thought, be ascribed to the fact that the team seemed to be made up of college kids. For while college teams successfully supply fresh talent, year after year, to the NFL and NBA, soccer is not a college sport. Soccer is the people's game, played with empty tin cans in the back streets of Brazilian cities. Soccer is working-class self-expression. If the United States is to have a first-rate soccer team, its administrators must look away from the colleges and into the heart of the minority communities who could be found crowding around their televisions in those summer weeks, sharing in the world's excitement over the world championship of *o jogo bonito,* the Beautiful Game.

How to convey to America the idea of beauty as applied to a ball game it knows and cares so little about? How to explain the links that exist between soccer teams and national character? For all soccer fans know what it means to play like Brazilians (that is, with flair, flamboyance, and intoxicating rhythm), or like Germans (with great discipline, unwearying physical strength, and iron determination) or Italians (defensively, but with devastating bursts of counterattacking play).

This essay seeks to answer such questions by avoiding them. It seeks to find common ground between those who, like me, love soccer, and those to whom it feels like an alien irrelevance. It sets out not to describe the arcana of the game itself but to explore a related condition that crosses all sporting boundaries: that of being a fan.

A fan doesn't just tune in once every four years to cheer his country's team at the time of the World Cup. The true soccer fan is the club fan, for whom continuity is everything, and so is loyalty in times of adversity, and small gratifications offer great emotional rewards. Which is why, one rainy Sunday afternoon in March, I set out for Wembley Stadium, London, to watch my favorite club, Tottenham Hotspur, take on Leicester City in the final of the Worthington Cup.

There are three major competitions in English soccer each season, one played in leagues—the elite Premiership and the three lower divisions of the Football League—and two on a knockout basis (i.e., whoever loses is eliminated): the ancient and glamorous Football Association Challenge Cup (the "FA Cup"), and the johnny-come-lately, cheap-and-cheerful League Cup, which has metamorphosed, in this era of sponsorship, into the Milk Cup, the Coca-Cola Cup, and now the Worthington Cup. (At least milk, Coke, and Worthington beer are all things you can pour into cups. Cricket, also a much-sponsored sport, has had its Cups sponsored by the manufacturers of cigarettes and razor blades.)

In spite of the third-out-of-three status of the Worthington Cup, the chance to watch one's team play at Wembley lifts the heart and quickens the pulse. Wembley is the hallowed heart of the English game, the turf on which the England team won its only World Cup way back in 1966. I've been a Spurs fan since the early 1960s, but I've never made it to Wembley to watch them in a final until now.

What's more, the nineties have been lean years for this once-great soccer club. But now, here we are in a cup final again. A win may herald the beginning of a new golden era. I make my way to the great stadium, full of hope.

2. FIRST LOVE

I came to London in January 1961 as a boy of thirteen and a half, on my way to boarding school and accompanied by my father. It was a cold month, with blue skies by day and green fogs by night. We stayed at a huge barracks of a hotel, the Cumberland at Marble Arch, and soon after we settled in, my father asked if I would like to see a professional soccer game.

In Bombay, where I had grown up, there was no soccer to speak of; the local sports were cricket and field hockey. The only part of India where soccer was taken seriously was Bengal, and although the fame of the Mohun Bagan team of Calcutta had reached my ears, I had never seen the game played.

The first game my father took me to see was a friendly match between the North London club, Arsenal, and the Spanish champions, Real Madrid. I did not then know that the visitors were rated as perhaps the greatest club side ever seen anywhere. Or that they had just won the European Cup, the annual tournament held to determine the champion of all Europe's national champions, five years running (an achievement that nobody before or since has matched). Or that among their players were two of the game's all-time immortals, the Hungarian Ferenc Puskas, "the little general" who masterminded his national side's humiliating drubbings of the England team, and the Argentinian center-forward Alfredo di Stefano. Other Real players—the flying winger Gento, the defensive colossus Santamaria—were rated almost as highly as the two superstars.

This is the way I remember the game:* in the first half, Real Madrid tore the Arsenal apart. The London club was and is renowned for its tough defensive style of play—"Boring Arsenal" is a label they were stuck with for years—but Real went through them almost at will, and at the halftime break led 3–0. Then, because this was after all just a friendly game with nothing riding on it, Real took off their star players and replaced them for the second half with a bunch of kids. Arsenal stubbornly kept all their first-team players on the field and the game ended up tied, 3–3; but not even the most die-hard Arsenal fans at the game could pretend that the result accurately reflected the quality of the two teams. On the way back to the hotel my father asked me for my views. "I didn't think much of that English team," I told him, "but I liked that Spanish side. Can you find out if there's an English team that plays like Real Madrid?" Unknown to me, I had asked for the near-impossible; as if, in Michael Jordan's airborne heyday, I had asked, "Can you find out if there's a team that plays like the Chicago Bulls?" My father, almost as much an innocent in these matters as myself, said, "I'll ask at the front desk." What he learned from that long-forgotten hotel clerk changed my life, because a few days later we went to watch the other famous club of North London, Tottenham Hotspur, and I lost my heart.

There were still many things I didn't know. I didn't know that between Tottenham and Arsenal, the Spurs and the Gunners, there was a

---

* However, it is deeply disturbing to discover that the club records contain no reference to this game, although there was an Arsenal–Real Madrid friendly in September 1962, which Real won 4–0. It seems I have somehow constructed a phantom memory, on the veracity of which my mind continues to insist, in spite of the documentary evidence to the contrary. An early indication, perhaps, that my métier would turn out to be fiction.

long rivalry and a deep mutual loathing. I didn't know that the Spurs tradition was of cavalier attacking play, and that if Arsenal were jeered for their negativity (it was said that their fans would sing in celebration of a scoreless draw), then the leaky Spurs defense was also a traditional butt of ridicule for soccer fans everywhere. I didn't even know the words to the Spurs' version of "Glory, Glory, Hallelujah." ("Poor old Arsenal lies a-moldering in the grave / while the Spurs go marching on! on! on!")

Most of all I didn't know that under their manager, the taciturn Yorkshireman Bill Nicholson—"Billy Nick"—and their loquacious Irish captain, Danny Blanchflower, Tottenham had become the greatest team to emerge in Britain since the "Busby Babes" of Manchester United perished in the Munich air disaster of 1958. The hotel clerk had been right. This team could have given Real Madrid a fright. These were the Super Spurs in their greatest year, on their way to capturing British soccer's Holy Grail, the League and Cup Double; that is to say, victory in a single season both in the First Division of the Football League and in the country's premier knockout competition, the FA Cup.

I don't remember who Spurs thrashed that day, but I do recall understanding that I had in some profound and unalterable way been changed by my visit to this bleak northern borough of a city in which I was still a complete stranger. The boy who left the Spurs' stadium at White Hart Lane after the final whistle was no longer a spectator. He had become a fan.

Bill Brown, Peter Baker, Ron Henry, Danny Blanchflower, Maurice Norman, Dave Mackay, Cliff Jones, John White, Bobby Smith, Les Allen, Terry Dyson. To this day I can recite the names of the first team without needing to look them up. I can even do most of the reserves. Johnny Hollowbread, Mel Hopkins, Tony Marchi, Terry Medwin, Eddie Clayton, Frank Saul . . . Sorry. Sorry. I'll stop.

I can remember, too, the horror with which I greeted the series of mishaps that broke the side up. I felt them as personal tragedies: Blanchflower's knee injury, Norman's broken leg, Mackay breaking the same leg *twice,* and above all the death of John White, killed by lightning while sheltering under a tree on a golf course. White's nickname at Spurs had been the Ghost.

Spurs did the Double in the 1960–61 season, narrowly missed repeating the feat in 1961–62, and in the following thirty-seven years they have often been "a good Cup side," winning many British and European knockout trophies, but they have never won a League Championship again. This is what it means to be a fan: to wait for a miracle, enduring decades of disillusion, and yet to have no choice in the matter of allegiance. Each weekend, I turn to the sports pages, and my eye automatically seeks out the Spurs' result. If they have won, the weekend feels richer. If they have lost, a black cloud settles. It's pathetic. It's an addiction. It's monogamous, till-death-us-do-part love.

In that glorious 1960–61 season, however, Blanchflower's Tottenham did, just that once, take the First Division championship by storm. Then, on the first Saturday in May, they went down the road to Wembley for the Cup Final, the Double's second leg. They won the game 2–0, even though they didn't play well on the day, as even their manager, Bill Nicholson, later admitted. They were, in fact, lucky to win.

The team they beat was Leicester City.

3. GOALKEEPERS

The 1999 Worthington Cup Final would turn out to be a tale of two opposing goalkeepers. The Spurs goalie, Ian Walker, had only recently regained his first-team place after a slump in form, and many of us still worried about his vulnerability. Leicester, on the other hand, had the U.S. international keeper, Kasey Keller, in goal. Walker and Keller would make one bad mistake apiece at crucial moments of the match. One of them got away with it. The other's fumble decided the game.

Goalkeepers aren't like other players, perhaps because they are allowed to handle the ball within the delineated confines of the "penalty area," perhaps because they are the last line of their team's defense, but mainly because, for goalkeepers, there is no middle register of performance; each time they play, they know they will come off the field either as heroes or as clowns.

A good goalkeeper must be brave enough to dive at the feet of an opponent arriving at speed. He must command the area around his goal and exude an air of swift decisiveness. He must know when to catch the ball and when to punch it, and whenever high crosses are aimed into the penalty area from the wings, he must, if he can, rise above the throng of players and make the ball his own.

In spite of (or because of) the goalie's vital importance, English soccer has goalkeeper jokes the way rock 'n' roll has drummer jokes. There was once a goalie nicknamed Dracula, because he was afraid of crosses. Also a goalie nicknamed Cinderella, because he was always late for the ball.

The keeper in the "Super Spurs" Double side was the Scottish international, Bill Brown. He was gaunt and unsmiling and brilliant and had an old-fashioned short-back-and-sides haircut, and nobody ever cracked a joke about him.

One day in the mid-1960s, however, Billy Nick splashed out 30,000 pounds, then a world-record transfer fee for a goalkeeper, to bring a huge raw Irish kid the short distance from the little Watford Football Club to mighty Spurs. His name was Pat Jennings, and he wore his hair fashionably long and wavy, with sideburns. The Spurs faithful distrusted him at once.

He did his time in the reserve side but soon enough got his turn in goal. The home fans gave him a hard time that day until, at a crucial moment, he flew across his goalmouth to save a shot that was heading at high velocity for the far top corner, and not only made the save but *caught the flying ball cleanly in a single outstretched hand.*

We looked at one another, aghast, with the same question in all our eyes: *exactly how big are this guy's paws?* After that save, Jennings had no more trouble with the Spurs crowd, who took him to their hearts until, many seasons later, the management did an unthinkable thing. Deciding that Pat—our by now beloved Pat, Ireland's international keeper as well as ours, Pat who was regularly rated as the finest in the world!— was over the hill, they transferred him to Arsenal. To Arsenal, of all clubs, where he went on to enjoy year after year of triumph! Even now, it's hard to put into words the outrage I felt. The outrage I still feel. I can only say what Spurs fans said to each other in those days, furiously, mirthlessly, often adding, as intensifiers, a series of unrepeatable expletives: "It's a joke."★

★ A joke with legs. In 2001 it happened again. Sol Campbell, the Spurs' captain and star defender, decided to switch allegiances to Arsenal as well.

4. THE SOUNDTRACK

Ossie's going to Wembley
His knees have gone all trembly
Come on, you Spurs.
Come on, you Spurs.

Soccer is a sung game, lustily and thoroughly sung. Teams have their individual anthems—"Glory, Glory" for Spurs, "You'll Never Walk Alone" for Liverpool—and a collection of other so to speak patriotic songs. Ossie was Osvaldo Ardiles, a member of Argentina's 1978 world-champion team, who came to Spurs immediately after his World Cup victory and endeared himself to the supporters both by the neat brilliance of his play and by his inability to master the sound of the English language. ("Tottingham," he called his chosen club or, alternatively, "the Spoors.")

Ossie went to Wembley to play for Spurs against Manchester City in the 1981 FA Cup Final, and he had, as a teammate, a fellow Argentinian, Ricardo "Ricky" Villa. The game was drawn, but in the replay Villa scored one of the most inspired goals of modern times, jinking and twisting past most of the opposing defense before he buried the ball in the net. Thus Ossie's final became Villa's triumph. Ricky won the Cup for "Tottingham," but Ossie still has the song.

Soccer has many other aural codes. There is, for example, the rhythm of the scores. Each Saturday we hear the results being read on radio and TV, and so formalized is the reading that you can divine the result simply from the announcer's stresses and intonation. Then there's the music of the roars. In the middle 1980s I lived for a time at one end of Highbury Hill, the long road at whose other end is the Arsenal stadium. Match days, when the crowd surged past our house, were often a little wild. (Once somebody stuck a flayed pig's head on the iron railings of my front yard. Why? The pig didn't say.) But I could always work out how the game was going without leaving my study, just by the way the crowd roared. One kind of roar—uninhibited, chest-beating, triumphant—invariably followed a goal by the home team. Another, groanier noise indicated a near miss, a shrieky third informed me of a near miss by the opposition, and a dull grunt, a flayed pig's head of a grunt, would follow a goal by the visitors.

There are also the chants, non–team specific formulae adapted by each set of supporters for local use. I once took Mario Vargas Llosa to White Hart Lane, and he was bewildered and delighted when he realized that the fans' cry of "One team in Europe! There's only one team in Europe!" was being chanted to, more or less, the tune of "Guantanamera."

That year, Spurs had a right-back called Gary Stevens. A rival soccer club, Everton, also had a right-back called Gary Stevens, and, to make matters worse, both players had at different times played right-back for England. Thus, to Vargas Llosa's further mystification, another version of the "Guantanamera" chant went "Two Gary Stevens! There's only two Gary Stevens!"

All together now: "We all agree . . . Arsenal are rubbish!" Or, when your team is winning well: "Are you watching, are you watching, are you watching, Arsenal?" Or, in the same circumstances, but more ambitiously: "At last they're gonna believe us, at last they're gonna believe us, at last they're gonna believe us! . . . We're going to win the League." (Or, if more appropriate, "Cup.")

Or, vindictively, after one's team has taken the lead, and while pointing at the visiting team's supporters in their corral: "You're not singing, you're not singing, you're not singing anymore!"

5. DAVID AND THE GENT

One week before the Worthington Cup Final, Tottenham's French superstar, the gifted left-winger David Ginola, had scored a solo goal in a league match that was almost a replay of Ricky Villa's famous Cup-winning masterpiece. Ginola has movie-star good looks and Pat Jennings's hair: tresses long and silky enough to win him a featured role—this is true—in a L'Oréal television commercial. ("Because I'm worth it" became, in Ginola's heavily accented version, "Because I'm worse eat.")

There is no doubt that Ginola is worth it. His skills are even more lustrous than his locks. Ginola can shimmy like your sister Kate. His balance, his feinting, his tight ball control at high speed, his ability to score from thirty yards out, or by waltzing past defenders like the great matadors who work closest to the bulls, make him a defender's nightmare. Two criticisms have been made of him, however. First, that he is lazy, a luxury player, uninterested in the hard graft of the game. Second, that he dives.

Diving is a form of gamesmanship. A diver pretends to be fouled when he hasn't been. A great diver is like a salmon leaping, twisting, falling. A great dive can last almost as long as the dying of the swan. And it can, of course, influence the referee, it can earn free kicks or penalty kicks, it can get an opponent cautioned or even sent off.

The course of the 1999 Worthington Cup Final between Spurs and Leicester would be greatly altered by a dive.

An earlier Spurs star, the great German goalscorer Jürgen Klinsmann, also used to be accused of diving. Spurs fans screamed "cheat" at Ginola when he was playing for Newcastle United. England fans booed and howled at Klinsmann when he plunged to the ground while playing for Germany. But when the two of them signed for Spurs, the fans understood that these noble spirits were in truth more sinned against than sinning. Oh, now we saw the subtle pushes with which cynical defenders knocked them off balance, the surreptitious little trips and ankle-taps in whose existence we had so vocally disbelieved. Now we understood the tragedy of genius, we saw how grievously Ginola and Klinsmann had been wronged. Was this just our self-serving fickleness? Certainly not. Reader, it was because the scales fell from our eyes.

As for the other criticism leveled at Ginola, that he was lazy, that all changed when, during the course of the 1998–1999 season, Spurs acquired a new manager. His name is George Graham, and he was known, when he was an elegant player (one of the stars of the Scotland team), as "Gentleman George." As a manager, he has acquired a less cultured image as the hardest of hard men, a man whose teams are built on the granite of an impregnable defense. In a few short months, he has transformed that well-known joke, the Tottenham defense, into a well-drilled, stingy unit. He has taught the back four to imagine they are joined by a rope, and now, instead of running in opposite directions like Mack Sennett's Keystone Kops, they move as one.

What would a grim fellow like George Graham make of the blessed butterfly, Ginola? It was widely believed that the L'Oréal model would be the first player Graham unloaded after taking charge at Spurs. Instead, the winger has blossomed toward greatness, and nowadays he and Graham sing each other's praises almost daily. The manager has inspired the player to work hard, and the player has, well, inspired the manager the way he inspires us all. "Do something extraordinary,"

Graham now tells Ginola before each game, and it's astonishing how often Ginola obliges.*

Oh, there's one more thing about George Graham. First as a player and then as a manager, he made his name, and won a shelf of trophies, at Highbury. Spurs have hired the former manager of their arch-enemies, Arsenal.

6. DECLINE AND FALL

How did such a thing come to pass? The answer lies in Spurs' recent history. They last won a major trophy, the FA Cup, in 1991. After that the club's fortunes started a long, depressing slide. Boardroom incompetence had landed Tottenham in serious financial trouble, and the team's star player, England's moron-genius, the child-man Paul Gascoigne, as famous for bursting into tears during a World Cup game as for his exceptional talent, had to be transferred to Lazio in Rome, Italy, to help pay off the club's debts.

The "sale" of Paul Gascoigne was a traumatic event for the fans. Gascoigne was what we thought of as a true Spurs player, fabulously gifted, a playmaker at least as influential as the late John White. Now Gascoigne, too, had been struck down, and was gone.

As the club declined, the fans were left with their memories. Spurs have had more than their share of genuinely great players: the lethal goalscoring partnership of the "goal-poacher" Jimmy Greaves and Alan Gilzean (he of the "cultured forehead"); the stealthy beauty of the play of Martin Peters, a member of England's 1966 World Champion team. Later Tottenham teams offered us the high-velocity skills of Gary Lineker, a Leicester City player many years before he joined Spurs, and the long-range passing accuracy of Ardiles and Villa's English teammate Glenn Hoddle.

(This same Hoddle was fired from his job as coach to the England national team because of a series of confused remarks he made about reincarnation. By jumbling together the languages of Buddhism, Hin-

---

* This love affair didn't last. Eventually Graham's true nature reasserted itself and Ginola was sent packing. But not so long afterward, Graham was sent packing too. That's soccer, as they say.

duism, Christianity, and spiritualist mumbo-jumbo, he managed to give the impression that he believed disabled people were to blame for their disabilities; but in spite of the predictable tabloid uproar, I found it hard to condemn poor "Glenda" for what seemed more like stupidity than malice. I remembered the grandeur of his game in the old days, and the joy it had given me, and I hated to see him turn out to be such a doofus. "At the end of the day I never said them things," he mumbled miserably as he shuffled off into the darkness, making one wish he could still leave the talking to his feet.)★

The low point of Spurs' fortunes was reached in the 1997–98 season, when the team's owner, the computer-industry millionaire Alan Sugar, appointed as manager a Swiss person called, alas, Christian Gross. He never managed to command the team's respect or to attract first-rate players to the club, and under his regime Tottenham came close to losing their elite Premiership status.

At the start of the present season, the team looked even worse, and Gross was duly sacked. Five days after his exit I saw them thrashed 3–0 at home by Middlesbrough, a team that the great Spurs sides of the past would have effortlessly demolished. The Tottenham players and supporters were utterly demoralized. Then Alan Sugar, to the consternation of many Spurs fans, turned to the ex-Gunner, Gentleman George.

George Graham had taken some hard knocks of his own. In the last decade there has been much concern about the growth of corrupt practices in soccer. There have been allegations that Far Eastern betting syndicates have sought to influence senior players to throw matches. In France in 1997, Bernard Tapie, the multi-millionaire proprietor of the country's then-champion side, Marseille, was found guilty and jailed on charges of match-fixing and corruption.

As a player, George Graham was a member of the Arsenal team that did the Double in 1971, thus emulating the Spurs' great achievement. (They've since done it again, damn it, just a year ago; and they played so brilliantly, so much like a classic Spurs side, that I was forced to set aside a lifetime's prejudices and cheer them on.) As a manager, Graham led the Gunners to two League Championships and four other major honors. But in the mid-nineties he, too, faced accusations of wrongdoing. He was found guilty by the Football Association of receiving "bungs," under-the-counter cash payments worth approxi-

---

★ George Graham's sacking made possible the Second Coming of Glenda. He took over at White Hart Lane and kept the spiritual stuff to himself.

mately £425,000, made as "sweeteners" during the course of big-money transfer deals. In spite of all the success he had brought to Arsenal, Gentleman George lost his job.

However, he's a tenacious character, and he slowly fought his way back into the big time. By the time Sugar made his approach, Graham had become the manager of another Premiership club, Leeds United, where he had put together one of the most promising young sides in the league. But the lure of one of the country's traditional "big five" clubs proved irresistible, and he came back to London.

If some Spurs fans mistrusted him, the speed of the team's improvement has shut them up. Tottenham still don't have a great side; as I write this they're stuck in the middle of the Premiership table. But getting to Wembley is the most glamorous event in a club player's life. George Graham must take the credit for bringing a little of the old glamour back to depressed White Hart Lane.

7. A RESULT TEAM

A man on his way to the big game passes a pub near the stadium and grimaces at the sidewalk, which is ankle-deep in used plastic beer glasses and empty cans. "That's why the game will never catch on in the States, right there," he says, a little shamefacedly. A second man chimes in. "That, and the food," he says. "The meat pies, the fucking burgers." The first man is still shaking his head at the garbage. "Americans would never leave this mess." He sighs. "They wouldn't stand for it."

A third man, passing, recognizes the first and greets him gaily: "You're like bleeding dogshit, mate—you're everywhere, you are."

The three men go off happily toward Wembley.

Inside the stadium, the field of play is covered in two giant shirts and a pair of giant soccer balls. There is much razzamatazz—great flocks of blue and white balloons are released, and giant flares begin to burn as the teams arrive—and this has plainly been learned from studying American sporting occasions. But as ever, the point of being there is not this sort of thing but the crowd. You'd have to be made of stone not to be affected by the communal release of shared excitement, by the simple sense of standing together against the world, or the opposing team, anyhow. The chanting swells and surges from one end of the grand old stadium to the other. Next year Wembley is to be demolished and a new third-millennium super-stadium built in its place. This is almost the old lady's last hurrah.★

The game begins. I quickly see that it isn't going to be a classic. Leicester look distinctly second-rate, and although Spurs settle first into a rhythm, they don't inspire full confidence. In the twenty-first minute Sol Campbell, an England international player, completely misses a crucial tackle, and Leicester are kept at bay only by a fine covering tackle by Spurs Swiss defender Ramon Vega, another player whose form has improved dramatically since Graham arrived.

My heart's in my mouth, but Ginola gives me something to enjoy: a couple of fast, swerving runs with no fewer than three Leicester players trying to shut him down, and one moment of breathtaking ball control, in which he pulls down an awkwardly high ball with one touch of the outside of his right boot, and passes it away almost instantly, the speed of his artistry setting up a dangerous Tottenham break.

No goals in the first half. In the second, however, high drama. In the sixty-third minute, the Tottenham full-back Justin Edinburgh is crudely tackled by Leicester's blond-thatched Robbie Savage. Irritated by the clumsiness of the tackle, Edinburgh stupidly reaches out with an open hand and smacks Savage somewhere on the head. Blond hair flies. Then, after a comically long pause, Savage executes a perfect backflip of a dive and collapses to the ground.

The referee, Terry Heilbron, has been fooled. He cautions Savage for his unfair tackle, but then shows Edinburgh the dreaded red card for his "foul" on Diving Robbie. Edinburgh has been sent off, expelled from the game, and Spurs are down to ten men against Leicester's eleven.

"Cheat, cheat," chant the Spurs fans, and then boo. The noise made by thirty-five thousand or so soccer fans booing in unison is unearthly, monstrous; but in our hearts we fear that the day may be lost. And for the next several minutes, as Leicester City charge forward, our fears seem justified. In the Spurs goal, Ian Walker has to stretch hard to catch a loose ball. Then Leicester burst through Spurs' depleted defenses again, and this time Vega is cautioned for a "professional foul"—the

★ They haven't knocked it down yet. Instead, in the great tradition of British fiascoes—cf. the Bouncing Bridge across the Thames, the Millennium Dome—the superstadium plan has hit snag after snag. Will there be a new stadium in North London or not? Who knows?

deliberate fouling of a player whom he couldn't have stopped by fair means.

It's all Leicester City, but slowly—and this is an indication of the steely confidence Graham has engendered—Tottenham regroup. Their fans sing a rousing chorus of "Glory, Glory, Hallelujah" to encourage them, and, surprisingly, Spurs begin once more to have the better of the exchanges. David Ginola on the left wing is having a quiet game by his exalted standards, but Leicester are still being forced to use two or even three players to stop him. This means that, in spite of being a man down, Spurs actually often have a man over on their right flank, and it is down this flank that their best attacks now come. The Tottenham right-back Stephen Carr is making more and more threatening runs. The England international midfield player Darren Anderton (once nicknamed "Sicknote" because he got injured so often, but fit at last these days) is also beginning to show, with his trademark long-legged stride and his dangerous floated crosses. Spurs main goalscorer, Les Ferdinand, is looking livelier, and so is the team's duo of Scandinavian stars: the Norwegian striker Steffen Iversen and the Danish midfielder Allan Nielsen, who has been picked only because the team's new signing, the England player Tim Sherwood, is ineligible, have a shot each, and then combine fluently to allow Nielsen another shot, well saved by Kasey Keller.

Meanwhile, Leicester's Savage, clearly rattled by the boos that fill the stadium whenever he touches the ball, is involved in another bit of rough stuff, but gets away with it. The game goes into its last five minutes. If there is no result after ninety minutes' play, there will be half an hour of extra time, and if the scores are still level, the game will be decided by penalty kicks. (Soccer fans hate the arbitrariness of the sudden-death penalty shoot-out. We always hope it won't come to that.) In the eighty-sixth minute, Ian Walker moves to the edge of his penalty area to gather a loose ball, slips, misses the ball completely, and allows Leicester's Tony Cottee to send it bouncing and bobbling across the face of Tottenham's undefended goal. Amazingly, there isn't a single Leicester player on hand to tap it into the empty net. Walker scrambles back into position. Tottenham's moment of greatest danger has passed.

The game enters the last minute of normal time. Leicester, already playing for extra time, take the precaution of bringing off the much-reviled Robbie Savage, who would be sent off if cautioned a second time, and the way he's been playing, he's lucky not to have been shown the red card already. On, in his place, comes Theo Zagorakis, captain of Greece's international side. Before Leicester have time to settle down to the change in their formation, however, lightning strikes.

A whipped pass from Ferdinand in midfield releases Iversen, whose fast run down the right catches the Leicester defense cold. He cuts in toward goal and shoots. It isn't a great shot, on target but weak. Somehow, however, Kasey Keller fails to hold the ball, and palms it feebly right onto the forehead of the charging Allan Nielsen. Boom! As the Univision commentators would say, "Góóóóóóóóóóóól!!!!!!"

It's all over in an instant, and Tottenham have won 1–0. And then there are the celebrations to enjoy, the presentations, the jeering. *You're not singing, you're not singing, you're not singing anymore.* The oddly three-handled Worthington Cup is held high by each Tottenham player in turn. In victory they suddenly stop looking like rich, pampered superstar athletes and become, instead, innocent young men bright with the realization that they are experiencing one of the great moments of their lives. The massed joy of the Spurs fans is itself a joy to behold. Never mind the scrappiness of the game. It's the result that counts.

George Graham is famous as a manager of "result teams," teams that will somehow grind out the result they need without bothering too much about providing entertainment along the way. I can't remember when the term was last applied to a Spurs lineup. It's an Arsenal kind of concept. "Boring Arsenal" were also "Lucky Arsenal," because of their habit of stealing games like this one. Well, who's boring and lucky now?

As I left the ground, beaming foolishly, a fellow Spurs fan recognized me and waved cheerily in my direction. "Gawd bless yer, Salman," he yelled. I waved back, but I didn't say what I wanted to say: Nah, not Gawd, mate, he doesn't play for our team. Besides, who needs him when you've already got David Ginola; when you're leaving Wembley Stadium with a win?

April 1999

Farming Ostriches

[*Originally delivered as a keynote address to the American Society of Newspaper Editors*]

It's a somewhat daunting privilege to face so distinguished a "press conference" at an hour of the morning at which I'm usually barely capable of speech. Although I must say that after my recent American book tour, 9:00 A.M. feels like child's play. On one January day in Chicago I found myself sitting up in President Reagan's hotel bed—I should say not at the same time as President Reagan—and giving, by telephone, no fewer than eleven radio interviews before eight o'clock: a personal best. When I came to Washington four years ago to participate in a free-speech conference, an aide of President Bush, explaining why no member of that administration was willing to meet me, remarked that, after all, I was "just an author on a book tour." It is hard to put into words how sweetly satisfying it felt this January, what a sense of overcoming it gave me, in spite of all those early starts, finally to be, indeed, just an author on a book tour. An author on a book tour *sleeping in the president's bed.*

Speaking of presidents, it may interest you to know that when I was finally able to visit the White House, the meeting was arranged for the day before Thanksgiving, and scheduled to take place immediately before President Clinton's unbreakable appointment on the White House lawn with a certain Tom the Turkey, whom he was to "pardon" before the assembled press corps. It was therefore understandably unclear whether the president would have time to be involved in my own visit. On the way to the meeting I found myself hysterically inventing the next day's headlines: "Clinton Meets Turkey—Rushdie Gets Stuffed," for example. Fortunately, this imaginary headline turned out to be incorrect, and my encounter with Mr. Clinton took place, and proved interesting and, to speak politically, extremely useful.

I was wondering what I might usefully and interestingly say to *you* today—wondering what, if any, common ground might be occupied by novelists and journalists—when my eye fell upon the following brief text in a British national daily: "In yesterday's *Independent* we stated that Sir Andrew Lloyd Webber is farming ostriches. He is not."

One can only guess at the brouhaha concealed beneath these admirably laconic sentences: the human distress, the protests. As you know, Britain has been going through a period of what one might call heightened livestock insecurity of late. As well as the mentally challenged cattle herds, there has been the alarming case of the great ostrich-farming bubble, or swindle. In these overheated times, a man who is not an ostrich farmer, when accused of being one, will not take the allegation lightly. He may even feel that his reputation has been slighted.

Plainly, it was quite wrong of *The Independent* to suggest that Sir Andrew Lloyd Webber was actually breeding ostriches. He is of course a celebrated exporter of musical turkeys. But if we agree for a moment to permit the supposedly covert and allegedly fraudulent farming of ostriches to stand as a metaphor for all the world's supposedly covert and allegedly fraudulent activities, then must we not also agree that it is vital that these ostrich farmers be identified, named, and brought to account for their activities? Is this not at the very heart of the project of a free press? And might there not be occasions on which every editor in this room would be prepared to go with such a story—one might call it Ostrichgate—on the basis of less-than-solid evidence, in the national interest?

I am arriving by degrees at my point: which is that the great issue facing writers both of journalism and of novels is that of determining, and then publishing, the truth. For the ultimate goal of both factual and fictional writing is the truth, however paradoxical that may sound. And truth is slippery, and hard to establish. Mistakes, as in the Lloyd Webber case, can be made. And if truth can set you free, it can also land you in hot water. Fine as the word sounds, truth is all too often unpalatable, awkward, unorthodox. The armies of received ideas are marshaled against it. The legions of all those who stand to profit by useful untruths will march against it. Yet it must, if at all possible, be told.

But, it may be objected, can there really be said to be any connection between the truth of the news and of the world of the imagination? In the world of facts, either a man is an ostrich farmer or he is not. In fiction's universe, he may be fifteen contradictory things at once.

Let me attempt an answer.

The word "novel" derives from the Latin word for *new;* in French, *nouvelles* are both stories and news reports. A hundred years ago, people read novels, among other things, for information. From Dickens's *Nicholas Nickleby,* British readers got shocking information about poor schools like Dotheboys Hall, and such schools were subsequently abolished. *Uncle Tom's Cabin, Huckleberry Finn,* and *Moby-Dick* are all, in this newsy sense, information-heavy.

So: until the advent of the television age, literature shared with print journalism the task of telling people things they didn't know. This is no longer the case, for either literature or print journalism. Those who read newspapers and novels now get their primary information about the world from the TV, Internet, and radio. There are exceptions: the success of that lively novel *Primary Colors* shows that novels can just occasionally still lift the lid on a hidden world more effectively than reporting; and of course the broadcast news is highly selective, and newspapers provide far greater breadth and depth of coverage. But many people now read newspapers, I suggest, *to read the news about the news.* We read for opinion, attitude, spin. We read not for raw data, not for Gradgrind's "facts, facts, facts," but to get a "take" on the news that we like. Now that the broadcasting media fulfill the function of being first with the news, newspapers, like novels, have entered the realm of the imagination. They both provide versions of the world.

Perhaps this is clearer in a country like Britain, with its primarily national press, than in the United States, where the great proliferation of local papers allows print journalism to provide the additional service of answering to local concerns and adopting local characteristics. The successful quality papers in Britain—among dailies, *The Guardian, Times, Telegraph,* and *Financial Times*—are successful because they have clear pictures of who their readers are and how to talk to them. (The languishing *Independent* once did, but appears latterly to have lost its way.) They are successful because they share, with their readers, a vision of British society and of the world.

The news has become a matter of opinion. And this puts a newspaper editor in a position not at all dissimilar from that of a novelist. It is for the novelist to create, communicate, and sustain over time a personal and coherent vision of the world that entertains, interests, stimulates, provokes, and nourishes his readers. It is for the newspaper editor to do very much the same thing with the pages at his disposal. In that specialized sense—and let me emphasize that I mean this as a compliment!—we are all in the fiction business now.

Sometimes, of course, the news in newspapers seems fictive in a less complimentary sense. Over Easter, a leading British Sunday newspaper ran a front-page lead story announcing the discovery of the tomb—indeed, of the very bones—of Jesus Christ himself; a discovery, as the newspaper was quick to point out, with profound significance for the Christian religion, whose adherents were, at that very moment, celebrating Jesus's physical ascension into heaven, presumably accompanied by his bones. Not only Jesus but Joseph, Mary, someone called Mary II (presumably Magdalene), and even a certain Judah, son of Jesus, had been discovered, banner headlines proclaimed. A long way down the article—far further than most readers would have read—it was revealed that *the only evidence* that this was indeed the family of Jesus was the simple coincidence of names, which, the journalist admitted, were among the most common names of the period. Nevertheless, she insisted, the mind could not resist the speculation . . .

Such nonsense has perhaps always been a part of newspapers' entertainment value. But the spirit of fiction permeates the press in other ways as well.

One of the more extraordinary truths about the soap opera that is the British Royal Family is that to a large extent the leading figures have had their characters invented for them by the British press. And such is the power of the fiction that the flesh-and-blood Royals have become more and more like their print personae, unable to escape the fiction of their imaginary lives.

The creation of "characters" is, in fact, rapidly becoming an essential part of print journalism's stock-in-trade. Never have personality profiles and people columns—never has *gossip*—occupied as much of a newspaper's space as they now do. The word "profile" is apt. In a profile, the subject is never confronted head-on but receives a sidelong glance. A profile is flat and two-dimensional. It is an outline. Yet the images created in these curious texts (often with their subjects' collusion) are extraordinarily potent—it can be next to impossible for the actual person to alter, through his own words and deeds, the impressions they create—and, thanks to the mighty Clippings File, they are also self-perpetuating.

A novelist, if he is talented and lucky, may in the course of a lifetime's work offer up one or two characters who enter the exclusive pantheon of the unforgotten. A novelist's characters hope for immortality; a profile journalist's, perhaps, for celebrity. We worship, these days, not images but Image itself: and any man or woman who strays into the public gaze becomes a potential sacrifice in that temple. Often, I repeat, a willing sacrifice, willingly drinking the poisoned chalice of Fame. But for many people, including myself, the experience of being profiled is perhaps closest to what it must feel like to be used as a writer's raw material, what it must feel like to be turned into a fictional character, to have one's feelings and actions, one's relationships and vicissitudes, transformed, by writing, into something subtly—or unsubtly—different. To see ourselves mutated into someone we do not recognize. For a novelist to be thus rewritten is, I recognize, a case of the biter bit. Fair enough. Nevertheless, something about the process feels faintly—and, I stress, *faintly*—improper.

In Britain, intrusions into the private lives of public figures have prompted calls from certain quarters for the protection of privacy laws. It is true that in France, where such laws exist, the illegitimate daughter of the late President Mitterrand was able to grow up unmolested by the press; but where the powerful can hide behind the law, might not a good deal of covert ostrich farming go undetected? I'm still against laws that curtail the investigative freedoms of the press. But, speaking as someone who has had the uncommon experience of becoming, for a time, a hot news story—of, as my friend Martin Amis put it, "vanishing into the front page"—it would be dishonest to deny that when my family and I have been the target of press intrusions and distortions, my principles have been sorely strained.

Still, my overwhelming feelings about the press are ones of gratitude. No writer could have wished for a more generous response to his work—or for fairer, more civil profiles!—than I have received in America and around the world—this year. And in the long unfolding of the so-called Rushdie affair, American newspapers have been of great importance in keeping the issues alive, ensuring that readers have kept sight of the essential points of principle involved, and even pressuring America's leaders to speak out and act. But there is more than that to thank you for. I said earlier that newspaper editors, like novelists, need to create, impart, and maintain a vision of society. In any vision of a free society, the value of free speech must rank the highest, for that is the freedom without which all the other freedoms would fail. Journalists do more than most of us to protect those values; for the exercise of freedom is freedom's best defense, and that is something you all do, every day.

However, we live in an increasingly censorious age. By this I mean that the broad, indeed international, acceptance of First Amendment principles is being steadily eroded. Many special-interest groups, claiming the moral high ground, now demand the protection of the censor. Political correctness and the rise of the religious right provide the pro-censorship lobby with further cohorts. I would like to say a little about just one of the weapons of this resurgent lobby, a weapon used, interestingly, by everyone from anti-pornography feminists to religious fundamentalists: I mean the concept of "respect."

On the surface, "respect" is one of those ideas nobody's against. Like a good warm coat in winter, like applause, like ketchup on your fries, everybody wants some of *that*. Sock-it-to-me-sock-it-to-me, as Aretha Franklin puts it. But what we used to mean by respect—what Aretha meant by it; that is, a mixture of good-hearted consideration and serious attention—has little to do with the new ideological usage of the word.

Religious extremists, these days, demand *respect* for their attitudes with growing stridency. Very few people would object to the idea that people's rights to religious belief must be respected—after all, the First Amendment defends those rights as unequivocally as it defends free speech—but now we are asked to agree that to dissent from those beliefs—to hold that they are suspect, or antiquated, or wrong; that, in fact, they are *arguable*—is incompatible with the idea of respect. When criticism is placed off limits as "disrespectful," and therefore offensive, something strange is happening to the concept of respect. Yet in recent times both the American National Endowment for the Arts and the very British BBC have announced that they will use this new version of "respect" as a touchstone for their funding decisions.

Other minority groups—racial, sexual, social—have also demanded that they be accorded this new form of respect. To "respect" Louis Farrakhan, we must understand, is simply to agree with him. To "diss" him is, equally simply, to disagree. But if dissent is also to be thought a form of "dissing," then we have indeed succumbed to the Thought Police. I want to suggest to you that citizens of free societies, democracies, do not preserve their freedom by pussyfooting around their fellow-citizens' opinions, even their most cherished beliefs. In free societies, you must have the free play of ideas. There must be argument, and it must be impassioned and untrammeled. A free society is not a calm and eventless place—that is the kind of static, dead society dictators try to create. Free societies are dynamic, noisy, turbulent, and full of radical disagreements. Skepticism and freedom are indissolubly linked; and it is the skepticism of journalists, their show-me, prove-it unwillingness to be impressed, that is perhaps their most important contribution to the freedom of the free world. It is the *disrespect* of journalists—for power, for orthodoxies, for party lines, for ideologies, for vanity, for arrogance, for folly, for pretension, for corruption, for stupidity, maybe even for editors—that I would like to celebrate this morning, and that I urge you all, in freedom's name, to preserve.

April 1996

A Commencement Address

FOR BARD COLLEGE, N.Y.

Members of the Class of 1996, I see in the paper that Southampton University on Long Island got Kermit the Frog to give the commencement address this year. You, unfortunately, have to make do with me. The only Muppet connection I can boast is that Bob Gottlieb, my former editor at Alfred Knopf, also edited that important self-help text *Miss Piggy's Guide to Life*. I once asked him how it had been to work with such a major star and he replied, reverentially, "Salman: the pig was divine."

In England, where I went to college, we don't do things quite this way on graduation day, so I've been doing a little research into commencement and its traditions. The first American friend I asked told me that in her graduation year—not at this college, I hasten to add—she and her fellow-students were so incensed at the choice of commencement speaker, whom I suppose I should not name—oh, all right then, it was Jeane Kirkpatrick—that they boycotted the ceremony and staged a sit-in in one of the college buildings instead. It is a considerable relief, therefore, to note that you are all here.

As for myself, I graduated from Cambridge University in 1968—the great year of student protest—and I have to tell you that I almost didn't make it. This story has nothing to do with politics or demonstrations; it is, rather, the improbable and cautionary tale of a thick brown gravy-and-onion sauce. It begins a few nights before my graduation day, when some anonymous wit chose to redecorate my room, in my absence, by hurling a bucketful of the aforesaid gravy-and-onions all over the walls and furniture, to say nothing of my record player and my clothes. With that ancient tradition of fairness and justice upon which the colleges of Cambridge pride themselves, my college instantly held me solely responsible for the mess, ignored all my representations to the contrary, and informed me that unless I paid for the damage *before the ceremony,* I would not be permitted to graduate. It was the first but, alas, not the last occasion on which I would find myself falsely accused of muck-spreading.

I paid up, I have to report, and was therefore declared eligible to receive my degree. In a defiant spirit, possibly influenced by my recent gravy experience, I went to the ceremony wearing brown shoes, and was promptly plucked out of the parade of my gowned and properly black-shod contemporaries, and ordered back to my quarters to change. I am not sure why people in brown shoes were deemed to be dressed improperly, but I was again facing a judgment against which there could be no appeal.

Again I gave in, sprinted off to change my shoes, got back to the parade in the nick of time; and at length, after these vicissitudes, when my turn came, I was required to hold a university officer by his little finger, and to follow him slowly up to where the vice-chancellor sat upon a mighty throne. As instructed, I knelt at his feet, held up my hands, palms together, in a gesture of supplication, and begged in Latin for the degree, for which, I could not help thinking, I had worked extremely hard for three years, supported by my family at considerable expense. I recall being advised to hold my hands way up above my head, in case the elderly vice-chancellor, leaning forward to clutch at them, should topple off his great chair and land on top of me.

I did as I was advised; the elderly gentleman did not topple; and, also in Latin, he finally admitted me to the degree of Bachelor of Arts.

Looking back at that day, I am a little appalled by my passivity, hard though it is to see what else I could have done. I could have *not* paid up, *not* changed my shoes, *not* knelt to supplicate for my B.A. I preferred to surrender and get the degree. I have grown more stubborn since. I have come to the conclusion, which I now offer you, that I was wrong to compromise; wrong to make an accommodation with injustice, no matter how persuasive the reasons.

Injustice, today, still conjures up, in my mind, the memory of gravy.

Injustice, for me, is a brown, lumpy, congealing fluid, and it smells pungently, tearfully, of onions. Unfairness is the feeling of running back to your room, flat out, at the last minute, to change your outlawed brown shoes. It is the business of being forced to beg, on your knees, in a dead language, for what is rightfully yours.

This, then, is what I learned on my own graduation day; this is the message I have derived from the parables of the Unknown Gravy-Bomber, the Vetoed Footwear, and the Unsteady Vice-Chancellor upon his Throne, and which I pass on to you today: first, if, as you go through life, people should someday accuse you of what one might call Aggravated Gravy Abuse—and they will, they will—and if in fact you are innocent of abusing gravy, do not take the rap. Second: those who would reject you because you are wearing the wrong shoes are not worth being accepted by. And third: kneel before no man. Stand up for your rights.

I like to think that Cambridge University, where I was so happy for three marvelous years, and from which I gained so much—I hope your years at Bard have been as happy, and that you feel you have gained as much—that Cambridge University, with its finely developed British sense of irony, intended me to learn precisely these valuable lessons from the events of that strange graduation day.

Members of the Class of 1996, we are here to celebrate with you one of the great days of your lives. We participate today in the rite of passage by which you are released from this life of preparation into that life for which you are now as prepared as anyone ever is. As you stand at the gate of the future, I should like to share with you a piece of information about the extraordinary institution you are leaving, which will explain the reason why it is such a particular pleasure for me to be with you today. In 1989, within weeks of the threat made against me by the mullahs of Iran, I was approached by the president of Bard, through my literary agent, and asked if I would consider accepting a place on the faculty of this college. More than a place; I was assured that I could find, here in Annandale, among the Bard community, many friends and a safe haven in which I could live and work. Alas, I was not able, in those difficult days, to take up this courageous offer, but I have never forgotten that at a moment when red-alert signals were flashing all over the world, and all sorts of people and institutions were running scared, Bard College did the opposite—that it moved toward me, in intellectual solidarity and human concern, and made not lofty speeches but a concrete offer of help.

I hope you will all feel proud that Bard, quietly, without fanfares, made such a principled gesture at such a time. I am certainly extremely proud to be a recipient of Bard's honorary degree, and to have the privilege of addressing you today.

—

Hubris, according to the Greeks, was the sin of defying the gods, and could, if you were really unlucky, unleash against you the terrifying, avenging figure of the goddess Nemesis, who carried in one hand an apple-bough and, in the other, the Wheel of Fortune, which would one day circle around to the inevitable moment of vengeance. As I have been, in my time, accused not only of gravy abuse and wearing brown shoes but of hubris, too, and since I have come to believe that such defiance is an inevitable and essential aspect of what we call freedom, I thought I might commend it to you. For in the years to come you will find yourselves up against gods of all sorts, big and little gods, corporate and incorporeal gods, all of them demanding to be worshiped and obeyed—the myriad deities of money and power, of convention and custom, that will seek to limit and control your thoughts and lives. Defy them; that's my advice to you. Thumb your noses. For, as the myths tell us, it is by defying the gods that human beings have best expressed their humanity.

The Greeks tell many stories of quarrels between us and the gods. Arachne, the great artist of the loom, sets her skills of weaving and embroidery against those of the goddess of wisdom herself, Minerva or Pallas Athena; and impudently chooses to weave versions of only those scenes that reveal the mistakes and weaknesses of the gods—the rape of Europa, Leda and the Swan. For this—for the irreverence, not for her lesser skill—for what we would now call *art,* and *chutzpah*—the goddess changes her mortal rival into a spider.

Queen Niobe of Thebes tells her people not to worship Latona, the mother of Diana and Apollo, saying, "What folly is this!—To prefer beings whom you never saw to those who stand before your eyes!" For this sentiment, which today we would call *humanism,* the gods murder her children and husband, and she metamorphoses into a rock, petrified with grief, from which there trickles an unending river of tears.

Prometheus the Titan steals fire from the gods and gives it to mankind. For this—for what we would now call the desire for *progress,* for improved scientific and technological capabilities—he is bound to a pillar while a great bird gnaws eternally at his liver, which regenerates as it is consumed.

The interesting point is that the gods do not come out of these stories at all well. If Arachne is overly proud when she seeks to compete with a goddess, it is only an artist's pride, joined to youthful gutsiness; whereas Minerva, who could afford to be gracious, is merely vindictive. The story increases Arachne's shadow, as they say, and diminishes Minerva's; it is Arachne who gains, from the tale, a measure of immortality.

And the cruelty of the gods to the family of Niobe proves her point. Who could *prefer* the rule of such cruel gods to self-rule, the rule of men and women by men and women, however flawed that may be? Once again, the gods are weakened by their show of strength, while the human beings grow stronger, even though—even *as*—they are destroyed.

And tormented Prometheus, of course, Prometheus with his gift of fire, is the greatest hero of all.

—

It is men and women who have made the world, and they have made it in spite of their gods. The message of the myths is not the one the gods would have us learn—"behave yourself and know your place"—but its exact opposite. It is that we must be guided by our natures. Our worst natures can, it's true, be arrogant, venal, corrupt, or selfish; but in our best selves, we—that is, *you*—can and will be joyous, adventurous, cheeky, creative, inquisitive, demanding, competitive, loving, and defiant.

Do not bow your heads. Do not know your place. Defy the gods. You will be astonished how many of them turn out to have feet of clay. Be guided, if possible, by your better natures. Great good luck and many congratulations to you all.

May 1996

"Imagine There's No Heaven"

A LETTER TO THE SIX BILLIONTH WORLD CITIZEN

[Written for a UN-backed anthology of such letters]

Dear little Six Billionth Living Person,

As the newest member of a notoriously inquisitive species, you'll probably soon be asking the two sixty-four-thousand-dollar questions with which the other 5,999,999,999 of us have been wrestling for some time: How did we get here? And, now that we are here, how shall we live?

Oddly—as if six billion of us weren't enough to be going on with—it will almost certainly be suggested to you that the answer to the question of origins requires you to believe in the existence of a further, invisible, ineffable Being "somewhere up there," an omnipotent creator whom we poor limited creatures are unable even to perceive, much less to understand. That is, you will be strongly encouraged to imagine a heaven, with at least one god in residence. This sky-god, it's said, made the universe by churning its matter in a giant pot. Or, he danced. Or, he vomited Creation out of himself. Or, he simply called it into being, and lo, it Was. In some of the more interesting creation stories, the single mighty sky-god is subdivided into many lesser forces—junior deities, avatars, gigantic metamorphic "ancestors" whose adventures create the landscape, or the whimsical, wanton, meddling, cruel pantheons of the great polytheisms, whose wild doings will convince you that the real engine of creation was lust: for infinite power, for too easily broken human bodies, for clouds of glory. But it's only fair to add that there are also stories which offer the message that the primary creative impulse was, and is, love.

Many of these stories will strike you as extremely beautiful, and therefore seductive. Unfortunately, however, you will not be required to make a purely literary response to them. Only the stories of "dead" religions can be appreciated for their beauty. Living religions require much more of you. So you will be told that belief in "your" stories, and adherence to the rituals of worship that have grown up around them, must become a vital part of your life in the crowded world. They will be called the heart of your culture, even of your individual identity. It is possible that they may at some point come to feel inescapable, not in the way that the truth is inescapable but in the way that a jail is. They may at some point cease to feel like the texts in which human beings have tried to solve a great mystery and feel, instead, like the pretexts for other, properly anointed human beings to order you around. And it's true that human history is full of the public oppression wrought by the charioteers of the gods. In the opinion of religious people, however, the private comfort that religion brings more than compensates for the evil done in its name.

As human knowledge has grown, it has also become plain that every religious story ever told about how we got here is quite simply wrong. This, finally, is what all religions have in common. They didn't get it right. There was no celestial churning, no maker's dance, no vomiting of galaxies, no snake or kangaroo ancestors, no Valhalla, no Olympus, no six-day conjuring trick followed by a day of rest. Wrong, wrong, wrong. But here's something genuinely odd. The wrongness of the sacred tales hasn't lessened the zeal of the devout in the least. If anything, the sheer out-of-step zaniness of religion leads the religious to insist ever more stridently on the importance of blind faith.

As a result of this faith, by the way, it has proved impossible, in many parts of the world, to prevent the human race's numbers from swelling alarmingly. Blame the overcrowded planet at least partly on the misguidedness of the race's spiritual guides. In your own lifetime, you may well witness the arrival of the nine billionth world citizen. If you're Indian (and there's a one in six chance that you are) you will be alive when, thanks to the failure of family-planning schemes in that poor, God-ridden land, its population surges past China's. And if too many people are being born as a result, in part, of religious strictures against birth control, then too many people are also dying because religious culture, by refusing to face the facts of human sexuality, also refuses to fight against the spread of sexually transmitted diseases.

There are those who say that the great wars of the new century will once again be wars of religion, jihads and crusades, as they were in the Middle Ages. I don't believe them, or not in the way they mean it. Take a look at the Muslim world, or rather the *Islamist* world, to use the word coined to describe Islam's present-day "political arm." The divisions between its great powers (Afghanistan versus Iran versus Iraq versus Saudi Arabia versus Syria versus Egypt) are what strike you most forcefully. There's very little resembling a common purpose. Even after the non-Islamic NATO fought a war for the Muslim Kosovar Albanians, the Muslim world was slow in coming forward with much-needed humanitarian aid.

The real wars of religion are the wars religions unleash against ordinary citizens within their "spheres of influence." They are wars of the godly against the largely defenseless—American fundamentalists against pro-choice doctors, Iranian mullahs against their country's Jewish minority, the Taliban against the people of Afghanistan, Hindu fundamentalists in Bombay against that city's increasingly fearful Muslims.

The victors in that war must not be the closed-minded, marching into battle with, as ever, God on their side. To choose unbelief is to choose mind over dogma, to trust in our humanity instead of all these dangerous divinities. So, how did we get here? Don't look for the answer in storybooks. Imperfect human knowledge may be a bumpy, potholed street, but it's the only road to wisdom worth taking. Virgil, who believed that the apiarist Aristaeus could spontaneously generate new bees from the rotting carcass of a cow, was closer to a truth about origins than all the revered old books.

The ancient wisdoms are modern nonsenses. Live in your own time, use what we know, and as you grow up, perhaps the human race will finally grow up with you and put aside childish things.

As the song says, "It's easy if you try."

As for morality, the second great question—how to live? What is right action, and what wrong?—it comes down to your willingness to think for yourself. Only you can decide if you want to be handed down the law by priests, and accept that good and evil are somehow external to ourselves. To my mind religion, even at its most sophisticated, essentially infantilizes our ethical selves by setting infallible moral Arbiters and irredeemably immoral Tempters above us; the eternal parents, good and bad, light and dark, of the supernatural realm.

How, then, are we to make ethical choices without a divine rulebook or judge? Is unbelief just the first step on the long slide into the brain-death of cultural relativism, according to which many unbearable things—female circumcision, to name just one—can be excused on culturally specific grounds, and the universality of human rights, too, can be ignored? (This last piece of moral unmaking finds supporters in some of the world's most authoritarian regimes and also, unnervingly, on the op-ed pages of The Daily Telegraph.)

Well, no, it isn't, but the reasons for saying so aren't clear-cut. Only hard-line ideology is clear-cut. Freedom, which is the word I use for the secular-ethical position, is inevitably fuzzier. Yes, freedom is that space in which contradiction can reign, it is a never-ending debate. It is not in itself the answer to the question of morals but the conversation about that question.

And it is much more than mere relativism, because it is not merely a never-ending talk-shop, but a place in which choices are made, values defined and defended. Intellectual freedom, in European history, has mostly meant freedom from the restraints of the Church, not the State. This is the battle Voltaire was fighting, and it's also what all six billion of us could do for ourselves, the revolution in which each of us could play our small, six-billionth part: once and for all we could refuse to allow priests, and the fictions on whose behalf they claim to speak, to be the policemen of our liberties and behavior. Once and for all we could put the stories back into the books, put the books back on the shelves, and see the world undogmatized and plain.

Imagine there's no heaven, my dear Six Billionth, and at once the sky's the limit.

July 1997

"Damme, This Is the Oriental Scene for You!"

——————

I once gave a reading to university students in Delhi, and when I'd finished a young woman put up her hand. "Mr. Rushdie, I read through your novel *Midnight's Children*," she said. "It is a very long book, but never mind, I read it through. The question I want to ask is this: fundamentally, what's your point?"

Before I could attempt an answer, she spoke again. "Oh, I know what you're going to say. You're going to say that the whole effort—from cover to cover—that is the point of the exercise. Isn't that what you were going to say?"

"Something like that, perhaps . . ." I got out.

She snorted. "It won't do."

"Please," I begged, "do I have to have just one point?"

"Fundamentally," she said, with impressive firmness, "yes."

Contemporary Indian literature remains largely unknown in the United States, in spite of its considerable present-day energy and diversity. The few writers that have made an impression (R. K. Narayan, Vikram Seth) are inevitably read in a kind of literary isolation: texts without context. Some writers of Indian descent (V. S. Naipaul, Bharati Mukherjee) reject the ethnic label of "Indian writers," perhaps in an effort to place themselves in other, better-understood literary contexts. Mukherjee sees herself nowadays as an American writer, while Naipaul would perhaps prefer to be read as an artist from nowhere and everywhere. Indians (and, since the partition of the subcontinent almost fifty years ago, one should also say Pakistanis) have long been migrants, seeking their fortunes in Africa, Australia, Britain, the Caribbean, and America, and this diaspora has produced many writers who lay claim to an excess of roots; writers like the Kashmiri American poet Agha Shahid Ali, whose verses look toward Srinagar from Amherst, Massachusetts, by way of other catastrophes:

> what else besides God disappears at the altar?
> O Kashmir, Armenia once vanished. Words are nothing,
> just rumors—like roses—to embellish a slaughter.

How, then, to make any simple, summarizing statement— "fundamentally, what's your point?"—about so multiform a literature, hailing from that huge crowd of a country (close to a billion people at the last count), that vast, metamorphic, continent-sized culture that feels, to Indians and visitors alike, like a non-stop assault on the senses, the emotions, the imagination, and the spirit? Put India in the Atlantic Ocean and it would reach from Europe to America; put India and China together and you've got almost half the population of the world.

These days, new Indian writers seem to emerge every few weeks. Their work is as polymorphous as the place, and readers who care about the vitality of literature will find at least some of these voices saying something they want to hear. The approaching fiftieth anniversary of Indian independence is a useful pretext for a survey of half a century of post-liberation writing. For many months now, I have been reading my way through this literature, and my Delhi interrogator may be pleased to hear that the experience has indeed led me to a single— unexpected, and profoundly ironic—conclusion.

This is it: the prose writing—both fiction and non-fiction—created in this period by Indian writers working in English is proving to be a more interesting body of work than most of what has been produced in the sixteen "official languages" of India, the so-called vernacular languages, during the same time.

It is a large claim, though it may be an easy one for Western readers to accept; if most of India's English-language writers are still largely unknown in the West, the problem is far greater in the case of the vernacular literatures. Of India's non–English language authors, perhaps only the name of the Nobel Prize–winning Bengali writer Rabindranath

Tagore would be recognized, and even his work, though still popular in Latin America, is pretty much a closed book elsewhere.

However, it is a claim that runs counter to almost all the received critical wisdom within India itself.* It is also not a claim that I ever expected to make.

Admittedly, I did my reading only in English, and there has long been a genuine problem of translation in India—not only into English but between the vernacular languages—and it is possible that good writers have been ill served by their translators' inadequacies. Nowadays, however, such bodies as the Indian Sahitya Akademi and UNESCO, as well as Indian publishers themselves, have been putting substantial resources into the creation of better translations, and the problem, while not eradicated, is certainly much diminished.

I should add that I exclude poetry from my thesis. The rich poetic traditions of India continue to flourish in many languages; the English-language poets, with a few distinguished exceptions—Arun Kolatkar, A. K. Ramanujan, Jayanta Mahapatra, Dom Moraes—do not match the quality of their counterparts in prose.

Ironically, the century before Independence contains many vernacular-language writers who would merit a place in any anthology: Bankim Chandra Chatterjee, Rabindranath Tagore, Dr. Muhammad Iqbal, Mirza Ghalib, Bibhutibhushan Banerjee (the author of *Pather Panchali*, on which Satyajit Ray based his celebrated Apu Trilogy of films), and Premchand, the prolific (and therefore rather variable) Hindi author of, among many others, the famous novel of rural life *Godaan,* or *The Gift of a Cow.*

This is not to say that there aren't excellent writers to be found outside English. The leading figures include Mahasveta Devi (Bengali), O. V. Vijayan (Malayalam), Nirmal Verma (Hindi), U. R. Ananthamurthy (Kannada), Suresh Joshi (Gujarati), Amrita Pritam (Punjabi), Qurratulain Haider (Urdu), and Ismat Chughtai (Urdu). But these artists are scattered across many languages; it's the concentration of new talent in English that has created the phenomenon, the "boom." For my money, the finest Indian writer available in translation—a greater writer than

---

* When first published in two slightly different versions, this essay caused howls of protest and condemnation. Almost all Indian critics and most Indian writers disagreed with its central assertion. Readers are accordingly warned that mine is an improper view. Which doesn't necessarily mean it's wrong.

most of the English-language ones—is Saadat Hasan Manto, an immensely popular Urdu writer of low-life fictions, sometimes scorned by conservative critics for his choice of characters and milieus, much as Virginia Woolf snobbishly disparaged the fictional universe of James Joyce's *Ulysses*. Manto's masterpiece is perhaps the short story "Toba Tek Singh," a parable of the Partition of India, in which a lunatic asylum near the new frontier decides that the lunatics, too, must be partitioned: Indian lunatics to India, Pakistani lunatics to the new country of Pakistan. But everything is unclear: the exact location of the frontier, and of the places of origin of the insane persons, too. The lunacies in the asylum become, in this savagely funny story, a perfect metaphor for the greater insanity of history.

For some Indian critics, English-language Indian writing will never be more than a post-colonial anomaly, the bastard child of Empire, sired on India by the departing British; its continuing use of the old colonial tongue is seen as a fatal flaw that renders it forever inauthentic. "Indo-Anglian" literature evokes, in these critics, the kind of prejudiced reaction shown by some Indians toward the country's community of "Anglo-Indians"—that is, Eurasians.

Fifty years ago Jawaharlal Nehru delivered, in English, the great "freedom at midnight" speech that marked the moment of independence:

> At the stroke of the midnight hour, when the world sleeps, India will awake to life and freedom. A moment comes, which comes but rarely in history, when we step out from the old to the new, when an age ends, and when the soul of a nation, long suppressed, finds utterance."

Since that indisputably Anglophone oration, the role of English itself has often been disputed in India. Attempts in India's continental shelf of languages to coin medical, scientific, technological, and everyday neologisms to replace the commonly used English words sometimes succeeded, but more often comically failed. And when the Marxist government of the state of Bengal announced in the mid-1980s that the supposedly elitist, colonialist teaching of English would be discontinued in government-run primary schools, many on the Left denounced the decision itself as elitist, as it would deprive the masses of the many economic and social advantages of speaking the world's language; only the affluent private-school elite would henceforth have that privilege. A well-known Calcutta graffito complained, "My son won't learn English. Your son won't learn English. But Jyoti Basu [the Chief Minister] will send his son abroad to learn English." One man's ghetto of privilege is another's road to freedom.

Like the Greek god Dionysus, who was dismembered and afterward reassembled—and who, according to the myths, was one of India's earliest conquerors—Indian writing in English has been called "twice-born" (by the critic Meenakshi Mukherjee) to suggest its double parentage. While I am, I must admit, attracted by the Dionysian resonances of this supposedly double birth, it seems to me to rest on the false premise that English, having arrived from outside India, is and must necessarily remain an alien there. But my own mother-tongue, Urdu, the camp-argot of the country's earlier Muslim conquerors, was also an immigrant language, forged out of a blend between the conquerors' imported tongue and the local languages they encountered. However, it became a naturalized subcontinental language long ago; and by now that has happened to English, too. English has become an Indian language. Its colonial origins mean that, like Urdu and unlike all other Indian languages, it has no regional base; but in all other ways, it has emphatically come to stay.

(In many parts of South India, people will prefer to converse with visiting North Indians in English rather than Hindi, which feels, ironically, more like a colonial language to speakers of Tamil, Kannada, or Malayalam than does English, which has acquired, in the South, an aura of lingua franca cultural neutrality. The new Silicon Valley–style boom in computer technology that is transforming the economies of Bangalore and Madras has made English, in those cities, an even more important language than before.)

Indian English is not "English" English, to be sure, any more than Irish or American or Caribbean English is. And it is a part of the achievement of English-language Indian writers to have found literary voices as distinctively Indian, and also as suitable for any and all of the purposes of art, as those other Englishes forged in Ireland, Africa, the West Indies, and the United States.

However, Indian critical assaults on this new literature continue to be made from time to time. Its practitioners are denigrated for being too upper-middle-class; for lacking diversity in their choice of themes and techniques; for being less popular in India than outside India; for possessing inflated reputations on account of the international power of the English language, and of the ability of Western critics and publishers to impose their cultural standards on the East; for living, in many cases, outside India; for being deracinated to the point that their work lacks the spiritual dimension essential for a "true" understanding of the soul of India; for being insufficiently grounded in the ancient literary traditions of India; for being the literary equivalent of MTV culture, of globalizing Coca-Colonization; even, I'm sorry to report, for suffering from a condition that one waspish recent commentator, Pankaj Mishra, calls "Rushdie-itis . . . [a] condition that has claimed Rushdie himself in his later works."

It is interesting that so few of these criticisms are literary in the pure sense of the word. For the most part they do not deal with language, voice, psychological or social insight, imagination, or talent. Rather, they are about class, power, and belief. There is a whiff of political correctness about them: the ironical proposition that India's best writing since Independence may have been done in the language of the departed imperialists is simply too much for some folks to bear. It ought not to be true, and so must not be permitted to be true. (That many of the attacks on English-language Indian writing are made in English by writers who are themselves members of the college-educated, English-speaking elite is a further irony.)

Let us quickly concede what must be conceded. It is true that most of these writers come from the educated classes of India; but in a country still bedeviled by high illiteracy levels, how could it be otherwise? It does not follow, however—unless one holds to a rigid, class-war view of the world—that writers with the privilege of a good education will automatically write novels that seek only to portray the lives of the bourgeoisie. It is true that there tends to be a bias toward metropolitan and cosmopolitan fiction, but there has been, during this half century, a genuine attempt to encompass as many Indian realities as possible, rural as well as urban, sacred as well as profane. This is also, let us remember, a young literature. It is still pushing out the frontiers of the possible.

The point about the power of the English language, and of the Western publishing and critical fraternities, also contains some truth. Perhaps it does seem, to some "home" commentators, that a canon is being foisted on them from outside. The perspective from the West is rather different. Here, what seems to be the case is that Western publishers and critics have been growing gradually more and more excited by the voices emerging from India; in England at least, British writers are often chastised by reviewers for their lack of Indian-style ambition and verve. It feels as if the East is imposing itself on the West, rather than the other way around.

And, yes, English is the most powerful medium of communication in the world; should we not then rejoice at these artists' mastery of it, and at their growing influence? To criticize writers for their success at "breaking out" is no more than parochialism (and parochialism is perhaps the main vice of the vernacular literatures). One important dimension of literature is that it is a means of holding a conversation with the world. These writers are ensuring that India or, rather, Indian voices (for they are too good to fall into the trap of writing *nationalistically*) will henceforth be confident, indispensable participants in that literary conversation.

Granted, many of these writers do have homes outside India. Henry James, James Joyce, Samuel Beckett, Ernest Hemingway, Gertrude Stein, Mavis Gallant, James Baldwin, Graham Greene, Gabriel García Márquez, Mario Vargas Llosa, Jorge Luis Borges, Vladimir Nabokov, Muriel Spark were or are wanderers, too. Muriel Spark, accepting the British Literature Prize for a lifetime's achievement in March 1997, went so far as to say that travel to other countries was essential for all writers. Literature has little or nothing to do with a writer's home address.

The question of religious faith, both as a subject and as an approach to a subject, is clearly important when we speak of a country as bursting with devotions as India; but it is surely excessive to use it, as does one leading academic, the redoubtable Professor C. D. Narasimhaiah, as a touchstone, so that Mulk Raj Anand is praised for his "daring" merely because, as a leftist writer, he allows a character to be moved by deep faith, while Arun Kolatkar's poetry is denigrated for "throwing away tradition and creating a vacuum," and so "losing relevance," because in *Jejuri,* a cycle of poems about a visit to a temple town, he skeptically likens the stone gods in the temples to the stones on the hillsides nearby ("and every other stone / is god or his cousin"). In fact, many of the writers I admire have profound knowledge of the "soul of India"; many have deeply spiritual concerns, while others are radically secular, but the need to engage with, to make a reckoning with, India's religious self is everywhere to be found.

The cheapening of artistic response implied by the allegations of de-racination and Westernization is notably absent from these writers' work. As to the claims of excessive Rushdie-itis, I can't deny that I used on occasion to feel something of the sort myself. However, it was a short-lived virus. Those whom it affected soon shook it off and found their own true voices. And these days more or less everyone seems immune to the disease.

At any rate, there is not, need not be, should not be, an adversarial relationship between English-language literature and the other literatures of India. In my own case, and I suspect in the case of every Indian writer in English, knowing and loving the Indian languages in which I was raised has remained of vital personal and artistic importance. As an individual, I know that Hindi-Urdu, the "Hindustani" of North India, remains an essential aspect of my sense of self; as a writer, I have been partly formed by the presence, in my head, of that other music, the rhythms, patterns, and habits of thought and metaphor of my Indian tongues.

Whatever language we write in, we drink from the same well. India, that inexhaustible horn of plenty, nourishes us all.

———

The first Indian novel in English was a dud. *Rajmohan's Wife* (1864) is a poor melodramatic thing. The writer, Bankim Chandra Chatterjee, reverted to Bengali and immediately achieved great renown. For seventy years or so there was no English-language fiction of any quality. It was the generation of Independence, "midnight's parents," one might call them, who were the true architects of this new tradition. (Jawaharlal Nehru himself was a fine writer; his autobiography and letters are important, influential works. And his niece, Nayantara Sahgal, whose early memoir *Prison and Chocolate Cake* contains perhaps the finest evocation of the heady time of Independence, went on to become a major novelist.)

In that generation, Mulk Raj Anand was influenced by both Joyce and Marx but most of all, perhaps, by the teachings of Mahatma Gandhi. He is best known for social-realist works like the novel *Coolie*, a study of working-class life reminiscent of post-war Italian neo-realist cinema (De Sica's *Bicycle Thief*, Rossellini's *Open City*). Raja Rao, a scholarly Sanskritist, wrote determinedly of the need to make an Indian English for himself, but even his much-praised portrait of village life,

Kanthapura, now seems dated, its approach at once grandiloquent and archaic. The centenarian autobiographer Nirad C. Chaudhuri has been, throughout his long life, an erudite, contrary, and mischievous presence. His view, if I may paraphrase and summarize it, is that India has no culture of its own, and that whatever we now call Indian culture was brought in from outside by the successive waves of conquerors. This view, polemically and brilliantly expressed, has not endeared him to many of his fellow-Indians. That he has always swum so strongly against the current has not, however, prevented *The Autobiography of an Unknown Indian* from being recognized as the masterpiece it is.

The most significant writers of this first generation, R. K. Narayan and G. V. Desani, have had opposite careers. Narayan's books fill a good-sized shelf; Desani is the author of a single work of fiction, *All About H. Hatterr,* and that singleton volume is already fifty years old. Desani is almost unknown, while R. K. Narayan is, of course, a figure of world stature, for his creation of the imaginary town of Malgudi, so lovingly made that it has become more vividly real to us than most real places. (But Narayan's realism is leavened by touches of legend; the river Sarayu, on whose shores the town sits, is one of the great rivers of Hindu mythology. It is as if William Faulkner had set his Yoknapatawpha County on the banks of the Styx.)

Narayan shows us, over and over again, the quarrel between traditional, static India, on the one hand, and modernity and progress, on the other; represented, in many of his stories and novels, by a confrontation between a "wimp" and a "bully"—The Painter of Signs and his aggressive beloved with her birth control campaign; The Vendor of Sweets and the emancipated American daughter-in-law with the absurd "novel writing machine"; the mild-mannered printer and the extrovert taxidermist in *The Man-Eater of Malgudi.* In his gentle, lightly funny art, he goes to the heart of the Indian condition and, beyond it, into the human condition itself.

The writer I have placed alongside Narayan, G. V. Desani, has fallen so far from favor that the extraordinary *All About H. Hatterr* is presently out of print everywhere, even in India. Milan Kundera once said that all modern literature descends from either Richardson's *Clarissa* or Sterne's *Tristram Shandy,* and if Narayan is India's Richardson then Desani is his Shandean other. *Hatterr's* dazzling, puzzling, leaping prose is the first genuine effort to go beyond the Englishness of the English language. His central figure, "fifty-fifty of the species," the half-breed as unabashed anti-hero, leaps and capers behind the work of many of his successors:

> The earth was blotto with the growth of willow, peach, mango-blossom, and flower. Every ugly thing, and smell, was in incognito, as fragrance and freshness. Being prone, this typical spring-time dash and activity, played an exulting phantasmagoria-note on the inner-man. Medically speaking, the happy circumstances vibrated my duct-less glands, and fused me into a wibble-wobble *Whoa, Jamieson!* fillip-and-flair to *live, live!*

Or, again:

> The incidents take place in India. I was exceedingly hard-up of cash: actually, in debts. And, it is amazing, how, out in the Orient, the short-age of cash gets mixed up with romance and females somehow! In this England, they say, if a fellah is broke, females, as matter of course, forsake. Stands to reason. Whereas, out in the East, they attach them-selves! Damme, this is the Oriental scene for you!

This is "babu-English," the semi-literate, half-learned English of the bazaars, transmuted by erudition, highbrow monkeying around, and the impish magic of Desani's unique phrasing and rhythm, into an entirely new kind of literary voice. Hard to imagine I. Allan Sealy's more recent, Eurasian comic-epic *The Trotter-Nama,* an enormous tome full of interpolations, exclamations, resumptions, encomiums, and catastrophes, without Desani. My own writing, too, learned a trick or two from him.

———

Ved Mehta is well known both for his astute commentaries on the Indian scene and for his several distinguished volumes of autobiography. The first of these is the most moving: *Vedi,* a memoir of a blind boyhood that describes cruelties and kindnesses with equal dispassion and great affect. (More recently, Firdaus Kanga, in his autobiographical fiction *Trying to Grow,* has also transcended physical affliction with high style and comic brio.)

Ruth Prawer Jhabvala, author of the Booker Prize–winning *Heat and Dust* (afterward made into a Merchant-Ivory movie), is a renowned master of the short-story form. As a writer, she is sometimes underrated in India because, I think, the voice of the rootless intellectual (so quintessentially her voice) is such an unfamiliar one in that country where people's self-definitions are so rooted in their regional identities.

That Ruth Jhabvala has a second career as an award-winning screenwriter is well known. But not many people realize that India's greatest film director, the late Satyajit Ray, was also an accomplished author of short stories. His father edited a famous Bengali children's magazine, *Sandesh,* and Ray's biting little fables are made more potent by their childlike charm.

Anita Desai, one of India's major living authors, merits comparison with Jane Austen. In novels such as *Clear Light of Day*—written in a clear, light English full of subtle atmospherics—she displays both her exceptional skill at social portraiture and an unsparing, Austen-like mordancy of insight into human motivations. *In Custody,* perhaps her best novel to date, finely uses English to depict the decay of another language, Urdu, and the high literary culture that lived in it. Here the poet, the last, boozing, decrepit custodian of the dying tradition, is (in a reversal of Narayan) the "bully"; and the novel's central character, the poet's young admirer Deven, is the "wimp." The dying past, the old world, Desai tells us, can be as much of a burden as the awkward, sometimes wrongheaded present.

Though V. S. Naipaul approaches India as an outsider, his engagement with it has been so intense that no account of its modern literature would be complete without him. His three non-fiction books on India, *An Area of Darkness, India: A Wounded Civilization,* and *India: A Million Mutinies Now,* are key texts, and not only because of the hackles they have raised. Many Indian critics have taken issue with the harshness of his responses. Some have fair-mindedly conceded that he does attack things worth attacking. "I'm anti-Naipaul when I visit the West," one leading South Indian novelist told me, "but I'm often pro-Naipaul back home."

Some of Naipaul's targets, like—this is from *A Wounded Civilization*—the intermediate-technology institute that invents "reaping boots" (with blades attached) for Indian peasants to use to harvest grain, merit the full weight of his scorn. At other times he appears merely supercilious. India, his migrant ancestors' lost paradise, cannot stop disappointing him. By the third volume of the series, however, he seems more cheerful about the country's condition. He speaks approvingly of the emergence of "a central will, a central intellect, a national idea," and disarmingly, even movingly, confesses to the atavistic edginess of mood in which he had made his first trip almost thirty years earlier: "The India of my fantasy and heart was something lost and irrecoverable. . . . On that first journey, I was a fearful traveler."

In *An Area of Darkness,* Naipaul's comments on Indian writers elicit in this reader a characteristic mixture of agreement and dissent. When he writes,

> The feeling is widespread that, whatever English might have done for Tolstoy, it can never do justice to the Indian "language" writers. This is possible; what I read of them in translation did not encourage me to read more. Premchand . . . turned out to be a minor fabulist. . . . Other writers quickly fatigued me with their assertions that poverty was sad, that death was sad . . . many of the "modern" short stories were only refurbished folk tales,

then he is expressing, in his emphatic, unafraid way, what I have also felt. (Though I think more highly of Premchand than he.) When he goes on to say,

> The novel is part of that Western concern with the condition of men, a response to the here and now. In India thoughtful men have preferred to turn their backs on the here and now and to satisfy what President Radhakrishnan calls "the basic human hunger for the unseen." It is not a good qualification for the writing and reading of novels,

then I can go only some of the way with him. It is true that many learned Indians go in for a sonorously impenetrable form of critico-mysticism. I once heard an Indian writer of some renown, and much interest in India's ancient wisdoms, expounding his theory of what one might call Motionism. "Consider Water," he advised us. "Water without Motion is—what? Is a lake. Very well. Now, Water plus Motion is—what? Is a river. You see? The Water is still the same Water. Only Motion has been added. By the same token," he continued, making a breathtaking intellectual leap, "Language is Silence, to which Motion has been added."

(A fine Indian poet, who was sitting beside me in the great man's audience, murmured in my ear: "Bowel without Motion is—what? Is constipation! Bowel plus Motion is—what? Is shit!")

I agree with Naipaul that mysticism is bad for novelists. But in the India I know, for every obfuscating Motionist, there is a debunking Bowelist whispering in one's ear. For every unworldly seeker for the ancient wisdoms of the East, there is a clear-eyed witness responding to the here and now in precisely that fashion which Naipaul inaccurately calls uniquely Western. And when Naipaul concludes by saying that in the aftermath of the "abortive" Indo-British encounter, India is little more than a very Naipaulian community of mimic men—that the country's artistic life has stagnated, "the creative urge" has "failed"; that "Shiva has ceased to dance"—then I fear we part company altogether. *An Area of Darkness* was written as long ago as 1964, a mere seventeen years after Independence, and a little early for an obituary notice. The growing quality of Indian writing in English may yet change his mind.

In the 1980s and 1990s, the flow of that good writing has become a flood. Bapsi Sidhwa is technically Pakistani, but literature has no need of Partitions, particularly as Sidhwa's novel *Cracking India* is one of the finest responses to the horror of the division of the subcontinent. Gita Mehta's *A River Sutra* is an important attempt by a thoroughly modern Indian to make her reckoning with the Hindu culture from which she emerged. Padma Perera, Anjana Appachana (*Listening Now*), and Githa Hariharan, less well known than Sidhwa and Mehta, confirm the quality of contemporary writing by Indian women.

A number of different styles of work are evolving: the Stendhalian realism of a writer like Rohinton Mistry, the author of two acclaimed novels, *Such a Long Journey* and *A Fine Balance,* and of a collection of stories, *Tales from Firozsha Baag;* the equally naturalistic but lighter, more readily charming prose of Vikram Seth (there is, admittedly, a kind of perversity in invoking lightness in the context of a book boasting as much sheer avoirdupois as *A Suitable Boy*); the elegant social observation of Upamanyu Chatterjee (*English, August*), the more flamboyant manner of Vikram Chandra (*Love and Longing in Bombay*). Amitav Ghosh's most impressive achievement to date is the non-fiction study of India and Egypt *In an Antique Land.* It may be that his greatest strength will turn out to be as an essayist of this sort. Sara Suleri, whose memoir *Meatless Days* is, like Bapsi Sidhwa's *Cracking India,* a visitor from across the Pakistani frontier, is a non-fiction writer of immense originality and grace. And Amit Chaudhuri's languorous, elliptic, beautiful prose is impressively impossible to place in any category at all.

Most encouragingly, yet another talented generation has begun to emerge. The Keralan writer Arundhati Roy has arrived to the accompaniment of a loud fanfare. Her novel, *The God of Small Things,* is full of ambition and sparkle, and written in a highly wrought and utterly personal style. Equally impressive are the debuts of two other first novelists. Ardashir Vakil's *Beach Boy* and Kiran Desai's *Hullabaloo in the Guava Orchard* are, in their very unalike ways, highly original books. The Vakil book, a tale of growing up near Juhu Beach, Bombay, is sharp, funny, and fast; the Kiran Desai, a Calvino-esque fable of a misfit boy who climbs a tree and becomes a sort of petty guru, is lush and intensely imagined. Kiran Desai is the daughter of Anita: her arrival establishes the first dynasty of modern Indian fiction. But she is very much her own writer, and welcome proof that India's encounter with the English language, far from proving abortive, continues to give birth to new children, endowed with lavish gifts.

The map of the world, in the standard Mercator projection, is not kind to India, making it look substantially smaller than, say, Greenland. On the map of world literature, too, India has been undersized for too long. Fifty years after India's independence, however, that age of obscurity is coming to an end. India's writers have torn up the old map and are busily drawing their own.

March 1997

India's Fiftieth Anniversary

[*Originally commissioned and published by* Time *magazine*]

There are really only two ways of arriving at your fiftieth birthday. You can (1) do it defiantly—by thumbing your nose at Father Time, throwing the mother of all parties, and announcing your intention of growing old disgracefully; or, (2) you can deal with it grumpily—by pretending it isn't happening, hiding your head under the pillows, and wishing the day would just go away. On the occasion of my own recently completed half century, my inclinations led me unequivocally down route 1. Now it's India's turn; but though the fiftieth anniversary of the end of British rule is being loudly trumpeted around the world, India herself, while not entirely ignoring the event, is reacting with a halfhearted, shoulder-shrugging sourness, a certain category 2 lack of celebratory spirit that has raised many international observers' eyebrows. You get the feeling the lady wishes she had lied about her age.

Indians have always been less susceptible to anniversary-itis than Westerners. The annual Republic Day (January 26) parades, popular with visitors to India largely on account of the participation of glamorously caparisoned elephants, have been mostly ignored by the locals. Independence Day itself (August 15) is also traditionally a lackluster affair. Ten years ago, on the fortieth anniversary of the end of the Raj,

I was at the Red Fort in Delhi, filming the then prime minister Rajiv Gandhi's speech to a crushingly indifferent nation. The audience was so unimpressed, in fact, that very large numbers of people simply walked away while Rajiv was still speaking.

The Indian governing elite has long been wary about sanctioning public resources for mere display. It is believed that the public would disapprove of money wasted on, for example, fireworks displays, when it could be used for much-needed irrigation schemes. Against this, one could argue that the Indian public's estimation of their leaders has fallen so low, because of recent corruption scandals and endemic inter-party bickering, that it's hard to see how a little fun would make things worse. And there aren't actually any special proposals for worthy new schemes on the table.

One could, therefore, wish for a touch more subcontinental hoopla as the big five-oh comes around. In India, such plans as have been un-veiled range from the conventionally tedious (members of the Indian National Assembly will listen to recordings of speeches by the founders of the nation, Gandhi and Nehru), to the shoestring amateur dramatics of "restaging" the passing of the 1942 Quit India Resolution in Bombay, to the plainly bizarre—viz., the apparently serious proposal that the an-niversary be marked by erecting a statue of Gandhiji (clad, no doubt, only in his legendary loincloth) *in Antarctica*. And in Pakistan—after all, it's Pakistan's fiftieth anniversary, too—even less is promised; accord-ing to the Pakistani High Commission in London, the Nawaz Sharif government has decided to "celebrate humbly." Pakistani politicians are not noted for their humility, so this is, in its way, something of a first.

Fifty years ago, Mr. Nehru, taking office as India's first prime minis-ter, described Independence as the moment ". . . when the soul of a nation, long suppressed, finds utterance." The explanation for the na-tion's present unwillingness to throw its *Nehru topi* in the air lies in the subsequent battering administered by history to that newly liberated soul. If, in August 1947, many Indians had idealistic hopes of a great new beginning, then August 1997 is suffused by the sense of an ending. Another age is ending: the first age, one might say, of the history of post-colonial India. It has not been the promised golden age of free-dom. The prevailing mood is one of disenchantment. Private citizens and public commentators alike readily provide a long, convincing list of reasons for this disenchantment, starting with the dark side of Inde-pendence itself; that is, of course, Partition. The decision to carve a

Muslim homeland, Pakistan, out of the body of subcontinental India led to bloody massacres in which over a million Hindus, Sikhs, and Muslims lost their lives. Partition has poisoned the subsequent history of relations between the two newborn states ever since. Why on earth would anyone want to celebrate the fiftieth anniversary of one of the century's great tragedies?

Like many secularist Indians, I would argue that Partition was an avoidable mistake, the result not of historical inevitability or the true will of the people but of political antagonisms—between Gandhi and M. A. Jinnah, between the Congress and the Muslim League—which gradually turned Mr. Jinnah, originally a strong opponent of the idea of a separate Muslim state, into its most ardent advocate and eventual founder. (Of course, the divide-and-rule tactics of the British did nothing to help.) My own family, like so many of Muslim origin, was cut in half by Partition. My parents opted to stay in Bombay, and so did my two uncles and their families, but my aunts and their families went to West Pakistan, as it was called until 1971, when East Pakistan seceded and became Bangladesh. We were lucky, escaping the worst of the bloodletting, but our lives were defined and shaped by the frontier separating us. Who would celebrate the descent of the Iron Curtain, the building of the Berlin Wall?

The period after Partition gives rise to a further, familiar litany of woes. The nation's great social ills have not been cured. Mrs. Indira Gandhi's famous slogan, *Garibi Hatao,* "Remove Poverty," was an empty promise; India's poor are as poor as ever, and more numerous than ever, thanks in part to her son Sanjay's hated forcible-sterilization campaign during Mrs. G.'s mid-1970s period of dictatorial "emergency rule," which set back other efforts at birth control by more than a generation. Illiteracy, child labor, infant mortality, the privations imposed by casteism on those of lower or no caste, all these great questions remain unanswered. (The placing of a garland of shoes, an old Indian insult, around the neck of a statue of the Dalit or Untouchable leader Dr. Ambedkar recently led to days of rioting in Bombay.)

Ancient violence takes on new forms. The practice of burning brides for their dowries is on the increase. There is terrifying evidence that ritual child sacrifice is being practiced by some followers of the cult of the goddess Kali. Communal violence erupts regularly. Terrorists advocating a separate Sikh state plant bombs in the Punjab, and terrorists advocating Kashmiri separatism abduct tourists in the beautiful Valley.

Large-scale bloodshed has been seen in Meerut, in Assam, and in Ayodhya, Uttar Pradesh, after the destruction by Hindu nationalists of the Babri Masjid, a mosque believed by some to stand on the birthplace of the Hindu deity Lord Ram.

My hometown, Bombay, for a long time believed itself immune to the worst of India's communal evils; a series of explosions in 1993 destroyed that myth, giving proof that the idealisms, the innocence, of the first post-Independence age had been blown away, perhaps forever—and doing so in the heart of that great metropolis which contains all that is best and worst in the new, modernizing India, all that is most dynamically innovative and most hopelessly impoverished, most internationally minded and most narrowly sectarian.

And then there's corruption. In my novel *The Moor's Last Sigh,* a character offers his definitions of modern Indian democracy ("one man one bribe") and of what he calls the Indian theory of relativity ("everything is for relatives"). Like most things written about India, this looks like an exaggeration but is actually an understatement. The scale of public corruption is now almost comically great. From the Maruti scandal of the 1970s (huge sums of public money disappeared from a "people's car" project headed by Sanjay Gandhi) to the Bofors scandal of the 1980s (huge sums of public money went astray from an international arms deal that besmirched the reputation of Rajiv Gandhi) to the 1990s attempts to fix the movements of the Indian stock market by using, naturally, huge sums of public money, things have been going from bad to worse. Dozens of leading political figures, including the last Congress prime minister, P. V. Narasimha Rao, are under investigation for corruption. And then there is Laloo Prasad Yadav, chief minister of the state of Bihar (one of the poorest parts of India), who has been charged with involvement in Bihar's so-called Fodder Scam, a swindle involving the diversion of, yes, huge sums of public money to support the rearing over many years of great herds of wholly fictitious cattle. More than $150 million is alleged to have vanished in a scheme that even the immortal Chichikov, anti-hero of Gogol's great scam-novel *Dead Souls,* could never have invented.

It would be easy to continue in this vein. There is the rise of extremist Hindu nationalism, the decay of the Civil Service on which Indian democracy has depended for so long, and the tendency of the coalition supporting the minority Indian government of Prime Minister I. K. Gujral to fragment. Bits of it have been breaking off with distressing frequency—the Yadav faction has gone, and the Southern DMK party has also threatened to leave the coalition—and the government survives only because nobody really wants a general election; nobody, that is, except the militant Hindu Bharatiya Janata Party (BJP), the largest single party in Parliament, presently excluded from power but likely to win even more seats next time around, and thus be harder to gang up against. And, if you're old-fashioned, you can complain about the effect of MTV culture on Indian youth, and if you're a sports fan you can lament India's lack of world-class athletes.

And yet I do feel like celebrating. The news is not all bad. (For example, the election of India's first Untouchable president, Mr. Kocheril Raman Narayanan, will perhaps result in an assault on the worst excesses of casteism.) Above all, however, I want to extol the virtues of the most important thing that came into being on that midnight fifty years ago, the thing which has survived all that history could throw at it: that is, the so-called idea of India. I have spent much of my adult life thinking and writing about this idea. At the time of the last bout of anniversary-itis, in 1987, I traveled all over India asking ordinary Indians what they thought the idea was, and whether they found it to be a valuable one. Remarkably, given India's size and diversity, and Indians' strong regional loyalties, everyone I spoke to was entirely comfortable with the term "India," entirely certain that they understood it and "belonged to" it; and yet, when one examined the matter more closely, one saw that their definitions differed radically, as did their ideas of what "belonging" might entail.

And that multiplicity, finally, was the point. In the modern age, we have come to understand our own selves as composites, often contradictory, even internally incompatible. We have understood that each of us is many different people. Our younger selves differ from our older selves; we can be bold in the company of our lovers and timorous before our employers, principled when we instruct our children and corrupt when offered some secret temptation; we are serious and frivolous, loud and quiet, aggressive and easily abashed. The nineteenth-century concept of the integrated self has been replaced by this jostling crowd of "I" 's. And yet, unless we are damaged, or deranged, we usually have a relatively clear sense of *who we are*. I agree with my many selves to call all of them "me." This is the best way to grasp the idea of India. India has taken the modern view of the self and enlarged it to encompass almost one billion souls. The selfhood of India is so capacious, so elastic, that it manages to accommodate one billion kinds of difference. It agrees with its billion selves to call all of them "Indian." This is a notion far more original than the old pluralist ideas of "melting pot" or "cultural mosaic." It works because the individual sees his own nature writ large in the nature of the state. This is why individual Indians feel so comfortable about the strength of the national idea, why it's so easy to "belong" to it, in spite of all the turbulence, the corruption, the tawdriness, the disappointment of fifty overwhelming years.

Churchill said India wasn't a nation, just an "abstraction." John Kenneth Galbraith, more affectionately, and more memorably, described it as "functioning anarchy." Both of them, in my view, underestimated the strength of the India-idea. It may be the most innovative national philosophy to have emerged in the post-colonial period. It deserves to be celebrated; because it is an idea that has enemies, within India as well as outside her frontiers, and to celebrate it is also to defend it against its foes.

July 1997

Gandhi, Now

A thin Indian man with not much hair and bad teeth sits alone on a bare floor, wearing nothing but a loincloth and a pair of cheap spectacles, studying the clutch of handwritten notes in his hand. The black-and-white photograph takes up a full page of the British newspaper. In the top left-hand corner of the page, in full color, is a small rainbow-striped apple. Below this, there's a slangily, ungrammatically American injunction to "Think Different." Such is the present-day power of international big business. Even the greatest of the dead may summarily be drafted into its image campaigns. Once, half a century ago and more, this bony man shaped a nation's struggle for freedom. But that, as they say, is history. Fifty years after his assassination, Gandhi is modeling for Apple. His thoughts don't really count in this new incarnation. What counts is that he is considered to be "on-message," in line with the corporate philosophy of the Mac.

The advertisement is odd enough to be worth deconstructing a little. Obviously, it is rich in unintentional comedy. M. K. Gandhi, as the photograph itself demonstrates, was a passionate opponent of modernity and technology, preferring the pencil to the typewriter, the loincloth to the business suit, the plowed field to the belching manufactory. Had the word processor been invented in his lifetime, he would almost certainly have found it abhorrent. The very term "word processor," with its overly technological ring, is unlikely to have found favor.

"Think Different." Gandhi, in his younger days a sophisticated and Westernized lawyer, did indeed change his thinking more radically than most people do. Ghanshyam Das Birla, one of the merchant princes who backed him, once said, "Gandhi was more modern than I. But he made a conscious decision to go back to the Middle Ages." This is not, presumably, the revolutionary new direction in thought that the good folks at Apple are seeking to encourage. What they saw was an "icon," a man so famous that he was still instantly recognizable half a century after his assassination. Double-click on this icon and you opened up a set of "values," with which Apple plainly wished to associate itself: "morality," "leadership," "saintliness," "success," and so on. They saw "Mahatma" Gandhi, the "great soul," an embodiment of virtue to set beside, oh, Mother Teresa, the Dalai Lama, the Pope.

Perhaps, too, they found themselves identifying with a little guy who vanquished a big empire. It's true that Gandhi himself saw the independence movement as a kind of Indian David struggling against the Philistines of the empire-on-which-the-sun-never-sets, calling it "a battle of Right against Might." The struggling Apple company, battling with the cohorts of the all-powerful Bill Gates, wished perhaps to comfort itself with the thought that if a "half-nude gent"—as a British viceroy, Lord Willingdon, once called Gandhi—could bring down the Brits, then maybe, just maybe, a well-flung apple might yet fell the Microsoft Goliath.

In other words, Gandhi today is up for grabs. He has become abstract, ahistorical, postmodern, no longer a man in and of his time but a free-floating concept, a part of the available stock of cultural symbols, an image that can be borrowed, used, distorted, reinvented, to fit many different purposes, and to the devil with historicity or truth.

Richard Attenborough's movie *Gandhi* struck me, when it was first released, as an example of this type of unhistorical Western saint-making. Here was Gandhi-as-guru, purveying that fashionable product, the Wisdom of the East; and Gandhi-as-Christ, dying (and, before that, frequently going on hunger strike) so that others might live. His philosophy of non-violence seemed to work by embarrassing the British into leaving; freedom could be won, the film appeared to suggest, by being more moral than your oppressor, whose own moral code would then oblige him to withdraw.

But such is the efficacy of this symbolic Gandhi that the film, for all its simplifications and Hollywoodizations, had a powerful and positive effect on many contemporary freedom struggles. South African anti-apartheid campaigners and democratic voices all over South America have enthused to me about the film's galvanizing effects. This posthumous, exalted "international Gandhi" has evidently become a totem of real, inspirational force.

The trouble with the idealized Gandhi is that he's so darned dull, little more than a dispenser of homilies and nostrums ("an eye for an eye will make the whole world go blind") with just the odd flash of wit (asked what he thought of Western civilization, he gave the celebrated reply "I think it would be a good idea"). The real man, if it is still possible to use such a term after the generations of hagiography and re-invention, was infinitely more interesting, one of the most complex and contradictory personalities of the century. His full name, Mohandas Karamchand Gandhi, was memorably—and literally—translated into English by the novelist G. V. Desani as "Action-Slave Fascination-Moon Grocer," and he was as rich and devious a figure as that glorious name suggests.

Entirely unafraid of the British, he was nevertheless scared of the dark and always slept with a light burning by his bedside.

He believed passionately in the unity of all the peoples of India, yet his failure to keep the Muslim leader Jinnah within the Congress fold led to the partition of the country. (His opposition denied Jinnah the presidency of the Congress, which might have kept him from assuming the leadership of the separatist Muslim League; his withdrawal, under pressure from Nehru and Patel, of a last-ditch offer to Jinnah of the prime ministership itself ended the last faint chance of avoiding Partition. And for all his vaunted selflessness and modesty, he made no move to object when Jinnah was attacked during a Congress session for calling him plain Mr. Gandhi, instead of the more worshipful Mahatma.)

He was determined to live the life of an ascetic, but as the poet Sarojini Naidu joked, it cost the nation a fortune to keep Gandhi living in poverty. His entire philosophy privileged the village way over that of the city, yet he was always financially dependent on the support of industrial billionaires like Birla. His hunger strikes could stop riots and massacres, but he also once went on hunger strike to force his capitalist patron's employees to break their strike against their harsh conditions of employment.

He sought to improve the conditions of India's Untouchables, yet in

today's India, these peoples, now calling themselves Dalits, and forming an increasingly well organized and effective political grouping, have
rallied round the memory of their own leader, Dr. Ambedkar, an old
rival of Gandhi's. As Ambedkar's star has risen among the Dalits, so
Gandhi's stature has been reduced.

The creator of the political philosophies of passive resistance and
constructive non-violence, he spent much of his life far from the political arena, refining his more eccentric theories of vegetarianism,
bowel movements, and the beneficial properties of human excrement.

Forever scarred by the knowledge that, as a sixteen-year-old youth,
he'd been making love to his wife, Kasturba, at the moment of his father's death, Gandhi forswore sexual relations but went on into his old
age with what he called his brahmacharya experiments, during which
naked young women, often the wives of friends and colleagues, would
be asked to lie with him all night, so that he could prove that he had
mastered his physical urges. (He believed that the conservation of his
"vital fluids" would deepen his spiritual understanding.)

He, and he alone, was responsible for the transformation of the
demand for independence into a nationwide mass movement that mo-
bilized every class of society against the imperialist; yet the free India
that came into being, divided and committed to a program of modern-
ization and industrialization, was not the India of his dreams. His
sometime disciple, Jawaharlal Nehru, was the arch-proponent of mod-
ernization, and it is Nehru's vision, not Gandhi's, that was eventually—
and perhaps inevitably—preferred.

Gandhi began by believing that the politics of passive resistance
and non-violence could be effective in any situation, at any time, even
against a force as malign as Nazi Germany. Later, he was obliged to revise his opinion, and concluded that while the British had responded to
such techniques, because of their own nature, other oppressors might
not. This is not so different from the Attenborough movie's position,
and it is, of course, wrong.

Gandhian non-violence is widely believed to be the method by
which India gained independence. (The view is assiduously fostered
inside India as well as outside it.) Yet the Indian revolution did indeed
become violent, and this violence so disappointed Gandhi that he
stayed away from the Independence celebrations in protest. Moreover,
the ruinous economic impact of World War II on the United Kingdom,
and—as the British writer Patrick French says in Liberty or Death—the

gradual collapse of the Raj's bureaucratic hold over India from the mid-1930s onward, did as much to bring about freedom as any action of Gandhi's, or indeed of the nationalist movement as a whole. It is probable, in fact, that Gandhian techniques were not the key determinants of India's arrival at freedom. They gave Independence its outward character and were its apparent cause, but darker and deeper historical forces produced the desired effect.

These days, few people pause to consider the complex character of Gandhi's personality, the ambiguous nature of his achievement and legacy, or even the real causes of Indian independence. These are hurried, sloganizing times, and we don't have the time or, worse, the inclination to assimilate many-sided truths. The harshest truth of all is that Gandhi is increasingly irrelevant in the country whose "little father"— *Bapu*—he was. As the analyst Sunil Khilnani has pointed out, India came into being as a secularized state, but Gandhi's vision was essentially religious. However, he "recoiled" from Hindu nationalism. His solution was to forge an Indian identity out of the shared body of ancient narratives. "He turned to legends and stories from India's popular religious traditions, preferring their lessons to the supposed ones of history."

It didn't work. The last Gandhian to be effective in Indian politics was J. P. Narayan, who led the movement that deposed Indira Gandhi at the end of her period of Emergency rule (1974–1977). In today's India, Hindu nationalism is rampant, in the form of the BJP and its thuggish sidekick, the Shiv Sena. During the present elections, Gandhi and his ideas have scarcely been mentioned. Most of those who are not seduced by sectarian politics are in the thrall of an equally potent, equally anti-Gandhian force: money. And organized crime, too, has moved into the public sphere. In Gandhi's beloved rural heartland, actual gangsters are being elected to office.

Twenty-one years ago, the writer Ved Mehta spoke to one of Gandhi's leading political associates, a former governor-general of independent India, C. Rajagopalachari. His verdict on Gandhi's legacy is disenchanted, but in today's India, on the fast track to free-market capitalism, it still rings true: "The glamour of modern technology, money, and power is so seductive that no one—I mean no one—can resist it. The handful of Gandhians who still believe in his philosophy of a simple life in a simple society are mostly cranks."

What, then, is greatness? In what does it reside? If a man's project fails, or survives only in irredeemably tarnished form, can the force of his example still merit the supreme accolade? For Jawaharlal Nehru, the defining image of Gandhi was "as I saw him marching, staff in hand, to Dandi on the Salt March in 1930. Here was the pilgrim on his quest of Truth, quiet, peaceful, determined, and fearless, who would continue that quest and pilgrimage, regardless of consequences." Nehru's daughter, Indira Gandhi, later said: "More than his words, his life was his message." These days, that message is better heeded outside India. Albert Einstein was one of the many to praise Gandhi's achievement; Martin Luther King, Jr., the Dalai Lama, and all the world's peace movements have followed in his footsteps. Gandhi, who gave up cosmopolitanism to gain a country, has become, in his strange after-life, a citizen of the world. His spirit may yet prove resilient, smart, tough, sneaky, and—yes—ethical enough to avoid assimilation by global McCulture (and Mac culture, too). Against this new empire, Gandhian intelligence is a better weapon than Gandhian piety. And passive resistance? We'll see.

February 1998

The Taj Mahal

[*Written for a* National Geographic *survey of the great marvels of the world*]

The trouble with the Taj Mahal is that it has become so overlaid with accumulated meanings as to be almost impossible to see. A billion chocolate-box images and tourist guidebooks order us to "read" the Mughal emperor Shah Jehan's marble mausoleum for his wife Mumtaz Mahal, known as Taj Bibi, as the World's Greatest Monument to Love. It sits at the top of the West's short list of images of the Exotic (and also Timeless) Orient. Like the *Mona Lisa,* like Andy Warhol's screenprinted Elvis, Marilyn, and Mao, mass reproduction has all but sterilized the Taj.

Nor is this by any means a simple case of the West's appropriation or "colonization" of an Indian masterwork. In the first place, the Taj, which in the mid-nineteenth century had been all but abandoned, and had fallen into a severe state of disrepair, would probably not be standing today were it not for the diligent conservationist efforts of the colonial British. In the second place, India is perfectly capable of over-merchandising itself.

When you arrive at the outer walls of the gardens in which the Taj is set, it's as if every hustler and hawker in Agra is waiting for you to make the familiarity-breeds-contempt problem worse, peddling imitation Mahals of every size and price. This leads to a certain amount of shoulder-shrugging disenchantment. Recently, a British friend who was about to make his first trip to India told me that he had decided to leave the Taj off his itinerary because of its over-exposure. If I urged him not to, it was because of my own vivid memory of pushing my way for the first time through the jostling crowd, not only of imitation-vendors but also of prescribed readings, past all the myriad hawkers of meaning and interpretation, and into the presence of the *thing-in-itself,* which utterly overwhelmed me and made all my notions about its de-valuation feel totally and completely redundant.

I had been skeptical about the visit. One of the legends of the Taj is that the hands of the master masons who built it were cut off by the emperor, so that they could never build anything lovelier. Another is that the mausoleum was constructed in secrecy behind high walls, and a man who tried to sneak a preview was blinded for his interest in ar-chitecture. My personal imagined Taj was somewhat tarnished by these cruel tales.

The building itself left my skepticism in shreds, however. Announc-ing itself as itself, insisting with absolute force on its sovereign au-thority, it simply obliterated the million million counterfeits of it and glowingly filled, once and forever, the place in the mind previously oc-cupied by its simulacra.

And this, finally, is why the Taj Mahal must be seen: to remind us that the world is real, that the sound is truer than the echo, the original more forceful than its image in a mirror. The beauty of beautiful things is still able, in these image-saturated times, to transcend imitations. And the Taj Mahal is, beyond the power of words to say it, a lovely thing, perhaps the loveliest of things.

June 1999

The Baburnama

Zahiruddin Muhammad Babur (1483–1530), the founder of the Mughal Empire in India, is best remembered for three things: the story of his death, the controversy over his mosque, and the extraordinary reputation of *The Baburnama,* his book.

I first heard the legend of Babur's death when I was still a boy. His son and heir Humayun was ill, the story went. His fever rose and the court's doctors despaired of saving him. Then Babur, after consulting a mystic, walked three times around Humayun's bed and offered himself to God in his son's place. Whereupon Humayun strengthened and recovered, and Babur weakened and—on December 21, 1530—died. This story struck me with an almost mythic force. I remember being horrified by Abraham's unnatural readiness to sacrifice his allegedly beloved son—Isaac according to the Old Testament, but Ismail in the Muslim version. Was that what the love of God made fathers willing to do? It was enough to make one regard one's own parent with a somewhat worried eye. Babur's story served as an antidote. Here the love of God was used to make possible the opposite and somehow more "natural" sacrifice: the father dying that the child might live. Babur and Humayun's story lodged deep within me as the paradigmatic tale of fatherly love.

These days, Babur's name is still associated with legends, but of a different and more controversial kind. The Babri Masjid, the mosque he built in Ayodhya, a city in what was once the kingdom of Awadh (Oudh) and is now the heartland state of Uttar Pradesh, was demolished in 1992 by Hindu extremists who believed that it had been built on the ruins of a Hindu temple sacred to the mythic hero of the Ramayana, Lord Ram (or Rama) himself; a temple, moreover, which had been constructed to mark the site of the Ramjanmabhoomi—the actual birthplace of the hero-god.

Ayodhya was indeed the name of Ram's city, whence he set forth to rescue his beloved Sita from her abductor, Lord Ravan. But there's little reason to believe that modern-day Ayodhya stands on the same site as the Ramayana's fabled realm. And, at the risk of rousing the ire of militant Hindus, there is no real proof that the mythological Lord Ram, an incarnation of the great god Vishnu, was a historical personage at all. Even the simplest facts remain in doubt; archaeologists disagree about the site, and as to it being the "real" Ramjanmabhoomi, that's about as likely as Christ being born in modern Bethlehem's Manger Square. (It is also pointed out that many Hindu temples in India are built over the ruins of Buddhist shrines.)

All these doubts and caveats are swept aside by the zealots' wrath. Babur, the bloodthirsty slayer of infidels, the devoted destroyer of temples, is in their eyes guilty as charged, and all India's Muslims are indirectly tainted by his crime. (There's a Hindu nationalist view that India is a country of many peoples: Hindus, Sikhs, Parsis, Buddhists, Jains, Christians—and Mughals.) They claim, moreover, that the Babri Masjid is only the first of the mosques on their hit list. In Mathura, they allege, another mosque stands on the demolished birthplace of another divinity—another incarnation of Vishnu, actually—Lord Krishna, he of the milkmaids and the lustrous blue skin.

The autobiography that is Babur's third and most enduring claim to fame is inconveniently silent—or, in the opinion of his more strident critics, conveniently so—on the time Babur spent in and around the Ayodhya region. In all surviving manuscripts there's a five-month gap between April and September 1528, the period during which Babur was in Oudh, and during which the Babri Masjid was built. Thus there's no proof that anything at all was demolished to build the mosque, or, alternatively, that it wasn't. In our paranoid age it's perhaps necessary to point out that there's nothing suspicious about this gap. Four hundred and seventy-plus years is a long time. Things get lost in four and a half centuries, sometimes the things (Thomas Kyd's *Hamlet,* for example) that we most want to find.

A man's character can get blurred by the passage of time. Where facts are insufficient, what fills the space is interpretation. Take two recent depictions of a single scene from the emperor's life: the temporary capture in the Punjab of the founder of Sikhism, Guru Nanak, by Babur's conquering army. The critic N. S. Rajaram, a deconstructionist of Indian "secularist myths," an apologist for the destruction of the Babri Masjid, and in general no fan of Babur's, writes that "in his *Babur Vani*, Nanak denounced him in no uncertain terms, giving a vivid account of Babur's vandalism in Aimanabad." Against this, Amitav Ghosh tells us in a recent essay that Sikhs

> have long cherished a story, preserved in their scriptural tradition, about an encounter between Babur and the founder of their faith, Guru Nanak. . . . Learning of a miracle performed by the Guru, Babur visited him in prison. Such was the presence of the Guru that Babur is said to have fallen at his feet, with the cry: "On the face of this faqir one sees God himself."

Ghosh concedes that Sikhs became "dedicated adversaries of the Mughal state in the seventeenth century" but argues powerfully that the flowering of Hinduism, including the Vaishnavite development of the theology and sacred geography of Krishna-worship, which took place in northern India under Babur and his successors, would have been impossible in a climate of persecution. "Hinduism would scarcely be recognizable today," Ghosh writes,

> if Vaishnavism had been actively suppressed in the sixteenth century: other devotional forms may have taken its place, but we cannot know what those would have been. It is a simple fact that contemporary Hinduism as a living practice would not be what it is if it were not for the devotional practices initiated under Mughal rule. The sad irony of the assault on the Babri mosque is that the Hindu fanatics who attacked it destroyed a symbol of the very accommodations that made their own beliefs possible.

Rajaram argues back, with almost equal force, that Babur

> was more than ordinarily ruthless. He pursued to the limit the concept of Jihad—a total war for the annihilation of his adversaries as prescribed by Islam of which he was a practitioner. He was a product

of his age and his environment, and that is exactly how we must see him. Whitewashing his blood-soaked record to turn him into a figure of chivalry and prince charming is an exercise in juvenile fantasy. Babur saw ruthlessness as a virtue, and terror as a useful tactical tool. In this he was a true descendant of Timur and Chengiz Khan—both of whom were his ancestors. Guru Nanak's eyewitness account gives a better picture of Babur and his methods than almost any modern history book. The same holds true for *The Baburnama*: it is a primary source of great importance that goes to demolish romantic tales about him.

(Somewhat coarsely, Rajaram reminds us that the phrase *Babur ki aulad,* "offspring of Babur," is a common term of abuse leveled at Indian Muslims.)

How contemporary this dispute sounds! Today, once again, we are tossed between Islam's apologists and detractors. In part because of these modern disagreements, those who would defend India's Muslims against the accusations of Hindu nationalists naturally stress the civilization and tolerance of Mughal Islam. As many writers have said, the dynasty Babur founded—his true *aulad*—was noted for its polytheistic inclusiveness. At the height of the Mughal Empire, Babur's grandson Akbar went so far as to invent a new creed—the Din-i-Illahi—that sought to be a fusion of all that was best in Indian spirituality. Against this, however, it's argued that the last of the so-called Grand Mughals, Aurangzeb, did his iconoclastic best to undo his predecessors' good work, rampaging across the country destroying temples. (Some of India's most precious antiquities, such as the temple complex at Khajuraho, survive only because in Aurangzeb's time these extraordinary edifices with their famous erotic carvings had faded from prominence and weren't marked on his maps.)

Who, then, was Babur—scholar or barbarian, nature-loving poet or terror-inspiring warlord? The answer is to be found in *The Baburnama,* and it's an uncomfortable one: he was both. It could be said that the struggle taking place within Islam in our own era, the struggle which has, I believe, been a feature of the history of Islam from its beginnings to the present day—between conservatism and progressivism, between Islam's male-dominated, aggressive, ruthless aspect and its gentler, deeply sophisticated culture of books, philosophers, musicians, and artists, that same contradictory doubleness which modern commentators have found so hard to understand—was, in the case of Babur, an internal conflict. Both Baburs are real, and perhaps the strangest thing about *The Baburnama* is that they do not seem to be at odds with one another. When the book's author looks inward and reflects, he is often melancholy, but the dark clouds that gather over him do not seem to be the product of a storm within. Mostly, they have to do with his sense of loss. The first Mughal emperor of India was also an exile and a homesick man. His soul pined for what we would now call Afghanistan.

Afghanistan's new significance in the world after September 11, 2001, changes the way we now read *The Baburnama*. Hitherto, the book's Indian section has been of most interest, with its firsthand account of the birth of an empire that lasted two hundred years, until the British supplanted it. But suddenly it is the work's "Afghan" beginnings that fascinate us. Place names from Kunduz to Kabul, made newly familiar by the bulletins of a modern war, leap out at us. The ancient treacheries of the region's warlords seem to have things to teach us about the power struggles of today. Babur is fascinatingly frank about all of this. (It's plain that in his time the best response to the death of a parent was to dive for cover and plot your siblings' death, knowing that those siblings would be filled with similarly loving thoughts about you.)

Yet this treacherous land was the place Babur loved. Read him on Kabul, "a petty little province," and vivid detail enlivens his simple declaratory sentences. "At the end of the canal is an area called Gulkana, a secluded, cozy spot where much debauchery is indulged in." *The Baburnama,* not unattractively, finds sex and booze wherever it goes. "Kabul wine is intoxicating. The wine from the slopes of Khwaja Khawand Sa'id mountain is known for being strong." Tropical and cold-weather fruits are eulogized, melons are disparaged, meadows are praised for being free of flies while others are flyblown and to be avoided. Mountain roads and passes, which became the subjects of nightly analyses on the world's media during the recent battles against the Taliban and Al-Qaida forces, are here meticulously described. Muskrats scuttle and partridges rise. A world leaps into view.

In India, which he so famously disliked, Babur's powers of description grow, if anything, stronger. Sometimes he succumbs to fantasy. "It is said that . . . there are elephants ten yards tall." Usually, however, he confines his remarks to what he has seen with his own eyes. "[Rhinoceroses] wield their horns in an amazing way. . . . During one hunt a page named Maqsud had his horse thrown a spear length by one. Thereafter he was nicknamed Rhinoceros Maqsud." He describes the cows, the monkeys, the birds, the fruits of India; but in spite of his evident respect for the "excellent" system of numbering and the "wonderful" systems of weights and measures, he can't resist going on to the attack. "Hindustan is a place of little charm. There is no beauty in its people . . . the arts and crafts have no harmony or symmetry. . . . There is no ice. . . . There are no baths." He likes the monsoon, but not the humidity. He likes the winter, but not the dust. The summer isn't as hot as it is in Balkh and Kandahar, and that's a plus. He admires the "craftsmen and practitioners of every trade." But what he likes most is the wealth. "The one nice aspect of Hindustan is that it is a large country with lots of gold and money."

The contradictions in Babur's personality are well illustrated by his account of the conquest of Chanderi in 1528. First comes a bloodthirsty description of the killing of many "infidels" and the apparent mass suicide of two or three hundred more. ("They killed each other almost to the last by having one man hold a sword while the others willingly bent their necks. . . . A tower of infidels' skulls was erected on the hill on the northwest side of Chanderi." Then, just three sentences later, we get this: "Chanderi is a superb place. All around the area are many flowing streams. . . . The lake . . . is renowned throughout Hindustan for its good, sweet water. It is truly a nice little lake."

The Western thinker whom Babur most resembles is his contemporary the Florentine Niccolò Machiavelli. In both men, a cold appreciation of the necessities of power, of what would today be called realpolitik, is combined with a deeply cultured and literary nature, not to mention the love, often to excess, of wine and women. Of course, Babur actually was a prince, not simply the author of *The Prince,* and could practice what he preached; while Machiavelli, the natural republican, the survivor of torture, was by far the more troubled spirit of the pair. Yet both these unwilling exiles were, as writers, blessed, or perhaps cursed, with a clear-sightedness that looks amoral, as truth so often does.

The Baburnama, the first autobiography in Islamic literature, was originally written in Chaghatay Turkish, the language of Babur's ancestor Temur-i-Lang, "lame Temur," better known in the West as Tamerlane. Wheeler M. Thackston's translation replaces the inadequate Beveridge version, and is so fluently readable, and so thoroughly backed up by the detailed scholarship of Thackston's many annotations, as to feel definitive. From Thackston's footnotes we learn about much that Babur leaves unsaid—about, for example, Persian verse forms such as the qasida and the ghazal; or peaked Mongolian caps; or the place in the heavens of the star Canopus. He is not afraid to argue with Babur. When Babur speculates that the name of a province, Lamghan, is derived from the Islamic version of the name of Noah, "Lamkan," Thackston ripostes: "He is quite mistaken in this, for the -ghan and -qan endings on so many toponyms in the area are of Iranian origin." Babur should feel well pleased to have so unsubmissive a translator and editor. A great translation can unveil—can, literally, dis-cover—a great book; and in Thackston's translation, one of the classic works of world literature arrives in English like a marvelous discovery.

January 2002

A Dream of Glorious Return

I have left India many times. The first time was when I was thirteen and a half and went to boarding school in Rugby, England. My mother didn't want me to go, but I said I did. I flew west excitedly in January 1961, not really knowing that I was taking a step that would change my life forever. A few years later, my father, without telling me, suddenly sold Windsor Villa, our family home in Bombay. The day I heard this, I felt an abyss open beneath my feet. I think that I never forgave my father for selling that house, and I'm sure that if he hadn't I would still be living in it. Since then my characters have frequently flown west from India, but in novel after novel their author's imagination has returned to it. This, perhaps, is what it means to love a country: that its shape is also yours, the shape of the way you think and feel and dream. That you can never really leave.

Before the Partition Massacres of 1947, my parents left Delhi and moved south, correctly calculating that there would be less trouble in secular, cosmopolitan Bombay. As a result I grew up in that tolerant, broad-minded city, whose particular quality—call it freedom—I've been trying to capture and celebrate ever since. *Midnight's Children* (1981) was my first attempt at such literary land reclamation. Living in London, I wanted to get India back; and the delight with which Indian readers clasped the book to themselves, the passion with which they, in turn, claimed me, remains the most precious memory of my writing life.

In 1988, I was planning to buy myself an Indian base with the advances I'd received for my new novel. But that novel was *The Satanic Verses,* and after it was published the world changed for me, and I was no longer able to set foot in the country that has been my primary source of artistic inspiration. Whenever I made inquiries about getting a visa, the word invariably came back that I would not be granted one. Nothing about my plague years, the dark decade that followed the Khomeini fatwa, has hurt more than this rift. I felt like a jilted lover left alone with his unrequited, unbearable love. You can measure love by the size of the hole it leaves behind.

It has been a deep rift, let's admit that. India was the first country to ban *The Satanic Verses*—which was proscribed without following India's own stipulated due process in such matters, banned before it entered the country by a weak Congress government led by Rajiv Gandhi, in a desperate, unsuccessful bid for Muslim votes. After that, it sometimes seemed as if the Indian authorities were determined to rub salt in the wound. When *The Moor's Last Sigh* was published in the fall of 1995, the Indian government, in an attempt to appease Bal Thackeray's brutal Shiv Sena in Bombay (which has done much to damage the city's old free-spirited openness, and which I therefore satirized in the novel), blocked the book's import through customs but backed down quickly when challenged in the courts. Then BBC Television's efforts to make a prestigious five-hour dramatization of *Midnight's Children,* with a screenplay I myself adapted from the novel, were thwarted when India refused permission to film. That *Midnight's Children* was deemed unfit to be filmed in its own country, the country which had so recently celebrated its publication with so much recognition and joy, was a bad and miserable shock.

There were smaller but still wounding slights. For years I was declared persona non grata by the Indian High Commission in London's cultural arm, the Nehru Centre. And at the time of the fiftieth anniversary of Indian independence, I was similarly barred from the Indian consulate's celebrations in New York.

Meanwhile, in some Indian literary quarters, it has become fashionable to denigrate my work. And the ban on *The Satanic Verses* is, of course, still in place.

———

After the September 24, 1998, agreement between the British and Iranian governments that effectively set aside the Khomeini fatwa, things began to change for me in India too. India granted me a five-year visa just over a year ago. But at once there were threats from Muslim hardliners like Imam Bukhari of the Delhi Juma Masjid. More worryingly, some commentators told me not to visit India because if I did so I might look like a pawn of the Hindu-nationalist Bharatiya Janata Party government. I have never been a BJP man, but that wouldn't stop them using me for their own sectarian ends.

"Exile," it says somewhere in *The Satanic Verses,* "is a dream of glorious return." But the dream fades, the imagined return stops feeling glorious. The dreamer awakes. I almost gave up on India, almost believed the love affair was over for good.

But, as it turns out, not so. As it turns out, I'm about to leave for Delhi after a gap of twelve and a half years. My son Zafar, twenty, is coming with me. He hasn't been to India since he was three, and is very excited. Compared to me, however, he's the very picture of coolness and calm.

FRIDAY, APRIL 7

The telephone rings. The Delhi police are extremely nervous about my impending arrival. Can I please avoid being spotted on the plane? My bald head is very recognizable; will I please wear a hat? My eyes are also easily identified; will I please wear sunglasses? Oh, and my beard, too, is a real giveaway; will I wear a scarf around that? The temperature in India is close to 100°F, I point out: a scarf might prove a little warm. Oh, but there are cotton scarves . . .

These requests are relayed to me in a don't-shoot-the-messenger voice by my usually unflappable Indian attorney, Vijay Shankardass. How about, I suggest hotly, if I just spend the entire journey with my head in a paper bag? "Salman," says Vijay, carefully, "there's a lot of tension out here. I'm feeling fairly anxious myself."

The organizers of the Commonwealth Writers' Prize, at whose invitation I am traveling to Delhi, are sending mixed messages. Mr. Pavan Varma, a civil servant who is also in charge of media relations for the event, ignores all requests for discretion and holds a press conference to say that I'll probably be at the prize banquet. Contrariwise, Colin Ball, head of the Commonwealth Foundation, whose prize it is, tells Vijay that if police protection is not extended to all the twenty or so foreign visitors arriving at Claridge's Hotel for the ceremony, he may have to withdraw my invitation, even though I won't be staying at Claridge's, and nobody has ever threatened the delegates, who are not deemed by the Indian authorities to be in any danger. The only threats around right now are Mr. Ball's.

I'm going to India because things are better now and I judge that it's time to go. I'm going because if I don't go I'll never know if it's okay to go or not. I'm going because in spite of everything that has happened between India and myself, in spite of the bruises on my heart, the hook of love is in too deeply to pull out. Most of all, I'm going because Zafar asked to come with me. High time he was reintroduced to his other country.

But the truth is I don't know what to expect. Will I feel welcomed or spurned? *I don't know if I'm going back to say hello or good-bye.* Oh, stop being so melodramatic, Salman. Don't meet trouble halfway. Just get on the plane and go.

So: I fly to Delhi, and nobody sees me do it. Here's the invisible man in his business class seat. Here he is, watching the new Pedro Almodóvar movie on a little pop-up screen, while the plane flies over, er, Iran. Here's the invisible man sleep-masked and snoring.

And here I am at journey's end, stepping out into the heat of Delhi's international airport with Zafar at my side, and only Vijay Shankardass can see us. *Abracadabra!* Magic realism rules. Don't ask me how it's done. The shrewd conjurer never explains the trick.

I feel an urge to kiss the ground or, rather, the blue rug in the airport "finger," but am embarrassed to do so beneath the watchful eyes of a small army of security guards. Leaving the rug unkissed, I move out of the terminal into the blazing, bone-dry Delhi heat, so different from the wet-towel humidity of my native Bombay. The hot day enfolds us like an embrace. A road unrolls before us like a carpet. We climb into a cramped, white Hindustan Ambassador, a car that is itself a blast from the past, the British Morris Oxford, long defunct in Britain but alive and well here in this Indian translation. The Ambassador's air-conditioning system isn't working.

I'm back.

SATURDAY, APRIL 8

India doesn't stand on ceremony, and rushes in from every direction, thrusting me into the middle of its unending argument, clamoring for my total attention as it always did. *Buy Chilly cockroach traps! Drink Hello mineral water! Speed Thrills But Kills!* shout the billboards. There are new kinds of messages, too. *Enroll for Oracle 81. Graduate with Java as well.* And, as proof that the long protectionist years are over, Coca-Cola is back with a vengeance. When I was last here it was banned, leaving the field clear for the disgusting local imitations, Campa-Cola and Thums Up. Now there's a red Coke ad every hundred yards or so. Coke's slogan of the moment is written in Hindi transliterated into Roman script: *Jo Chaho Ho Jaaye.* Which could be translated, literally, as "whatever you desire, let it come to pass."

I choose to think of this as a blessing.

HORN PLEASE, demand the signs on the backs of the one million trucks blocking the road. All the other trucks, cars, bikes, motor-scooters, taxis, and *phut-phut* autorickshaws enthusiastically respond, welcoming Zafar and me to town with an energetic rendition of the traditional symphony of the Indian street.

Wait for Side! Sorry-Bye-Bye! Fatta Boy!

The news is just as cacophonous. Between India and Pakistan, as usual, acrimony reigns. Pakistan's ex–Prime Minister Nawaz Sharif has just been sentenced to life imprisonment after what looked very like a show trial stage-managed by the latest military strongman to seize power, General Pervez Musharraf. India's army of vociferous commentators, linking this story to the unveiling by Pakistan of a new missile, the Shaheen-II, warn darkly of the worsening relations between the two countries. A politician from the Bharatiya Janata Party (BJP) accuses Imam Bukhari of "seditious utterances" for some allegedly pro-Pakistani, anti-Indian statements. *Plus ça change.* Tempers, as ever, run high.

Inevitably, Bill Clinton, on his recent visit to the subcontinent, was drawn into these old antagonisms. From an Indian point of view, he said most of the right things. In particular, his toughness toward Pakistan, its dictatorship, its nuclear bomb, its illiberalism, won him many friends, and this after many years during which Indians were convinced that the basis of American foreign policy in the region was, in Dr. Kissinger's phrase, to "tilt toward Pakistan."

India is, on the whole, basking in the afterglow of the Clinton visit when I arrive. The roseate old charmer has done it again. Bombay's movie world is agog. "Hindustani hearts," reports a showbiz magazine in the city's inimitable prose style, "went bonkers over the Grand daddy of Uncle Sam." A starlet, Suman Ranganathan, variously described as a "sexy babe" and "apni sizzling mirchi," that is, "our very own sizzling hot chili," is much taken by Big Bill, who is, she declares, "amazing, approachable, and someone who knows the pulse of the people."

In India, as my friend the distinguished art critic Geeta Kapur reminds me, people have very rarely been bothered by politicians' private lives. One very senior BJP leader is known to have kept a mistress for years without it affecting his career in the slightest. Indians, therefore, view the Lewinsky scandal with bemused puzzlement. If various hot chilis choose to sizzle at the world's most powerful man, who could be surprised?

—

I've been back only for an instant, and already everyone I talk to—Vijay Shankardass, friends I'm eagerly ringing up to announce my arrival, even policemen—is regaling me with opinions on the new shape of Indian politics. If Bombay is India's New York—glamorous, glitzy, vulgar-chic, a merchant city, a movie city, a slum city, incredibly rich, hideously poor—then Delhi is like Washington. Politics is the only game in town. Nobody talks about anything else for very long.

Once, India's minorities looked for protection to the left-leaning Congress, then the country's only organized political machine. Now the disarray of the Congress Party, and its drift to the right, is everywhere apparent. Under the leadership of Sonia Gandhi, the once mighty machine languishes and rusts.

People who have known Sonia for years urge me not to swallow the line that she was never interested in politics and allowed herself to be drafted into the leadership only because of her concern for the party. A portrait is painted of a woman completely seduced by power but unable to wield it, lacking the skill, charm, vision, indeed everything except the hunger for power itself. Around her fawn the sycophantic courtiers of the Nehru-Gandhi dynasty, working to prevent the emergence of new leaders—P. S. Chidambaram, Madhavrao Scindia, Rajesh Pilot—who just might have the freshness and will to revive the party's fortunes, but who cannot be permitted to usurp the leadership role that, in the Sonia clique's view, belongs to her and her children alone.

I was last in India in August 1987, making a television documentary about the fortieth anniversary of Independence. I have never forgotten being at the Red Fort listening to Rajiv Gandhi delivering a stunningly tedious oration in broken schoolboy Hindi, while the audience simply and crushingly walked away. Now, here on television is his widow, her Hindi even more broken than his, a woman convinced of her right to rule but convincing almost nobody except herself.

I remember another widow. In that 1987 documentary we included an interview with a Sikh woman, Ravel Kaur, who had seen her husband and sons murdered before her eyes by gangs known to be led and organized by Congress people. Indira Gandhi had recently been assassinated by her Sikh bodyguards, and the whole Sikh community of Delhi was paying the price. The Rajiv Gandhi government prosecuted nobody for these murders, in spite of much hard evidence identifying many of the killers.

For Vijay Shankardass, who had known Rajiv for years, those were disillusioning days. He and his wife hid their Sikh neighbors in their own home to keep them safe. He went to see Rajiv to demand that something be done to stop the killings, and was deeply shocked by Rajiv's seeming indifference. "Salman, he was so *calm.*" One of Rajiv's close aides, Arjun Das, was less placid. *"Saalón ko phoonk do,"* he snarled. "Blow the bastards away." Later, he too was killed.

Through the Indian High Commission in London (my friend and namesake, Salman Haidar, then the deputy high commissioner, was pressed into censorious service), the Rajiv government did its level best to prevent our film from being shown, because of the interview with the Sikh widow. Even though she was no Sikh terrorist but a victim of anti-Sikh terrorism; even though she remained opposed to radical Sikh demands for a state of their own, and asked no more than justice for the dead, India sought to stifle her voice. And, I'm pleased to say, failed.

So many widows. In *Midnight's Children,* I satirized the first widow to take power in India, Mrs. Indira Gandhi, for her abuse of that power during the quasi-dictatorial Emergency years in the mid-seventies. I could not have foreseen how resonant—by turns tragic and bathetic— the trope of the widow would continue to be.

Widows also feature prominently in the Indian Canadian film director Deepa Mehta's unfinished film *Water,* which is partly set in a widows' hostel in the holy city of Benares, where bereaved women come to pray and mourn by the banks of the sacred Ganges. Threats of violence from extremist Hindu groups stopped the filming. Mehta has abandoned her efforts to complete the picture and returned to Canada in despair.

Years ago, the climactic scenes of *Midnight's Children* were also set in a Benares widows' hostel. This, of course, is pure coincidence, but another writer, Sunil Gangopadhyay of Bengal, is making serious allegations against Deepa Mehta. He accuses her of plagiarism, claiming that substantial passages of his novel *Those Days* have been "lifted" and incorporated in Ms. Mehta's screenplay. She accepts that she was "inspired" by Gangopadhyay's book but denies the charge of plagiarism. The author's translator, Aruna Chakravati, retorts that Mehta's screenplay is far inferior to Gangopadhyay's epic historical novel: not "enlightened" but "stagnant."

The plagiarism charge is one reason why much of the Indian cultural elite has given Deepa Mehta only halfhearted support against her bully-boy opponents. People say she shouldn't have sought to ingratiate herself with the BJP's information minister, Arun Jaitley, who, like the BJP in general, is abhorred by much of the arts community. Also that she did herself and her movie no favors by making so many outspoken public statements, which hardened her opponents' attitudes and made it less likely that the film would ever be completed. She should have got her film made first and screamed later, people say.

The painter Vivan Sundaram argues that the episode shows us with great clarity the two faces of the BJP: the "moderate" stance of Atul Behari Vajpayee's government, which initially gave the filmmaker permission to film, and the "hard-line" position of the party's rank and file, whose gangs threw part of the film set into the Ganges and threatened Mehta's life, until the BJP leadership was forced to stop the filming.

—

Congress has strange bedfellows these days. Its decay can perhaps best be measured by the poor quality of its allies. In the state of Bihar, the bizarre political double-act of Laloo Prasad Yadav and his wife, Rabri Devi—on whom the wholly fictitious, and wildly corrupt, Bombay politicians Piloo and Golmatol Doodhwala in *The Ground Beneath Her Feet* were very loosely modeled—is once again taking center stage. Some years ago, Laloo, then Bihar's chief minister, was implicated in the Fodder Scam, a swindle in which large amounts of public livestock subsidies were claimed for the maintenance of cows that didn't actually exist. (In my novel, Piloo, India's "Scambaba Deluxe," runs a similar scheme involving non-existent goats.) Laloo was jailed but managed to secure the chief ministership for Rabri, and blithely went on running the state, by proxy, from his prison cell.

Since then he has been in and out of the clink. At present he's inside, and Rabri is at least technically in the driving seat, and another juicy corruption scandal is emerging. The tax authorities want to know how Laloo and Rabri manage to live in such high style (they have a particularly grand house) on the relatively humble salaries that even senior ministers in India pull down. Rabri has been "chargesheeted"—indicted—but refuses to resign; or rather, Laloo, from jail, announces that there is no question of his wife the chief minister vacating her post.

As a writer with satirical inclinations, I'm delighted by the Yadav saga, the barefaced skulduggery of it, the shameless wholeheartedness, the glee with which Laloo and Rabri just go on being their appalling selves. But their survival is also a sign of the growing corruption of Indian political culture. This is a country in which known gangsters have been elected to the national parliament, and where a man who runs a state from his prison cell can receive the vocal support of no less a figure than the Congress Party leader, Sonia Gandhi herself.

SUNDAY, APRIL 9

*Z*afar at twenty is a big, gentle young man who, unlike his father, keeps his emotions concealed. But he is a deeply feeling fellow and is engaging with India seriously, attentively, beginning the process of making his own portrait of it, which may unlock in him an as yet unknown other self.

At first he notices what first-time visitors notice: the terrible poverty of the families living by the railway tracks in what look like trash cans and bin liners, the men holding hands in the street, the "terrible" quality of Indian MTV and the "awful" Bollywood movies. We pass through the sprawling Army cantonment and he asks if the armed forces are as much of a political factor here as they are in neighboring Pakistan, and looks impressed when I tell him that soldiers in India have never sought political power.

I can't tempt him into Indian national dress. I myself put on a cool, loose kurta-pajama outfit the moment I arrive, but Zafar is mutinous. "It's just not my style," he insists, preferring to stay in his young Londoner's uniform of T-shirt, cargo pants, and sneakers. (By the end of the trip he is wearing the white pajamas, but not the kurtas; still, progress of a kind has been made.)

Zafar has never read more than the first three chapters of *Midnight's Children* in spite of its dedication ("For Zafar Rushdie who, contrary to all expectations, was born in the afternoon"). In fact, apart from *Haroun and the Sea of Stories* and *East, West,* he hasn't finished any of my books. The children of writers are often this way. They need their parents to be parents, not novelists. Zafar has always had a complete set of my books proudly on display in his room, but he reads Alex Garland and Bill Bryson and I pretend not to care.

Now, poor fellow, he's getting a crash course in my work as well as my life. In the Red Fort after Partition, my aunt and uncle, like many Muslims, had to be protected by the Army from the violence raging outside; a version of this appears in my novel *Shame*. And here, off Chandni Chowk, the bustling main street of Old Delhi, are the lanes winding into the old Muslim *mohallas* or neighborhoods in one of which, Ballimaran, my parents lived before they moved to Bombay; and it's also where Ahmed and Amina Sinai, the parents of the narrator of *Midnight's Children,* faced the gathering pre-Independence storm.

Zafar takes all this literary tourism in good part. Look, here at Purana Qila, the Old Fort supposedly built on the site of the legendary city of Indraprastha, is where Ahmed Sinai left a sack of money to appease a gang of arsonist blackmailers. Look, there are the monkeys who ripped up the sack and threw the money away. Look, here at the National Gallery of Modern Art are the paintings of Amrita Sher-Gil, the half-Indian, half-Hungarian artist who inspired the character of Aurora Zogoiby in *The Moor's Last Sigh* . . . Okay, enough, Dad, he plainly thinks but is too nice to say. Okay, I'll read them, this time I really will. (He probably won't.)

There are signs at the Red Fort advertising an evening *son et lumière* show. "If Mum was here," he says suddenly, "she'd insist on coming to that." Zafar's bright, beautiful mother, my first wife, Clarissa Luard, the British Arts Council's highly esteemed literature officer, guardian angel of young writers and little magazines, died of a recurrence of breast cancer last November, aged just fifty. Zafar and I had spent most of her final hours by her bedside. He was her only child.

"Well," I say, "she was here, you know." In 1974, Clarissa and I spent more than four months traveling around India, roughing it in cheap hotels and long-distance buses, using the advance I'd received for my first novel, *Grimus,* to finance the trip, and trying to stretch the money as far as it would go. Now, I begin to make a point of telling Zafar what his mother thought of this or that—how much she liked the serenity of this spot, or the hubbub over there. What began as a little father-and-son expedition acquires an extra dimension.

———

I've always known that, after everything that has happened, this first visit would be the trickiest. Don't overreach yourself, I thought. If it goes well, things should ease. The second visit? "Rushdie returns again" isn't much of a news story. And the third—"Oh, here he is once more"—barely sounds like news at all. In the long slog back to "normality," habituation, even boredom, has been a useful weapon. "I intend," I start telling people in India, "to bore India into submission."

I should have worked out that if I myself was a little uncertain of how things would go, everyone around me would be in a blue funk. Things have improved in England and America, and normal service has very largely been resumed. I have grown unaccustomed to the problems of a maximum-security protection operation. What's happening in India feels, in this regard, like entering a time warp and being taken back to the bad old early days of the Iranian attack.

My protection team couldn't be nicer or more efficient, but gosh, there are a lot of them, and they are jumpy. In Old Delhi, where many Muslims live, they are especially on edge, particularly whenever, in spite of my cloak of invisibility, a member of the public commits the faux pas of recognizing me.

"Sir, there has been exposure! Exposure has occurred!" my protectors mourn. "Sir, they have said the name, sir! The name has been spoken!" "Sir, please, the hat!"

It's useless to point out that I do tend to get recognized a fair bit because, well, I look like this and other people don't; or that, on every single "exposure," the reaction of the persons concerned has been friendly, even delighted. My protectors have a nightmare scenario in their heads—rioting mobs, et cetera—and mere real life isn't enough to wipe it away.

This has been one of the most frustrating aspects of the last few years.

People—journalists, policemen, friends, strangers—all write scripts for me, and I get trapped inside those fantasies. What none of the scenarists ever seems to come up with is the possibility of a happy ending—one in which the problems I've faced are gradually overcome, and I resume the ordinary literary life that is all I've ever wanted. Yet this, the wholly unanticipated story line, is what has actually transpired.

My biggest problem these days is waiting for everyone to let go of their nightmares and catch up with the facts.

—

I dine with Vivan Sundaram and Geeta Kapur, at their home in the Shanti Niketan district of South Delhi. Before I go, I am required by the police to ask Vivan and Geeta not to tell anyone I'm coming. During our meal, they are telephoned by a senior police officer who asks them not to tell anyone I've been there. The next day, they receive another follow-up phone call urging discretion. They are amused, but I am irritated. This is getting ridiculous.

Vivan is Amrita Sher-Gil's nephew, and some of her best canvases are on the walls of his home, as is his own luminous family portrait of Amrita's world. This is a big picture set in the Sher-Gil drawing room, and it's a work that endlessly draws you in yet remains beautifully mysterious. The directness of Amrita's gaze—she alone looks straight out of the picture at us—is balanced by the dreamlike inwardness of the other family members. A lost-world atmosphere pervades the room, at once golden and stifling; and there is the gun. I have a passion for contemporary Indian art, and just to see this great painting again feels like a homecoming.

"So, do things feel different?" Vivan asks, and I say, not as much as I thought they would. People don't change, the heart of the place is the same. But of course there are changes. One friend has been gravely ill but is recovering. Another dear friend is still seriously unwell. And of course the obvious changes. The BJP in power. The new technology boom that has given even more impetus and affluence to the Indian bourgeoisie.

I mention Clinton's visit, which Geeta and Vivan portray as a defining moment for the rich India that has grown exponentially since my last visit, fueled by new technology. In America, 40 percent of the people working in Silicon Valley are now of Indian origin, and in India itself the new electronic age has made many fortunes. Clinton lavished praise on these new techno-boomers, making a point of visiting Hyderabad, one of the new boomtowns. For the Indian rich, his coming was both a validation and an apotheosis.

"You can't believe how they loved it," Geeta says. "So many people longing to bow down and say, sir, sir, we just love America."

"India and the U.S. as the two great democracies," Vivan adds. "India and America as partners and equals. That was the idea, and it was said without any sense of irony at all."

The India that remains in thrall to religious-communalist sectarians of the most extreme and medievalist type; the India that's fighting something like a civil war in Kashmir; the India that cannot feed or educate or give proper medical care to its people; the India that can't provide its citizens with drinkable water; the India in which the absence of simple toilet facilities obliges millions of women to control their natural functions so that they can relieve themselves under cover of darkness; these Indias were not paraded before the president of the United States. Instead, gung-ho nuclear India, fat-cat entrepreneurial India, super-nerd computer-India, glam-rock high-life India all pirouetted and twirled in the international media spotlight that accompanies the Leader of the Free World wherever he goes.

MONDAY, APRIL 10

A somewhat paranoid start to my day. I learn that the head of the British Council in India, Colin Perchard, has refused me permission to use the council's auditorium for a press conference at the end of the week. In addition, the British high commissioner, Sir Rob Young, has been instructed by the Foreign Office to stay away from me—he is "not to come out of the stables," he tells Vijay.

Robin Cook, the British foreign secretary, is arriving in India the day I am due to leave and, it would appear, is anxious not to be too closely associated with me. He is scheduled to travel to Iran soon, and naturally that trip must not be compromised. (Later: Cook's trip is canceled anyway, because of the closed-court "spy trials" of Jews in Iran. So it goes.)

Better news comes from the Commonwealth Foundation's Colin Ball, who has moderated his stance and is no longer threatening to withdraw my invitation to his awards dinner. Like Cinderella, it would appear, I shall go to the Ball. But in my paranoid mood I think that if the foundation is so nervous about my mere presence, they are unlikely to want the closer association with me that giving me the prize would inevitably create.

I remind myself why I'm really here. The Commonwealth Writers' Prize is only a pretext. To have made this trip with Zafar is the real victory. For both of us, India is the prize.

—

The Hansie Cronje cricket scandal pushes politics off the front pages and my own little grumbles out of my head. Cronje, the captain of the South African cricket team and poster boy for the new South Africa, is being accused by the Indian police of having been involved, along with three of his teammates, Herschelle Gibbs, Nicky Boje, and Pieter Strydom, of taking money from the Indian bookies Sanjiv Chawla and Rajesh Kalra to fix the results of one-day international games.

It's sensational news. The Indian police claim to have transcripts of telephone conversations that leave no room for doubt. There are hints of a link to underworld crime-syndicate bosses like the notorious Dawood Ibrahim. People start speculating about this being the tip of an enormous iceberg. Can cricket itself survive if spectators don't know if they're watching a fair contest or a sort of pro-wrestling bout in white flannels? "We treated them like gods," a fan says, "and they turned out to be crooks."

Rumors of match-fixing have been flying around for years, clouding the reputations of some of the game's leading players: Pakistan's Salim Malik, Australia's Shane Warne, and India's own former captain, Mohammed Azharuddin, who was accused of corruption by a teammate, Manoj Prabhakar. A former England international star, Chris Lewis, has given the British cricket authorities the names of three allegedly corrupt England stars. (These names have not been made public.) But, so far, none of the charges have been proven, and not much of the mud has stuck.

It's no secret that as the one-day version of the game has become a big money-spinner, and as the numbers of such matches have proliferated, the interest of Far Eastern betting syndicates and bookmakers with underworld links has grown. But no cricket-lover wants to believe that his heroes are jerks. Such chosen blindness is a form of corruption, too.

Within moments, the denials begin. Hansie is a gent, clean as a whistle, honest as the day is long. And why were Indian policemen bugging South African players' phones in the first place? And the voices on the tapes don't even sound South African.

Cronje himself gives a press conference denying the charges, insisting that his teammates and his bank accounts will confirm that he never tried to throw a match or received any cash for doing so. And behind all the backlash is what sounds, to Indian ears, suspiciously like racism. Commentators from the white cricket-playing countries have been the fastest out of the blocks, rubbishing the allegations, casting doubt on the professionalism and even the integrity of the Indian policemen investigating the case.

The officer in charge of my protection team is the kindly-natured Akshey Kumar, who loves literature, can speak with knowledge about the work of Vikram Seth and Vikram Chandra, Rohinton Mistry and Arundhati Roy, and is proud of having two daughters at college in Boston, at Tufts. K. K. Paul, who has been running the Cronje investigation, is a friend of his, a superb detective, says Kumar, and a man of great probity. What's more, South Africa being a friendly nation, the Indian authorities would never allow these accusations to be made public unless they're 110 percent convinced of the strength of the case that Paul and his team have built. Therefore, Kumar advises with great prescience, just wait on and see.

—

We're off on a road trip to show the boy the sights: Jaipur, Fatehpur Sikri, Agra. For me, the road itself has always been the main attraction.

There are more trucks than I remembered, many more, blaring and lethal, often driving straight at us down the wrong side of the carriageway. There are wrecks from head-on smashes every few miles. Look, Zafar, that is the shrine of a prominent Muslim saint; all the truckers stop there and pray for luck, even the Hindus. Then they get back into their cabs and take hideous risks with their lives and ours as well.

Look, Zafar, that is a tractor-trolley loaded with men. At election time the *sarpanch* or headman of every village is ordered to provide such trolleyloads for politicians' rallies. For Sonia Gandhi, ten tractor-trolleys per village is the requirement. People are so disillusioned with politicians these days that nobody would actually go to the rallies of their own free will.

Look, those are the polluting chimneys of brick kilns smoking in the fields. Outside the city the air is less filthy, but it still isn't clean. But in Bombay between December and February, think of this, aircraft can't land or take off before 11:00 A.M. because of the smog.

The new age is here all right. Zafar, if you could read Hindi you'd see the new age's new words being phonetically transliterated into that language's Devanagiri script: *Millennium Tires. Oasis Cellular. Modern's Chinese "Fastfood."*

He wants to learn Hindi. He is good at languages and wants to learn Hindi and Urdu and come back without all the paraphernalia that presently surrounds us: without, to be blunt, me. Good. He's got the bug. Once India bites you, Zafar, you'll never be cured.

Behold, Zafar, the incomprehensible acronyms of India. What is a WAKF board? What is an HSIDC? But one acronym reveals a genuine shift in reality. You see it everywhere now, every hundred yards or so: STD-ISD-PCO. PCO is personal call office, and now anyone can pop into one of these little booths, make calls to anywhere in India or, indeed, the world, and pay on the way out. This is the genuine communications revolution of India. Nobody need be isolated anymore.

In the roadside *dhabas* where we stop for refreshments, they're talking about Hansie Cronje. Nobody is in any doubt that he is guilty as sin.

———

Bill Clinton visited the hilltop fortress-palace of Amber, outside Jaipur, but his security people wouldn't allow him to indulge in the famous local tourist treat. At the bottom of Amber's hill is a taxi-rank of elephants. You buy a ticket at the Office of Elephant Booking and then lurch uphill on the back of your rented pachyderm. Where the president failed, Zafar and I succeed. I feel glad to know—in a moment of schadenfreude—that somebody else's security was tighter and more restrictive than mine.

Clinton did, however, watch dancing girls twirling and cavorting for him in Amber's Saffron Garden. He'd have liked that. Rajasthan is colorful. People wear colorful clothes and perform colorful dances and ride on colorful elephants to colorful ancient palaces, and these are things a president should know.

He should also know that at a test site near Pokhran in Rajasthan's Thar desert Indian know-how brought India into the nuclear age. Rajasthan is, therefore, the cradle of the new India that must be thought of as America's partner and equal. (Clinton did raise the subject of the Test Ban Treaty but failed to persuade India to sign. After all, the United States hasn't ratified it, either.)

What should not be drawn to Clinton's attention—because it has no place in either the colorful, touristic, elephant-taxi India or the new, thrusting, Internet-billionaire, entrepreneurial India that is presently being sold to the world—is that Rajasthan, along with its neighboring state of Gujarat, is currently dying of thirst, in the grip of the worst drought for over a century.

What the president must not be permitted even to think is that the money spent on India's ridiculous Bomb could have helped care for and feed the sick and hungry. Or that it's absurd for Prime Minister Vajpayee to appeal to the people of India to help fight the massive destruction wrought by the drought by making charitable contributions, "no matter how small," while the Indian government is still spending a fortune on Rajasthan's other weapon of mass destruction.

It's hot: almost 110°F, over 40°C. The rains have failed for the last two years, and it's still two months to the next monsoon. Wells are running dry, and villagers are being forced to drink dirty water, which gives them diarrhea, which causes dehydration, and so the vicious circle tightens its grip.

When I was last here, a dozen years ago, the region was in the grip of the previous worst-ever drought. I traveled in Gujarat then and saw much the same sort of devastation as is apparent everywhere in rural Rajasthan today. As the gulf between the feast of the haves and the famine of the have-nots widens, the stability of the country must be more and more at risk. I have been smelling a difference in the air, and reluctant as I am to put into words what isn't much more than an instinct, I do feel a greater volatility in people, a crackle of anger just below the surface, a shorter fuse.

At dinner, Zafar eats a bad shrimp. I blame myself. I should have known to remind him of the basic rules for travelers in India: always drink bottled water, make sure you see the seal on the bottle being broken in front of you, never eat salad (it won't have been washed in bottled water), never put ice in your drinks (it won't have been made with bottled water) . . . and *never, never eat seafood unless you're by the sea.*

Zafar's desert shrimp knocks him flat. He has a sleepless night: vomiting, diarrhetic. In the morning he looks terrible, and we have a long, hard journey ahead of us, on bumpy, difficult roads. Now he, too, needs to guard against dehydration. Unlike the villagers we're leaving behind, however, we have plenty of bottled water to drink, and proper medication. And, of course, we're leaving.

TUESDAY, APRIL 11

A day to grind through. Long, grueling journey to Agra, then back to Delhi. Zafar suffers but remains stoical. He's too weak to walk around the magnificent Fatehpur Sikri site, and only just manages to drag himself around the Taj, which he declares to be smaller than expected. I am very relieved when I can finally get him into a comfortable hotel bed.

I turn on the television news. Cronje has confessed.

WEDNESDAY, APRIL 12

CRONJE: I AM A CROOK say the banner headlines in the morning papers. The erstwhile cricketing demigod has admitted to having feet of clay: he has "been dishonest," he has taken money, and now he has been fired from the South African captaincy and kicked out of the national team. K. K. Paul and his men have been thoroughly and dramatically vindicated.

The money Cronje took was paltry, as it turns out: a mere $8,200. Not much of a price for a man's good name.

Meanwhile, back in South Africa, the predominantly white cricket-loving public (South African blacks are much more interested in soccer) rallies behind its beloved Hansie. Put him back in the team, say the opinion polls, and the media, too, back him to the hilt. In Durban, a crowd of whites attacks Sadha Govender, chairman of the KwaZulu-Natal Cricket Development Programme, who is repeatedly slapped and kicked. "Charros brought Cronje down," the whites shout. (Govender is of Indian origin. Charros are Indians.)

Hansie Cronje's locker-room nickname—given him long before the present scandal—was Crime. As in crime doesn't pay. He was notoriously stingy, the story goes, about buying a round of drinks. Now, as the South African government moves toward agreeing to his extradition to stand trial in India, and his lawyers warn him to expect a jail term, he must have started thinking of that nickname as a prophecy.

I am impressed by the relative lack of triumphalism in the Indian response to Cronje's downfall. "What are we gloating over?" warns Siddharth Saxena in *The Hindustan Times*: meaning, let's not be self-righteous about this. The bookmakers were Indians, after all, and in the revelations that should now begin to flood out, we may learn that we're no angels, either. One of the bookies, Rajesh Khalra, is already under arrest, and a suspected middleman, the movie actor Kishen Kumar, will be arrested as soon as he gets out of the hospital, where he is being treated for a sudden heart problem.

At a roadside *dhaba* earlier today, Zafar saw a smiling young man in a Pepsi poster. "Who's that?" he wanted to know. "That" was Sachin Tendulkar, India's great cricketing superstar, the best batsman in the world. My God, I thought, if one day a scandal should touch Tendulkar, it really would destroy the game. People wouldn't be able to stand it.

Another alleged go-between, Hamid "Banjo" Cassim, a South African businessman, is named by the Indian police. He is said to have links with the bookie Sanjiv Chawla, as well as Mohammed Azharuddin . . . and Sachin Tendulkar. Azharuddin's and Tendulkar's denials of wrong-doing are instant and furious, and nobody actually accuses them of anything. But a shadow falls across the sun.

———

Roper Starch Worldwide, a market research agency, has issued a World Happiness Barometer. On average, apparently, just 24 percent of the world's population describes itself as happy. The happiest countries are the USA (46 percent), India (37 percent), and the United Kingdom (36 percent). India's in the Happiness Silver Medal Position! Her right to a place at the world's top table is confirmed!

The unhappiest countries in the world are China (9 percent) and Russia (3 percent). Figures for the present happiness level of cricket fans in South Africa are not included.

———

India's national happiness level has been raised, this morning, by the good news that Indian-born Jhumpa Lahiri has won the Pulitzer Prize for her first book of stories, *The Interpreter of Maladies*. She's on the front page of every paper, beaming at her good fortune, and in spite of the somewhat ambiguous attitude in these parts to the work "Diaspora Indians," she is given glowing write-ups everywhere. She is a very talented writer, and I share the general feeling of pride in her achievement.

———

Sri Lanka wants the United Kingdom branded a terrorist state, because it harbors so many terrorist groups: the LTTE (Tamil Tigers), Hamas from Palestine, the Kurdish PKK, the Kashmiri Harkat-ul-Ansar, and, according to the Sri Lankans, sixteen other groups on the U.S. terrorism list. I can't help feeling that Sri Lanka has a point. The United States is presently accusing Pakistan and Afghanistan of forming a "terror hub" because they give house room to Osama bin Laden and various Kashmiri separatists. If it isn't too sad-sack a question in the midst of all this happiness, why isn't Britain being "chargesheeted" as well?

———

Sometime in the 1930s my paternal grandfather, Mohammed Din Khaliqi, a successful Delhi businessman, acquired a hot-season retreat for his family, a modest stone cottage in the pretty little town of Solan in the Shimla Hills. He named it Anis Villa after his only son, Anis Ahmed. That son, my father, who later took the surname Rushdie, gifted the house to me on my twenty-first birthday. And eleven years ago, the state government of Himachal Pradesh took it over without so much as a by-your-leave.

It isn't easy to seize a man's property in India, even for a state government. In order to get hold of Anis Villa, the local authorities falsely declared it to be "evacuee property." The law pertaining to evacuee property was devised after Partition to enable the state to take possession of homes left behind by individuals and families who had gone to Pakistan. This law did not apply to me. I was an Indian citizen until I became a British one by naturalization, and I have never held a Pakistani passport or been a resident of that country. Anis Villa had been wrongfully seized, and provably so.

Vijay Shankardass and I became close friends because of Solan. One of the most distinguished attorneys in India with, incidentally, a proud history of anti-censorship victories to his name, he took on the Himachal authorities on my behalf. The case took seven years, and we won. Both parts of this sentence are impressive. Seven years, by Indian standards, is *incredibly fast*. And to defeat a government, even when right is quite clearly on your side, takes some doing. Vijay's victory has been much admired in India, and he deserves all the kudos he has received.

For Vijay, the Solan case was just one part of the larger task of putting right my relationship with India, which has become, for him, something of a personal crusade. He has dedicated much time to it, testing the waters, lobbying politicians, working tirelessly on my behalf. The present trip would have been impossible without him. He is softly spoken, has quite exceptional gifts of negotiation and persuasion, and I owe him a debt of gratitude that can never be repaid.

We regained possession of the Solan villa in November 1997. Since then, the roof has been fixed, the house cleaned and painted, and one bathroom modernized. Impressively, the electricity, plumbing, and telephone all work. In preparation for our visit, furniture and furnishings have been rented for a week from a local store, at the surreal cost, for a six-bedroom house, of one hundred dollars. A caretaker and his family live on the premises. Solan has grown out of all recognition, but the villa's view of the hills remains clear and unspoiled.

Zafar is just a few weeks shy of his own twenty-first birthday. Going to Solan with him today closes a circle. It also discharges a responsibility I have long felt to the memory of my father, who died in 1987. You see, Abba, I have reclaimed our house. Four generations of our family, living and dead, can now forgather there. One day it will belong to Zafar and his little brother, Milan. In a family as uprooted and far-flung as ours, this little acre of continuity stands for a very great deal.

To get to Solan you take a three-hour ride in an air-conditioned "chair car" on the Shatabdi Express from New Delhi to Le Corbusier's city of Chandigarh, the shared capital city of both Punjab and Haryana. Then you drive for an hour and a half, up into the hills. At least, this is what you do if you're not me. The police do not want me to take the train. "Sir, exposure is too great." They are upset because the manager of the hotel in Jaipur has blabbed to Reuters that I was there. Vijay has managed to squash the Reuters story for the moment, but the shield of invisibility is wearing thin. At Solan, as even the police accept, or say they accept, the cat will surely spring from the bag. It's where everyone expects me to go. The day before yesterday, the Indian state TV service Doordarshan sent a team up to Anis Villa to nose around and quiz

Govind Ram, the caretaker, who stonewalled nobly. Once I'm actually there, however, the story will surely break.

One rather unattractive development: the police high-ups who telephone Akshey Kumar every five minutes to ask how things are going have developed the notion that the Jaipur leak was engineered by Vijay and myself. This germ of suspicion will shortly blossom into a full-blown disease.

Zafar is feeling better, but I refuse to inflict what will be a seven-hour car journey on him. I put him on the train, lucky dog. I am to meet him at Chandigarh station with my inconspicuous "car-cade" of four black sedans.

———

There's another train leaving Delhi, a train whose existence wasn't dreamed of the last time I was in India. This is the Samjhauta Express, the non-stop direct rail link between the Indian capital and the city of Lahore in Pakistan. Just as I'm preparing to celebrate this sign of improving relations between the old adversaries, however, I discover that the continuance of the service is now at risk. Pakistan complains that India isn't providing its share of the rolling stock. India complains, more seriously, that Pakistan is using the train to smuggle drugs and counterfeit money into India.

Drugs are a huge issue, of course, but the counterfeit money issue is also a big one. In Nepal, these days, people are reluctant to accept Indian five hundred rupee notes, because of the quantity of forgeries in circulation. Not long ago a diplomat from the Pakistan mission in Delhi went to pay his young son's school fees, and used a mixture of genuine and funny money to do so. The boy was expelled, and although he was later reinstated, the link between the Pakistani government and the bad money had been clearly established.

(On Friday the fourteenth, India and Pakistan agree to let the train continue running for the moment. But it can no longer be said to symbolize the spirit of friendly cooperation. Rather, it's just another problem, another location of the struggle between the two neighbors.)

———

I collect Zafar at Chandigarh, and as we go up into the hills my heart lifts. Mountains have a way of cheering up plains dwellers. The air freshens, tall conifers lean from steep slopes. As the sun sets, the lights of the first hill stations glow in the twilight above us. We pass a narrow-gauge railway train on its slow, picturesque way up to Shimla. For me this is the emotional high point of the trip to date, and I can see that Zafar, too, is moved. We stop at a *dhaba* near Solan for dinner, and the owner tells me how happy he is that I'm there, and someone else runs up for an autograph. I ignore the worried expression on Akshey Kumar's face. Even though I've hardly ever been here in my life, and not at all since I was twelve years old, I feel like I'm home.

It's dark when we reach the villa. From the road we have to climb down 122 steps to reach it. At the bottom there's a little gate, and Vijay, also in a state of high feeling, formally welcomes me to the home he has won back for my family. Govind Ram runs up and astonishes Zafar by stooping down to touch our feet. I am not a superstitious man, but I feel the presence at my shoulder of my grandfather, who died before I was born, and of my parents' younger selves. The sky is on fire with stars. I go into the back garden by myself. I need to be alone.

THURSDAY, APRIL 13

I am woken at 5:00 A.M. by amplified music and chanting from a *mandir,* a Hindu temple, across the valley. I get dressed and walk around the house in the dawn light. With its high-pitched pink roofs and little corner turrets, it's more beautiful than I remembered, more beautiful than it looked in Vijay's photographs of it, and the view is as stunning as promised. It's a very strange feeling to walk around a house you don't know that somehow belongs to you. It takes a while for us to grow into each other, the house and I, but by the time the others wake up, it's mine.

We spend most of the day mooching around the premises, sitting in the garden under the shade of big old conifers, eating Vijay's special scrambled eggs. I know now that the trip has been worthwhile: I know it from the expression on Zafar's face.

In the afternoon we make an excursion to the next town, the former British summer capital. They called it Simla, but it's gone back to being Shimla now that they have left. Vijay shows me the law courts where he fought for Anis Villa, and we go, too, to the former Viceregal Lodge, a big old pile that once staged the crucial pre-Independence Simla Conference of 1945 and now houses a research establishment called the Indian Institute of Advanced Studies. The fabric of the building, of course, is badly neglected, and may soon become unsafe.

Zafar walks gravely around the conference table where the shades of Gandhi, Nehru, and Jinnah are seated, but when we get outside again he asks, "Why is that stone lion still holding up an English flag?" The probable answer, I hypothesize, is that nobody noticed until he did. India has been independent for over half a century, but the flag of St. George is still up there on the roof.

———

A little ducking and swerving in the grounds to dodge the BJP-wallah who now runs the institute. Alas, I am here not only as observer but also as observed, and I mustn't fall into the trap of looking like the BJP's man. A handshake that would certainly be photographed is worth a little fancy footwork to avoid.

Unlike V. S. Naipaul (who is also in India, I gather), I do not see the rise of Hindu nationalism as a great outpouring of India's creative spirit. I see it as the negation of the India I grew up in, as the triumph of sectarianism over secularism, of hatred over fellowship, of ugliness over love. It is true that Prime Minister Vajpayee has tried to lead his party in a more moderate direction, and that Vajpayee personally is surprisingly popular among Muslims, but his attempt to reshape his party in his own image has failed.

The BJP is the political manifestation of the extremist Hindu movement, the RSS (Rashtriya Swyamsevak Sangh), rather as Sinn Fein in Northern Ireland is the political offspring of the Provisional IRA. In order to change the BJP, Vajpayee would have to carry the leadership of the RSS with him. Regrettably, the opposite is happening. The relatively moderate RSS chief, Professor Rajendra Singh—"Rajju Bhaiyya"—has been ousted by the hard-line K. S. Sudarshan, who has started warning Vajpayee to toe the RSS line.

The prime minister's options are limited. He could give in and unleash the dogs of religious strife. He could try doing what Indira Gandhi brilliantly carried off in 1969, when the kingmakers of the Congress attempted to turn her into their puppet. (She resigned from her own party, formed the Congress-I or Indira Congress, took most of her MPs with her, called a general election, and destroyed the old guard at the polls.) Or, as seems most likely, he could soldier on until the next election and then stand down. At that point the BJP's moderate mask will slip, it will no longer be able to hold together the kind of broad-based coalition that presently underpins its hold on power, and, given the shambles the Congress Party's in, India will enter another phase of splintered, unstable governments. It's not a happy prediction, but it's what the probabilities suggest. And it's a good enough reason for keeping away from BJP apparatchiks, however low-level they may be.

There is a conference under way at the institute. Professor B. B. Lal, using grayware pottery shards found at sites associated with the great Kuru-Pandava war as evidence, concludes that the age of the revered *Mahabharata* may be only three thousand years, not the supposed five thousand. What will the BJP/RSS make of so radical a rewriting of the story of this sacred Hindu text?

—

My metamorphosis from observer to observed, from the Salman I know to the "Rushdie" I often barely recognize, continues apace. Rumors of my presence in India are everywhere. I am profoundly depressed to hear that a couple of Islamic organizations have vowed to make trouble, and trouble is news, and so maybe, I think, this will be seen as the meaning of my trip to India, which will be very, very sad, and bad, indeed.

At dinner in Solan's Himani restaurant, I'm tucking into the spicy Indian version of Chinese food when I'm approached by a Doordarshan reporter called Agnihotri, who just by chance happens to be vacationing up here with his family. And there it is: he has his scoop and the story's out. Within moments a local press reporter arrives and asks me a few friendly questions. None of this is very unexpected, but as a result of these chance encounters the jitteriness of the police reaches new heights, and boils over into a full-scale row.

Back at Anis Villa, Vijay receives a call on his cell phone from a police officer named Kulbir Krishan in Delhi. Krishan is somewhere in the middle of the invisible chain of command of Delhi desk-pilots, but what he says makes Vijay lose his composure for the first time in all the years of our friendship. He is almost trembling as he tells me, "We are accused of having called those journalists to the restaurant. This man says we have not been gentlemen, we have not kept our word, and we have, if you can believe the phrase, 'talked out of turn.' Finally the fellow says, 'There will be riots in Delhi tomorrow, and if we fire on the crowds and there are deaths, the blood will be on your heads.'"

I am horrified. It quickly becomes clear to me that there are two issues here. The first, and lesser, issue is that after a week of accepting all manner of limitations and security conditions, we are being accused of dishonesty and bad faith. That is insulting and unjust, but it isn't, finally, dangerous. The second issue is a matter of life and death. If the Delhi police have become so trigger-happy that they are preparing to kill people, then they must be stopped before it's too late.

No time now for niceties. Zafar looks on, dazed, while I blow my stack at poor, decent Akshey Kumar (who is not at all to blame) and tell him that unless Kulbir Krishan gets back on the phone *right now,* apologizes to Vijay and me personally, and assures me that there are no plans to murder anybody tomorrow, I will insist on our driving through the night back to New Delhi so that I can be waiting at Prime Minister Vajpayee's office door at dawn, to ask him to deal with the problem personally.

After a certain amount of this kind of raging—"I'll go to the British high commissioner! I'll call a press conference! *I'll write a newspaper article!*"—the hapless Kulbir does call back to speak of "misunderstandings," and promises that there will be no shootings or deaths.

"If I spoke out of context," he memorably concludes, "then I am very sorry indeed." I burst out laughing at the sheer absurdity of this formulation and put down the phone. But I do not sleep well. The meaning of this entire journey will be defined by what happens in the next two days, and even though I hope and believe that the police are overreacting, I can't be sure. Delhi is their town, and me, I'm Rip Van Winkle.

FRIDAY, APRIL 14

We leave Solan at dawn and drive Zafar and Vijay to Chandigarh station. (I, of course, am going all the way by road.) Zafar is recovering from the shrimp attack, but Vijay looks worn out, frazzled. He repeats several times that he has never been spoken to so rudely, and doesn't propose to let the matter rest. I can see that he's had it with the police, with all the traveling, and probably with me. Tomorrow night, I tell him, all this will be over and you can go back to being a lawyer and not think about Salman Rushdie and his problems even once. He laughs weakly and gets on the train.

It's the day of the Commonwealth Writers' Prize banquet, but I'm not thinking about that. All the way back to Delhi, I'm wondering whose instincts will prove the sharper: mine or my protectors'. How will my return-of-the-native trip end: happily or badly? I'll soon know.

At half past twelve I'm closeted in a meeting with R. S. Gupta, the special assistant commissioner in charge of security for the whole city of Delhi. He is a calm, forceful man, used to getting his way. He paints a dark picture. A Muslim politician, Shoaib Iqbal, plans to go to Friday midday prayers at the city's most important mosque, the Juma Masjid in Old Delhi, and there get support for a demonstration against me, and against the Indian government for allowing me to enter the country. The congregation will be in six figures, and if the mosque's imam— it's Bukhari—supports the call to demonstrate, the numbers could be huge and bring the city to a standstill. "We are negotiating with them," Gupta says, "to keep the numbers small, and the event peaceful. Maybe we will succeed."

After a couple of hours of high-tension waiting, during which I am effectively confined to quarters—"Sir, no movements, please"—the news is good. Fewer than two hundred people have marched—and two hundred marchers, in India, is a number smaller than zero—and it has all gone off without a hitch. The nightmare scenario has not come to pass. "Fortunately," Mr. Gupta tells me, "we have been able to manage it."

What really happened in Delhi today? The security worldview is always impressive and often persuasive, but it remains just one version of the truth. It is one of the characteristics of security forces everywhere in the world to try and have it both ways. Had there been mass demonstrations, they would have said, "You see, all our nervousness has been amply justified." But there were no such marches; and so I'm told, "We were able to prevent the trouble because of our foresight and skill."

Maybe so. But it might also be the case that for the vast majority of Indian Muslims, the controversy over *The Satanic Verses* is old hat now, and in spite of the efforts of the politician and the imam (both of whom made blood-and-thunder speeches) nobody could really be bothered to march. Oh, there's a novelist in town to go to a dinner? What's his name? Rushdie? So what?

This, certainly, is the view taken, almost without exception, by the Indian press in its analysis of the day's events. The small demonstration that has occurred is noted, but the private political agendas of its organizers are also pointed out.

It's a hot day in Delhi, and there's a hot wind blowing. A dust storm rages across the city. As we all take in the news that the only storm in Delhi today is meteorologically induced, we can finally begin to relax, and to concede that perhaps everyone has been more nervous than was necessary and that the long dispute that has kept me away from India is really over at last.

The script in people's heads is being rewritten. The foretold ending has not come to pass. What happens instead is extraordinary and, for Zafar and myself, an event of immense emotional impact, exceeding in its force even the tumultuous reception of *Midnight's Children* almost twenty years ago. What bursts out is not violence but joy.

—

At a quarter to eight in the evening, Zafar and I walk into the Commonwealth Prize reception at the Oberoi hotel, and from that moment until we leave India, the celebrations never stop. Journalists and photographers surround us, their faces wreathed in most unjournalistic smiles. Friends burst through the media wall to embrace us. The actor Roshan Seth, recently recovered from serious heart problems, hugs me and says, "Look at us, yaar, we're both supposed to be dead but still going strong." The eminent columnist Amita Malik, a friend of my family's from the old days in Bombay, quickly gets over her embarrassment at mistaking Zafar for my bodyguard and reminisces wonderfully about the past, praising my father's wit, his quick gift for repartee, and telling tales of my favorite uncle, Hameed, who died too young, too long ago.

Gifted young writers—Raj Kamal Jha, Namita Gokhale, Shauna Singh Baldwin—come up to say generous things about the significance of my writing for their own work. One of the great ladies of English-language Indian literature, the novelist Nayantara Sahgal, clasps my hands and whispers, "Welcome home." I look around and there's Zafar being interviewed for television and speaking fluently and touchingly about his own happiness at being here. My heart overflows. I had not really dared to expect this, had been infected by the fears of the police, and had defended my heart against many kinds of disappointment. Now I can feel the defenses falling away one by one, the happiness rising like a tropical dawn, fast and brilliant and hot. There are few such moments in a lifetime. Forgive me for saying perhaps too much about this one. It is a rare thing to be granted your heart's desire.

Somewhere in there the Commonwealth Writers' Prize goes to J. M.

Coetzee, thanks to the deciding vote of the specter at the feast, the stone-faced Indian judge Shashi Deshpande. But this is a party even her curdled judgments cannot poop. India is the prize.

SATURDAY, APRIL 15

R ushdie in India: like Solzhenitsyn regaining home, but without the anger or medieval prophecies. There is only joy, lots of joy." As the *Indian Express*'s hyperbolically affectionate front-page lead demonstrates, the party spirit is spilling into the media, drowning the few, muted negative voices. In all my conversations with the press I've tried to avoid reopening old wounds, to tell Indian Muslims that I'm not and have never been their enemy, and to stress that I'm in India to mend broken links and to begin, so to speak, a new chapter. Today the *Asian Age* concurs: "Let's turn a page." Elsewhere, in *Outlook,* there is pleasure that India has "made some amends for being the first to ban *The Satanic Verses* and subjecting him to the persecution and agony that followed." The *Pioneer* expresses its satisfaction that India is, once again, standing up for "democratic values and the individual's right to express himself." It also, in less elevated mood, improbably but delightfully accuses me of "turning the city's sophisticated party women into a bunch of giggling schoolgirls" who tell their men, "Dahling, [he] could send Bollywood hunks back to school."

Dilip Padgaonkar of *The Times of India* puts it most movingly: "He is reconciled with India and India with him . . . something sublime has happened to him which should enable him to continue to mesmerise us with his yarns. He has returned to where his heart has always been. He has returned home." In *The Hindustan Times,* there is an editorial headed "Reconsider the Ban." This sentiment is echoed right across the media. In *The Times of India* an Islamic scholar, among other intellectuals, backs an end to the ban. On the electronic media, opinion polls run 75 to 25 percent in favor of allowing *The Satanic Verses* to be freely published in India at long last.

—

Vijay throws a farewell party for me. His wife, Rani, an expert on prison systems and penal reform, has returned from a conference in Vienna just in time. And there's a surprise: my two actress aunts, Uzra Butt and her sister Zohra Segal, are there, with my cousin Kiran Segal, Zohra's daughter and one of the country's foremost exponents and teachers of the Odissi school of Indian classical dancing. This is the zany wing of the family, sharp of tongue and mischievous of eye. Uzra and Zohra are the grand old ladies of the Indian theater, and we were all in love with Kiran at one time or another. Zohra and Kiran lived in an apartment in Hampstead for a time in the 1960s, and when I was at boarding-school at Rugby, I sometimes spent vacations in their spare bedroom, next to Kiran's bedroom door, on which there was a large, admonitory skull and crossbones sign. I now discover that Vijay Shankardass and Roshan Seth both stayed in the same spare room in the same period. All three of us would look wistfully at the skull and crossbones, and none of us ever got past it.

"I haven't seen you dance for years," I say to Kiran.

"Come back soon," she says. "Then I'll dance."

June 2000

PART II

Messages from the Plague Years

This is a selection made from the large number of pieces I published during the long campaign against the *Satanic Verses* fatwa.

[*First, from a speech to the International Conference on Freedom of Expression, Washington, D.C., April 1992*]

I'd like to thank all those who helped make this trip possible. It wasn't a simple matter, and how odd that is! For a writer interested in freedom of expression to attend a conference on the subject should be a simple matter. It should not be necessary for his travel plans to be shrouded in secrecy. The security forces should not need to pay me any special attention. It feels a little like being inside one of those science-fiction yarns in which the present has been altered, so that the Inquisition appears in Piccadilly Circus, and there are witch-burnings on the Potomac.

The fatwa of Imam Khomeini bent the world out of shape. Ancient blood-lusts were unleashed, armed with state-of-the-art modern technology. Battles that we thought no longer needed to be fought—battles against such concepts as "blasphemy" and "heresy," which throughout human history have been the storm troopers of bigotry—were re-enacted in our streets. Many people who should have known better defended the real and threatened violence and blamed its victims. Even now, in Britain, there is a powerful lobby that regularly denigrates my character. It is hard for me to be my own advocate in this matter, hard for me to insist on my own value. When I do, I am accused of arrogance and ingratitude. But when I don't fight my corner, my case is swiftly forgotten. Quite a double-bind.

As we used to say in the sixties, there is a fault in reality. Do not adjust your minds. What has been done to *The Satanic Verses,* its author, publishers, translators, and booksellers, is a crime against freedom. The novel is not the crime; the author is not the criminal.

Of course I know I'm not the only writer under attack. I have tried hard during the past three years to point out that those words, "blasphemy" and "heresy," have been launched against writer after writer, especially in the Muslim world. I have tried repeatedly to remind people that we are witnessing a war against independence of mind, a war for power.

> The peculiar evil of silencing the expression of an opinion is that it is robbing the human race, posterity as well as the existing generation— [robbing] those who dissent from the opinion, still more than those who hold it. [For] if the opinion is right, they are deprived of the opportunity of exchanging error for truth; if wrong, they lose what is almost as great a benefit, the clearer perception and livelier impression of truth produced by its collision with error.

Those words are from John Stuart Mill's great essay "On Liberty." It is extraordinary how much of Mill's essay applies directly to the case of *The Satanic Verses.* The demand for the banning of this novel and indeed the eradication of its author is precisely what Mill called the "assumption of infallibility." Those who make such demands do so, just as Mill anticipated, because they find the book and its author "immoral and impious."

"But," he writes, "this is the case in which [the assumption of infallibility] is most fatal. These are exactly the occasions on which the men of one generation commit those dreadful mistakes which excite the astonishment and horror of posterity." Mill gives two examples of such occasions: the cases of Socrates and of Jesus Christ. To these can be added a third case, that of Galileo. All three men were accused of blasphemy and heresy. All three were attacked by the storm troopers of bigotry. And yet they are, as is plain to anyone, the founders of the philosophical, moral, and scientific traditions of the West. We can say, therefore, that blasphemy and heresy, far from being the greatest evils, are the methods by which human thought has made its most vital advances. The writers of the European Enlightenment, who all came up against the storm troopers at one time or another, knew this. It was because of his nervousness of the power of the Church, not of the State, that Voltaire suggested it was advisable for writers to live in close proximity to a frontier, so that, if necessary, they could hop across it into safety. Frontiers will not defend a writer now, not if this new form of terrorism, terrorism by edict and bounty, is allowed to have its day.

Many people say that the Rushdie case is a one-off, that it will never be repeated. This complacency, too, is an enemy to be defeated. I return to John Stuart Mill. "The dictum that truth always triumphs over persecution is one of those pleasant falsehoods which all experience refutes. History teems with instances of truth put down by persecution. If not suppressed for ever, it may be thrown back for centuries. . . . Persecution has always succeeded, save where the heretics were too strong a party to be effectually persecuted." There it is in a nutshell. Religious persecution is never a matter of morality, always a question of power. To defeat the modern-day witch-burners, it is necessary to show them that our power, too, is great—that our numbers are greater than theirs, and our resolve, too. This is a battle of wills.

Free societies are societies in motion, and with motion comes friction. Free people strike sparks, and those sparks are the best evidence of freedom's existence. Totalitarian societies seek to replace the many truths of freedom by the one truth of power, be it secular or religious; to halt the motion of society, to snuff out its spark. Unfreedom's primary purpose is invariably to shackle the mind.

The creative process is rather like the processes of a free society. Many attitudes, many views of the world, jostle and conflict within the artist, and from these frictions the spark, the work of art, is born. This inner multiplicity is frequently very difficult for the artist to bear, let alone explain. Denis Diderot, the great novelist-philosopher of the French Enlightenment, spoke of the dispute within him between atheistic, materialistic rationalism and a profound need for spiritual and moral depth. "It infuriates me," he said, "to be enmeshed in a devilish philosophy which my mind is forced to accept but my heart to disown."

An even greater writer, Fyodor Dostoevsky, also agonized about the coexistence in his heart of absolute faith and absolute unbelief. And before him, William Blake said approvingly that Milton, that devout genius, was, as a poet, naturally, of the devil's party. Within every artist—within, perhaps, every human imagination—there exists, to paraphrase Blake, a marriage between Heaven and Hell.

[*An open letter published in Japan in July 1992, on the anniversary of the murder of Hitoshi Igarashi, the Japanese translator of* The Satanic Verses]

One year has passed since the vicious murder of Professor Igarashi, but I have still not become accustomed to the fact. It still feels as appalling, as enraging, as evil as it did when I first heard the news. The celebratory response of some Japanese-based Muslims also remains in the memory as a sour, unpleasant taste.

I have come to understand that what is important is precisely not to become accustomed to the intolerable. In our modern world, with its rapid shifts of focus and its short attention span, it is all too easy to lose interest in a particular case, no matter how vivid the story once was. But to do so in this case would be an insult to Professor Igarashi's memory. It simply can never be acceptable to murder a man in the name of any god or ideology. In such a case, morality is never on the side of the murderers.

I did not know Professor Igarashi, but he knew me, because he translated my work. Translation is a kind of intimacy, a kind of friendship, and so I mourn his death as I would that of a friend. I do not believe that the people of Japan will find his murder acceptable.

I have read that there is now evidence linking the murder to Middle Eastern terrorists. I would say this: whoever the murderers were (and we know that many Middle Eastern terrorists have their paymasters in Tehran), it was Khomeini's fatwa that was the real murderer.

For this reason, and to do honor to the name of the fallen man, a distinguished scholar and my translator, Hitoshi Igarashi, I call upon the people and government of Japan to demand an end to this terrorist threat. A Japanese citizen has been the first to lose his life to the fatwa. Japan can help ensure that he is also the last.

[*First published on February 7, 1993, under the title "The Last Hostage"*]

F our years. It's been four years and I'm still here. Strange how that feels simultaneously like a victory and a defeat.

Why a victory? Because when, on February 14, 1989, I heard the news from Tehran, my instant reaction was: I'm a dead man. I remembered a poem by my friend Raymond Carver about being told by his doctor he had lung cancer.

> He said are you a religious man do you kneel down
> in forest groves and let yourself ask for help . . .
> I said not yet but I intend to start today

But I'm not a religious man. I didn't kneel down. I went to do a TV interview and said I wished I'd written a more critical book. Why? Because when the leader of a terrorist state has just announced his intention to murder you in the name of god you can either bluster or gibber. I did not want to gibber. And because when murder is ordered in the name of god you begin to think less well of the name of god.

Afterward I thought: if there is a god I don't think he's very bothered by *The Satanic Verses,* because he wouldn't be much of a god if he could be rocked on his throne by a book. Then again, if there isn't a god, he certainly isn't bothered. So this quarrel's not between me and god but between me and those who think—as Bob Dylan once reminded us—they can do any damn thing because they have god on their side.

The police came to see me and said, stay put, don't go anywhere, plans are being made. Police officers on short patrol watched over me that night. I lay unsleeping and listened out for the angel of death. One of my favorite films was and is Luis Buñuel's *The Exterminating Angel.* It is a film about people who cannot get out of a room.

The next afternoon—when the television was roaring with hatred and blood-lust—I was offered Special Branch protection. The officers who came said I should go somewhere for a few days while the politicians sorted things out. Do you remember? Four years ago we all thought this crisis would be solved in a matter of days. That in the late twentieth century a man should be threatened with murder for writing a book, that the leader of a religious-fascist state should threaten the free citizen of a free country far away from his own, was too crazy. It would be stopped. The police thought so. I thought so too.

So off we went, not to any deep-secret safe house, but to a hotel in the countryside. In the room next door to mine was a reporter from the *Daily Mirror* who had checked in with a lady who was not his wife. I kept out of his way, not wishing to intrude. And that night, when every journalist in the country was trying to find out where I'd gone, this gentleman—how shall I put this?—missed his scoop.

It was going to be over in a few days, but four years later, it's still going on. And I am told the level of threat against my life has not diminished at all. I am told there is nobody protected by the Special Branch whose life is in more danger than mine. So, a victory and a defeat: a victory because I'm alive, in spite of being described by a "friend" as a dead man on leave. A defeat because I'm still in this prison. It goes where I go. It has no walls, no roof, no manacles, but I haven't found a way out in four years.

I was under political pressure. I do not think it is generally known how heavy this pressure was. The issue of the British hostages kept cropping up. I was asked to make an apologetic statement: otherwise something might happen to a British hostage and that, it was hinted, would be my fault. The statement that I agreed to make was not even written by me, but by the late John Lyttle, the Archbishop of Canterbury's man on the hostage case, and by other worthies and eminences. I changed two words, and even that alteration required a bit of a fight. It did no good to anyone. It was done to help the hostages but was portrayed as my first failure to save my wretched neck. Khomeini restated his fatwa. Multi-million-dollar bounties were offered.

Now there was official pressure on me simply to disappear. The argument was that I'd made enough trouble already. I should not speak up on the issue, I should not defend myself. There was a big enough public-order problem, and since the authorities were doing so much to protect me I should not make life harder for them. Go nowhere, see nobody, say nothing. Be an un-person and be grateful to be alive. Listen to the vilifications, the misrepresentations, the murderous speeches, the appeasements, and shut up.

For almost a year and a half I had no contact with any member of the British government or any civil servant, in either the Home Office or the Foreign Office. I was in limbo. I have been told that the Home Office vetoed any meeting with me, because this would allegedly be bad for race relations. In the end I telephoned William Waldegrave, at that time a Foreign Office minister, and asked if it might not be a good idea for us to meet. He was not able—not permitted, I think—to meet me. But I did at last have a meeting with a Foreign Office diplomat, and on one occasion with the foreign secretary Douglas Hurd himself. These meetings were held on the basis that they must be kept entirely secret, "so that the hostages should not suffer."

Incidentally, I do not recall Tehran or the hostage-holders in Lebanon ever making this linkage. But maybe I am mistaken about this. If I reveal these details now, it is because it is safe to do so. Until the day Terry Waite was released, I was a sort of hostage to the hostages. I accepted that their cases had to be resolved first; that, to an extent, my rights had to be set aside for the sake of theirs. I hoped only that, once they were free, it would be my turn; that the British government and the world community would seek the end of this crisis, too.

I had a long wait, with many bizarre moments during it. A Pakistani film portraying me as a torturer, murderer, and drunkard wearing an appalling variety of Technicolor safari suits was refused a certificate in Britain. I saw a video of the film; it was awful. It ended with my "execution" by the power of god. The ugliness of those images stayed with me for a while. However, I wrote to the British Board of Film Classification promising them that I would not take legal action against them or the film, and asking them to license it. I told them I did not want the dubious protection of censorship. The film was un-banned and promptly vanished from sight. An attempt to screen it in Bradford was greeted by rows of empty seats. It was a perfect illustration of the argument for free speech: people really can make up their own minds. Still, it was weird to be pleased at the release of a film whose subject was my death.

—

Sometimes I stayed in comfortable houses. Sometimes I had no more than a small room in which I could not approach the window lest I be seen from below. Sometimes I was able to get out a bit. At other times I had trouble doing so.

I tried to visit the USA and France, and the governments of those countries made it impossible for me to enter.

Once I had to go into the hospital to have my wisdom teeth extracted. I learned afterward that the police had made emergency plans to have me removed. I would have been anesthetized and carried out in a body bag, in a hearse.

I became friendly with my protection teams and learned a good deal about the internal workings of the Branch. I learned how to find out if you're being followed on a motorway and I grew accustomed to the hardware that was always lying around and I learned the slang of the police force—drivers, for example, are known as OFDs, which stands for Only Fucking Drivers.★ Motorway police are Black Rats. My own name was never used. I learned to answer to other names. I was "the Principal."

I have become familiar with much that was unthinkably strange four years ago, but I have never become used to it. I knew from the start that habituation would be a surrender. What has happened to my life is a grotesque thing. It is a crime. I will never agree that it has become my normal condition.

"What's blond, has big tits, and lives in Tasmania? Salman Rushdie." I got letters, sometimes I still get letters, saying, give up, change your name, have an operation, start a new life. This is the one option I have never considered. It would be worse than death. I don't want some other person's life. I want my own.

The protection officers have shown great understanding and helped me get through the worst times. I will always be grateful to them. These are brave men. They are putting their lives on the line for me. Nobody ever did that for me before.

———

Here is a thing that needs saying. I suspect that because I have not been killed, many people think there is nobody trying to kill me. Many people probably think it's all a bit theoretical. It isn't. In the early months an Arab terrorist blew himself up in a Paddington hotel. Afterward I was told by a journalist who had visited the Hizbollah redoubts in the Beka'a Valley in Lebanon that she had seen this man's photograph on an office "wall of martyrs," with a caption stating that his target had been me. And, at the time of the Gulf War, I heard that the Iranian government had paid out money for a contract killing. After

---

★ One OFD who managed to allow a bullet-proof Jaguar to be stolen while in his care was instantly named the king of Spain by his colleagues, because the king of Spain (say it aloud) is Juan Carlos.

months of extreme caution I was told that the killers had been—to use the euphemistic language of the intelligence services—"frustrated." I thought it best not to inquire into the causes of their frustration.

And in 1992 three Iranians were expelled from Britain. Two of them worked at the Iranian mission in London, the third was a "student." I was told by the Foreign Office that these were spies and they were undoubtedly in Britain on matters related to the fulfillment of the fatwa.

And the Italian translator of *The Satanic Verses* was nearly killed, and the Japanese translator *was* killed. In 1992 the Japanese police announced the results of their twelve-month investigation. In their view the killers were professional Middle Eastern terrorists who had entered from China. Meanwhile, an Iranian hit-squad assassinated former prime minister Shapour Bakhtiar in Paris. They cut his head off. Another squad killed a dissident Iranian singer in Germany. They chopped him up and put the bits in a bag.

Nothing very theoretical about that.

———

England is a small country and it is full of people and many of these people are naturally inquisitive. It is not an easy country in which to disappear. Once I was in a building that I needed to leave, but there was a burst central heating pipe just off the hallway, and a plumber had been called in. A police officer had to distract the plumber's attention so that I could slip past him while his head was turned away. Once I was in a kitchen when a neighbor turned up unexpectedly. I had to dive down behind a kitchen cabinet and remain there, crouching, until he left. Once I was in a traffic jam outside the Regent's Park mosque just as the faithful were emerging from Eid prayers. I sat in the back of an armored Jaguar with my nose deep in *The Daily Telegraph.* My protectors joked that it was the first time they had seen me so interested in the *Telegraph.*

To live like this is to feel demeaned every day, to feel little twists of humiliation accumulating around your heart. To live like this is to allow people—including your ex-wife—to call you a coward on the front page of the newspapers. Such people would no doubt be prepared to speak well of me at my funeral. But to live, to avoid assassination, is a greater victory than to be murdered. Only fanatics go looking for martyrdom.

I am forty-five years old, and I can't leave my places of residence without permission. I do not carry keys. Sometimes there are "bad patches." During one "bad patch" I slept in thirteen different beds in twenty nights. At such times a great wild jangle fills your body. At such times you begin to come unstuck from your self.

I have learned to let things go: the anger, the bitterness. They will come back later, I know. When things are better. I'll deal with them then. Right now my victory lies in not being broken, in not losing my self. It lies in continuing to work. There are no hostages anymore. For the first time in years, I am able to fight my corner without being accused of damaging anyone else's interests. I have been fighting as hard as I can.

Like everyone else I rejoiced at the end of the Lebanon hostages' terrible ordeal. But the people most active in my defense campaign, Frances D'Souza and Carmel Bedford at Article 19, knew that the huge relief we all felt at the closing of that awful chapter was also a danger. Maybe people wouldn't want to pay attention to someone saying, excuse me, there's still one more problem. Maybe I'd be seen as a sort of party-pooper. On the other hand there were persistent rumors that the British government was on the verge of normalizing relations with Iran and forgetting the "Rushdie case" entirely. What to do? Shut up and go on relying on "silent diplomacy," or speak out?

In my view there was no choice. The hostages' release had set my tongue free at last. And it would be absurd to fight a war for freedom of speech by remaining silent. We agreed to make the campaign as noisy as possible, to demonstrate to the British government that it couldn't afford to ignore the case, and to try and rekindle the kind of international support that would demonstrate to the Iranian terror-state that the fatwa was damaging their self-interests as well as mine.

In December 1991, a few days after the release of the last American hostage, Terry Anderson, I was finally permitted to enter the United States to speak at Columbia University's celebration of the two hundredth anniversary of the Bill of Rights. The plans for the trip were a nightmare. I did not know until twenty-four hours before I left that I would be allowed to go. I was given leave to travel in a military aircraft, a great favor for which I was immensely grateful. (This would have remained entirely secret except that a British tabloid saw fit to publish the fact and then blame me for endangering the RAF.)

The moment of departure was overwhelming. It was my first time out of Britain in almost three years. For a moment, the cage seemed a little bigger. Then, in New York, I was met by an eleven-vehicle motorcade, complete with motorcycle outriders. I was placed in an armored white limo and rushed through Manhattan at high speed. "It's what we'd do for Arafat," explained the operation's leader, known for the day as Hudson Commander. I inquired timidly, "How about the president?" For the president they would close down a lot more side streets, Hudson Commander explained, "but in your case we thought that might be a little too conspicuous." This entirely without irony. The New York Police Department is very thorough, but it doesn't make many jokes.

I spent that day in a fourteenth-floor suite with at least twenty armed men. The windows were blocked by bullet-proof mattresses. Outside the door were more armed men with Schwarzenegger-sized muscles and weaponry. In this suite I had a series of meetings that must remain secret, except, perhaps, for one. I was able to meet with the poet Allen Ginsberg for twenty minutes. The moment he arrived, he pulled cushions off the sofas and set them on the floor. "Take off your shoes and sit down," he said. "I'm going to teach you some simple meditation exercises. They should help you handle your terrible situation." Our mutual literary agent, Andrew Wylie, was there, and I made him do it, too, which, squawking somewhat, he did. While we did our breathing and chanting, I thought how extraordinary it was for an Indian by birth to be taught Buddhism by an American poet sitting cross-legged in a room full of men armed to the gills. There's nothing like life; you can't make this stuff up.

That night the huge motorcade took me to Columbia and I was able to make my contribution. Free speech is life itself, I remember saying. The next day the American press was sympathetic and positive. It was clear that Americans saw the issue, as I did, as one in which an old, taken-for-granted freedom had become a life-and-death affair. Back home it was a different matter. I got back to Britain to be faced by such headlines as RUSHDIE INFLAMES MUSLIM ANGER AGAIN (because I had asked for the publication of a paperback edition of *The Satanic Verses*).

During the next year, as I visited more and more countries, this dichotomy became ever more apparent. In the rest of the free world, the "Rushdie case" is about freedom of expression and state terrorism. In Britain, it seems to be about a man who has to be saved from the consequences of his own actions. Elsewhere, people know that the outrage has been committed not by me but against me. In certain quarters of my own country, people take a contrary view.

———

The paperback was published in the spring of 1992, not by Penguin, who refused to do so, but by a consortium. I was able to be in Washington for its launch, and at a free-speech conference I produced the first copy. As I did so my emotions assaulted me without warning. It was all I could do to keep back the tears. (I should mention here that the paperback publication of *The Satanic Verses* passed off without incident, in spite of many people's forebodings and some people's chickenings-out. I was reminded, as I have often been reminded, of Roosevelt's famous saw about fear itself being the thing most to be feared.)

I had come to Washington mainly to address members of both houses of Congress. On the evening before the meeting, however, I was told that Secretary of State James Baker had personally rung the leaders of both houses to say he did not wish the meeting to take place. The Bush administration made dismissive remarks about my presence. Marlin Fitzwater, explaining the administration's refusal to meet me, said, "He's just an author on a book tour."★

In spite of the Bush people's best efforts, I did manage to meet a group of U.S. senators—led by New York's Daniel Patrick Moynihan and Vermont's Patrick Leahy—who invited me to lunch at the Capitol and, to my amazement, brought along copies of my books for me to sign. After lunch, at a press conference, Moynihan and others spoke passionately on my behalf. This was a crucial moment. It now became possible to approach parliamentarians and governments all over Europe and the Americas. I was even invited to the British House of Commons to address an all-party group, after which Iran's Majlis (parliament) instantly demanded that the fatwa be carried out.

———

In the summer of 1992 it was made possible for me to go to Denmark as the guest of Danish PEN. Once again, the security was very heavy. There was even a small gunboat in Copenhagen harbor that I was told was "ours." This resulted in many jokes about the need to guard against an attack by the Iranian fleet in the Baltic, or perhaps by fundamentalist frogmen.

★ See page 129, in "Farming Ostriches."

During the time in Denmark the government kept away from me (though by enabling my visit and providing protection, they had clearly shown a certain level of support). The risk to Denmark's feta cheese exports to Iran was cited as one reason for the government's reticence. However, I was given enthusiastic support by politicians of all other parties, notably Anker Jorgensen, the Labor once-and-probably-future prime minister, with whom I gave a joint press conference aboard a boat in the harbor. Jorgensen promised to hold discussions with the ruling party to develop a policy of all-party support for my case. It was less than I'd hoped for, but it was a step on the road.

I made a brief visit to Spain. (I am glossing over the immense difficulties of organization, but believe me, none of these trips was easy.) There I was made an offer of mediation by Gustavo Villapalos, the rector of Madrid's Complutense University, a man very close to the Spanish government and also extremely well connected in Iran. Soon he reported to me that he had received encouraging signals from persons high in the Iranian regime: it was an excellent time to resolve this matter, he had been told. Iran knew that this case was the biggest single obstacle to its economic strategies. All sorts of distinguished people were letting it be known that they wanted a solution: the names of Khomeini's widow and surviving elder brother were mentioned. A few weeks later, however, European newspapers quoted Villapalos as having said that I had agreed to rewrite parts of *The Satanic Verses*. I had said no such thing. Villapalos told me he had been misquoted and asked for a meeting in London. I agreed. Since then I have not heard from him.

A breakthrough came in late summer, in Norway. Once again my hosts were the international writers' organization, PEN, and my courageous publishers, Aschehoug. Once again, the media and people of the country showed me fantastic warmth and support. And this time I had meetings with the ministers for culture and education, received a message of friendship from the prime minister, Gro Harlem Brundtland, and elicited firm promises of government support at the United Nations and in other international forums as well as in bilateral contacts between Norway and Iran.

The Nordic countries, with their traditionally strong concern for human-rights issues, were beginning to come aboard. In October I was invited to address a Nordic Council conference in Helsinki: an opportunity to push for a joint Nordic initiative. And indeed the Nordic Council did make a strong resolution of support, and many delegates to the conference undertook to bring the matter back to their own parliaments and governments.

There was one snag, however. The British ambassador, invited by the Nordic Council to the session I was to address, refused to come. I was told by the organizers that they had been shocked by the rudeness of his refusal.

Back home, I was abruptly informed by a chief superintendent who was clearly very embarrassed by what she was saying that my protection would shortly end, even though there was no reason to believe that things were any safer. "Many people live in danger of their lives in Britain," I was told, "and some of them die, you know." However, soon after Article 19 took the matter up with Number 10, this policy was reversed, and the defense campaign received a letter from the prime minister's office assuring us unequivocally that the protection would continue as long as the threat did.

I am—to say it once again—very grateful for the protection. But I also know that it will take a bigger push to force Iran to change its policy, and the purpose of my visits abroad was to try and create the force for that push.

———

On October 25, 1992, I went to the German capital, Bonn. Germany is Iran's number-one trading partner. I had been led to believe I would get nowhere. What happened in Germany felt, therefore, like a small miracle.

My visit was arranged by a small miracle of a woman, an SPD member of the Bundestag called Thea Bock. Her English was as rotten as my German, and even though we often had to speak in sign language we got along famously. By a mixture of cajoling, strong-arm tactics, and sheer trickery, and with the help of other members, notably Norbert Gansel, she managed to arrange meetings for me with most of the people at the heart of the German state—the very powerful and popular speaker of the Bundestag, Rita Süssmuth; high-ranking officials in the Foreign Ministry; the leading members of the foreign affairs committee; and the leader of the SPD himself, Bjorn Engholm, who astonished me by standing next to me on TV and calling me his "brother in spirit." He committed the SPD to total support for my cause and since then has worked hard on my behalf. In short, I was promised support from Germany by people at the very highest levels of the State. Since then that support has been made concrete. "We will protect Mr. Rushdie," the German government has announced. The Bundestag has passed an all-party resolution stating that Germany will hold Iran legally responsible for my safety and that, should any injury befall me, Iran will face economic and political consequences. (The Swedish and Canadian parliaments are presently considering similar resolutions.) Also, the enormous German-Iranian cultural agreement has been put on hold, and Foreign Minister Klaus Kinkel has stated that it will not be taken off the shelf until the cancellation of the fatwa.

Germany's willingness to use economic and cultural leverage on my behalf rattled Iran into its latest restatement of the fatwa and renewal of bounty offers. This was foolish; it only strengthened the resolve of a growing number of sympathetic governments to take up the case. After Germany came Sweden, where the government and Swedish PEN jointly awarded me the Kurt Tucholsky Prize, traditionally given to writers suffering human-rights abuses. Sweden's deputy prime minister Bengt Westerberg made a passionate speech to the press promising the government's complete and vigorous support. The leader of Sweden's Social Democratic Party, Ingvar Carlsson, promised to work with other European socialist parties on my behalf. I know that he has now taken up this case with the British Labour Party, urging it to do more. At the moment of writing, neither I nor Article 19 has been contacted by the Labour Party leadership to tell us of their position and intentions. I invite John Smith or Jack Cunningham to rectify this as soon as possible.

A diplomat more experienced in the ways of the Middle East than most* said to me: "The secret of diplomacy is to be standing in the station when the train arrives. If you aren't in the station, don't complain if you miss the train. The trouble, of course, is that the train can arrive at many stations, so make sure you're standing at all of them."

In November, Iran's prosecutor general, Morteza Moqtadaei, said that all Muslims were obliged to kill me, thus revealing the falsehood of Iran's claim that the fatwa had nothing to do with the Iranian government. Ayatollah Sanei, the man behind the bounty, said that volunteer hit-squads were to be dispatched. Then, at the beginning of December, I made it across the Atlantic again: to Canada, as the guest of Canadian

---

* Gianni Pico, who negotiated the release of many of the Lebanon hostages.

PEN. (Was any writer ever given more help by his colleagues? If I ever get out of this, it will be my life's work to try and give back just a little of the aid, and passion, and affection I've been given.) At a PEN benefit night in Toronto, so many writers spoke on my behalf that somebody whispered to me, "This is one hell of a bar mitzvah you're getting"; and it was. The premier of Ontario, Bob Rae, bounded onstage and embraced me. He thus became the first head of any government to stand with me in public. (Backstage, before the event, he actually kissed me for a photographer. Naturally, I kissed him back.)

The next day in Ottawa I met, among others, Canada's secretary of state for external affairs, Barbara MacDougall, and the leader of the opposition, Jean Chrétien. I also gave testimony to the parliamentary subcommittee on human rights. The effect of all this was electrifying. Within forty-eight hours, resolutions demanding that the Canadian government take this issue to the United Nations and pursue it in many other places such as the International Court of Justice had been rushed through the Canadian parliament with all-party support and the government had agreed to act upon them.

Another train in another station. Since then I've had a series of very friendly meetings in Dublin, with the new foreign minister, Dick Spring, and two other cabinet members, and, at her invitation, with President Mary Robinson at Phoenix Park. Next stop, perhaps, President Clinton?

—

I always knew this would be a long struggle; but at least, now, there's movement. In Norway, a projected oil deal with Iran is being blocked by politicians sympathetic to the campaign against the fatwa; in Canada, a $1 billion line of credit that Iran had been promised has also been blocked.

I say wherever I go that the struggle isn't just about me. It isn't even primarily about me. The great issues here are freedom of expression, and national sovereignty too. Also, the case of *The Satanic Verses* is just the best-known of all the cases of writers, intellectuals, progressives, and dissidents being jailed, banned, and murdered throughout the Muslim world. Iran's artists and intellectuals know this, which is why they have so courageously made statements giving me unqualified support. Leading Muslim intellectuals—the poet Adonis, the novelist Tahar Ben Jalloun, and scores of others—have called for the end of

Iran's threats, not only because they care about me but because they know that this is their fight, too. To win this fight is to win one skirmish in a much greater war. To lose would have unpleasant consequences for me, but it would also be a defeat in that larger conflict.

As this goes to press there is news that Yasser Arafat has denounced the fatwa as being against Islam; while, here in Britain, even the infamous demagogue Dr. Kalim Siddiqui believes it is time for "both sides to forgive and forget." After four years of intimidation and violence, there is certainly plenty to forgive. Still, I welcome even this most improbable of olive branches.

[*From an address delivered in King's College Chapel, Cambridge, on the morning of Sunday, February 14, 1993*]

To stand in this house is to be reminded of what is most beautiful about religious faith: its ability to give solace and to inspire, its aspiration to these great and lovely heights, in which strength and delicacy are so perfectly conjoined. In addition, to be asked to speak here on this day, the fourth anniversary of the notorious fatwa of the late Imam Khomeini, is a particular honor. When I was an undergraduate at this college, between 1965 and 1968, the years of flower-power and student power, I would have found the notion of delivering an address in King's Chapel pretty far-out, as we used to say; and yet, such are the journeys of one's life that here I stand. I am grateful to the chapel and the college for extending this invitation, which I take as a gesture of solidarity and support, support not merely for one individual but, much more importantly, for the high moral principles of human rights and human freedoms that the Khomeini edict seeks so brutally to attack. For just as King's Chapel may be taken as a symbol of what is best about religion, so the fatwa has become a symbol of what is worst.

It feels all the more appropriate to be speaking here because it was while in my final year of reading history at Cambridge that I came across the story of the so-called satanic verses or temptation of the Prophet Muhammad, and of his rejection of that temptation. That year, I had chosen as one of my special subjects a paper on Muhammad, the rise of Islam, and the caliphate. So few students chose this option that the lectures were canceled. The other students switched to different special subjects. However, I was anxious to continue, and Arthur Hibbert, one of the King's history dons, agreed to supervise me. So as it happened I was, I think, the only student in Cambridge who took the paper. The next year, I'm told, it was not offered again. This is the kind of thing that almost leads one to believe in the workings of a hidden hand.

The story of the "satanic verses" can be found, among other places, in the canonical writings of the classical writer al-Tabari. He tells us that on one occasion the Prophet was given verses which seemed to accept the divinity of the three most popular pagan goddesses of Mecca, thus compromising Islam's rigid monotheism. Later he rejected these verses as being a trick of the devil—saying that Satan had appeared to him in the guise of the Archangel Gabriel and spoken "satanic verses."

Historians have long speculated about this incident, wondering if perhaps the nascent religion had been offered a sort of deal by the pagan authorities of the city, which was flirted with and then refused. I felt the story humanized the Prophet, and therefore made him more accessible, more easily comprehensible to a modern reader, for whom the presence of doubt in a human mind, and human imperfections in a great man's personality, can only make that mind, that personality, more attractive. Indeed, according to the traditions of the Prophet, even the Archangel Gabriel was understanding about the incident, assuring him that such things had befallen all the prophets, and that he need not worry about what had happened. It seems that the Archangel Gabriel, and the God in whose name he spoke, was rather more tolerant than some of those who presently affect to speak in the name of God.

Khomeini's fatwa itself may be seen as a set of modern satanic verses. In the fatwa, once again, evil takes on the guise of virtue; and the faithful are deceived.

It's important to remember what the fatwa is. One cannot properly call it a sentence, since it far exceeds its author's jurisdiction; since it contravenes fundamental principles of Islamic law; and since it was issued without the faintest pretense of any legal process. (Even Stalin thought it necessary to hold show trials!) It is, in fact, a straightforward terrorist threat, and in the West it has already had very harmful effects. There is much evidence that writers and publishers have become nervous of publishing any material about Islam except of the most reverential and anodyne sort. There are instances of contracts for books being canceled, of texts being rewritten. Even so independent an artist as the filmmaker Spike Lee felt the need to submit to Islamic authorities the script of his film about Malcolm X, who was for a time a member of the Nation of Islam and performed the hajj or pilgrimage to Mecca. And to this day, almost one year after the paperback of *The Satanic Verses* was published (by a specially constituted consortium) in the United States, and imported into Britain, no British publisher has had the nerve to take on distribution of the softcover edition, even though it has been in the bookstores for months without causing the tiniest frisson.

In the East, however, the fatwa's implications are far more sinister. "You must defend Rushdie," an Iranian writer told a British scholar recently. "In defending Rushdie you are defending us." In January, in Turkey, an Iranian-trained hit-squad assassinated the secular journalist Ugur Mumçu. Last year, in Egypt, fundamentalist assassins killed Farag Fouda, one of the country's leading secular thinkers. Today, in Iran, many of the brave writers and intellectuals who defended me are being threatened with death-squads.

Last summer, I was able to participate in a literary seminar staged in a Cambridge college and attended by scholars and writers from all over the world, including many Muslims. I was touched by the friendship and enthusiasm with which the Muslim delegates greeted me. A distinguished Saudi journalist took my arm and said, "I want to embrace you because you, Mr. Rushdie, are a free man." He was fully aware of the ironies of what he was saying. He meant that freedom of speech, freedom of the imagination, is that freedom which gives meaning to all the others. He could walk the streets, get his work published, lead an ordinary life, and did not feel free, because there was so much he could not say, so much he hardly dared to think. I was protected by the Special Branch; he had to watch out for the Thought Police.

Today, as Professor Fred Halliday says in this week's *New Statesman & Society*, "the battle for freedom of expression, and for political and gender rights, is being fought out not in the senior common rooms and dinner tables of Europe, but in the Islamic world." In his essay, he gives some instances of the way in which the case of *The Satanic Verses* is being used as a symbol by the oppressed voices of the Muslim world. One of the many Iranian exile radio stations, he tells us, has even named itself Voice of the Satanic Verses.

The Satanic Verses is a committedly secular text that deals in part with the material of religious faith. For the religious fundamentalist, especially, at present, the Islamic fundamentalist, the adjective "secular" is the dirtiest of dirty words. But here's a strange paradox: in my country of origin, India, it was the secular ideal of Nehru and Gandhi that protected the nation's large Muslim minority, and it is the decay of that ideal that leads directly to the bloody sectarian confrontations which the subcontinent is now witnessing, confrontations that were long foretold and could have been avoided had not so many politicians chosen to fan the flames of religious hatred. Indian Muslims have always known the importance of secularism; it is from that experience that my own secularism springs. In the past four years, my commitment to that ideal, and to the ancillary principles of pluralism, skepticism, and tolerance, has been doubled and redoubled.

I have had to understand not just what I am fighting against—in this situation, that's not very hard—but also what I am fighting for, what is worth fighting for with one's life. Religious fanaticism's scorn for secularism and for unbelief led me to my answer. It is that values and morals are independent of religious faith, that good and evil come before religion: that—if I may be permitted to say this in the house of God—it is perfectly possible, and for many of us even necessary, to construct our ideas of the good without taking refuge in faith. That is where our freedom lies, and it is that freedom, among many others, which the fatwa threatens, and which it cannot be allowed to destroy.

[*From an article that was not, in the end, offered for publication, April 1993*]

O n Monday, February 22, the prime minister's office announced that Mr. Major had agreed in principle to a meeting with me, as a demonstration of the government's determination to stand up for freedom of expression and for the right of its citizens not to be murdered by thugs in the pay of a foreign power. More recently a date was set for that meeting. Immediately a vociferous Tory backbench campaign sought to have the meeting canceled, because of its interference with Britain's "partnership" with the murderous mullahs of Tehran. The date—which I had been assured was "as firm as can be"—has today been postponed without explanation. By a curious coincidence, a proposed British trade delegation to Iran in early May can now take place without embarrassment. Iran is hailing this visit—the first such mission in the fourteen years since the Khomeini revolution—as a "breakthrough" in relations. Its news agency states that the British have promised that lines of credit will be made available.

It is becoming harder to retain confidence in the Foreign Office's decision to launch a new "high-profile" international initiative against the notorious fatwa. For not only are we scurrying off to do business with the tyrannical regime that the U.S. administration calls an "international outlaw" and brands as the world's leading sponsor of terrorism, but we also propose to lend that regime the money with which to do business with us. Meanwhile, I gather I am to be offered a new date for my little meeting. But nobody from Number 10 Downing Street has spoken or written to me.

The Tory "anti-Rushdie" pressure group—its very description demonstrates its members' desire to turn this into an issue of personality rather than principle—includes Sir Edward Heath and Emma Nicholson, as well as that well-known apologist for Iranian interests Peter Temple-Morris.★ Emma Nicholson tells us that she has grown to "respect and like" the Iranian regime (whose record of killing, maiming, and torturing its own people has recently been condemned by the United Nations as being among the worst in the world), while Sir Edward, still protected by Special Branch because, twenty years ago, the British people suffered under his disastrous premiership, criticizes the decision to offer similar protection to a fellow Briton who is presently in greater danger than himself.

All these persons agree on one point: the crisis is my fault. Never mind that over two hundred of the most prominent Iranians in exile have signed a statement of absolute support for me. That writers, thinkers, journalists, and academics throughout the Muslim world— where the attack upon dissenting, progressive, and above all secularist ideas is daily gathering force—have told the British media that "to defend Rushdie is to defend us." That *The Satanic Verses,* a legitimate work of the free imagination, has many defenders (and where there are at least two views, why should the book-burners have the last word?), or that its opponents have felt no need to understand it.

Iranian officials have admitted that Khomeini never so much as saw a copy of the novel. Islamic jurisprudents have stated that the fatwa contradicts Islamic law, never mind international law. Meanwhile, the Iranian press has awarded a prize of sixteen gold pieces and a pilgrim-

---

★ Nicholson and Temple-Morris have both left the Conservatives: Nicholson is now a Liberal Democrat MEP, and Temple-Morris joined Labour.

age to Mecca for a cartoon "proving" that *The Satanic Verses* is not a novel at all but a carefully engineered Western conspiracy against Islam. Does this whole affair not feel, at times, like the blackest of black comedy—a circus sideshow enacted by murderous clowns?

In the last four years I have been slandered by many people. I do not intend to keep turning the other cheek. If it was proper to attack those on the Left who were the fellow-travelers of Communism, and those on the Right who sought to appease the Nazis, then the friends of revolutionary Iran—businessmen, politicians, or British fundamentalists—deserve to be treated with equal contempt.

I believe we have reached a turning point. Either we are serious about defending freedom, or we are not. If we are, then I hope Mr. Major will very soon be willing to stand up and be counted as he has promised. I should very much like to discuss with him how pressure on Iran can be increased—in the European Commission, through the Commonwealth and the UN, at the International Court of Justice. Iran needs us more than we need Iran. Instead of quaking when the mullahs threaten to cut trade links, let us be the ones to turn the economic screws. I have discovered, in my conversations across Europe and North America, widespread all-party interest in the idea of a ban on offering credit to Iran, as a first stage. But everyone is waiting for the British government to take a lead. In today's London *Times,* however, Bernard Levin suggests that fully two-thirds of all Tory MPs would be delighted if Iranian assassins succeeded in killing me. If these MPs truly represent the nation—if we are so shruggingly unconcerned about our liberties—then so be it: lift the protection, disclose my whereabouts, and let the bullets come. One way or the other. Let's make up our minds.

[*From* The Observer, *July 1993*]

I met the writer and journalist Mr. Aziz Nesin in 1986, when I took part in an event organized by British writers to protest against the Turkish authorities' decision to confiscate his passport. I hope that Mr. Nesin remembers my small effort on his behalf, because recently he has done me no favors at all. Mr. Nesin is now editor-in-chief of the Turkish newspaper *Aydinlik,* and a publisher. Recently *Aydinlik* began the publication of extracts from *The Satanic Verses,* "to promote debate and discussion." These extracts appeared over a period of weeks, under the heading "Salman Rushdie—Thinker or Charlatan?" At no time did Mr. Nesin or *Aydinlik* seek my permission to publish any extracts. Nor did they discuss with me what extracts would be used, or allow me to confirm the accuracy or quality of the translation. I never saw the published texts. Ever since 1989, Iranian mullahs and Islamic zealots around the world have been quoting and reproducing de-contextualized segments of *The Satanic Verses* to use as propaganda weapons in the larger war against progressive ideas, secularist thought, and the modern world, a war in which the so-called Rushdie affair is no more than a skirmish. I was appalled to find that these Turkish secular-ists and anti-fundamentalists were using my work in exactly the same unscrupulous fashion, albeit to serve different political purposes. Once again, I was a pawn in somebody else's game.

I asked my agents to write to Mr. Nesin and ask: why had his news-paper pirated my work? What were his motives for wishing to publish me in the first place? Was he, for example, interested in my work as a writer? And if, as he claimed, he had fought on behalf of writers' rights for many years, would he be prepared to protest against *Aydinlik*'s in-fringement of those rights? After a long silence, Nesin's reply was to print my agents' letter in *Aydinlik* together with a riposte that must rank as one of the most malicious, untruthful and, paradoxically, revealing texts I have ever read. He scolded me for daring to ask about his mo-tives and then said that he didn't care about my situation: "What con-cern is Salman Rushdie's cause to me?" He further said that he had asked for permission to publish only as a courtesy. If we refused, he said, "I will be forced to publish the book without your sanction . . . you may take us to court."

Plainly, Nesin and his associates wished to use me, and my work, as cannon fodder in their struggle against religious zealotry in Turkey. And here is where I find myself in difficulties. For I, too, am a commit-ted secularist. I, too, deplore, and have used every opportunity in the last five years to struggle against, the spread of religious fanaticism across the face of the earth. Only last week I was able to attend a gather-ing in Paris of the Académie Universelle des Cultures, an organization created by President Mitterrand under the presidency of the Nobel lau-reate Elie Wiesel and attended by, among others, Wole Soyinka, Um-berto Eco, Cynthia Ozick, the great Arab poet Adonis, and, from Turkey, the novelist Yashar Kemal. As members of this académie we spent a good part of the day protesting against attacks on secularists by fundamentalists in Algeria, Egypt, and, yes, Turkey. I have believed from the beginning that the true context of the attack on *The Satanic Verses* was this wider war. But Mr. Nesin did not see me as a combatant. For him, my work was simply a weapon, to use as he saw fit.

Now, tragically, Mr. Nesin has been involved in a violent confrontation with the fundamentalists in Sivas, Turkey. The news reports say he is alive.* But many, many people are dead. And the newspaper reports call this a "Rushdie riot." It is hard to express how I feel today.

However, we must not fail to lay the blame for these horrible killings where it truly belongs. Murder is murder, and the guilt for the crime must be laid at the feet of the criminals. And the criminals are, of course, the religious zealots who hounded a meeting of secularist writers, who set fire to their hotel and then prevented the rescue services from reaching the scene. I am utterly appalled by these God-driven mobs and by their wild lust for the blood of unbelievers, and I send my grief, my sympathy, and my outraged support to the families of the dead; to all those who fight against religious bigots; yes, also to Mr. Aziz Nesin.

Will any good come out of this tragedy? Will the world's leaders, now assembling for the G7 meeting in Japan, assume the moral responsibility of saying, enough is enough, terrorism cannot be supported, and countries that promote it, that train and arm and finance the killers, that point fingers across the world and demand the heads of innocent men, will suffer for their misdeeds? Will the much-spoken-of New World Order be a triumph of cynicism, of business-as-usualism, of naked greed and raw power? Or might we, at last, start to draw the lines of a more humane society and inform terrorist states that their immoral acts will have political and economic consequences? I hope that every journalist arriving in Tokyo will ask the G7 politicians to condemn the fanatical murderers of Sivas, and their "spiritual" leaders and paymasters too. These are not only the enemies of secularists and Westerners; they are also the real enemies of Islam.

---

* Aziz Nesin did survive the Sivas attack. He died in 1995.

[*This article appeared in* The New York Times *in July 1993 under the title "The Struggle for the Soul of Islam"*]

T he following news stories are all taken from the first half of 1993. In Pakistan, an elderly poet, Akhtar Hameed Khan, seventy-eight, is quoted as saying that while he admires Muhammad, his real inspiration has been Buddha. He denies saying this but is nevertheless accused by mullahs of blasphemy. In 1992, he had been arrested for insulting the Prophet's descendants by writing a poem about animals that the fundamentalists alleged had hidden, allegorical meanings. He managed to beat that charge, but now, once again, his life is in danger.

In Sharjah, one of the United Arab Emirates, an Indian theater group who in 1992 performed a play entitled *Corpse-Eating Ants,* which was held to be blasphemous, and who had been sentenced to six-year jail sentences for blasphemy, appeal against the sentence. Some members of the group are freed, but one has his sentence increased to ten years, and another has his six-year term upheld by the appeals court.

In Istanbul, one of the country's most respected secularist journalists, Ugur Mumçu, is gunned down in the street. Turkish fundamentalists take credit for the attack, and the Turkish government says it has evidence linking the murderers to Iran. The interior minister, Ismet Sezgin, says that at least three killings have been carried out by a group called Islamic Movement, whose members have been trained in assassination techniques "at an official Iranian facility between Tehran and Qom."

In Egypt, the assassins who in 1992 murdered the distinguished secular thinker Farag Fouda are currently being tried; however, extremist bombings and killings continue.

In Algeria, the writer Tahar Djaout is one of six secularists murdered in a killing spree by what the security forces call "Muslim terrorists."

In Saudi Arabia, a number of distinguished intellectuals forms the country's first human-rights group. Within days, many of them are fired from their posts, including university professorships; many of them are arrested and jailed. Trials are pending.

In Egypt, Professor Nasr Abu-Zeid, who teaches literature at Cairo University, is charged with apostasy because of his criticisms of the Islamists. Fundamentalists ask the courts to dissolve his marriage, since it is illegal for a Muslim to be married to an apostate. The alternative would be for his wife to be stoned to death as an adulteress.

In Turkey, thirty-six secularist writers, dancers, musicians, and artists gathered for a conference in the town of Sivas are burned to death in their hotel by a mob of Islamic fundamentalists which accuses them of being atheists and therefore, in the fanatics' view, deserving of being burned alive.

The United States has recently become all too painfully familiar with the nature of the holy—or, rather, unholy—terrorists of Islam. The crater beneath the World Trade Center and the uncovering of a plot to set off more gigantic bombs and to assassinate leading political figures have shown Americans how brutal these extremists can be. These and other cases of international Islamic terrorism have shocked the world community; whereas the cases of domestic terrorism previously listed have captured relatively little of the world's "share of mind." I should like to suggest that this imbalance in our attention represents a kind of victory for fanaticism. If the worst, most reactionary, most medievalist strain in the Muslim world is treated as the authentic culture, so that the bombers and the mullahs get all the headlines while progressive, modernizing voices are treated as minor, marginal, "Westoxicated"—as small news—then the fundamentalists are being allowed to set the agenda.

The truth is that there is a great struggle in progress for the soul of the Muslim world, and as the fundamentalists grow in power and ruthlessness, those courageous men and women who are willing to engage them in a battle of ideas and of moral values are rapidly becoming as important for us to know about, to understand, and to support as once the dissident voices in the old Soviet Union used to be. The Soviet terror-state, too, denigrated its opponents as being overly Westernized and enemies of the people; it, too, took men from their wives in the middle of the night, as the poet Osip Mandelstam was taken from Nadezhda. We do not blame Mandelstam for his own destruction; we do not blame him for attacking Stalin, but rather, and rightly, we blame Stalin for his Stalin-ness. In the same spirit, let us not fall into the trap of blaming the Sharjah theater-folk for their rather macabre-sounding ants, or Turkish secularists for "provoking" the mob that murdered them.

Rather, we should understand that secularism is now the fanatics' Enemy Number One, and its most important target. Why? Because secularism demands a total separation between Church and State; philosophers such as the Egyptian Fouad Zakariya argue that free Muslim societies can exist only if this principle is adhered to. And because secularism rejects the idea that any society of the late twentieth century can be thought of as "pure," and argues that the attempt to purify the modern Muslim world of its inevitable hybridities will lead to equally inevitable tyrannies. And because secularism seeks to historicize our understanding of the Muslim verities: it sees Islam as an event within history, not outside it. And because secularism seeks to end the repressions against women that are instituted wherever the radical Islamists come into power. And, most of all, because secularists know that a modern nation-state cannot be built upon ideas that emerged in the Arabian desert over thirteen hundred years ago.

The weapons used against the dissidents of the Muslim world are everywhere the same. The accusations are always of "blasphemy," "apostasy," "heresy," "un-Islamic activities." These "crimes" are held to "insult Islamic sanctities." The "people's wrath," thus aroused, becomes "impossible to resist." The accused become persons whose "blood is unclean" and therefore deserves to be spilled.

The British writer Marina Warner once pointed out that the objects associated with witchcraft—a pointed hat, a broomstick, a cauldron, a cat—would have been found in most women's possession during the great witch-hunts. If these were the proofs of witchcraft, then all women were potentially guilty; it was only necessary for accusing fingers to point at one and cry, "Witch!" Americans, remembering the example of the McCarthyite witch-hunts, will readily understand how potent and destructive the process can still be. And what is happening in the Muslim world today must be seen as a witch-hunt of exceptional proportions, a witch-hunt being carried out in many nations, and often with murderous results. So the next time you stumble across a story such as the ones I've repeated here, perhaps a story tucked away near the bottom of an inside page in this newspaper, remember that the persecution it describes is not an isolated act—that it is part of a deliberate, lethal program, whose purpose is to criminalize, denigrate, and even to assassinate the Muslim world's best, most honorable voices: its voices of dissent. And remember that those dissidents need your support. More than anything, they need your attention.

[*From a letter to* The Independent, *July 1993*]

I find it impossible to avoid the conclusion that the world community's shameful response to the continuing annihilation of the Bosnian Muslims is in some way connected to their being Muslims. It is
worth mentioning, however, that outrage at this fact is by no means
confined to the Muslim community—if only because, according to
your correspondent Yasmin Alibhai-Brown, the "underlying issue" is
that "for years the majority of Muslims have felt misunderstood and
demonised in the West. . . . Bosnia is seen as the culmination of their
process of alienation."

This kind of them-and-us rhetoric of victimization, no matter how
legitimate it may seem, creates as many cultural problems as it addresses.

It creates intellectual confusions, as when British Muslims rightly
excoriate Europe for failing to defend its very own citizens but denigrate these same Muslims for being "Muslims in name only." Bosnia's
Muslims are indeed secularized and humanistic, representing an attractive blend of Muslim and European values. By sneering at this hybrid
culture, British Muslims undermine their own case.

It creates moral confusions, too: when German racists burn Muslims in their houses, the blame is very properly laid on the perpetrators;
but when Islamic fanatics burn dozens to death in a hotel in Turkey,
some Muslim commentators at once try to blame the targets of the
mob, accusing them of such inflammatory offenses as atheism.

Worst of all, it creates the risk that the community will fall under the
spell of leaders who will ultimately damage them more than their
present (real or perceived) enemies. Germany's sense of national humiliation after World War I was exploited by Hitler during his rise
to power; the Iranian people's wholly justified hatred of the regime of
the shah led them toward the great historical mistake of supporting
Khomeini; in India today, the cry of "Hinduism under threat" is rally-
ing people to the banner of Hindu fundamentalism; and now, here in
Britain, Alibhai-Brown tells us that "moderation seems an obscenity."
Will the fatuous Dr. Siddiqui be followed by more formidable extremist figures?

British Muslims may not wish to hear this from the author of *The
Satanic Verses,* but the real enemies of Islam are not British novelists or

Turkish satirists. They are not the secularists murdered by fundamentalists in Algeria recently. Nor do they include the distinguished Cairo professor of literature and his scholarly wife who are presently being hounded by Egyptian fanatics for being apostates. Neither are they the intellectuals who lost their jobs and were arrested by the authorities in Saudi Arabia because they founded a human-rights organization. However weak, however few the progressive voices may be, they represent the best hope in the Muslim world for a free and prosperous future. The enemies of Islam are those who wish the culture to be frozen in time, who are, in Ali Shariati's phrase, in "revolt against history," and whose tyranny and unreason are making modern Islam look like a culture of madness and blood. Alibhai-Brown's interviewee Nasreen Rehman wisely says that "we must stop thinking in binary, oppositional terms." May I propose that a starting place might be the recognition that, on the one hand, it is the Siddiquis and Hizbollahs and blind sheikhs and ayatollahs who are the real foes of Muslims around the world, the real "enemy within"; and that, on the other hand—as in the case of the campaign on behalf of Bosnia's Muslims—there are many "friends without."

[*From a letter to* The Nation, August 1993]

Alexander Cockburn accuses me of "spiteful abuse" of Turkish secularists (*The Nation,* July 26). This is a grave charge, and I hope you will permit me space to reply. I heard the news of the atrocity in Sivas, Turkey, on the evening of Friday, July 2. Within half an hour I put out a statement condemning the fundamentalist murderers, and elaborated on this in a live telephone interview with the main BBC radio news program of the evening. The next day, I appeared on BBC-TV, ITN, and Sky Television, and spoke on the telephone to journalists from several British newspapers. In every case the primary importance of denouncing the murderers formed the main thrust of my contribution.

In the week that followed, I wrote a further text (July 6), published as the leading letter in the London *Independent,* in which I tried to speak up for Bosnia's Muslims and also defended those who died in Sivas against the charge that "such inflammatory offences as atheism" had provoked their murderers into murdering them. I gave interviews on this subject to several European newspapers. Finally, I published a text that some of your readers may have seen in *The New York Times* (July 11), discussing the need to pay attention to and support the dissidents of the Muslim world—including those in Turkey—who are at present under such vicious and lethal attack.

It is a pity Cockburn did not trouble to check the facts—he made no attempt to contact me or my agents or the Rushdie Defence Campaign based at Article 19 in London—before letting fly. After almost two weeks in which hardly a day has passed without my speaking up for secularist principles and against religious fanaticism, it is really quite extraordinary to be vilified in your pages for not having done so.

The *Observer* piece itself—as Cockburn concedes—also laid the blame for the Sivas massacre firmly on the local religious fanatics, and expressed my outrage at what they had done. It is true, however, that I criticized the behavior of the journalist Aziz Nesin, in whose newspaper *Aydinlik* unauthorized extracts from *The Satanic Verses* had been published in May.

Cockburn quotes Nesin thus: "I had met Rushdie in London and discussed the possibility of publishing his book in Turkish." This is untrue. In 1986—the only time I ever met Nesin—*The Satanic Verses* was not even finished. Nesin goes on: "The only thing he lately cares for is whether he receives his copyright fees or not." Not so. I have no interest in receiving whatever monies may be due to me from *Aydinlik*. I am, however, vitally interested in how, and by whom, my work is published.

Nesin and *Aydinlik* published the pirated extracts from my novel in the most polemical manner possible, denigrated my work, attacked my integrity as a man and as an artist, and made a lot of money by doing so—Cockburn reveals that the paper's circulation trebled during the period of publication. Certainly these were not people I would have chosen to be the first publishers of *The Satanic Verses* in a Muslim country. Yet Cockburn believes I was wrong to defend myself, even though British Muslim "spokesmen" and sections of the British media were attempting to make me the person responsible for the Sivas killings. It appears to be Cockburn's view that all this—the theft of my work, the assaults on my character, the lies about my public positions, and the responsibility for having caused a "Rushdie riot"—is just fine, whereas my wish to set the record straight is evidence of an even deeper perfidy. In a letter from the Turkish writer Murat Belge, one of the friends whose advice I sought, he says: "It is quite legitimate to criticize Nesin for his rather childish behavior. However, the way all the politicians are now blaming him for everything is infuriating. . . . It is as if Nesin has killed these people, and the murderers who actually burned them alive are innocent citizens." This is exactly my view, which I have expressed over and over again in the past fortnight. I am sad that it has not managed to get through to Alexander Cockburn.

[*From* The Guardian, *September 1993*]

I have just returned from Prague, where President Vaclav Havel reaffirmed his belief that the so-called Rushdie affair was a test case of democratic values, a test case, as he put it, for himself. The story has been widely reported—except in Britain, where, as far as I can see, it has not been mentioned by a single newspaper, nor has anyone thought it interesting until now to print the photograph of the meeting that was made freely available to the press. However, an unpleasant little story about Iran giving gold coins and tickets to Mecca to the winners of a Rushdie cartoon contest has been given space by several papers.

In late July, I was able to visit Portugal, and President Mario Soares went on national television with me to declare his passionate support for the fight against the fatwa, and committed himself to helping in every way he could. Once again, this was treated as a big story by many European countries; in Britain, however, nothing.

In my meetings with John Major, Douglas Hogg, and Foreign and Commonwealth Office diplomats, I have repeatedly been told that the British government considers such trips to be matters of the highest importance and utility. They remind Iran about the wide international consensus on this issue, and demonstrate, too, the international community's growing impatience with Iran's failure to withdraw its threats, and its determination to make Iran do so. In my view they also serve the important symbolic function of showing the fundamentalists that their intimidation isn't working. The trips take enormous amounts of planning, and I couldn't make them without the help and support of many individuals, organizations (notably the Rushdie Defence Campaign at Article 19), and security forces; so it is frustrating, to say the least, that they are so comprehensively ignored at home.

It is plain that Iran is feeling the heat. In a recent interview with *Time* magazine, President Rafsanjani said that in his view the Rushdie case was a Western conspiracy to put pressure on Iran, which takes some beating as a case of upside-down, Humpty-Dumpty thinking. But if one ignores the paranoia in the first half of his comment, the second half shows that he is feeling under pressure. This is excellent news. In recent months, Speaker Nateq-Nouri of the Iranian Majlis, the same man who less than a year ago was demanding my head on a plate, has said that it is not Iran's policy to have me killed; and Rafsanjani, in his *Time* interview, confirmed this. Amusing as such wide-eyed, who-me-guv innocence can seem, it is at least evidence that the penny has begun to drop. It is possible that Iran is trying to find the language that will solve the problem, for the fatwa, as a senior Western diplomat with deep knowledge of the region told me, is essentially a matter of Iran's internal politics: how are they to do what the world demands and still manage to play to the home audience as well?

If I'm right that Iran has begun to get the message, then this is the time to increase the pressure. The public support of Presidents Havel and Soares therefore matters a great deal, which is why the sudden jadedness of the British media is so worrying. As the mullahs' little cartoon contest shows, the problem has not gone away just because I've been getting out more. It won't go away until Iran backs down. If news editors are getting bored, that boredom plays into the hands of the terrorist censors.

Three years ago, Vaclav Havel came to Britain on a state visit and asked to meet me. The British government prevented the meeting, fearing, perhaps, for the British hostages in Lebanon. Havel had wished to make a major gesture of solidarity in front of the world's press but was restricted to speaking to me on the phone. How ironic that the meeting should finally take place with the support of the British ambassador in Prague and the Foreign and Commonwealth Office back home, and then be ignored by the press!

There is a problem of news values here that goes far beyond my own case. It seems that nasty stories are news but constructive developments are not. When religious bigots recently burned thirty-six Turkish intellectuals and artists to death in the town of Sivas, the event was widely—and inaccurately—reported in our papers. When, days later, literally hundreds of thousands of Turks marched peacefully through the streets in defense of secularism and tolerance, their deeds were ignored. In this case and in others, it seems as if an old cliché is being inverted—it is not the terrorists who are being starved of the oxygen of publicity but their adversaries. It is unsettling to find the processes and values of our editorial decision-makers becoming—to use a Czech analogy—so Kafkaesque.

[*From the* Daily Mail, *September 1993*]

M ay I congratulate the *Daily Mail* on its consistency? Mary Kenny's spiteful piece, in which I am called bad-mannered, sullen, grace-less, silly, curmudgeonly, unattractive, small-minded, arrogant, and egocentric—she apparently doesn't see how funny it is to insist so sourly that someone else should "try a little sweetness"—is, after all, only the latest in your long campaign to make me the villain of the so-called Rushdie affair.

Regarding the expense of my protection, I question Kenny's figures★ but have expressed my gratitude for that protection publicly on many, many occasions—you don't seem to have been listening—and have also done so privately, to the police and prime minister. I *am* grateful for it. It has, in all probability, saved my life. But it's not only my freedom that is being defended but also British sovereignty—the right of British citizens not to be assassinated by a foreign power—and principles of free speech. This is a fight against state terrorism. My death would mean that Iran had won the battle. Is the defeat of terrorism and the

★ The cost of my protection has always stuck in the throat of many British com-mentators. Estimates ranging from the wild (one million pounds a year) to the surreal (ten million pounds a year) have been repeated so often that they have become pseudo-facts. The British authorities have over the years placed me in an invidious position by refusing to clarify the facts while "senior Home Office sources" regularly leaked mis-leading information. The truth is as follows. First, although the "thirty different safe houses" provided for me, according to the *Mail,* at "an estimated cost . . . of ten million pounds" are by now a well-established myth, the fact is that *no safe house was provided for me at any time.* I always found, and met the cost of, my own accommodation. The cost to the British taxpayer was nil. Second, I was protected by officers who, had they not been allocated to me, would still have been on the police payroll; the additional cost to Brit-ish taxpayers of protecting me was therefore limited to overtime expenses. Third, dur-ing these dark years I have paid a great deal of income tax on those big book deals and large royalties of which segments of the media—and Islamic members of the House of Lords—so disapprove. I would suggest that the British exchequer has actually made a net profit on our strange relationship. Finally, the U.K. taxpayer has never footed the bill when I've been out of Britain.

preservation of free speech and national integrity worth so little to you that you must so frequently carp about the cost?

The thrust of Mary Kenny's attack on me is that I have made criticisms of aspects of British society, and that I do not vote Conservative. She derides me for having pointed to elements of racism in Britain; in the week of the horrific attack on young Quddus Ali, can the existence of that racism really be denied? She blames me for having criticized the police in the past—does she really believe, after the recent flood of reversed convictions and discoveries of widespread police malpractice, that I have no right to do so? I have always given credit where it's due, and the Special Branch officers who guard me know very well how deeply I appreciate their work.

Kenny also sneers at my 1983 general election essay about "Nanny-Britain"; but wasn't it the Tory Party who gave Mrs. Thatcher the ultimate bad review by dumping her so unceremoniously? It's true that I am not a Tory voter; after recent by-election results, how many Britons still are? The Conservative Party is not the State. To vote Labour is not an act of treason. (Not that I am able to vote; one of the deprivations of a life at an "unknown address" is that I cannot register. Does Mary Kenny care that I have been deprived of the most basic democratic right?)

Kenny goes on to suggest that I have "special social responsibilities"—but were I to suggest the same, she would no doubt instantly scream about my "arrogance." She demands that I "turn my attention to healing the rifts between mankind." I would describe the writer's role a little more modestly than that myself, but in recent weeks and months I have spoken out for justice in Bosnia, supported the fragile PLO-Israeli pact, criticized the growth of religious sectarianism that is endangering India's secular constitution, demanded the world's attention for progressive, democratic voices throughout the Muslim and Arab world, and tried repeatedly to draw attention to the crimes against such people—the murders and persecutions of journalists, writers, and artists in Turkey, Algeria, Sharjah, Egypt, and Pakistan, to say nothing of my old friend the Islamic Republic of Iran. None of these efforts were reported in the *Daily Mail*.

As for Prince Charles, his attack on me and my protection has been reported in the French, Spanish, and British press.* It has been con-

---

* The *Mail* had attacked me for responding to the Prince of Wales's reported view that too much public money was being spent on me. I had been asked by a Spanish journalist what I thought of Ian McEwan's remark that Prince Charles cost much more to protect than I did but had never written anything of interest. I had replied light-

firmed to me by the French philosopher Bernard-Henri Lévy, who was present when the Prince of Wales's remarks were made. This is why I treat Buckingham Palace's denials with a degree of skepticism. And yes, it's true, I did poke fun at him in return; am I—even after Camillagate—the only Briton to be denied the right to join in this national pastime?

Let me be very clear: I do not attack the country that protects me. All countries are many countries, and there are many Britains that I love and admire; why else would I have chosen to live here for the last thirty-two years? However, I have the same right as any other citizen— the same right as the *Daily Mail*—to say what it is about this society and its leadership that I dislike. I will give up that right only (to coin a phrase) over my dead body. The real arrogance lies in assuming, as the *Daily Mail* and its columnists assume, that their view of this country, "their Britain," is the only legitimate one; the real bad-mannered behavior is that of a paper which daily reviles and bullies all those who don't fit into its narrow-minded, complacent worldview.

Mary Kenny is right to say that, in the Rushdie affair, freedom of speech is something we are all paying for. I am fighting with all my might to bring about the day when the financial burden can be lifted. In the meanwhile, it would be absurd—would it not?—to give up that very freedom. So I shall continue to speak my mind, and you at the *Daily Mail* will, I'm sure, continue to speak yours.

[*From a statement in the Swedish newspaper* Expressen, *October 1993*]

Your newspaper's decision to campaign against the continued political, economic, and cultural involvement of the civilized world with the Iranian terror-state is very important, and I welcome it. No intelligence experts doubt that the hand of Iran was behind the cowardly attack on my distinguished Norwegian publisher and dear friend William Nygaard, an attack which he survived only by a kind of miracle. Iran's is also the hidden hand behind the killing of more than twenty Iranian

---

heartedly that I agreed with Ian. The wrath of the *Mail*—that same *Mail* which had devoted dozens of pages to Prince Charles's desire to be Ms. Parker-Bowles's tampon!—knew no bounds.

dissidents in Europe during the presidency of the so-called moderate Rafsanjani, who also sits on the National Security Council, in which such decisions are made.

How many more murders and assaults on innocent men and women will the Free World tolerate? If we go on reacting to violence with a shrug and a cry of "business as usual," then are we not collaborating in terrorism by turning a blind eye to it? Of course Iran uses "cut-out" mechanisms and smoke screens to conceal its role; but the UN has condemned Iran's human-rights violations and use of terrorism; the United States has named it the world's major sponsor of terrorism; the EC has insisted that it improve its record in these matters before relations with it can improve. Yet this past week Germany welcomed Iran's secret service head as an honored guest—the very man, Fallahian, who is behind all the Iranian assassination teams at work around the world! This is an almost laughably cynical act.

The Nordic countries have always supported my campaign against the Iranian terrorist regime; I have long been grateful for that support. Now the terrorists have attempted revenge, by shooting an unarmed man in the back. This time they must not be permitted to get away with it. I ask that Sweden, Norway, the other Nordic countries, and all the free nations of Europe cast Iran into the outer darkness where it belongs. I ask for an instant and complete break in all political, economic, financial, and cultural links. Let the evildoers be isolated. If they seek to destroy our fragile but precious freedoms, then they themselves are asking to be destroyed. And make no mistake: tyrannical as they are, cruel as they are, murderous as they are, their hated and feared regime is fragile, too. Without the support of the West, it will fall.

Does the West wish to be responsible for keeping the fanatical mullahs of Iran in power? It is time to make a choice in this matter; not for my sake, not only for William Nygaard's sake, but for the sake of freedom itself.

[From the introduction to a documentary film on television]

Tahar Djaout was one of the most eloquent voices in the struggle against bigotry now being waged throughout the Muslim world. He was killed because he fought against the new Islamic inquisition, which is every bit as vicious as the old Christian one. We should feel his death as a wound in our own world. The battle between progressive and regressive elements in Muslim culture—between, as Djaout says, those who move forward and those who go back, who recoil—is of immense importance to us all. Its outcome may shape the next age of human history.

Tahar Djaout wrote in French, which gave him an international as well as a national voice, and earned him the hatred of the fanatics, for it is in the nature of fanatics to be parochial. I feel close to his plurality of self as well as tongue, and to his vulnerability. Those who embrace difference are always in danger from the apostles of purity. Ideas of purity—racial purity, cultural purity, religious purity—lead directly to horrors: to the gas oven, to ethnic cleansing, to the rack.

I introduce this film tonight, even though there is a danger that the endorsement of one as demonized as myself may give the mullahs a rhetorical weapon, because I believe that the killings will be stopped only when the world community cries out in outrage, and forces the Thought Police to desist. After all, the weapon that killed Tahar Djaout was not rhetorical. It was a gun.

No religion justifies murder. If assassins disguise themselves by putting on the cloak of faith, we must not be fooled. Islamic fundamentalism is not a religious movement but a political one. Let us, in Djaout's memory, at least learn to call tyranny by its true name.

[*A statement read out at an evening for Sarajevo in New York, November 1993*]

There is a Sarajevo of the mind, an imagined Sarajevo whose present ruination and torment exiles us all. That Sarajevo represented something like an ideal, a city in which the values of pluralism, tolerance, and coexistence have created a unique and resilient culture. In that Sarajevo there actually exists that secularist Islam for which so many people are fighting elsewhere in the world. The people of that Sarajevo do not define themselves by faith or tribe but simply, and honorably, as citizens. If that city is lost, then we are all its refugees. If the culture of Sarajevo dies, then we are all its orphans. The writers and artists of Sarajevo are therefore fighting for us as well as for themselves. On the airwaves of Radio Zid, or in the sessions of the recent Sarajevo Film Festival—what an achievement, to stage a festival of over a hundred movies in the midst of such a war!—the candle is kept burning.

To define the people of Sarajevo simply as entities in need of basic supplies would be to visit upon them a second privation: by reducing them to mere statistical victimhood, it would deny them their personalities, their individuality, their idiosyncrasies—in short, their humanity. So, whatever the world's governments and the UN protection force may say, let us insist that culture is as important to Sarajevo as medicines or food; that the people of Bosnia need cultural convoys, too. Let us insist that in wartime, when the forces of inhumanity are at their height, culture is not a luxury; and that the fight for the survival of the unique culture of Sarajevo is also a fight for what matters most to us about our own.

[Written for the International Parliament of Writers, February 1994]

A DECLARATION OF INDEPENDENCE

Writers are citizens of many countries: the finite and frontiered country of observable reality and everyday life, the boundless kingdom of the imagination, the half-lost land of memory, the federations of the heart which are both hot and cold, the united states of the mind (calm and turbulent, broad and narrow, ordered and deranged), the celestial and infernal nations of desire, and—perhaps the most important of all our habitations—the unfettered republic of the tongue. These are the countries that our Parliament of Writers can claim, truthfully and with both humility and pride, to represent. Together they comprise a greater territory than that governed by any worldly power; yet their defenses against that power can seem very weak.

The art of literature requires, as an essential condition, that the writer be free to move between his many countries as he chooses, needing no passport or visa, making what he will of them and of himself. We are miners and jewelers, truth-tellers and liars, jesters and commanders, mongrels and bastards, parents and lovers, architects and demolition men. The creative spirit, of its very nature, resists frontiers and limiting points, denies the authority of censors and taboos. For this reason it all too frequently is treated as an enemy by those mighty or petty potentates who resent the power of art to build pictures of the world that quarrel with, or undermine, their own simpler and less open-hearted views.

Yet it is not art that is weak but artists who are vulnerable. The poetry of Ovid survives; the life of Ovid was made wretched by the powerful. The poetry of Mandelstam lives on; the poet was murdered by the tyrant he dared to name. Today, around the world, literature continues to confront tyranny—not polemically but by denying its authority, by going its own way, by declaring its independence. The best of that literature will survive, but we cannot wait for the future to release it from the censor's chains. Many persecuted authors will also, somehow, survive; but we cannot wait silently for their persecutions to end. Our Parliament of Writers exists to fight for oppressed writers and against all those who persecute them and their work, and to renew continually the declaration of independence without which writing is impossible; and not only writing but dreaming; and not only dreaming but thought; and not only thought but liberty itself.

[*An open letter to Taslima Nasrin, July 1994*]

Dear Taslima Nasrin, I am sure you have become tired of being called the female Salman Rushdie—what a bizarre and comical creature that would be!—when all along you thought you were the female Taslima Nasrin. I am sorry my name has been hung around your neck, but please know that there are many people in many countries working to make sure that such sloganizing does not obscure your own identity, the unique features of your situation, and the importance of fighting to defend you and your rights against those who would cheerfully see you dead.

In reality it is our adversaries who seem to have things in common, who seem to believe in divine sanction for lynching and terrorism. So instead of turning you into a female me, the headline writers should be describing your opponents as "the Bangladeshi Iranians." How sad it must be to believe in a god of blood! What an Islam they have made, these apostles of death, and how important it is to have the courage to dissent from it!

Taslima, I have been asked to inaugurate a series of open letters in your support, letters that will be published in about twenty European countries. Great writers have agreed to lend their weight to the campaign on your behalf: Czeslaw Milosz, Mario Vargas Llosa, Milan Kundera, and many more. When such letter-writing campaigns were run on my behalf, I found them immensely strength-giving and cheering, and I know that they helped shape public opinion and government attitudes in many countries. I hope that our letters will bring you similar comfort and cheer, and that the pressure they will exert will be of use.

You have spoken out about the oppression of women under Islam, and what you said needed saying. Here in the West there are too many eloquent apologists working to convince people of the fiction that women are not discriminated against in Muslim countries; or that, if they are, it has nothing to do with the religion. The sexual mutilation of women, according to this argument, has no basis in Islam; which may be true in theory, but in practice, in many countries where this goes on, the mullahs wholeheartedly support it. And then there are the countless (and uncounted) crimes of violence within the home, the inequalities of legal systems that value women's evidence less than men's, the driving of women out of the workplace in all countries where Islamists have come to, or even near to, power, and so on.

You have spoken out, too, about the attacks on Hindus in Bangladesh after the destruction of the Ayodhya mosque in India by Hindu extremists. For this your novel *Lajja* has been attacked by zealots, for this your life was first placed in danger. Yet any fair-minded person would agree that a religious attack by Muslims on innocent Hindus is as bad as an attack by Hindus on innocent Muslims. Such simple fairness is the target of the bigots' rage and, in defending you, we also defend that fairness.

You are accused of having said that the Qur'an should be revised (though you have said that you were referring only to the Sharia). You may have seen that only last week the Turkish authorities have announced a project to revise the Sharia, so in that regard at least you are not alone. And here is another simple point: even if you did say that the Qur'an should be revised to remove its ambiguities about the rights of women, and even if every Muslim man in the world were to disagree with you, it would remain a perfectly legitimate opinion, and no society that wishes to jail or hang you for expressing it can call itself free.

Simplicity is what fundamentalists always say they are after, but in fact they are obscurantists in all things. What is *simple* is to agree that if one may say, "God exists," then another may also say, "God does not exist"; that if one may say, "I loathe this book," then another may also say, "But I like it very much." What is not at all simple is to be asked to believe that there is only one truth, one way of expressing that truth, and one punishment (death) for those who say this isn't so.

As you know, Taslima, Bengali culture—and I mean the culture of Bangladesh as well as Indian Bengal—has always prided itself on its openness, its freedom to think and argue, its intellectual disputatiousness, its lack of bigotry. It is a disgrace that your government has chosen to side with the religious extremists against their own history, their own civilization, their own values. Bengalis have always understood that free expression is not only a Western value; it is one of their own great treasures, too. It is that treasure-house, the treasure-house of the intelligence, the imagination, and the word, that your opponents are trying to loot.

I have seen and heard reports that you are all sorts of dreadful things—a difficult woman, an advocate (horror of horrors) of free love. Let me assure you that those of us who are working on your behalf are well aware that character assassination is normal in such situations, and must be discounted. And simplicity again has something valuable to say on this issue: even difficult advocates of free love must be allowed to stay alive, otherwise we would be left only with those who believe that love is something for which there must be a price—perhaps a terrible price—to pay.

Taslima, I know that there must be a storm inside you now. One minute you will feel weak and helpless, another strong and defiant. Now you will feel betrayed and alone, and now you will have the sense of standing for many who are standing silently with you. Perhaps in your darkest moments you will feel you did something wrong—that the processions demanding your death may have a point. This of all your goblins you must exorcise first. You have done nothing wrong. The wrong is committed by others against you. You have done nothing wrong, and I am sure that, one day soon, you will be free.

[*A statement for the French press regarding the cancellation of the visit of Taslima Nasrin, October 1994*]

The Bangladeshi writer Taslima Nasrin has been obliged to cancel her visit to France because of the French government's decision to limit her visa to twenty-four hours, on the bizarre grounds that France could not guarantee her safety.

This is disturbing news. *France* could not guarantee her safety? France, of all countries? How is it that she can stay safely in Lisbon, in Stockholm, in Stavanger, but not in Paris? France's minister of the interior, Charles Pasqua, likes to present himself as a strong man; why, then, does he make France itself look so weak? In my experience of these matters the "safety" argument is always a disguise for the real, cynical motives for such decisions. To those of us who admire French culture, who have found inspiration in France's contributions to the language of human freedom, it seems essential that the French government should think again. France should not shun those who are persecuted by freedom's enemies but rather embrace them; it should not be a no-go area for such people but a valued refuge. I urge M. Pasqua and the French government urgently to reconsider their decision in this case.

[*An introduction to* The Price of Free Speech *by William Nygaard, October 1995*]

The day William Nygaard was shot was one of the worst days of my life. (A worse day for him, of course.) I called Oslo constantly for news of his condition, and in between calls tried to reassure myself: he was a fit man, of athletic habits, he would be fine. But when I heard that he was going to survive I realized that until that moment I had not really believed he would. Then we learned that he was expected to make a full recovery, and I wondered if I should give up my lifelong skepticism about miracles. I went on to Norwegian television feeling relieved enough to make a joke. He had always had a back problem, I said, and now he would have an even bigger one.

In the days that followed there wasn't much to joke about. I couldn't help feeling that my friend and publisher had been struck by bullets that had been meant for me. I felt, at different times, or all at once, filled with rage, helplessness, determination, and, yes, guilt. Meanwhile William's colleagues at Aschehoug responded to the atrocity with great courage and principle. They did not waver in their resolve to keep my work in print; indeed, they printed extra copies. And when, finally, William was strong enough to take phone calls, I heard his strangely weakened voice saying an extraordinary thing: "I just want you to know," were his first words to me, "that I am very proud to be the publisher of *The Satanic Verses*." William doesn't like being called heroic, but that day I understood how deep his convictions were, how tough-minded his principles.

Since his recovery, William has been standing up for those principles, defending the freedoms he cares about, and expressing his anger that those who menace such freedoms continue to be treated with deference, in a series of remarkable essays and speeches. Reading his words, I sometimes come across statements that surprise me, such as the revelation that publishers felt *The Satanic Verses* to be a more "difficult" book than my earlier novels (all I can say is, they didn't tell me!); and sometimes there are things I don't quite agree with, such as his description of literary agents as the "killer whales" of modern literature—because I know that had it not been for my agents' passionate work on my behalf, *The Satanic Verses* would probably not have been published in, for example, France and Spain. But with the central thrust of his arguments, I am in complete accord.

The attack on all those concerned with the publication of *The Satanic Verses* is an outrage. It is a scandal. It is barbaric. It is philistine. It is bigoted. It is criminal. And yet, over the last seven years or so, it has been called a number of other things. It has been called religious. It has been called a cultural problem. It has been called understandable. It has been called theoretical. But if religion is an attempt to codify human ideas of the good, how can murder be a religious act? And if, today, people understand the motives of such would-be assassins, what else might they "understand" tomorrow? Burnings at the stake? If zealotry is to be tolerated because it is allegedly a part of Islamic culture, what is to become of the many, many voices in the Muslim world—intellectuals, artists, workers, and above all women—clamoring for freedom, struggling for it, and even giving up their lives in its name?

What is "theoretical" about the bullets that struck William Nygaard, the knives that wounded the Italian translator Ettore Capriolo, the knives that killed the Japanese translator Hitoshi Igarashi?

After nearly seven years, I think that we have the right to say that nobody has been angry enough about this state of affairs. I have been told in Denmark about the importance of cheese exports to Iran. In Ireland it was halal beef exports. In Germany and Italy and Spain other kinds of produce were involved. Can it really be the case that we are so keen to sell our wares that we can tolerate the occasional knifing, the odd shooting, and even a murder or two? How long will we chase after the money dangled before us by people with bloody hands?

William Nygaard's voice has been asking many such uncompromising questions. I salute him for his courage, for his obstinacy, and for his rage. Will the so-called Free World ever be angry enough to act decisively in this matter? I hope that it may become so, even yet. William Nygaard is a free man who chooses to exercise his rights of speech and action. Our leaders should recognize that their lack of sufficient anger indicates their own lack of interest in freedom. By becoming complaisant with terror, they become, in a very real sense, unfree.

[*Reflections on the fatwa's eighth anniversary, February 1997*]

Europe begins, as the Italian writer Roberto Calasso reminds us in *The Marriage of Cadmus and Harmony,* with a bull, and a rape. Europa was an Asian maiden abducted by a god (who changed himself, for the occasion, into a white bull) and was held captive in a new land that came, in time, to bear her name. The prisoner of Zeus's unending desire for mortal flesh, Europa has been avenged by history. Zeus is just a story now. He is powerless, but Europe is alive. At the very dawn of the idea of Europe, then, is an unequal struggle between human beings and gods, and an encouraging lesson: that while the bull-god may win the first skirmish, it is the maiden-continent that triumphs, in time.

I, too, have been engaged in a skirmish with a latter-day Zeus, though his thunderbolts have thus far missed their mark. Many others— in Algeria and Egypt as well as Iran—have been less fortunate. Those of us engaged in this battle have long understood what it's about. It's about the right of human beings, their thoughts, their works of art, their lives, to survive those thunderbolts—to prevail over the whimsical autocracy of whatever Olympus may presently be in vogue. It's about the right to make moral, intellectual, and artistic judgments, without worrying about Judgment Day.

The Greek myths are Europe's southern roots. At the continent's other end, the old Norse creation-legends also bring news of the supplanting of the gods by the human race. The final battle between the Norse gods and their terrible enemies has already taken place. The gods have slain their foes and been slain by them. Now, we are told, it is time for us to take over. There are no more gods to help us. We're on our own. Or, to put it another way (for gods are tyrants, too): we're free. The loss of the divine places us at the center of the stage, to build our own morality, our own communities; to make our own choices; to make our own way. Once again, in the earliest ideas of Europe, we find an emphasis on what is human over and above what is, at one moment or another, held to be divine. Gods may come and gods may go, but we, with any luck, go on forever. This humanist emphasis is, to my mind, one of the most attractive aspects of European thought. It's easy, of course, to argue that Europe has also stood, during its long history, for conquest, pillage, exterminations, and inquisitions. But now that we are being asked to join in the creation of a new Europe, it's helpful to remind ourselves of the best meanings of that resonant word. Because there is a Europe that many, if not most, of its citizens care about. This is not a Europe of money, or bureaucracy. Since the word "culture" has been debased by over-use, I'd prefer not to use it. The Europe that is worth talking about, worth re-creating, is anyhow something broader than a "culture." It is a civilization.

Today, I am listening to the melancholy echoes of one small, intellectually impoverished, pathetically violent assault on the values of that civilization. I refer, I'm sorry to say, to the Khomeini fatwa, whose eighth anniversary this is, and to the latest barbaric noises about "bounty money" emerging from the Iranian government's front organization, the 15 Khordad Foundation. I'm also sorry to say that the EU's response to such threats has been little more than tokenist. It has achieved nothing. The Europe for which Europeans care would have done more than merely state that it found such an assault unacceptable. It would have placed maximum pressure on Iran while removing as much pressure as possible from the lives of those threatened. What has happened is the exact opposite. Iran is under very little (I would even say no) pressure on this matter. But for eight years, some of us have been under a fair amount of stress.

During these eight years, I have come to understand the equivocations at the heart of the new Europe. I have heard Germany's foreign minister say, with a shrug, that "there is a limit" to what the EU is prepared to do for human rights. I have heard Belgium's foreign minister tell me that the EU knows all about Iran's terrorist activities against its own dissidents on European soil. But as to action? Just a world-weary smile; just another shrug. In Holland, I actually found myself obliged to explain to Foreign Ministry officials why it would not be a good idea for the EU to accept the fatwa's validity on religious grounds!

This new Europe has looked to me like not a civilization but an altogether more cynical enterprise. EU leaders pay lip service to the Enlightenment ideals—free expression, human rights, the right to dissent, the importance of the separation of Church and State. But when these ideals come up against the powerful banalities of what is called "reality"—trade, money, guns, power—then it's freedom that takes a dive. Speaking as a committed European: it's enough to make a Euro-skeptic of you.

Like so many of my fellow-Britons, I hope there will soon be a New Labour government. I have been urging that government-in-waiting to understand the importance of the arts in conveying the sense of national renewal which Labour must seek swiftly to create. I have also asked Mr. Blair to bring a new spirit of urgency to the fight against the Zeus of Iran and his attempt to kidnap our freedoms and, by doing so, to show New Labour's commitment to the true spirit of Europe—not just to an economic community, or monetary union, but to European civilization itself.

Tony Blair's New Labour government duly took office, winning a landslide victory on May 1, 1997. On Thursday, September 24, 1998, during the UN General Assembly in New York, the foreign ministers of the United Kingdom and Iran issued the joint statement that has effectively brought the story of the fatwa to an end: not immediately [see February 1999 in "Columns"] but gradually. As they say in the movies:

(Slow fade.)

PART III

Columns

DECEMBER 1998: THREE LEADERS

M an is by nature a political animal, said Aristotle, and so the public
life of a "good" society must reflect the nature of its members.
Many of the great Macedonian's assertions—that the slave is "naturally" inferior to his master, the female to the male, the "barbarian" to
the Greek—now sound archaic. And yet Aristotle's basic proposition
still rings true. The travails of three leading political figures—Bill Clinton, Saddam Hussein, and Augusto Pinochet—reveal how deeply we
believe in natural justice.

President Clinton's probable escape from his domestic pursuers can
be ascribed in part to his foes' astonishing folly. He has been lucky in
his enemies: the sex-crazed, mealymouthed Kenneth Starr and his
backers on the Christian Right, who remind us that "fundamentalism"
is a term born in the USA; Newt Gingrich, who overplayed a winning
hand and lost his shirt; and Linda Tripp, the wicked witch of the wire,
who, like Nixon, didn't understand that by bugging herself she would
only prove her own villainy, even with the expletives deleted. When an
ancient force, puritanical fanaticism, combines with the contemporary
tabloid dogma that public figures have no right to privacy, and when
the Washington political and media elites work themselves up into a
mighty pompous froth, even the president rocks on his throne. But

Clinton survives, because he has human nature on his side. Human nature distinguishes between sexual dalliance and political misconduct. It can be brutal; the word on Monica and Paula is that Americans just don't care about them. They have come to know Bill Clinton far more intimately than they normally know their leaders, and he, of course, has always known them better than any other politician. Clinton is winning his fight because he is like his people; because, you could say, he's a natural.

In the matter of Iraq, however, the U.S. administration's understanding of human nature has been deficient, to say the least. The hypothesis that bombing raids might provoke a coup against Saddam was always flawed. On the whole, people do not see as allies those who are dropping quantities of high explosives on them from the sky. Like Yossarian, the hero of *Catch-22,* they take the bombs personally.

Apparently some Iraqis seriously believe that Paula Jones and Monica Lewinsky were pawns in an international Zionist conspiracy designed to make Clinton bomb Baghdad. The recent aborted American-British attack has the merit of demonstrating the two ladies' declining international influence but otherwise plays right into Saddam's hands. Threatening to bomb and then not bombing has the advantage of killing fewer people but the disadvantage of making oneself look silly.

Those voices advocating a rapid end to sanctions, and a subsequent opening up of the Iraqi market to Western goods and ideas, may not find much favor with America's military analysts, but an Iraq freed from the privations of the embargo and the threat of aerial attack is more likely to think of the West as a friend. The best way to topple Saddam Hussein may be to help bring into being an Iraq in which his tyrannies are not only hateful but anachronistic.

The case of the month's other tyrant ought to be getting easier. Pinochet, after all, has earned the right to be called the most evil man presently alive on earth. (Sorry, Saddam.) The British law lords have decreed that he isn't immune from extradition. The crucial principle of universal accountability has thus been upheld. Atrocity is not to be excused by the occupancy of high office.

Why then has the British home secretary asked for extra time to decide Pinochet's future? The ex-tyrant was well enough to hang out with Lady Thatcher just the other day but now claims that the pressure he's under has provoked a stress-related mental ailment. The families of the dead must be disgusted by this ruse. Pinochet must not escape on such flimsy "compassionate" grounds. Jack Straw should confirm at once that for the mass murderers of the world, there can be no compassion.

"Human nature exists, and it is both deep and highly structured," writes Edward O. Wilson, the biologist and writer whom Tom Wolfe calls "a new Darwin." If it did not, let us be clear, then the idea of universals—human rights, moral principles, international law—would have no legitimacy.

It is the fact of our common humanity that allows most of us to forgive Bill Clinton his faults. It is why so few people think that bombing innocent Iraqis is the right way to punish Saddam Hussein. And it is why we want to see Pinochet brought to justice. A world that hounded Clinton but turned a blind eye to Pinochet would indeed be a world turned upside down.

JANUARY 1999: THE MILLENNIUM

If it's January, it must be the Year of the Millennium. Except that it isn't, because at the end of 1999 we'll have had, er, exactly 999 years since the last millennium. This year's millennium fever is like applauding a cricketer's century, or Mark McGwire's home-run record, at the beginning rather than the end of the crucial run.

We're also celebrating the two thousandth anniversary of the birth of Jesus Christ, as Catholic cardinals and British Domemakers and believers of all stripes continually remind us. Never mind that this puts Jesus in the odd position of having two birthdays in the space of a week (Christmas Day as well as the Millennial Instant), or that all serious scholars and even church leaders now agree that he wasn't actually born on either of them. Faux-Millennium or not, it's the only one we're going to get.

But will the faux-Millennium turn out to be a dark celebration of what one might call faux-Christianity? The year already boasts some striking examples of faux-Christian behavior, for instance General Pinochet attending Midnight Mass—which brings up the interesting question of the role of his confessor. Many of us would be very interested to hear the general's confession. But one man presumably already has. The issue of penance is therefore worth a moment's thought.

Exactly how many mea culpas and Hail Marys was the general asked to say to atone for his crimes?

Hard-line but essentially counterfeit Christian "values" have been the driving force behind the rabidly partisan attack by U.S. Republicans on their sexually deplorable president. To an observer whose admiration for American democracy was born at the time of the Watergate hearings, those grave, scrupulous, bipartisan deliberations over an earlier president's genuinely high crimes, the tawdry Clinton impeachment debate has been a disillusioning spectacle. Down into the dirt we tumble, in the name of the gentle Christ. But one of the Christian soldiers, Speaker-elect Robert Livingston, is already hoist on his own sanctimonious petard. Now the pornographer Larry Flynt's exposés may skewer several more, and no less a moral authority than the disgraced televangelist Jim Bakker has been seen on CNN, attacking his own Christian cohorts for their un-Christian uninterest in forgiveness and healing. How low can we go?

There's another name for the American Right's fork-tongued Christianity: hypocrisy. And Washington, that ugly School for Scandal full of Sneerwells, Backbites, and Snakes, has been for months in the grip of a kind of hypocrite fundamentalism. If the Senate now brings the sorry saga to a close, it will be because sober considerations of state have finally gained the ascendancy over mad-dog godliness; because worldly-wise politicians have put the faux-Christians back in their kennels at last.

President Clinton, who reportedly prayed with his spiritual advisers while the impeachment vote was being taken, is no slouch in the faux department himself. Of course his present, astonishing popularity rating is in part a reaction to the Starr troopers' sheer vileness, but it is also due to the popularity in America of his decision to bomb Iraq. Did Clinton discuss that with his spiritual advisers, too? Did his equally devout British ally, Prime Minister Blair, agree that those essentially pointless strikes were the moral, Christian way to go?

I well know that faux-religion isn't an exclusively Western vice. Believe me (to coin a phrase) I know something of the hypocritical fervor with which the militants of other faiths—Muslims, Hindus, Jews—invoke their god or gods to justify tyranny and injustice. No amount of Western hypocrisy can come close to Saddam Hussein's faux-Islam and the crimes committed in its name. Yet religious zealots have the nerve to accuse god-free secularists of lacking moral principles!

For an ungodly person like myself, the overarching issue in this millennium year is not any of the stuff on the god squads' agendas. It's the so-called Debt, the multi-trillions of owed dollars that keep the poorest countries of the world in hock to, and under the thumb of, the richest. Even in the most fiscally conservative circles, there is a growing consensus that the Debt must be wiped out, unless we want a third millennium marked by the resentment, violence, fanaticism, and despotism that must be the inevitable effects of this global injustice. Why not, then, make the cancellation of the Debt the human race's millennium gift to itself? Now, that could make 1999 a real milestone in human history. It's an idea in which our interests and principles coincide, wherever we come from, rich North or poor South, whoever we are, friend or faux. It's a policy that would erase the memory of 1998's shabby lewinskyings, and put Clinton's presidency into the history books for a genuinely high moral reason.

Cancel the Debt for the Millennium! It's even the Christian thing to do.

FEBRUARY 1999: TEN YEARS OF THE FATWA

Yes, all right, on February 14 it will be ten years since I received my unfunny Valentine. I admit to a dilemma. Ignore the politics (which I'd love to do), and my silence must look enforced or fearful. Speak, and I risk deafening the world to those other utterances, my books, written in my true language, the language of literature. I risk helping to conceal the real Salman behind the smoky, sulfurous Rushdie of the Affair. I have led two lives: one blighted by hatred and caught up in this dire business, which I'm trying to leave behind, and the life of a free man, freely doing his work. Two lives, but none I can afford to lose, for one loss would end both.

So I'll have my say, and because everybody loves an anniversary, no doubt much will be said elsewhere by the armies of bigotry and punditry. Let them volley and thunder. I'll speak of bookish things.

When asked about the effect on my writing of the ten-year-long assault upon it, I've answered lightheartedly that I've become more interested in happy endings; and that, as I've been told that my recent books are my funniest, the attacks have evidently improved my sense of humor. These answers, true enough in their way, are designed to deflect deeper inquiry. For how can I explain to strangers my sense of violation? It's as if men wielding clubs were to burst loudly into your home and lay it waste. They arrive when you're making love, or standing naked in the shower, or sitting on the toilet, or staring in deep inward silence at the lines you've scrawled on a page. Never again will you kiss or bathe or shit or write without remembering this intrusion. And yet, to do these things pleasurably and well, you must shut out the memory.

And how to describe the damage? As, perhaps, a heaviness. As something remembered from boarding-school childhood: I wake and, lying in bed, find I can't move. My arms, legs, and head have grown impossibly weighty. Nobody believes me, of course, and all the children laugh.

"I can't go on," says Beckett's Unnamable. "I'll go on." A writer's injuries are his strengths, and from his wounds will flow his sweetest, most startling dreams.

Amid the cacophony of the professionally opinionated and the professionally offended, may a voice still be heard celebrating literature, highest of arts, its passionate, dispassionate inquiry into life on earth, its naked journey across the frontierless human terrain, its fierce-minded rebuke to dogma and power, and its trespassers' fearless daring? In these years I've met and been inspired by some of the world's bravest fighters for literary freedom. I recently helped set up a house for refugee writers in Mexico City (more than twenty cities already belong to this refuge-city scheme) and was proud to be doing a little to ease the struggles of others in danger from intolerance. But as well as fighting the fight, which I will surely go on doing, I have grown determined to prove that the art of literature is more resilient than what menaces it. The best defense of literary freedoms lies in their exercise, in continuing to make untrammeled, uncowed books. So, beyond grief, bewilderment, and despair, I have rededicated myself to our high calling.

I am conscious of shifts in my writing. There was always a tug-of-war in me between "there" and "here," the pull of roots and of the road. In that struggle of insiders and outsiders, I used to feel simultaneously on both sides. Now I've come down on the side of those who by preference, nature, or circumstance simply do not belong. This unbelonging—I think of it as *disorientation,* loss of the East—is my artistic country now. Wherever my books find themselves, by a favored armchair, near a hot bath, on a beach, or in a late-night pool of bedside light: that's my only home.

Life can be harsh, and for a decade St. Valentine's Day has reminded me of that harshness. But these dark anniversaries of the appalling Valentine I was sent in 1989 have also been times to reflect upon the countervailing value of love. Love feels more and more like the only subject.

It's reported that the remains of St. Valentine himself are to come out of hiding. Instead of the cardboard box in which they were ignominiously stored for years, they will have a reliquary in Glasgow's roughneck Gorbals district. I like this image: the patron saint of fluffy romance discovers the gritty verities of life in the real world, while that world is enriched in turn by the flowering, in its mean streets, of love.

MARCH 1999: GLOBALIZATION

A couple of years ago a British literary festival (at Hay-on-Wye) staged a public debate on the motion that "it is the duty of every European to resist American culture." Along with two American journalists (one of whom was Sidney Blumenthal, now more famous as a Clinton aide and impeachment witness), I opposed the motion. I'm happy to report that we won, capturing roughly 60 percent of the audience's vote. But it was an odd sort of victory. My American co-panelists were surprised by the strength of the audience's anti-Americanism—after all, 40 percent of them had voted for the motion. Sidney, noting that "American culture" as represented by its armed forces had liberated Europe from Nazism not all that many years ago, was puzzled by the audience's apparent lack of gratitude. And there was a residual feeling that the case for "resistance" was actually pretty strong.

Since that day, the debate about cultural globalization and its military-political sidekick, intervention, has continued to intensify, and anti-American sentiment is on the increase. In most people's heads, globalization has come to mean the worldwide triumph of Nike, Gap, and MTV, the metamorphosis of Planet Earth into McWorld. Confusingly, we want these goods and services when we behave as consumers, but with our cultural hats on we have begun to deplore their omnipresence.

On the merits of intervention, even greater confusion reigns. We don't seem to know if we want a world policeman or not. If the "international community," which these days is little more than a euphemism for the United States, fails to intervene promptly in Rwanda, Bosnia, Kosovo, it is excoriated for that failure. Elsewhere, it is criticized just as vehemently when it does intervene: when American bombs fall on Iraq, or when American agents assist in the capture of the PKK leader Abdullah Ocalan.

Clearly, those of us who shelter under the pax Americana are deeply ambivalent about it, and the United States will no doubt continue to be surprised by the level of the world's ingratitude. The globalizing power of American culture is opposed by an improbable alliance that includes everyone from cultural-relativist liberals to hard-line fundamentalists, with all manner of pluralists and individualists, to say nothing of flag-waving nationalists and splintering sectarians, in between.

Much ecological concern is presently being expressed about the crisis in biodiversity, the possibility that a fifth or more of the earth's species of living forms may soon become extinct. To some, globalization is an equivalent social catastrophe, with equally alarming implications for the survival of true cultural diversity, of the world's precious localness: the Indianness of India, the Frenchness of France.

Amid this din of global defensiveness, little thought is given to some of the most important questions raised by a phenomenon that, like it or not, isn't going away anytime soon. For instance: do cultures actually exist as separate, pure, defensible entities? Is not mélange, adulteration, impurity, pick 'n' mix at the heart of the idea of the modern, and hasn't it been that way for most of this all-shook-up century? Doesn't the idea of pure cultures, in urgent need of being kept free from alien contamination, lead us inexorably toward apartheid, toward ethnic cleansing, toward the gas chamber? Or, to put it another way: are there other universals besides international conglomerates and the interests of super-powers? And if by chance there were a universal value that might, for the sake of argument, be called freedom, whose enemies—tyranny, bigotry, intolerance, fanaticism—were the enemies of us all; and if this "freedom" were discovered to exist in greater quantity in the countries of the West than anywhere else on earth; and if, in the world as it actually exists, rather than in some unattainable Utopia, the authority of the United States were the best current guarantor of that "freedom"; then might it not follow that to oppose the spread of American culture would be to take up arms against the wrong foe?

By agreeing what we are against, we discover what we are for. André Malraux believed that the third millennium must be the age of religion.* I would say rather that it must be the age in which we finally grow out of our need for religion. But to cease to believe in our gods is not the same thing as commencing to believe in nothing. There are fundamental freedoms to fight for, and it will not do to doom to their fates the terrorized women of Afghanistan or of the circumcision-happy lands of Africa by calling their oppression their "culture." And of course it is America's duty not to abuse its pre-eminence, and our right to criticize such abuses when they happen—when, for example, innocent factories in Sudan are bombed, or Iraqi civilians pointlessly killed.† But perhaps we, too, need to rethink our easy condemnations. Sneakers, burgers, blue jeans, and music videos aren't the enemy. If the young people of Iran now insist on rock concerts, who are we to criticize their cultural contamination? Out there are real tyrants to defeat. Let's keep our eyes on the prize.

APRIL 1999: ROCK MUSIC

I recently asked Vaclav Havel about his admiration for the American rock icon Lou Reed. He replied that it was impossible to overstate the importance of rock music for the Czech resistance during the years of darkness between the Prague Spring and the collapse of Communism. I was just relishing the mental image of the leaders of the Czech

---

* Or he didn't. It now looks probable that Malraux's much-quoted dictum, "The twenty-first century will be a century of religion or it will not be at all," which he is supposed to have come up with not long before he died, falls into the same category of never actually made remarks as "Play it again, Sam," and "Come up and see me sometime." I'm relieved to discover this. It's nice not to have to think of Malraux—for so long so sophisticated on the subject of religion—as an old fool at the last.

† Or, in the new world of the George W. Bush administration, when America tries to foist a useless missile shield, and maybe a new arms race, on us all; or when America withdraws from the Kyoto environmental accords, or refuses to sign a treaty designed to outlaw chemical weapons . . . In spite of all Bush's attempts to turn the USA into a pariah state, however, it remains the case that American culture isn't the enemy. Globalization itself isn't the problem; the inequitable distribution of global resources is.

underground grooving to the sound of the Velvet Underground playing "Waiting for the Man," "I'll Be Your Mirror," or "All Tomorrow's
Parties" when Havel added, with a straight face, "Why do you think we
called it the Velvet Revolution?" I took this to be an instance of Havel's
deadpan humor, but it was a joke of the sort that reveals another, less
literal truth; a generational truth, perhaps, because for popular music
fans of a certain age the ideas of rock and revolution are inseparably
linked. "You say you want a revolution," John Lennon had sneered at
us. "Well, you know, / We all want to change the world." And indeed
with the passage of the years I had come to think of this linkage as little
more than youthful romanticism. So the discovery that a real revolution had been inspired by rock music's glamorous snarl was pretty
moving. It felt like a sort of validation.★

Because now that nobody smashes guitars or protests about much
anymore, now that rock 'n' roll is middle-aged and corporate and the
turnover of the leading mega-groups exceeds that of small nation-
states, now that it's music for older people remembering their salad
days while the kids listen to gangsta rap, trance music, and hip-hop,
and Bob Dylan and Aretha Franklin get invited to sing at presidential
inaugurals, it's easy to forget the form's oppositional origins, its anti-
Establishment heyday. Yet rock 'n' roll's rough, confident spirit of rebellion may be one reason why this strange, simple, overwhelming
noise conquered the world nearly half a century ago, crossing all frontiers and barriers of language and culture to become only the third
globalized phenomenon in history after the two World Wars. It was the
sound of liberation, and so it spoke to the free spirits of young people
everywhere, and so also, of course, our mothers didn't like it.

After she became aware of my fondness for Bill Haley, Elvis, and
Jerry Lee Lewis, my own alarmed mother began eagerly to advocate the
virtues of Pat Boone, a man who once sang a sentimental ballad ad-
dressed to a mule. But singing to mules wasn't what I was after. I was
trying to imitate the curl of Presley's lips and the swoon-inducing rota-
tion of his hips, and I suspect boys everywhere, from Siberia to Patago-
nia, were doing the same.

What sounded and felt to us like freedom looked to the adult world
like bad behavior, and in a way both things are true. Pelvis-wiggling and

---

★ Apparently this wasn't a joke. I later found out he'd said the same thing, quite seriously, to Lou Reed as well.

guitar-smashing are indeed liberty's childish fringe; but it's also true, in all sorts of ways we have learned much more about as adults, that freedom is dangerous. Freedom, that ancient foot-tapping anarchy, the Dionysiac antithesis of Pat Boone: a higher and wilder virtue than good behavior and, for all its spirit of hairy late-night rebellion, far less likely than blind obedience and line-toeing convention to do serious damage. Better a few trashed hotel suites than a trashed world.

But there is that in us which doesn't want to be free; which prefers discipline and acceptance and patriotic local tunes to the wild loose-haired love-music of the world. There is that in us which wishes simply to go along with the crowd, and to blame all naysayers and pelvis-wigglers for rocking our comfortable boat. "Don't follow leaders," Bob Dylan warned in "Subterranean Homesick Blues," "Watch the parking meters." Yet we continue to want to be led, to follow petty warlords and murderous ayatollahs and nationalist brutes, or to suck our thumbs and listen quiescently to nanny states that insist they know what's best for us. So tyrants abound from Bombay to Mumbai, and even those of us who are notionally free peoples are no longer, for the most part, very rock 'n' roll.

The music of freedom frightens people and unleashes all manner of conservative defense mechanisms. As long as Orpheus could raise his voice in song, the Maenads could not kill him. Then they screamed, and their shrill cacophony drowned his music, and then their weapons found their mark, and he fell, and they tore him limb from limb.

Screaming against Orpheus, we too become capable of murder. The collapse of Communism, the destruction of the Iron Curtain and the Wall, was supposed to usher in a new era of liberty. Instead, the post–Cold War world, suddenly formless and full of possibility, scared many of us stiff. We retreated behind smaller iron curtains, built smaller stockades, imprisoned ourselves in narrower, ever more fanatical definitions of ourselves—religious, regional, ethnic—and readied ourselves for war.

Today, as the thunder of one such war drowns out the sweet singing of our better selves, I find myself nostalgic for the old spirit of independence and idealism that once, set infectiously to music, helped bring another war (in Vietnam) to an end. But at present the only music in the air is a dead march.

MAY 1999: MORON OF THE YEAR

In the battle for the hotly contested title of International Moron of the Year, two heavyweight contenders stand out. One is the Austrian writer Peter Handke, who has astonished even his most fervent admirers by his current series of impassioned apologias for the genocidal regime of Slobodan Milosevic; and who, during a recent visit to Belgrade, received the Order of the Serbian Knight for his propaganda services. Handke's previous idiocies include the suggestion that Sarajevo's Muslims regularly massacred themselves and then blamed the Serbs; and his denial of the genocide carried out by Serbs at Srebrenica. Now he likens the NATO aerial bombardment to the alien invasion in the movie *Mars Attacks!* and then, foolishly mixing his metaphors, compares the Serbs' sufferings to the Holocaust.

His rival in folly is the movie star Charlton Heston. As president of the U.S. National Rifle Association, Heston made a response to the massacre of innocents recently perpetrated by young Dylan Klebold and Eric Harris at Columbine High School in Littleton, Colorado, that was a masterpiece of the moronic. Heston thinks America should arm its teachers; he seems to believe that schools would be safer if staff had the power to gun down the children in their charge. (Little Johnny reaches into a pocket for a pencil—and Blam! Blam! his geography teacher blows him away.)

I will not draw glib parallels between NATO's aerial bombardments and the Colorado killings. No, the larger violence did not breed the lesser. Nor should too much be read into the accidental echo between Milosevic's Hitlerian tendencies and the lethal celebration of Hitler's birthday by the so-called Trench-coat Mafia; or the even more eerie assonance between the video-game mentality of the Colorado killers and the real-life aerial videos the NATO publicists show us every day.

In the matter of the war, let's agree, too, that it's okay to feel ambivalent about the confused, changing-policy-on-the-hoof manner of the NATO action. One minute we're told Milosevic's savage retaliatory assault on Kosovo couldn't have been foreseen; the next minute we hear that it should have been. Or again: we're not going to use ground troops. On second thought, maybe we are. And our war aims? Strictly limited; we seek only to create a safe haven to which the Kosovar refugees can return. No, no, we're going to march into Belgrade and get Milosevic, we're not making that old Saddam mistake again!

But objecting to vacillation and contradiction is not the same thing as Handke's half-crazy, half-cynical fellow-traveling with evil. The moral justification for NATO's intervention is the humanitarian disaster we see on TV every night. To blame NATO for the refugees' plight is to absolve the Serb army of its crimes. It needs to be said again and again: the people to blame for death and terror are those who terrorize and kill.

And in the matter of the Colorado killings, let's agree that guns aren't the sole cause of the horror. The killers learned how to make pipe bombs on the Internet, and got their trench coats from *The Matrix,* and learned to put a low value on human life from—whom? Their parents? Marilyn Manson? The Goths? Which is not at all to adopt Mr. Heston's unrepentant position. "This isn't a gun issue," he tells us. "It's a child issue." "Moses" Heston has new commandments to hand down these days: Thou shalt defend the right to bear arms in the teeth of all the evidence, and Thou shalt certainly not be blamed just because a few kids got iced.

Kosovo and Colorado do have something in common. They show that in our unstable world, incompatible versions of reality are clashing with one another, with murderous results. But we can still make moral judgments about the rival versions of the world that are at war. And the only civilized view of the Handke and Heston versions is that they are indefensible.

Never mind that Handke is co-writer of that great movie *Wings of Desire;* condemned as a "monster" by Alain Finkielkraut and Hans Magnus Enzensberger, by the Slovenian philosopher Slavoj Zizek and the Serbian novelist Bora Cosic, he deserves to be, as Susan Sontag pithily puts it, "finished." (Intellectually, that is, not literally. In case anyone was wondering.) Never mind, either, that Heston, his face as subtly mobile as Mount Rushmore, has helped millions of moviegoers snatch a few hours of peaceful sleep in darkened cinemas. He deserves to be "finished," too.

Who wins the prize? Peter Handke's folly makes him complicit with evil on a grand scale, but fortunately he is almost entirely powerless. As America's foremost gun lobbyist, however, Heston is doing his best to make sure that guns remain an integral part of the American household; and so, one day soon, somewhere in America, another young man will take up arms and begin to shoot his friends. So, by reason of his folly's greater effectiveness, I hand Charlton Heston the palm. But the year's not half done. Greater morons may yet step forward to challenge him. Watch this space.

JUNE 1999: KASHMIR

For over fifty years, India and Pakistan have been arguing and periodically coming to blows over one of the most beautiful places in the world, Kashmir, which the Mughal emperors thought of as Paradise on earth. As a result of this unending quarrel, Paradise has been partitioned, impoverished, and made violent. Murder and terrorism now stalk the valleys and mountains of a land once so famous for its peacefulness that outsiders made jokes about the Kashmiris' supposed lack of fighting spirit.

I have a particular interest in the Kashmir issue, because I am more than half Kashmiri myself, because I have loved the place all my life, and because I have spent much of that life listening to successive Indian and Pakistani governments, all of them more or less venal and corrupt, mouthing the self-serving hypocrisies of power while ordinary Kashmiris suffered the consequences of their posturings.

Pity those ordinary, peaceable people, caught between the rock of India and the hard place that Pakistan has always been! Now, as the world's newest nuclear powers square off yet again, their new weapons making their dialogue of the deaf more dangerous than ever before, I say: a plague on both their houses. "Kashmir for the Kashmiris" is an old slogan but the only one that expresses how the subjects of this dispute have always felt; how, I believe, the majority of them would still say they feel, if they were free to speak their minds without fear.

India has badly mishandled the Kashmir case from the beginning. Back in 1947 the state's Hindu maharaja "opted" for India (admittedly after Pakistan tried to force his hand by "allowing" militants to swarm across the borders), and in spite of UN resolutions supporting the largely Muslim population's right to a plebiscite, India's leaders have always rejected the idea, repeating over and over that Kashmir is "an integral part" of India. (The Nehru-Gandhi dynasty is itself of Kashmiri origin.) India has maintained a large military presence in Kashmir for decades, both in the Vale of Kashmir, where much of the population is based, and in mountain fastnesses such as the site of the present flash point. This force feels to most Kashmiris like an occupying army and is greatly resented. Yet until recently most Indians, even the liberal intelligentsia, refused to face up to the reality of Kashmiris' growing animosity toward them. As a result the problem has grown steadily worse, exacerbated by laws that threaten long jail sentences for any Kashmiri making anti-Indian statements in public.

Pakistan, for its part, has from its earliest times been a heavily militarized state, dominated by the Army even when under notionally civilian rule and spending a huge part of its budget—at its peak, well over half the total budgetary expenditure—on its armed forces. Such big spending, and the consequent might of the generals, depends on having a dangerous enemy to defend against and a "hot" cause to pursue. It has therefore always been in the interest of Pakistan's top brass to frustrate peacemaking initiatives toward India and to keep the Kashmir dispute alive. This, and not the alleged interests of Kashmiris, is what lies behind Pakistan's policy on the issue.

These days, in addition, the Pakistani authorities are under pressure from their country's mullahs and radical Islamists, who characterize the struggle to "liberate" (that is, to seize) Kashmir as a holy war. Ironically, Kashmiri Islam has always been of the mild, Sufistic variety, in which local *pirs*, or holy men, are revered as saints. This openhearted, tolerant Islam is anathema to the firebrands of Pakistan and might well, under Pakistani rule, be at risk. Thus, the present-day growth of terrorism in Kashmir has roots in India's treatment of Kashmiris but also in Pakistan's interest in subversion. Yes, Kashmiris feel strongly about the Indian "occupation" of their land; but it is also almost certainly true that Pakistan's Army and intelligence service has been training, aiding, and abetting the men of violence.

India's and Pakistan's possession of nuclear weapons makes urgent the need to move beyond the deadlock and the moribund fifty-year-old language of the crisis. What Kashmiris want, and what India and Pakistan must be persuaded to offer them, is a reunited land, an end to Lines of Control and warfare on high Himalayan glaciers. What they want is to be given a large degree of autonomy, to be allowed to run their own lives. (A dual-citizenship scheme, with frontiers guaranteed by both Pakistan and India, is one possible solution.)

The Kashmir dispute has already exposed the frailty of the Cold War theory of nuclear deterrence, according to which the extreme danger of nuclear arsenals should deter those who possess them from embarking on even a conventional war. That thesis now seems untenable. It was probably not deterrence but luck that prevented the Cold War from turning hot. So here we are in a newly dangerous world, in which nuclear powers actually are going to war. In such a time, the special-case status of Kashmir must be recognized and made the basis of the way forward. The Kashmir problem must be defused, or else, in the unthinkable worst-case scenario, it may end in the nuclear destruction of Paradise itself, and of much else besides.

JULY 1999: NORTHERN IRELAND

E ven before Tony Blair and Bertie Ahern spelled out the details of the latest Northern Ireland peace plan, the Ulster Unionist leader David Trimble was describing those urging him to accept the terms as "willing fools." Since then, his colleague Ken Maginnis has spoken of "betrayal," and Trimble has announced that he has "great difficulty in seeing how we can proceed with this." So are Blair and Ahern and Mo Mowlam and the other mediators really history's idiots, the IRA's foolish dupes and therefore fellow-travelers of evil, hell-bent on permitting terrorists "into the heart of government," as the Unionists imply they are?

Newspaper reports speak of a meeting between Blair and Sinn Fein's Martin McGuinness at which, after recording equipment was switched off, McGuinness said he was now speaking on behalf of the IRA, and made the offer that persuaded the British prime minister that the prize of IRA disarmament was within grasp.

Has Blair been deceived? We know that General John de Chastelain, head of the decommissioning body, thinks he has not. The general's report states that there is a basis for believing that the IRA and loyalist paramilitaries will fully disarm by May 2000. But Trimble and his team, suspicious of the reasons for delaying the report's release by a couple of days, are worried that de Chastelain had his arm twisted, and that the final version of his text was slanted toward the Republican position by British spin doctors.

Up to a point, it's possible to sympathize with Trimble, who took one courageous and politically risky step for peace a year ago, and who is now asked to endorse a further strategy that the unreconstructed masses of Drumcree marchers and the rest of the Unionist faithful will utterly detest. It's easy, in particular, to understand Unionists' exasperation with the infuriating brand of doublespeak still practiced by Sinn Fein, whose leaders insist, on the record, that their party is not to be confused with the IRA while, off the record, they speak powerfully on the Provos' behalf.

It's clear, too, that between Unionism and Sinn Fein there exists a mutual loathing so deep that no peace process can wipe it away. One remembers the distaste with which the late Israeli prime minister Yitzhak Rabin took Yasser Arafat's proffered hand. Trimble feels at least as much disgust for Gerry Adams as Rabin felt for the chairman of the PLO. And it probably hasn't escaped his memory that Rabin's handshake cost him his life. But, as Israelis and Palestinians know only too well, peace is not the same thing as reconciliation, it's not about kissing and making up with the foe you've fought for generations. Peace is simply the decision not to fight. Reconciliation may come after that, very very slowly, or it may not. And right now, most citizens of Northern Ireland—like most Israelis and most Palestinians—agree that peace without reconciliation is what they want. The silence of the guns will do.

This is the analysis—the gamble, really—on which the Blair-Ahern peace initiative is based: that the longer the cease-fire in Northern Ireland can be maintained, the harder it will be for the paramilitary war to resume. However imperfect the cessation of hostilities, however vicious the continued punishment beatings, however inflammatory the language still used by the two sides about each other, this lengthening stretch of minimal violence, this breathing space, may just enable peace to take deep enough root to last. It may get the distrustful communities of the Six Counties so used to their unreconciled peace as to make a return to war intolerable.

Risky as it is, this "peace gamble" remains the only game in town, and Unionist refusals will quickly come to be seen (as Tony Blair has warned) as unforgivable sabotage. Right now, Gerry Adams looks like he's dragging the IRA kicking and screaming toward the war's end, while Trimble is making us wonder whether he has become convinced that the peace on offer is a mirage, or simply that its price is too high. If he digs in his heels now, those conclusions will be hard to avoid. When, as Blair keeps saying, the prize is so great, then such intransigence looks like a greater folly than excessive "willingness."

David Trimble is right to insist that there must be no fudges, that disarmament must be real, prompt, and verifiable. But if Unionist stubbornness derails the peace train, the party will always stand accused of being history's "unwilling fools," who shirked the risk and refused to travel toward hope. And David Trimble may then be remembered as Northern Ireland's Netanyahu, not its Shamir or Rabin.

AUGUST 1999: KOSOVO

In the wake of the Gracko killings, British Prime Minister Tony Blair has appealed to the Albanians of Kosovo to set aside their enmities. "We fought this conflict," Mr. Blair said in the provincial capital Pristina last Friday, "because we believe in justice, because we believed it was wrong to have ethnic cleansing and racial genocide here in Europe towards the end of the twentieth century, and we didn't fight it to have another ethnic minority [the Kosovan Serb minority] repressed." These are good-hearted, high-minded, decent words, the words of a man who believes he has fought and won a just war, and for whom "justice" includes the idea of reconciliation. But they also indicate a failure of imagination. What happened to the Albanians in Kosovo was an atrocity whose dark effect on the spirit may lie beyond the power of decent men like Mr. Blair to wish away. What happened may be, quite simply, unforgivable.

Tragically, this is not the first such imaginative failure. In the conflict's early days, many Kosovar Albanians also failed to grasp the scale of the horror that was coming their way. In many villages, the men decided to flee, convinced that Milosevic's army was intent on massacring them. They vanished into the woods, over the mountains, out of the Army's murderous reach. But they made a miscalculation: they left their families behind, unable to believe that their wives, children, and infirm parents would be at risk from the advancing soldiers. They underestimated the human capacity for the atrocious.

Now let us imagine the refugees' terrible return at the conflict's end. Nervously, hoping for joy, they near their village. But before they get there they understand that the unimaginable has occurred. The fields are littered with bloodied garments and severed limbs. Carrion birds flap and strut. There are odors. The men of this village must now face a truth in which profound shame and humiliation mingle with great grief. They are alive because they ran away, but the loved ones whom they left behind have been murdered in their stead. The bodies that they now carry in farmyard carts to the burial ground speak accusations through their shrouds. *My son, in the weakness of my old age you were not there to save me. My husband, you allowed me to be raped and slaughtered. My father, you let me die.*

The village's survivors tell the returned refugees the story of the massacre. They tell them how some of the Serbs in the village put on Serbian Army uniforms and used their local knowledge to help the killers flush out the terrified Albanians from their bolt-holes. No, they said, don't bother to search that house, it has no cellar. Ah, but this house, there's a cellar under that rug, they'll be hiding in there.

These Kosovan Serbs have fled now. But Milosevic doesn't want them in Serbia, where they are the living proof of his defeat. And Mr. Blair, too, wants them to go home and be protected by K-FOR [the UN's Kosovo peacekeeping force]. They are reluctant to return, fearing vengeance. And guess what? They're right. They're right, and Tony Blair, with his vision of a new Kosovo—"a symbol of how the Balkans should be"—is wrong.

I supported the NATO operation in Kosovo, finding the human-rights evidence in favor of intervention to be powerful and convincing. Many writers, intellectuals, artists, and left-leaning bien-pensants thought otherwise. One of their arguments was, if Kosovo, then why not Kurdistan? Why not Rwanda or East Timor? Oddly, this kind of rhetoric actually makes the opposite point to the one it thinks it's making. For if it would have been right to intervene in these cases, and the West was wrong not to, then surely it was also right to defend the Kosovans, and the West's previous failures only serve to emphasize that this time, at least, they—"we"—got it right.

The anti-intervention camp's major allegation was and is that NATO's action in fact precipitated the violence it was intended to prevent; that, so to speak, the massacres were Madeleine Albright's fault. This seems to me both morally reprehensible—because it exculpates the actual killers—and demonstrably wrong. Set emotion aside and look at the cold logistics of Milosevic's massacre. It quickly becomes apparent that the atrocity was carefully planned. One does not make detailed plans to wipe out thousands of people just in case a speedy response to a Western attack should be needed. One plans a massacre because one intends to carry out a massacre.

True, the speed and enormity of the Serbian attack took the NATO forces by surprise (another failure of imagination). That doesn't make it right to blame NATO. Murderers are guilty of the murders they commit, rapists of their rapes.

But if "we" were right to go in, and the war was indeed fought for idealistic motives, the idealism of the present policy looks increasingly starry-eyed. The reality, as reported by experienced foreign correspondents who have returned from Kosovo to say that they have never seen anything like it, is that there are few Serbs left in Kosovo, and it is probably impossible to protect them. The old, multicultural Sarajevo was destroyed by the Bosnian war. The old Kosovo is gone too, very probably for good. Mr. Blair's ideal Kosovo is a dream. He and his colleagues should now support the construction of the free, ethnically Albanian entity that seems like a historical inevitability. The aftermath of a war is no time for dreaming.

SEPTEMBER 1999: DARWIN IN KANSAS

Some years ago, in Cochin in South India, I attended the World Understanding Day of the local Rotary Club. The featured speaker was an American creationist, Duane T. Gish, who attributed the malaise of Today's Youth to the propagation, by the world's school systems, of the pernicious teachings of poor old Charles Darwin. Today's Youth was being taught that it was descended from monkeys! Consequently, and understandably, it had become alienated from society, and "depressed." The rest—its drift, its criminality, its promiscuity, its drug abuse—inevitably followed.

I was interested to note that a few minutes into the lecture the habitually courteous Indian audience simply stopped listening. The hum of conversation in the room gradually rose until the speaker was all but drowned. Not that this stopped Duane. Like a dinosaur who hasn't noticed he's extinct, he just went bellowing on.

This summer, however, Mr. Gish's lizardy kind will have received cheering news. The Kansas Board of Education's decision to delete evolution from the state's recommended curriculum and from its standardized tests is, in itself, powerful evidence against the veracity of Charles Darwin's great theory. If Darwin were able to visit Kansas in 1999, he would find living proof that natural selection doesn't always work, that the dumbest and unfittest sometimes survive, and that the human race is therefore capable of evolving backward toward those youth-depressing apes. Nor is Darwin the only casualty. The Big Bang apparently didn't happen in the Kansas area, either—or, at least, it's just one of the available theories. Thus in one pan of the scales we have general relativity, the Hubble telescope, and all the imperfect but painstakingly accumulated learning of the human race; and, in the other, the Book of Genesis. In Kansas, the scales balance.

Good teachers, it must be said, are appalled by their state board's decision. As the new academic year begins, battle is about to be joined, and it may yet be that reason will prevail over superstition. But respected professors publicly concede that "it's going on everywhere, and the creationists are winning." In Alabama, for example, a sticker on textbooks hilariously suggests that since "no one was present when life first appeared on earth," we can't ever know the facts. Seems you just had to be there.

Or, not so hilariously. This stuff would be funny if it weren't so unfunny. American fundamentalists may be pleased to know that elsewhere in the world—Karachi, Pakistan, for example—the blinkered literalists of another faith have been known to come into university classes armed to the teeth and threaten lecturers with instant death if they should deviate from the strict Quranic view of science (or anything else). Might it be that America's notorious gun culture will now also take up arms against knowledge itself?

Nor should the rest of us feel too smug. The war against religious obscurantism, a war many people believed had been won long ago, is . breaking out all over, with ever greater force. Gobbledygook is back in style. The pull of stupidity grows everywhere more powerful. The young speak of the spiritual life as if it were a fashion accessory. A new dark age of unreason may be beginning. High priests and fierce inquisitors are cackling in the shadows. There are, once again, anathemas and persecutions.

Meanwhile, slowly, beautifully, the search for knowledge continues. Ironically, in the whole history of the sciences, there has never been so rich or revolutionary a golden age. Big science is unlocking the universe, tiny science is solving the riddles of life. And, yes, the new knowledge brings with it new moral problems, but the old ignorances are not going to help us solve these. One of the beauties of learning is that it admits its provisionality, its imperfections. This scholarly scrupulousness, this willingness to admit that even the most well supported of theories is still a theory, is now being exploited by the unscrupulous. But that we do not know everything does not mean we know nothing. Not all theories are of equal weight. The moon, even the moon over Kansas, is not made of green cheese. Genesis, as a "theory," is bunk.

If the over-abundant new knowledge of the modern age is, let's say, a tornado, then Oz is the extraordinary, Technicolor new world in which it has landed us, the world from which—life not being a movie—there is no way home. In the immortal words of Dorothy Gale, "I have a feeling we're not in Kansas anymore." To which one can only add: thank goodness, baby, and amen.

OCTOBER 1999: EDWARD SAID

All families invent their parents and children, give each of them a story, character, fate, and even a language. There was always something wrong with how I was invented." This is the opening of *Out of Place* by Edward Said, one of the finest memoirs of childhood and youth to be published in many a long year, a work that prompts the critic to reach for his highest comparisons. It can justly be likened to Proust's great novel-cycle because of its own recapturing of lost time; to Balzac, for the clarity of its social and historical perceptions; and to Conrad. The author is a Conradian scholar, but he is also, like the Nigger of the *Narcissus,* a sick man who is nevertheless determined to live until he dies. (Said suffers from CLL, a form of leukemia.) One of the many things to be said about this book is that it is a heroic instance of writing against death.

As its beginning shows, *Out of Place* is keenly aware of the inventions, blurrings, and imagination-figments that go to make up our sense of ourselves and our kin. It knows everything there is to know about displacement, about rootings and uprootings, about feeling wrong in the world, and it absorbs the reader precisely because such out-of-place experiences lie at or near the heart of what it is to be alive in our jumbled, chaotic times. How extraordinary, then, that so nuanced, so transparently honest a book, whose every page speaks to its author's immense honesty and integrity, should become the center of an intercontinental political storm! For Said has been malevolently accused of fraud, of having falsified his own life story and having based a lifetime of political involvement upon "thirty years of carefully crafted deception": of, in short, *not really being a Palestinian at all.*

The author of the current attack, Justus Reid Weiner, has unsavory backers: the Jerusalem Center for Public Affairs, primarily financed by the Milken Family Fund. Yes, that Michael Milken, the crooked financier jailed for, you've got it, fraud. But even though he boasts of having spent three years on Said's trail, his accusations are flimsy nothings. Weiner can't deny that Said actually was born in Jerusalem. To "prove" that Said and his family don't merit the status of Palestinian "refugees" or "exiles," however, Weiner does claim that Said didn't go to St. George's School in eastern Jerusalem and that the family house there never belonged to them. This is all hogwash. Fellow-students of Said's have come forward to confirm that he did indeed attend St. George's, and that the Saids were well known as an old Palestinian family. At least one of these students said as much to Weiner, who conveniently failed to mention the fact in his attack.

The house in Jerusalem was in the name not of Said's father but of close relatives. To use this as proof of anything is to ignore the everyday realities of extended-family living. And, anyway, how trivial can one get? Is it seriously proposed that Said's out-of-place early life, spent partly in Jerusalem, partly in Cairo, somehow disqualifies him from speaking as a Palestinian? That it's okay for Weiner, an American Jew transplanted to Israel, to speak as an Israeli but not for Said, a Palestinian re-rooted in New York, to speak for Palestine?

When a distinguished writer is attacked in this fashion—when his enemies set out not merely to give him a bad review but to destroy him—then there is always more at stake than the mere quotidian malice of the world of books. Professor Said is no stranger to controversy and, as a reward for being the most incisive and visible Palestinian intellectual of the last quarter century has received his share of death threats and abuse. This latest attack, however, is something new. And in spite of its flimsiness it has been given a great deal of credence, first in *Commentary* magazine and then in many leading U.S. newspapers, and in the British *Daily Telegraph*.

Even stranger is the fact that no American paper would publish Said's rebuttals, which eventually appeared, ironically, in the Israeli paper *Ha'aretz*. The Israeli media are thus shown to be fairer than those Western organs acting as Israel's defenders.

Said is a passionate advocate of reconciliation between Jews and Palestinians. It isn't hard to conclude that his enemies are not. The attack on Said is also an attack on what he stands for, on the world he has hoped for decades to argue into being: a world in which Palestinians are able to live with honor in their own country, yes, but also a world in which, by an act of constructive forgetting, the past can be worked through and then left in the past, so that Palestinians and Jews can begin to think about a different sort of future. That there are extremists in Israel determined to thwart this vision is not news. That so much of the Western press offers these extremists such ready collaboration ought to be news. It is certainly a scandal.

NOVEMBER 1999: PAKISTAN

Pakistan's new military strongman, Pervez Musharraf, has promised to purge the state of corruption before restoring democracy. Pakistan-watchers will recall that when an earlier cartoon of a dictator, General Zia of the waxed mustache and raccoon eyes, was in his prime he, too, used to speak of cleaning up the country and then holding elections. Zia promised and canceled elections so often that it became a joke. His title in those bad old days was CMLA, which officially stood for "Chief Martial Law Administrator" but which, people began to say, really stood for "Cancel My Last Announcement." Perhaps fearing such a reaction, General Musharraf has preferred not to announce elections at all. This is hardly an improvement.

Let's ignore for a moment the obvious fact that General Musharraf's refusal to give a timetable for restoring democracy is in itself a corrupt act, his second such misdeed, the coup he engineered being the first. Instead, let's take a look at the condition of the stables he has undertaken to clean up. The Nawaz Sharif government was economically incompetent, unpleasantly autocratic, deeply unpopular, and widely suspected of many forms of corruption, including election-rigging. Its actions merit the most thorough investigation. But how can General Musharraf, who has already accused Nawaz Sharif of trying to murder him, and has called that alleged attempt "treasonable," persuade us that his regime's inquiries will be dispassionate and credible? A generation ago, General Zia executed Prime Minister Z. A. Bhutto after a show trial. The echoes of that case can already be heard in Musharraf's pronouncements on Nawaz, and they're getting louder.

Benazir Bhutto, her People's Party, and her husband, Asif Zardari, also have many questions to answer. They, too, stand accused of large-scale corruption, and Zardari of being involved in the murder of Benazir's own brother as well. When Nawaz Sharif was prime minister, Benazir could and frequently did dismiss such charges as part of Sharif's political vendetta against her. Not very surprisingly, she has rushed to welcome the Musharraf coup. How will General Musharraf convince us that justice will be done in the Bhutto-Zardari case as well?

Look beyond the political parties and you see the real causes of the social wreckage of Pakistan. The poppy fields of the North-West Frontier have been producing opium for as long as anyone can remember. Nowadays they produce great quantities of heroin as well. To be exported, that heroin must travel a thousand miles south to Karachi—past Army units and octroi inspection points. In the opinion of every expert commentator I know, the Pakistani drug industry simply could not operate without the active cooperation of the bureaucracy and the Army. If General Musharraf would have us believe in his anti-corruption platform, he must first demonstrate that the Army has cleaned up its own act. How exactly does he propose to do this? And what does he intend to do about Karachi, which is presently a terrifyingly wild and all-but-lawless burg, in the grip not only of violent sectarian politics but also of the drug overlords and criminal mafias? Karachi's citizens speak every day of the collaboration between the city's police force and organized crime. What is General Musharraf's plan for the redemption of his country's most important city?

Beneath this suppurating surface lie deeper ills that a military regime is even less able to address. Pakistan is a country in which democratic institutions—make that democratic instincts—have never been permitted to take root. Instead, the country's elites—military, political, industrial, aristocratic, feudal—take it in turns to loot the nation's wealth, while increasingly extremist mullahs demand the imposition of draconian versions of Sharia law.

Nawaz Sharif's government grew more fanatically Islamist as it grew weaker. General Musharraf's quickly expressed determination not to permit fundamentalists to take over the state should be welcomed. But can any coup leader hope to create the kind of secular-democratic state in which coups become not only unnecessary but unthinkable? Can any elitist—and a man who believes he has the right to seize control of an entire nation-state is certainly that—be believed when he announces his desire to fight against elitism?

Musharraf has also made placatory noises toward India, and withdrawn some troops from the frontier. Yet he is the man responsible for planning this year's catastrophic military adventure in Kashmir, and he has made many ultra-hawkish comments about India in the recent past. Why should we trust his new softer line when he has shown every sign of having an itchy trigger finger—a finger that now sits upon Pakistan's nuclear button?

The Musharraf coup is, at present, very popular in Pakistan. So were the Pakistani nuclear tests. There are reports that after these tests ordinary Pakistanis went out to the blast sites and gathered up jars of radioactive earth as patriotic souvenirs. These jars, sitting in pride of place in Pakistani homes, may prove to be less worth having than they now seem. You could make much the same sort of hypothesis about the Pervez Musharraf regime.

DECEMBER 1999: ISLAM AND THE WEST

The relationship between the Islamic world and the West seems to be living through one of the famous "interregnums" defined by Antonio Gramsci, in which the old refuses to die, so that the new cannot be born, and all manner of "morbid symptoms" arise. Both between Muslim and Western countries and inside Muslim communities living in the West, the old, deep mistrusts abide, frustrating attempts to build new, better relations, and creating much bad blood. For example, the general suspicion felt by many ordinary Egyptians about America's motives has created a heightened, almost paranoiac atmosphere around the investigation of the crash of EgyptAir Flight 990. Now, all information pointing to the pilot Gameel al-Batouty's responsibility for the aircraft's fatal dive is believed to be tainted, in spite of indications that (a) he pulled rank to take over the controls from the co-pilot, even though it wasn't his shift, and (b) the now-notorious religious mutterings immediately preceded the aircraft's steep downward plunge. Meanwhile, theories exonerating the pilot are being propounded in Egypt almost daily—it was the Boeing malfunctioning, it was a bomb in the tail, it was a missile, and in any case it was America's fault. The many proponents of these "anti-American" theories see no contradiction in believing with great fervor notions for which there is as yet no shred of proof, while vilifying the FBI for seeking to draw premature conclusions from such evidence as there is.

A more dispassionate version of events is needed. The FBI is perhaps excessively prone to seeing air disasters as crimes rather than accidents. That was certainly a problem after the TWA 800 crash. On that occasion it was the National Transportation Safety Board that eventually made the case for a systems failure causing an explosion in a fuel tank. But this time it's the NTSB's preliminary examination of the data that has thrown up the possibility of a pilot suicide.

The much-criticized leakiness of the investigating bodies can also be seen as reassuring: with so many loose tongues around, in the end the truth will out. By contrast, the state-controlled press in Mubarak's Egypt is likely to reflect that government's nationalistic unwillingness to concede Egyptian responsibility for the crash, which could further damage the tourist trade.

Unreason and emotion have by now thoroughly politicized this investigation. Let us hope that those who fear a U.S. cover-up do not create an atmosphere in which American and Egyptian politicians and diplomats do in fact seek to cover up the truth in the interest of their bilateral relations.

Muslims living in the West also continue to feel defensive, suspicious, and persecuted. Hard on the heels of the dispute about the EgyptAir tragedy comes a demand in "multi-faith Britain" that all religious beliefs, not just the established Church of England, be protected from criticism. The West's alleged "Islamophobia" means that Islamic demands for the new law are by far the loudest.

It is true that in many Western quarters there is a knee-jerk reflex that leads to anti-Islamic rushes to judgment, so that British Muslims' sense of injury is frequently justified. But the proposed solution is the wrong cure, one that would make matters even worse than they are. *For the point is to defend people but not their ideas.* It is absolutely right that Muslims—that everyone—should enjoy freedom of religious belief in any free society. It is absolutely right that they should protest against discrimination whenever and wherever they experience it. It is also absolutely wrong of them to demand that their belief system—that any system of belief or thought—should be immunized against criticism, irreverence, satire, even scornful disparagement. This distinction be-tween the individual and his creed is a foundation truth of democracy, and any community that seeks to blur it will not do itself any favors. The British blasphemy law is an outdated relic of the past, has fallen into disuse, and ought to be abolished. To extend it would be an anachronistic move quite against the spirit of a country whose leader-ship likes to prefix everything with the word "new."

Democracy can only advance through the clash of ideas, can only flourish in the rough-and-tumble bazaar of disagreement. The law must never be used to stifle such disagreements, no matter how pro-found. The new cannot die so that the old can be reborn. That would indeed be a morbid symptom.

Once again, a clearer form of discourse is needed. Western societies urgently need to find effective ways of defending Muslims against blind prejudice. And Islamic spokesmen must likewise stop giving the im-pression that the way to better relations—the path to the new—requires the creation of new forms of censorship, of legal blindfolds and gags.

JANUARY 2000: TERROR VERSUS SECURITY

Now that the big Y2K party's over, think for a moment about the covert, worldwide battle that took place on and around Millen-nium Night. Behind the images of a world lit up by pyrotechnics, united for one evanescent instant by gaiety and goodwill, the new dia-lectic of history was taking shape. We already knew that capitalism ver-sus communism was no longer the name of the game. Now we saw, as clearly as the fireworks in the sky, that the defining struggle of the new age would be between Terrorism and Security.

I was one of the ten thousand gathered in London's Millennium Dome, that same dome off which James Bond bounces while fighting the forces of terror in the latest 007 film. The audience knew—after hours of waiting to be frisked on a cold railway platform, how could it not?—that a mammoth security operation had been launched to safe-guard the showpiece event. What few of us knew was that a bomb threat had been made, using an IRA code word, and that the dome came within an inch of being evacuated.

For days, the world had been hearing about nothing but terrorism. The United States had spoken the current bogeyman's name—Osama bin Laden—to frighten us children. There were arrests: a man with bomb-making equipment found at the U.S.-Canada border, a group in Jordan. Seattle canceled its celebrations. One of the leaders of the Aum Shinrikyo cult was released, and Japan feared a terrorist atrocity. President Chandrika Kumaratunga of Sri Lanka made history by surviving a suicide bomber's attack. There were bomb hoaxes at a British racetrack and at a soccer stadium. The FBI feared the worst from apocalyptic groups and lunatic-fringers. But in the end—apart from poor George Harrison, wounded by one such lunatic—we got off relatively lightly.

Almost all of us, that is, because there was also the Indian Airlines hijack. The events at Kandahar airport have left no fewer than four governments looking pretty bad. Nepal, proving that Kathmandu deserves its terrorist-friendly reputation, allowed men with guns and grenades to board a plane. The Indian government's capitulation to the terrorists was the first such surrender to hijackers in years; what will they do when the next aircraft is seized? And, finally, terrorists trained in Taliban camps and holding Pakistani passports disappeared from Afghanistan into, very probably, Pakistan. Thus was a largely defunct form of terrorism given a new lease on life.

Some knees jerked predictably. An Islamist journalist, writing in a liberal British paper of the sort that would be banned in Islamist countries, complained that the "terrorist" tag demonizes members of freedom movements struggling against violent, oppressive regimes. But terrorism isn't justice-seeking in disguise. In Sri Lanka it's the voices of peace and conciliation who are getting murdered. And the brutal Indian Airlines hijackers do not speak for the people of peaceable, vandalized Kashmir.

The security establishment rightly regards the non-explosive Millennium as a triumph. Security is, after all, the art of making sure certain things don't happen: a thankless task, because when they don't happen, there will always be someone to say the security was excessive and unnecessary. In London on New Year's Eve the security operation was on a scale that would have made citizens of many less fortunate nations convinced that a coup was in progress. But none of us thought so for an instant. This was security in the service of merrymaking, and that is something we can be impressed by and grateful for. And yet there is cause for concern. If the ideology of terrorism is that terror works, then the ideology of security is based on assuming the truth of the "worst-case scenario." The trouble is that worst-case scenarism, if I may call it that, plays right into the hands of the fear creators. The worst-case scenario of crossing the road, after all, is that you'll be hit by a truck and killed. Yet we all do cross roads every day, and could hardly function if we did not. To live by the worst-case scenario is to grant the terrorists their victory, without a shot having been fired.

It is also alarming to think that the real battles of the new century may be fought in secret, between adversaries accountable to few of us, the one claiming to act on our behalf, the other hoping to scare us into submission. Democracy requires openness and light. Must we really surrender our future into the hands of the shadow warriors? That most of the Millennial threats turned out to be hoaxes only underlines the problem; nobody wants to run from imaginary enemies. But how, in the absence of information, are we, the public, to evaluate such threats? How can we prevent terrorists and their antagonists from setting the boundaries within which we live?

Security saved President Kumaratunga, but many others died. The security at George Harrison's fortress-home didn't stop the would-be assassin's knife; it was his wife's well-swung table lamp that saved him. In the past, security didn't save President Reagan, or the pope. Luck did that. So we need to understand that even maximum security guarantees nobody's safety. The point is to decide—as the Queen decided on New Year's Eve—not to let fear rule our lives. To tell those bullies who would terrorize us that we aren't scared of them. And to thank our secret protectors, but to remind them, too, that in a choice between security and liberty, it is liberty that must always come out on top.

FEBRUARY 2000: JÖRG HAIDER

In April 1995, on the fiftieth anniversary of Austria's liberation from Nazism, an extraordinary rally took place on the Heldenplatz in central Vienna. Beneath the balcony from which Adolf Hitler had once harangued his roaring gang, Austrian artists, intellectuals, and politicians, as well as their friends and supporters from elsewhere, united to celebrate Hitler's downfall, and by doing so to cleanse the old square of its association with evil. It was my privilege to be one of the speakers that night, and it was clear to me that the event's more contemporary purpose was to give shape and voice to the "good Austria," that passionate and substantial anti-Haider constituency of which surprisingly little is heard outside Austria itself. Jörg Haider's supporters understood this too, and the rally accordingly became the focus of much ultra-rightist derision. Then, unfortunately, it began to rain.

It rained heavily, incessantly, relentlessly. This was neo-Nazi rain, absolutist, intolerant, determined to have its way. The rally's organizers were worried. A poor turnout would be celebrated by the Haiderites, and the whole event could backfire terribly. In a week's time, nobody would remember the weather, but nobody would be allowed to forget the sparse attendance. But there was nothing for it. The rally had to go ahead, and the rain kept bucketing down. When I came out onto the stage, however, I saw an unforgettable sight. The Heldenplatz was packed, as full as Times Square on Millennium Eve. The crowd was soaked to the skin, joyous, cheering, youthful. The rain crashed down on those young people all night and they didn't care. They had come in numbers to make a statement they cared greatly about, and they weren't going to let a little water get in the way. It was perhaps the most moving crowd I'd ever seen. The purpose of such rallies is to strengthen people's hope. It certainly strengthened mine.

These memories of the Heldenplatz rally make the news of Jörg Haider's surge toward power—eerily reminiscent of the career of the Hitlerish central figure in Brecht's *Resistible Rise of Arturo Ui*—all the more unpalatable. In his growing popularity I see the defeat of those idealistic young people standing shoulder to shoulder in the pouring rain.

But it won't do to describe Haider's triumph simply as a victory of evil over good. The success of extremist leaders is invariably linked to failures in the system they supplant. The tyranny of the shah of Iran created the tyranny of the ayatollahs. The lazy corruption of the old, secularist Algeria gave birth to the GIA and the FIS. In Pakistan, Nawaz Sharif's abuses of power have made possible the new abuses being perpetrated by his successor, General Musharraf. The incompetence and corruption of the Congress Party in India enabled the Hindu nationalist BJP and its sidekick, the Shiv Sena, to seize power. The failures of the old British Labour Party were the making of Thatcher's radical Conservatism. And the long-running Austrian "grand coalition," that backslapping, jobs-for-the-boys Establishment fix, has disillusioned the voters enough to make them turn toward Haider.

The papers are full of tales of fat-cat corruption these days, and the revelations are a gift to a populist demagogue of the Haider type. (When the heirs of the late Bettino Craxi shrug their shoulders and call the Kohl-Mitterrand-Craxi slush-fund story an irrelevance, they make things much worse. The more Europe looks like a "grand coalition" of arrogant leaders for whom ends easily justify means, the more ammunition the Haiders of Europe will have.)

Like Bombay's boss Bal Thackeray, Haider has said he will not himself enter the government—so much easier to run things through proxies and stooges, so much less, well, exposed. But Thackeray's support comes mainly from the ignored, disenfranchised urban poor. Haider, according to the political theorist Karl-Markus Gauss, has pulled off a more European trick. Like Le Pen in France or Bossi in Italy, he has won the support of the wealthy, successful bourgeoisie. What these people hate about immigrants, Gauss believes, is not their race but their poverty. (Credit where credit's due. The politician who invented this trick, who remained in power throughout the 1980s by persuading the employed to vote against the unemployed, is none other than General Pinochet's best friend, Margaret Thatcher.)

This system is corrupt, say the placards of the German anti-Kohl protesters. They're right, and the fight against that corruption and the fight against Jörg Haider are one and the same. The EU must devote as much energy to rooting out the slush-fund artists in its own ranks as to closing ranks against Haider and his Freedom Party.

At the end of Brecht's play, the actor playing Arturo Ui steps forward and addresses the audience directly, warning it against complacency. Ui-Hitler may have fallen, he reminds us, but "the bitch that bore him is in heat again." The European Union must set its house in order quickly, unless it wishes history to remember it as the latest incarnation of that sleazy, promiscuous canine.

MARCH 2000: AMADOU DIALLO

[*Amadou Diallo, a black immigrant from Guinea, was shot dead in the Bronx by four NYPD police officers—no fewer than forty-one shots being fired by the quartet—and all four shootists have just been acquitted of all wrongdoing, in a verdict that has stunned and divided New Yorkers.*]

English being the most elastic of languages, the word "mistake" is capable of a pretty big stretch, meaning anything from "innocent little gaffe" to "unforgivable, catastrophic error." This week in Albany, New York, the jury in the Amadou Diallo case stretched it a bit further still.

The jury decided Diallo's death was the result of a tragic mistake or, one might more accurately say, forty-one tragic mistakes, lethal, high-velocity mistakes, fired in quick succession by the four members of the Street Crime Unit, two of whom—Officers Carroll and McMellon—discharged their full sixteen-bullet (no, make that sixteen-*mistake*) clips into Diallo's body. After a pause, their colleagues, Officers Boss and Murphy, added, respectively, five and four tragic mistakes each.

These mistakes were themselves the consequences of earlier mistakes. The policemen saw a black man on his own doorstep and made the mistake of thinking he was a criminal. They thought he reminded them of a sketch they'd seen of a rapist but, er, they were mistaken. They thought he was reaching for a gun when in fact he was reaching for his wallet: um, *bad* mistake. They claimed to have seen a "muzzle flash," as if a bullet had been fired. (Wallets rarely emit such flashes.) Then Officer McMellon stumbled and fell; his colleagues erroneously concluded he'd been hit, presumably by Diallo's deadly wallet, and shot to kill. And they went on and on shooting because, bizarrely, they thought Diallo, who didn't fall down for a time, was wearing a bullet-proof vest. He wasn't. He was being shot so often and so hard that it was, almost certainly, the force of the bullets that was keeping him on his feet. In his dead body there were nineteen entry wounds and sixteen exit wounds.

When the police officers discovered their mistakes—"where's the fucking gun?"—they begged Amadou Diallo not to die. Later, in court, they wept for him. However, they plainly believe they have wept and suffered enough. They hope, according to press reports, to "ease back" into normal life. Through their lawyers, they express displeasure at suggestions that they should resign. They hint, however, that because of all the criticism they may not wish to remain police officers. Amazingly, it seems they have begun to see themselves as the injured parties. (Those courtroom tears are beginning to look even more crocodile-ish than they did at the time.)

And their senior officers, facing wrathful accusations of police racism, say that the NYPD feels "disheartened" by the flood of criticisms. There is much that should dishearten it. The Diallo killing has shown that the automatic assumptions within police culture—when coupled with the stop-and-frisk powers given to the police by Mayor Giuliani, and given the greater power of life and death by the omnipresence in America of the gun—are such that American minority groups now feel that their lives are seriously at risk. To put it bluntly: if you happen to be black, and a police officer stumbles while you are reaching for your wallet, his partners may shoot you dead.

But this is not, unfortunately, why the NYPD feels disheartened. The criticism is what depresses them, not their own mistakes. Because everybody makes mistakes, right? Right. But accusations of racism? Boy, those hurt.

One or two voices have begun to demand that the officers be dismissed from the NYPD, but at the moment of writing, the idea that men should be held accountable for their errors hasn't caught on. Mayor Giuliani, whose baby the much-enlarged Street Crime Unit is, has unsurprisingly defended the police. His political rival, Hillary Clinton, has issued her customary bland, having-it-both-ways nostrums. And the dead man's impressive mother, Kadiatou Diallo, is too brokenheartedly dignified to say anything that might be interpreted as a call for revenge.

But: *of course* the four officers should be fired at once. The idea that they might get their guns back and return to patrolling the streets of New York, with their poor judgment and macho slogans ("we own the night"), is unimaginably awful. No, worse: it's imaginably awful. In the aftermath of the beating of Rodney King in L.A., the sodomizing by baton of Abner Louima, and now the death of Amadou Diallo, people are beginning to be able to imagine the previously unimaginable.

Tragedy happens—"tragic mistakes" happen—when men act according to their flawed natures, in fulfillment of their preordained destinies. The tragedy of the four killers of Amadou Diallo is that their deeds were made possible by their general preconceptions about black people and poor neighborhoods; by a theory of policing that encouraged them to be rigid and punitive toward petty offenders; and by a social context in which the possession and use of firearms is so normative as to be almost beyond discussion. The tragedy of the street vendor Amadou Diallo is that he came as an innocent to the slaughter, made vulnerable by poverty and by the color of his skin. And the tragedy of America is that a nation which sees itself as leading the world toward a global future in which the American values of freedom and justice will be available for everyone fails so frequently and so badly to guarantee that freedom and that justice for so many people within its own frontiers.

APRIL 2000: ELIÁN GONZÁLEZ

When the world's imagination engages with a human tragedy as poignant as that of Elián González, the six-year-old refugee boy who survived a shipwreck only to sink deep into the political mire of Cuban-American Miami, it instinctively seeks to enter into the hearts and minds of each of the characters in the drama.

Any parent can grasp something of what Elián's father, Juan Miguel González, has been going through back in Elián's hometown of Cárdenas—the pain of losing his firstborn son, a child who arrived only after seven miscarriages; next the joy of learning that Elián had improbably survived, floating toward Florida on a rubber ring; and then the seismic shock of being told by a gang of estranged relatives and total strangers that they were resolved to stand between him and his child.

Perhaps we can understand Elián's inside-out state of mind a little, too. After all, this is a boy who saw his mother slip into the dark ocean and die, whose father hasn't been there. So if Elián now clutches at the hands of those who have been with him in Miami, if he holds on to them for dear life the way he clung to that rubber ring, who can blame him? If he has constructed a kind of provisional happiness in his new Florida backyard, we should understand that as a psychological survival mechanism, not as a permanent replacement for his father's love.

And if politicians play politics with a small boy's life, nobody likes it much, but nobody's very surprised, either. Al Gore weighs in with a poorly thought through scheme to turn Elián and his father into U.S.

residents (a scheme that Juan Miguel González instantly rejects), and we know that he's trying—and almost certainly failing—to win a few Cuban Republican votes. The mayor of Miami–Dade County, Alex Penelas, irresponsibly declares that his police force will not execute any order to hand Elián back to his father, and we know that he's playing to his particular gallery, too. Fidel Castro comes up with a succession of grandstand plays, turning Elián simultaneously into a symbol of national pride and of the folly of emigration to the USA, and this, too, comes as no surprise.

Elián González has become a political football. The first consequence of becoming a football is that you cease to be thought of as a living, feeling human being. A football is inanimate, and its purpose is to be kicked around. So you become what Elián has become in the mouths of most of those arguing over him—useful, but essentially a thing. You become the proof of the addiction of the United States to litigation, or of the pride and political muscle of a locally powerful immigrant community. You become the location of a battle between mob rule and the rule of law, between rabid anti-Communism and Third World anti-imperialism. You are described and redescribed, sloganized and falsified, until, for the howling combatants, you almost cease to exist. You become a sort of myth, an empty vessel into which the world can pour its prejudices, its poison, and its hate.

All of the foregoing is more or less comprehensible. But what's going on in the minds of Elián's Miami relatives—that's a tough one. This poor boy's flesh-and-blood family has elected to place its own ideological considerations over his obvious and urgent need for his father, which looks, to most of us on the outside, like an ugly, unnatural choice. There is strong evidence—for example, in a powerful *New York Times* article written by Gabriel García Márquez—that Juan Miguel González is a loving father; so when the Miami relatives' lawyers assault his good character, it sounds like a cheap shot. And while there is also evidence that Juan Miguel is being used by Castro for political ends, most of us would say, so what? Even if Señor González is a fully-fledged Red of the sort most hated by the Florida Cuban community, this does not override the rightness of returning his son to his care, and to argue that it does is, well, inhuman. When the Miami relatives hint that Elián will be "brainwashed" if he goes home, it only makes us think that they are even more blinkered than the ideologues they seek to condemn.

García Márquez concludes his article by deploring "the harm being done to Elián González's mental health by the cultural uprooting to which he is being subjected." This routinely anti-U.S. gibe is surely wide of the mark. President Clinton, Attorney General Janet Reno, and the U.S. federal courts have taken a sensible line throughout the protracted crisis, and American public opinion has generally backed their view that Elián's place is with his dad. This compares very favorably with, say, the actions of the German authorities, who have in a number of notorious recent cases refused to return children to non-German parents living abroad.

Plainly, the Elián story is not an American but a Cuban tragedy; and, yes, "cultural uprooting" is at its heart, but not in the sense that García Márquez meant. It is the Miami Cuban community that has evidently been harmed by being uprooted from its island in the sun. Their flight from tyranny has ended, or so it presently seems, in a flight not only from reason but from simple humanity, too.

MAY 2000: J. M. COETZEE

Just occasionally, a work of literature offers its readers a clearer, deeper understanding of the opaque events being reported in the press and on TV, whose shadowed truths the half-light of journalism fails to illumine. E. M. Forster's *A Passage to India* taught us that the great public quarrels of history can make it impossible for individuals to construct a private peace. History forbids the friendship between the Englishman Fielding and the Indian doctor Aziz. "Not yet, not yet," Aziz demurs. Not while imperialism's great injustice stands between us. Not until India is free.

After World War II, many German poets and novelists felt that their language had been reduced to rubble by Nazism, as thoroughly as the bomb-devastated cities. The "rubble literature" they created sought to rebuild German writing brick by brick.

Now, as the aftermath of Empire is acted out on the white-owned farmland of Zimbabwe while Kenya and South Africa watch with trepidation, J. M. Coetzee's acclaimed fiction *Disgrace* is proposed as another such age-defining work, a lens through which we can see more clearly much that was murky before. *Disgrace* is the story of David Lurie, a white professor who loses his job after sexual-harassment charges are laid against him by a female student with whom he has had a joyless series of sexual encounters. Lurie goes to stay with his daughter Lucy on her remote smallholding, where they are violently attacked by a group of black men. The consequences of this attack profoundly shake Lurie, darkening his view of the world.

There is something in *Disgrace* that harks back both to the Forsterian vision of the Indian struggle for independence and to the Germans' rubble literature. In Lucy's apparent readiness to accept her rape as her assailants' way of working out on her body the necessary revenges of history, we hear a much harsher, more discordant echo of Dr. Aziz's "not yet." And Lurie believes (like, one must conclude, his creator) that the English language is no longer capable of expressing the Southern African reality.

The bone-hard language Coetzee has found for his book has been much admired, as has the unflinchingness of his vision. The book unquestionably fulfills the first requirement for a great novel: it powerfully creates a dystopia that adds to the sum total of the imagined worlds at our disposal and, by doing so, increases what it is possible for us to think. Reading about Lurie and Lucy on their dangerous, isolated patch of land, we can more readily grasp the condition of those white farmers in Zimbabwe, as history comes calling for its revenge. Like the Byronic Lucifer—in whose name both "Lurie" and "Lucy" can be found—Coetzee's protagonist "acts on impulse, and the source of his impulses is dark to him." He has, perhaps, a "mad heart," and believes in something he calls "the rights of desire." This makes him sound passionate, but in fact he's cold and abstracted to an almost somnambulist degree.

This cold detachment, which also permeates the novel's prose, is the problem. "Rubble literature" didn't just strip language to its bones. It put new flesh on those bones, perhaps because its practitioners retained a belief in, even a love for, that language, and for the culture in which their renewed language was to flower. Lacking that loving belief, the discourse of *Disgrace* sounds heartless, and all its intelligence cannot fill up the hole.

To act on impulses whose source one claims not to understand, to justify one's plunges at women by one's "rights of desire," is to make a virtue of one's psychological and moral lacunae. For a character to justify himself by claiming not to understand his motives is one thing; for the novelist to collude in that justification is quite another.

Nobody in *Disgrace* understands anyone else. Lurie does not understand Melanie, the student he seduces, nor she him. He doesn't understand Lucy, his own daughter, and she finds his deeds and his "case" for his actions beyond her. He doesn't understand himself at the beginning, nor does he get any wisdom by the novel's end.

Inter-racial relations are conducted at the same level of ignorance. The whites don't understand the blacks and the blacks aren't interested in understanding the whites. Not one of the novel's black characters—not Petrus the "gardener and dog-man" who works with Lucy, and certainly not the gang of assailants—is developed into a living, breathing character. Petrus comes closest, but his motives remain enigmatic and his presence grows more menacing as the novel proceeds. To the novel's whites, its black inhabitants are essentially a threat—a threat justified by history. Because whites have historically oppressed blacks, it's being suggested, we must now accept that blacks will oppress whites. An eye for an eye, and so the whole world goes blind.

This, then, is the novel's acclaimed revelatory vision: one of a society of conflicting incomprehensions, driven by the absolutes of history. Certainly it's coherent enough—coherent in its privileging of incoherence, striving to make of its blindness a sort of metaphorical insight.

When a writer's created beings lack understanding, it becomes the writer's task to provide the reader with the insight lacked by the characters. If he does not, his work will not shine a light upon darkness but merely become a part of the darkness it describes. This, alas, is the weakness of *Disgrace*. It doesn't, finally, shed enough new light on the news. But the news does add a bit to our understanding of the book.

JUNE 2000: FIJI

They are trying to steal our land." Such is the emotive accusation made by the failed businessman George Speight and his gang of hooligan usurpers against Fiji's Indian community in general and the deposed Mahendra Chaudhry government in particular. By one of the bitter ironies of the Age of Migration, Speight's insistence on the basic cultural importance of land is very easy for people of Indian origin to grasp. (However, he goes too far, and by his insistence on what might be called the racial characteristics of land—for Speight plainly assumes that the land is, in its very nature, ethnically Fijian—he tips over into bigotry and folly.)

Land, home, belonging: to Indians these words have always felt more than ordinarily potent. India is a continent of deeply rooted peoples. Indians don't just own the ground beneath their feet; it owns them, too. An orthodox Hindu tradition goes so far as to warn that anyone who crosses the "black water"—the ocean—instantly loses caste. The so-called Indian diaspora, which has taken Indian communities and their descendants from their over-populous country across the world in every direction and as far as, well, Fiji, is therefore the most improbable of phenomena. Yet the journeyings of Indians all over the planet is one of the great sagas of our time, an epic replete with misadventures. Idi Amin's vicious expulsion of the Ugandan Asians, the tensions between the black and Indian populations of Trinidad and South Africa, "Paki-bashing" in Britain, the tough treatment of Indian workers in Gulf states, and now Fiji—it's tempting to conclude that the world has it in for these hardworking migrants and descendants of migrants, that their single-minded dedication to bettering their families' lot somehow comes across as reprehensible.

In the United States, many Indians speak almost shamefacedly of their lack of racially motivated trouble; not being the target of American racism, they have been until recently almost invisible as a community, and this invisibility has perhaps excused them from persecution. But there have been triumphs, too. With each generation, Indians have become more fully a part of Britain without losing their distinctive identity; while in America, the virtual takeover of Silicon Valley by Indian whiz-kids has got people's attention and earned their admiration.

In Fiji, the century-old Indian presence has been a success story. Indians have built the sugar industry that is the country's main resource; and—as the ethnic Fijian opposition to the Speight coup demonstrates—relations between the communities are by no means as bad as the rebels make out. In the Fijian Parliament, the Chaudhry government was supported by fifty-eight out of seventy-one members. Twelve out of eighteen members of the sacked cabinet were ethnic Fijians. Even among Speight's hostages, fourteen of the thirty-one prisoners are ethnic Fijians. Thus the Chaudhry government was in no sense a sectarian government of Indians lording it over Fijians. It was a genuine cultural mixture. Since its deposition, however, the Speight rebels, abetted by the craven Great Council of Chiefs and by the martial-law regime of Commodore Bainimarama, have dragged Fiji back toward its racially intolerant past. There has been much violence. Many Indians now say they'll have to leave. Meanwhile, the quality of debate deteriorates by the day. Speight's mob points approvingly to Mugabe's land grab in Zimbabwe, and says that the British should be responsible for the Indians they brought to Fiji, just as they "should" recompense the dispossessed Zimbabwean whites.

The fundamentals of the land question have been thoroughly obscured by such nonsense. The obvious truth is that, after a hundred years, Fiji's Indians have every right to be treated as Fijian, as the equals of ethnic Fijians. Preventing Indians from owning land was and is a great injustice—most of Fiji's land, particularly on the main island of Viti Levu, is owned by Fijians but held by Indians on ninety-nine-year leases, many of which are coming up for renewal—and the Speight idea of taking over the sugar farms as the Indians' ninety-nine-year leases expire compounds that injustice.

British Indians have fought to be recognized as British; Uganda's Indians were grievously wronged when Amin threw them out as "foreigners." Migrant peoples do not remain visitors forever. In the end, their new land owns them as once their old land did, and they have a right to own it in their turn. "We don't want Fijians fighting Fijians— our common enemy is the Indians," Speight says, but the final irony may be that his brand of ethnic cleansing is leading Fijians and Indians in western Fiji, the most prosperous part of the country, with most of the sugarcane operations, some gold mines, and the best tourist resorts, to make common cause against him. Secession is being seriously discussed. The choice facing Fiji's remarkably inept political class may therefore soon become a stark one: abandon the fundamentally racist notion that your land is ethnically tied to one racial group, or lose the best of that land to those who find your bigotry, and your weakness, impossible to bear.

JULY 2000: SPORT

France is the most powerful nation in Europe and probably, at present, the world; though Brazil would dispute that. The Germans, usually so organized and efficient, are in an uncharacteristic mess. Italians have flair but are profoundly defensive by nature. The Dutch are sometimes quarrelsome but, at their best, by far the most artistic of the Europeans; Belgium is dull by comparison. Spain is highly gifted but consistently under-achieves at the highest levels. Denmark, Norway, and Sweden seem to be in decline. Yugoslavia and Croatia can both be guilty (like Argentina) of hidden brutalities. Turkey, Nigeria, and the leading Arab nations are rapidly approaching parity with Europe and South America, while Japan and the USA remain very much second-class nations. And the English—alas, the English!—are pedestrian, tactically naïve, and, of course, hooligans.

The world according to soccer, like the whole sports-page cosmos, differs somewhat from the picture of reality to be found on the news pages but is instantly recognizable, except in the few remaining soccer-free corners of the globe. And in our sound bite–dominated era, the crude national stereotypes generated by sport have begun to inform the way we look at the "real" world as well as the narrower arena of sport itself. They even affect the way we—including those of us who lack any vestige of sporting prowess—look at ourselves.

Sporting success can have the most astonishing social, and even political, effects. A couple of years ago there was much talk of France's loss of cultural and national confidence, of a sort of crisis of French identity. The World Cup victory two years ago, and the Euro 2000 triumph last week, has silenced all such talk. And the genius of the French Muslim superstar Zinedine Zidane, scorer of the goal that won the World Cup and now the inspiration of the European champions, has done more to improve France's attitude toward its Muslim minority, and to damage the political aspirations of the ultra-right, than a thousand political speeches could hope to achieve.

Sporting failure likewise generates ripples far beyond the playing field. Thus England has reacted to its soccer team's mediocrity and its supporters' violence by plunging into a what's-wrong-with-us fit of self-criticism reminiscent of the gloomy worldview of A. A. Milne's immortal donkey, Eeyore. Not only can England's soccer players not play soccer, their tennis players can't play tennis, and one of them's Canadian anyway. In this Eeyore-ish mood, even victories look like less extreme forms of failure. The England cricket team actually wins a Test match, but the true Eeyore points out that when England lose, as they usually do, they get thrashed, but when they win, which is rare, they win by a whisker. The England rugby team beats mighty South Africa; Eeyore ripostes, ah, but they can't do it *regularly,* it's just a flash in the pan. The world heavyweight boxing champion is British, but Eeyore points out that Lennox Lewis, too, speaks with a transatlantic twang.

About one thing all commentators seem clear. A nation's sporting performance, its prowess or its ineptitude, like the behavior of its fans, has origins far removed from the closed universe of sport itself. It has deep roots in the Culture.

Culture is what we now have instead of ideology. We live in an age of culture wars, of groups using ever narrower self-definitions of culture both as a shield and as a sword. Culture is touchy. Use the wrong word and you'll be accused of racism by some cultural commissar or other. (In Philip Roth's magisterial new novel *The Human Stain,* the word is "spooks"; in a *New York Times* report from Akron, Ohio, last week it was "niggardly.")

These days everything is culture. Food is culture and religion is culture and so is gardening. Lifestyle is culture and politics is culture and race is culture and then there's the proliferation of sexual cultures and let's not forget subcultures, too. Sport, of course, is *major* culture. So, when British (and, to a lesser extent, other) louts were misbehaving in Holland and Belgium, it was their culture that was held responsible, and nobody saw the irony of using the term to explain the actions of such profoundly uncultured individuals. But if hooliganism is also a culture now, then the word has finally lost all meaning. Which matters only if you think that culture is something else, something to do with art, imagination, education, and ethics, something that broadens perceptions rather than narrowing them, which enables us to see beyond national stereotypes to the richer complexity of real life, in which not all Italians are defensive, not all Germans are efficient, and England, poor England, is not defined by its sportsmen, thugs, and Eeyores; in which "spooks" and "niggardly" are not racist words, and subtlety is valued more highly than sound bites, and a game is just a game.

AUGUST 2000: TWO CRASHES

The speed of life is now so great that we can't concentrate on anything for long. We need capsule meanings to be attached to news events instantly, explaining and pigeonholing their significance, so that we can move on, secure in the illusion of having understood something. In the days after two catastrophic crashes, of the Middle East peace process and the Air France Concorde, an army of commentators has been trying to come up with (on a postcard, preferably) the brief sound bites that bite.

Of the two disasters, the Concorde crash yields up its Instant Message more easily. It represents, as a thousand pundits have told us, the End of the Dream of the Future. In a world in which no Concorde had ever crashed, this most graceful of aircraft embodied our dreams of transcendence. In the new reality that is still smoldering on the ground in Gonesse, France, our expectations must be lowered. Transcendence kills. The pictures tell us so. In our airplanes, in our lives, in our fantasies of what we might be, we must give up the idea of breaking barriers. For a brief, fabulous period we exceeded our limits. Now we are gripped once more by the surly bonds of earth.

Unfortunately, the other crash seems, after analysis, to insist on meaning exactly the opposite thing. Everywhere I've been in the last week or so, and in much of what I've seen, heard, or read, one question has kept coming up: if it were left to you, how would you solve the riddle of Jerusalem? And the op-ed and dinner-table consensus seems to be that the old place must become a free city, a World City, neither Israeli nor Palestinian but capital of both. Seems fair and ultimately doable. Yes, we like that idea . . . What's that you say? There's a hot breaking news story? Quick, switch on CNN.

Oh, very well, we can go into this a bit more if you absolutely insist. It's simple, really. Barak's government has already given ground, but Israel must have its arm twisted by the United States until it agrees to this essential further concession. And, yes, Arafat was intransigent, in part because Hosni Mubarak persuaded his major backers to insist on the hard-line, we-get-East-Jerusalem-or-bust position. So, the Arab states must have their arms twisted by the United States until they agree to the Only Possible Solution . . .

You see, sometimes people just have to be bigger than what holds them back. We, they, just have to find it in ourselves, themselves, to transcend. Because peace is the Dream of the Future and cannot be denied . . .

Instant analysts are thus faced with an apparent black-and-white Message Contradiction. If the "meaning" of the Concorde crash is right, then the puncturing of human dreams is inevitable. There will therefore be no peace in the Middle East. And when the intifada returns in a more violent form—because now the Palestinians can fight with guns, not stones—Israel will retaliate with maximum force, and the region will slip toward war. But if, on the other hand, the post–Camp David, free Jerusalem can be conjured into being, it will give us all new hope, and reinvent the idea of the future as a potential *Star*

Trek utopia in which technological marvels—safer, cheaper Concordes, perhaps Concordes for All—arrive hand in hand with a universalist, brotherhood-of-man philosophy of human relations.

In reality, however, the contradiction doesn't exist. In the real world the present is always imperfect and the future is (almost) always a region of hope. The problem lies in the way we all now insist on reacting to the news. Is it a Good Thing? Is it a Bad Thing? What's in it for us? What do they tell us about ourselves? Or about the other guys? Where's the angle? Who's to blame? Gimme the zapper. Let's surf! In her famous essay "Illness as Metaphor," Susan Sontag pointed out the dangers of thinking in this quasi-mystical way, of, for example, seeing curses and judgments in sickness and disease. This argument also applies to the news or, rather, the current obsession with finding symbolic meaning in headline-worthy events. News as Instant Metaphor turns a random catastrophe like an air crash into a generalized cultural signifier or, more dangerously, over-interprets events like the Camp David negotiations until the overlaid resonances and echoes complicate and obscure the difficult, half-resolved, half-stymied thing itself.

News as Instant Metaphor is excessively emotive, often politically slanted, inevitably shallow. It idealizes or demonizes its subjects and dulls or inflames our responses. (The vile murder of young Sarah Payne in Britain, totemically represented as a symbol of innocence endangered by evil, has turned sections of the British media into a frothing lynch mob.)

The British government—among others—has recently been attacked for its preoccupation with spin rather than substance, presentation rather than reality; with, in other words, Government as Metaphor. But if the comment-heavy news media themselves—provocative opinion columns, however glib, are so much cheaper than old-fashioned journalism—were less eager to spin the news the moment it happens until it becomes a dazzling, hypnotic blur, we might see more clearly through the political spin doctors' smoke and mirrors.

SEPTEMBER 2000: SENATOR LIEBERMAN

According to Niccolò Machiavelli's classic manual of realpolitik, *The Prince,* a prince ought not to be religious but should be adept at simulating religiosity. It would come as something of a relief in this year's god-bothered American election campaign if it turned out that when the various candidates profess their various degrees of spiritual devotion, they don't really mean it. If they were just trying to look good in the eyes of the notoriously religious American electorate, one might almost be able to forgive them their protestations. To be cynical is merely to be a politician, after all, and anyhow, cynicism is greatly preferable to sanctimony.

No such luck, I'm afraid. Bill Clinton may very well be the most devout of believers, but the sheer enthusiasm and frequency with which he has confessed his sins, the brilliant volubility and star-quality performance of his fallen-sinner-sees-the-light act, has elevated the belief practices of the Leader to the level of major showbiz. His successors, none of them blessed (or cursed) with the fabled Clintonian charisma and pizzazz, have no option but to say what they mean, which means, unfortunately, that they also mean what they say.

The truly Machiavellian candidate would, for example, have noted the opinion polls that followed the announcement of Al Gore's selection of Senator Joe Lieberman for the second spot on the Democrat ticket. This American Prince—spotting that, while more than 90 percent of eligible voters said they had no difficulty in imagining themselves voting for a black, Jewish, or gay presidential candidate, only half of them were willing to consider voting for an atheist—would instantly pump up the spiritual volume, and if he wasn't already adept at feigning a deeply held faith, he would make darn sure he learned how to do so double quick.

So here, right on cue, comes Senator Joseph Lieberman himself, hauling George Washington out of his grave to cry that where there is no religion there can be no morality. But while Senator Lieberman may be many things, he's no Machiavelli, as is amply demonstrated by the two-left-feet clumsiness of this attempt to make religion even more important an issue in American public life than it already is. After the Anti-Defamation League's attack on his remarks, he's been backtracking fast. Now he's all for the separation of Church and State, always was, always will be, and no, he doesn't think that people without religious belief lack moral conviction, even though he did raise poor old George from the dead to say exactly that.

All this is alarming to those of us (the citizens of the rest of the world) who can't vote in November but whose fate will be profoundly influenced by the U.S. voters' choice. We're already disconcerted that only about 30 percent of American voters feel it's worth bothering to vote at all, and the thought that the relative perceived holiness of the candidates may be of decisive importance does nothing to reassure us.

In John Frankenheimer's classic sixties thriller *The Manchurian Candidate,* America's enemies try to seize control of the White House by getting a brainwashed American politician to run for president. Today, even the United States' friends are beginning to wish a Rest of the World candidate were permitted to run. We all live under the aegis of the American Empire's unchallenged might, so the victorious candidate will be our president, too. Of the actually available duo, it's plain that the Rest of the World's best bet is Al Gore. Not only is he smarter than his opponent, but he also does appear to know where the Rest of the World is, which gives him a definite edge in our admittedly self-interested opinion. For many of us, George W. Bush's failure to name the president of India was a mistake as irredeemable as Dan Quayle's "potatoe." Bush's fondness for frying his fellow human beings is also a reason for unease. If it was tough to forgive Clinton for executing a mentally retarded man, it's even tougher to accept George W.'s frequent human barbecues.

What a shame, then, that the sidekick chosen by Gore to prove he was "his own man" should turn out to be a moral throwback. Lieberman's attack on the movies in the name of "the family" should have been a straw in the wind. Neither this nor his use of Washington as a ventriloquist's dummy will be any easier to forget than Bush's ignorance of President Narayanan's name. Al Gore urgently needs to remind his running mate that people can be moral without being godly for the simple reason that morality precedes ideology—religion is a way of organizing our ideas about good and evil, and not necessarily the origin of those ideas. And to mention to Senator Lieberman that the Rest of the World would like him to be a little less of a putz.

OCTOBER 2000: THE HUMAN RIGHTS ACT

In the late 1970s, during the passage of the infamous British Nationality Act, I was a member of a delegation that lobbied the Conservative minister Geoffrey Finsberg. The proposed act, we argued, was not only racist in intent but a piece of constitutional highway robbery as well. It would arbitrarily abolish a nine-hundred-year-old birthright, the so-called *jus soli* under which British citizenship belonged to all those born on British soil. This was to be replaced by a new, multi-tiered concept of nationality as a gift of the state. "Full" British citizenship was to be based on a murky notion of "patriality"—i.e., having at least one British citizen among your four grandparents—which would allow most white South Africans and Zimbabweans to claim it while denying it to many British passport holders whose skin was black or brown and whose grandparents had unfortunately grown up in "the colonies" far away.

In the absence of a written constitution, Mr. Finsberg and the Conservatives were able to shrug the protests off, and the bill duly became law. It was presented as a defense against a flood of alien immigration, and under cover of such scare-mongering an ancient right of all citizens, white as well as black, was stolen away.

That experience convinced me that Britain's vaunted "unwritten constitution" wasn't worth the paper it wasn't written on. As a child of the post-colonial era, I knew that the British left every one of their colonies with a written constitution; why was Britain thought to be somehow above having one itself? Americans and Europeans have long found the British preference for vague, undefined freedoms not only anomalous but bizarre. If these things were worth having, why on earth were they not worth writing down? Yet movements for constitutional reform, such as Charter 88, of which I was a founding member, initially attracted media derision and met with political apathy. That we are celebrating the entry into British law of a statutory Human Rights Act a mere twelve years later indicates a great shift in British political consciousness, and for that shift pressure groups like Charter 88, Liberty, Index on Censorship, and Article 19 can take much credit. Membership in the EU has played its part as well. European ideas of liberty were pooh-poohed under the Tories, but now their beneficial influence is being felt.

If further proof were needed of the little-Englander unelectability of the British Conservative Party, its response to the Bill of Rights amply provides it. The party's present, in the form of Shadow Home Secretary Ann Widdecombe, its dinosaur past, represented by Lord Tebbit, and their friends in the media have united to attack the new legislation. The law courts will be jammed with "frivolous" cases, they protest. Illegal immigrants and criminals will be rubbing their hands in glee! And, oh, there will be gay sex in the schoolyard, and polygamy, because it's sanctioned by religions such as Islam, will no longer be a crime! This amazing display reveals just how profoundly the idea of entrenched freedoms upsets the British Right. The Human Rights Act has been law in Scotland for most of this year without destroying civil society, and the Scots must be puzzled by the Conservatives' alarmism. (Memo to anti-polygamists: even in Islam, there are legal loopholes. Muslim countries such as Pakistan, where polygamy is not tolerated, use them to outlaw the practice. Where there's a will, there's a way.)

Defenders of the Human Rights Act have emphasized the importance of creating a "culture of liberty." Obviously this doesn't mean that the British don't value freedom. But—as the Tory uproar suggests—some of them don't value it enough. A genuine culture of free expression, to give one example, would not tolerate the continued presence on the British statute books of the absurd, anachronistic blasphemy law. This law was tested in the European Court in the Visions of Ecstasy case (1996). In the written evidence I presented at Strasbourg, I argued that "the modern European concept of freedom of expression was developed, by the intellectuals of the eighteenth-century Enlightenment, in a struggle, not against the State, but against the Church. Since then, Europe has resisted the idea of Inquisitions, and has agreed that religious orthodoxies must not impose limits on what we think and say." In the end the Strasbourg judges did not overturn the blasphemy law, preferring to leave such decisions to the EU's individual member states. Now Britain is in a position to make the decision for herself. Let us hope that the abolition of the offense of blasphemy is one of the new act's earliest benefits. The likes of Ann Widdecombe and Lord Tebbit will be very upset if it is, which only enhances the attractiveness of the idea.

NOVEMBER 2000: GOING TO ELECTORAL COLLEGE

T he climax of this year's U.S. presidential election briefly conjured up the largely forgotten figure of Benjamin Harrison (1833–1901), the moderate Republican who, between 1889 and 1893, was the twenty-third president of the United States. You know: Benjamin Harrison? Ohio boy, grandson of the ninth president, William Henry Harrison, and described as a kindly man and stirring orator? Benjamin Harrison, who, as president, signed into law America's first-ever piece of anti-trust legislation, and who presided over the notorious "Billion Dollar Congress," with whose support he squandered the large budgetary surplus his administration had inherited? Well, no, I didn't know, either. But one fact about this now-obscure ex-president guarantees him a footnote in American electoral history. In the election of 1888, he polled 95,713 fewer votes than his opponent, Grover Cleveland—5,444,337 against 5,540,050—but still won the presidency, because the distribution of his votes earned him a majority in the electoral college, where he won handsomely, by 233 votes to Cleveland's 168.

The close-fought Gore-Bush battle has highlighted as never before the unusual way in which American democracy works. One thing we've all learned this year is that you don't need millions of votes to become president of the United States. You need exactly 270, in an electoral college that nowadays numbers 538.

A few days before the election, many political pundits suddenly woke up to the possibility that Al Gore could do a Harrison, get fewer votes than George W. Bush and still be elected president, because the voting intention polls in several battleground states, in the populous industrial North as well as Florida, had started swinging in the direction opposite to the nationwide surveys. As a result, the Gore people took to praising the electoral college effusively, extolling the wisdom of the Founding Fathers, who had made such a back-door victory constitutionally acceptable. Now that we've all experienced the drama of the tightest election in American history—one in which, surprisingly, it was Bush, not Gore, who lagged behind in the overall count—the Democrats have done a U-turn and are highlighting the injustice of losing an election to an opponent who received fewer votes. Dizzying as this reversal is, the question remains: how democratic is such a system of indirect election?

A variation on this type of two-step voting was the so-called Basic Democracy introduced in 1960 in Pakistan by President Ayub Khan, and now happily defunct. Ayub had come to power as so many generals have in Pakistan, by seizing it from an admittedly unsatisfactory civilian leader. His interest in representative government was therefore not great, and the system he devised was more basic than democratic. It divided up Pakistan's citizens into "constituencies" of around a thousand adults, each of whom elected a Basic Democrat, who then participated in a referendum that "confirmed" Ayub in power.

In 1965, the same system was used to defeat a strong challenge to the Ayub regime mounted by a combined opposition party led by Fatima Jinnah, sister of the nation's founder. It was widely believed in Pakistan that the biggest single advantage of Basic Democracy's electoral college was that its members could be coerced and bribed. Far easier to fix a limited election than to fix one in which all Pakistan's eligible voters participated fully.

Which is not to suggest that such a thing as a fixed election could ever happen in America, of course; perish the thought. True, the Cubans, Russians, and Chinese are laughing openly at American democracy, calling the USA a banana republic and worse. And when even CNN speaks of an "odor" hanging over the Florida election, and as stories continue to emerge of black voters intimidated by policemen, of polling stations remaining closed so that people were denied the chance to vote at all, and of would-be voters being told that the ballots had run out, those of us with experience of Third World elections can't help wondering why everyone in America is too fastidious even to mention that all this is happening in a state governed by the brother of the fiasco's principal beneficiary. But even if there hasn't been any hanky-panky, the bizarre Florida episode shows why, on the whole, direct elections feel cleaner than indirect ones. The wisdom of the minds that devised the collegiate system doesn't seem so self-evident anymore. My own country of origin, India, is like the United States a large federation of regionalisms, where people define themselves first as Bengalis, Tamils, Kashmiris, and so on, and only after that as Indians. But India, with far fewer resources than the USA, has managed—albeit imperfectly— to run a constituency-based, direct-election democracy for over half a century. It's hard to grasp why Americans can't do the same.

What the Founding Fathers have unquestionably given us, however, is a system filled with the kind of psephological arcana that political commentators adore. The fact that the electoral college contains an even number of votes creates the possibility of a tie. (An odd number of votes was evidently deemed Unwise, for reasons that were no doubt profound and remain incomprehensible.) Lovers of political esoterica will regret that such a 269–269 dead heat is unlikely to occur. If it did, the election would move on to the House of Representatives, where each state delegation would have just one vote. If that process were to result in a 25–25 tie, then the Senate would vote. And if they, too, were to end up deadlocked, 50–50, then they would have to elect a vice president to break the stalemate. Perhaps, after all, the Founding Fathers were wiser than I've allowed. In an electorate as ballot-shy as the United States, why not choose who becomes the world's most powerful leader by letting it all come down to a single, casting vote? It gives the phrase "one man, one vote" a whole new meaning.

DECEMBER 2000: A GRAND COALITION?

W e've all been put through electoral college by this time, and now most of us would like to "recuse" ourselves from the case or perhaps "vacate" our earlier judgments; we yearn for those innocent days when a butterfly wasn't a ballot and Chad was a place in Africa. Whoever wins this loses it, we sometimes say. Bush and Cheney will never live down their 300,000-vote defeat in the nationwide count. Gore-Lieberman will always be Sore-Loserman to half the country. But then again, nobody has a memory anymore. Two weeks after one of the combatants is sworn in, all this will fade. So maybe whoever loses it, loses it after all. We give up. We're confused.

We've stopped thinking it's funny, or even sad. This is still the election that Nader wrecked and Elián slanted and Katherine Harris's partisanship derailed and the media screwed up, but most of all it's just interminable and coated in foggy legalese and we almost don't care anymore. But under the boredom we know there has been damage. It will be a long time before America can preach to the world about electoral transparency. This election has been about as transparent as a Floridian swamp.

America reveres its democracy, its Constitution, its presidency, and the past weeks have done damage to American belief in all three. How then is the strength of the republic to be restored? Bush doesn't seem interested in reaching out to Gore, and Gore has been too committed to the fight to pay more than lip service to the notion of a reunited nation. The truth is that these United States have rarely been so divided. America, which so often casts itself as the world's peacemaker, now needs to make peace with itself; and so might benefit from the experience of other divided peoples.

I'm thinking, in particular, of Israel, and of the aftermath of the post-Begin election of 1984. The Israeli national unity government came into being after that election, once it was clear that neither Yitzhak

Shamir's Likud nor Shimon Peres's Labor Party could command a majority. The two major parties then came together in an uneasy, but nevertheless enduring, alliance. For two years Peres served as prime minister, Shamir as foreign minister; then they swapped portfolios. After the elections of November 1988 failed to shift the balance of power significantly, the coalition was renewed, with Shamir retaining the premiership, and Peres still serving as foreign minister. The arrangement finally broke down in 1990, because of the parties' incompatible views of the peace process. While it lasted, it wasn't the world's most effective government, but it did bring down the Israeli inflation rate and, more important, permitted Israel to present a united front to its adversaries for six long years: no mean achievement.

How could such a grand coalition be brought into existence in the USA? Well, if Bush becomes president, Dick Cheney, citing his ill health, might be persuaded to stand aside from the vice presidency, which could then be offered to the present vice president, Al Gore. And in the increasingly improbable event of a Gore presidency, Joe Lieberman could opt to take up his Senate seat instead of becoming Gore's veep, whereupon President Gore could offer the spot to Bush. After so radical a move, the creation of a genuine coalition cabinet would be relatively—and I mean relatively—simple. As to whether it would be constitutional for the president to step down after two years to allow his deputy a turn, that's an issue for the swarm of litigators presently buzzing around this election to consider.

Impossible? Maybe so. But everything about this election so far has strained credulity. What was once unthinkable might, in these odd circumstances, actually begin to make sense. It might even have become necessary. There's a satirical text from Zimbabwe, that great democracy, doing the rounds of the Internet at present. Asking us what we would think of the U.S. electoral fiasco if it had happened in a Third World country, this satire, supposedly written by "a Zimbabwean politician," pokes much predictable fun at the alleged corruption of the United States. If America can now be laughed at by Zimbabwean pols, then it's surely time for drastic remedies to be considered. A Bush-Gore alliance might just renew American (and international) faith in the honor of their leaders and restore some much-needed luster to their tarnished institutions. It would be a government of strange bedfellows, but better that, perhaps, than four more years of bitter partisan squabbling, which would inevitably drag America's democratic institutions—the Congress as well as the presidency, even the Supreme Court itself—further down into the Zimbabwean dirt.

"If only they could both lose." Why not stand the joke on its head? Let them both win. "The people have spoken," Bill Clinton said not so long ago. "It's just that we don't yet know what they meant." Maybe this sort of power-sharing formula comes closer to expressing the people's will than anything else.*

JANUARY 2001: HOW THE GRINCH STOLE AMERICA

[A verse for the inauguration, with apologies to Dr. Seuss]

Every *Vote* down in *Voteville* liked Voting a Lot,
But the GRINCH, who lived West of Voteville,
    did Not.
For Voting was *Counting*—not just Adding and such
But finding out if you Amounted to Much.
In this case, the question was, who, in a pinch,
Amounted to More? Did the Veep? Or the Grinch?

The Veep! What a creep!
What a CREEP! CREEP! CREEP! CREEP!
He simply could NOT be outdone by the Veep.

But the Veep was Experienced.
He'd done the big jobs,
He was smart. (He was smart-ass.)
He knew all the knobs
And the levers and buttons
That worked the State's Ship
And the Grinch?
Well, re: knowledge he was not too hip.
The President of India? The economy? Pass.
He'd never been close to the head of the class.

---

* Now that the Bush administration has revealed itself to be a hard-line, ideological right-wing regime, this article looks ridiculously naïve. It is the columnist's fate to be rendered absurd by events.

So far the poor Grinch hadn't Amounted to zip,
He just hadn't Counted. It gave him the pip.
(His father! His eminent Dad! His own blood!
Compared to him, Grinchy had proved quite a dud.)

And now that he'd actually reached his Big Day
Argh! Counting the Ballots could steal it away!

And what *was* a Ballot? Was it silver or gold?
Were they counting up treasure? A fortune untold?
No! Just some dumb punch-card! They were counting up *holes*!
Oh, the holes!
                    Yes, the holes!
Oh, the HOLES! HOLES! HOLES! HOLES!
The whole thing depended on Circles of Air—
Not to mention the half-holes,
    and holes that weren't there,
        but that wanted to be there,
            and thought that was fair.

All they would do was to add up! To Count!
And they'd *count*! And they'd *count*!
And they'd COUNT! COUNT! COUNT! COUNT!
And they'd probably end up with a
Quite Wrong Amount!
"If they go on counting,"
        the Grinch shuddered, "Eep!
"They may just wind up electing the Veep!

"How to stop it?" the Grinch exclaimed with a moan
And then he remembered he wasn't alone.
There were Grinches all over,
Big Grinches and small,
There were Grinches in Voteville and in City Hall,
He knew some news-Grinches,
And he could depend
On these inky fellows to shape and to bend
Their stories to help him win through in the end.

But the Grinches who'd give him
The edge and the win
Were the great Legal Grinches,
And Grinches of Spin.

So he called on his cohorts.
"My friends, we must Grinch
The election! 'Nuff Counting!
To work! Do not flinch!
We must Grinch! We must Grinch!
We must GRINCH! GRINCH! GRINCH! GRINCH!
We cannot be beaten by circles of air
Or circles that only imagine they're there.
Every day that they Count them, the total will creep
Up and up, until it elects that old Veep!"

So they Grinched the election.
They Grinched, day by day,
Until all the options were whittled away.
They Grinched it with lawyers,
They Grinched it with writs,
They split all the hairs
And they picked all the nits,
And when it came up to the Ultimate Bench
They Grinched it away with one final Wrench.
They ordered all Voteville to give up its Count,
Before it came up with that Quite Wrong Amount.

And the Votes down in Voteville?
They've run out of steam.
'Tis the season to party, to heal, and to dream.
Why worry? The Constitution is strong,
The judges who judge it can never be wrong,
The Veep may have won, but he's lost.
And that's that.
Voteville accepts the high judges' *fiat*.
There isn't a holler, there isn't a scream,
Think of the dollar! Let's play for the team!
So everyone okays the Grinch's regime,

And things are probably
        probably
          probably
            probably
Not as bad as they seem.

"Four whole years of Grinchdom!"
The Grinch cries with glee.
"There's Only One Person who Counts now
   . . . That's
     ME."

FEBRUARY 2001: SLEAZE IS BACK

One day after France's former foreign minister, the almost impossibly grand Roland Dumas, who is on trial for corruption, denounces the proceedings against him—that a personage as distinguished as he should be subjected to such an ordeal! *Zut! Alors!*—the fugitive businessman Alfred Sirven is arrested in the Philippines and immediately claims that he can provide evidence of corruption against "one hundred names"—that is, most of the political elite of the Mitterrand era.

Meanwhile, in Peru, the seizure of over two thousand secretly obtained videotapes reveals the power of the fallen President Fujimori's secret state over just about everyone in that country's ruling class. Journalists, politicians, generals were all being blackmailed for years.

Meanwhile, in India, the Bofors scandal bubbles to the surface again. The rumors of corruption surrounding this 1980s arms deal have already besmirched the reputations of the late Rajiv Gandhi—did he or did he not accept illegal kickbacks?—and the late Olof Palme—was he assassinated by a disgruntled middleman? Now, as the Indian courts turn their attention to the activities of the billionaire Hinduja brothers, the old scandal threatens to hurl new dirt across the oceans, at the British government, which became so improbably friendly with the Hindujas.

(A four-year-old child could have warned the Blairites against this association. Unfortunately, no four-year-old child was available, and as a result the British public presently believes New Labour to be almost as sleazy as the grubby Tories they replaced. Almost as sleazy as Neil Hamilton and Jonathan Aitken! Well . . . gosh.)

Meanwhile, in the United States, ex-President Clinton is under fire for having pardoned the fugitive financier Marc Rich, while his successor, "President" Bush, mouths platitudes about bilateralism while pursuing an agenda of the far right; and this in spite of the growing evidence that he lost the election he "won" thanks to the notorious Supreme Court coup; lost it, in Florida, by a margin of around 25,000 votes.

Yes, sleaze has resurfaced, grinning its slobbering grin, to remind us that it never really went away—that it remains the great occult force that bends and shapes the age, its existence perennially denied, its empire expanding daily. You can almost admire its inexhaustible inventiveness. Things you never imagined were sleazy—things that actually were never tarnished before—come daily under sleaze's slimy suzerainty, and are hopelessly compromised, or, like innocence or paradise, lost.

Thus, a feature of recent months has been the sleazing-up not only of politics, where it's almost expected, but of sport. Is racing fixed? asks the British press, and you can almost hear the horses laugh. About boxing, nobody even bothers to ask. And the former Liverpool goalkeeper Bruce Grobbelaar has at last been found guilty of taking bribes. Even cricket, whose very name was once a synonym for integrity, is now up to here in the dirt. As for athletics, the recent "doping Olympics" offered spectacular evidence of trouble: the shot-putter C. J. Hunter's four positive drug tests, the gold-medal gymnast Andreea Raducan's positive test for pseudoephedrine, Carl Lewis's astonishing comment on Linford Christie's positive test for nandrolone: "They got him at last." So our heroes are at it now, as well as our leaders. In fact, it looks as if they've been at it all along. Is there anything out there that isn't fixed? Reality-TV contests? Literary prizes? University entrance examinations? Your upcoming job interview? Or is it just that we haven't found out how the fixing is being done?

Welcome to the third millennium. The American novelist Thomas Pynchon's redefinition of paranoia has never seemed more firmly on the money: paranoia usefully seen as the crazy-making but utterly sane realization that our times have secret meanings, that those meanings are dreadful, immoral, and corrupt beyond our wildest imaginings, and that the surface of things is a fraud, an artifact designed to hide the awful truth from us ordinary deluded suckers, who keep wanting to believe that things might actually—you know?—be beginning to improve.

The sucker's reaction to much of the foregoing would be to point out that many of the sleaze merchants I've mentioned have received or are receiving their comeuppances. Dumas is on trial, Sirven is in custody, Fujimori has fallen, the Hindujas have been obliged to remain in India pending the outcome of their case, Clinton is history, the bent cricketers were banned, and the doping athletes were caught. So that's all right then.

The paranoid knows better. If the crimes of the past are only now being uncovered, the paranoid will retort, how long will it take before we know about the crimes of the present? Are the "innocent" merely the guilty whose guilt hasn't yet been established? Pynchonian analysis leaves true paranoids with few choices: to become obsessed investigators of the world's secret meanings; to accept their impotence and fall into one of a familiar selection of futile, addled, entropic hazes; or to explode into the kind of rage that wants to blow things up.

I knew a man once whose thing it was to wreck the toilets in office buildings and write a slogan on the ruined walls: "If the cistern cannot be changed it must be destroyed." I'm beginning to understand how he felt. And to remember how, in a younger, hairier, angrier phase of life, I often used to feel.

MARCH 2001: CROUCHING STRIKER, HIDDEN DANGER

Without Hollywood, they say, Los Angeles would just be Phoenix with a coastline. This year, as deadlines approach for strikes by actors and writers, L.A. is facing the possibility of becoming, for a time, exactly such a characterless, movie-less sprawl. Rumors are flying: the studios actually want the strikes, the actors don't, though their representatives are talking tough, and the writers? Well, they're only writers, after all. Talks keep breaking down an inch away from agreement. TV companies are preparing to flood the schedules with even more reality-TV programming—it's cheap! it's popular! it's not unionized!—to fill the holes created by The Strike. There's plenty of bad feeling in the air, and a growing sense of inevitability. The shutdown is "going to happen." (Which means either it will or it won't.)

And in the midst of this uncertainty, the movie community awaits its annual you-love-me-you-really-love-me festival of big business interests disguised as individual achievements. The lobbying season is over. The city is no longer being bombarded by "for your consideration" videotapes. Rock stars are no longer playing impromptu gigs in old folks' homes in the hope of garnering a few votes for Best Song from elderly academicians resident therein. The votes are in. The Oscars are coming.

The movies are L.A.'s culture. At the weekend, big audiences go to the new pictures the way the opera-loving Milanese go to an opening at La Scala. L.A. is a city of passionate moviegoers. I haven't seen such enthusiastically participatory audiences anywhere outside the Indian subcontinent. This can get irritating, for example when a big guy with his ass hanging out of his pants moans and groans loudly every time Penélope Cruz appears on screen in *All the Pretty Horses*—"my God, she's so beautiful!—Oh, oh, he's going to fall for her!—Uh-oh, here comes trouble!"—or when a five-year-old insistently asks her parents, during the interminable *Cast Away,* "Mommy, when is the volleyball going to talk?" (Footnote: Wilson the volleyball's performance is the best thing in this leaden movie. Why wasn't Wilson nominated for Best Supporting Actor? It's a scandal.)

Angeleno enthusiasm can, however, also be thrilling. I can't remember ever seeing a Western audience react to a new film the way a packed afternoon audience in a theater on La Brea responded to *Crouching Tiger, Hidden Dragon.* Even by L.A.'s standards, the whooping and cheering was astonishing. The audience knew it was sharing a very special experience—the arrival of a great, classic film—and was simply transported by its brilliance. Anyone who thinks DVDs will someday replace moviegoing should have been there.

Those PC killjoys who have denigrated *Crouching Tiger* as a piece of latter-day Orientalism, a Western appropriation of Eastern manner and material, would have seen an audience as diverse as America itself—Korean Americans, Chinese Americans, Hispanic Americans, African Americans easily outnumbered any WASP-y Orientalists who might have been there enjoying it for the wrong reasons. Akira Kurosawa and Satyajit Ray reached smaller audiences, in their native Japan and India, than the commercial movies of their contemporaries. That doesn't make *Seven Samurai* inauthentic, or the trashy products of the main-stream Bombay cinema "more Indian" than Ray's masterworks. So, yes, Jackie Chan sells a lot of tickets and, yes, *Crouching Tiger* draws on a long tradition of martial-arts movies. But Jackie Chan movies are cardboard fun, and Ang Lee's beautiful, intimate epic is—one would have thought self-evidently—a luminous work of art.

In the context of the Academy Awards and the shadow of the strike, the success of *Crouching Tiger* is especially significant. It's being talked about as the breakthrough movie that has taught Americans to accept subtitled foreign films into the giant cineplexes where the big money is made. And this is why the various players—but the studios above all—may be making a big mistake if they think they can ride out the strike without losing their stranglehold on the market. From the late 1950s to early 1970s, a flood of great non-American filmmakers prized Holly-wood's fingers off the cinema's throat for a few years. The result was the golden age of the sound cinema, the time of the great films of Kuro-sawa and Ray, of the French New Wave, of Fellini, Antonioni, and Vis-conti, of Wajda, Jancso, and Bergman. Now, once again, world cinema is blossoming, in China, in Iran, in Britain. And it may just be that the mass audience is ready, at long last, to enjoy rather more diversity in its cultural diet. After all, there are plenty of dreadful American films we could all cheerfully do without.

The Oscars usually show us how Hollywood sees itself. Ridley Scott's technically brilliant but woodenly scripted *Gladiator* is the big-studio candidate for honors, just as the latest sentimental Miramax con-fection, *Chocolat,* leads the charge of the smaller guys. Comedy comes off badly, as usual—the Coen brothers have to be content with screen-play and cinematography nominations for the wonderful *O Brother, Where Art Thou?* There's no nomination for George Clooney's delicious, hairnet-wearing performance in this movie, or, indeed, for Renée Zell-weger's moving, subtle work in the title role of *Nurse Betty.* But behind all this familiar maneuvering, the tiger is crouching, the dragon hides.

And if by some chance the one genuinely great movie to have been nominated this year runs away with the big prizes, it may just be the wake-up call that Hollywood needs. When the world's finest film-makers are coming after your audience, it may not be such a smart idea to shut your industry down.

APRIL 2001: IT WASN'T ME

The current hit single "It Wasn't Me" by Shaggy (featuring Rikrok) celebrates, with wickedly infectious glee, the uses of shamelessness. A man caught red-handed cheating on his girl—a man watched by said girl making love to someone else on the sofa, in the shower, on the bathroom floor—must, or so the song tells us, at all costs, and in the face of all the evidence, deny, deny, deny. Now, who does this remind us of?

There have been some great champions of brazen denial in recent years: Diego Maradona ignoring the video evidence of his notorious hand-balled goal against England and ascribing it to the "hand of God"; O. J. Simpson swearing to dedicate his life to finding his wife's "real" killer (any hot leads, O.J.?); the British Conservative politicians Neil Hamilton and Jonathan Aitken denying their proven corruption to the point of their economic ruination; and of course the great denier himself, Bill Clinton, passim, from "I did not have sexual relations with that woman, Miss Lewinsky," to the rejection of any improprieties in his last-gasp "Pardongate."

The barefaced denial, the giving of the lie direct, has become, in this age of saturation media coverage, an increasingly prominent feature of public life. It is now routine for even the age's greatest monsters—the war criminals of ex-Yugoslavia or Cambodia—to deny their atrocities, knowing that their power of access to the world's airwaves is almost certainly greater than any journalist's power of access to the truth. When great crimes are openly admitted—Timothy McVeigh boasting about the Oklahoma bombing, the Taliban taking pride in the destruction of the Bamiyan Buddhas—it's so unusual that you find yourself fighting the urge to praise the criminals for their plain speaking.

I once sat in a courtroom in Alice Springs, Australia, listening to the testimony of a truck driver accused of murder—of having deliberately crashed his vehicle into a bar he'd been thrown out of, killing and maiming many people. The man had clearly been carefully coached in the important contemporary art of saying the thing that is not. His dress was sober, his eyes downcast, his manner shocked and decent; and for a long time, he persuasively denied his guilt. But in the end the coaching couldn't save him. After he'd repeatedly denied that he could do such a thing, he made the mistake, under cross-examination, of saying why. "For me to half-destroy my truck," he explained reasonably, "is completely against my personality." The jury quickly found him guilty and threw away the key. What did him in was that flash of unpalatable truth. A more skillful liar—or rather, denier—would have known better.

"It wasn't me." Many such consummate exponents of the arts of brazen obfuscation are presently in the news. In Britain, successive governments have colluded with the British agricultural lobby to unleash not one but two plagues upon the world. The first, BSE [Bovine Spongiform Encephalopathy], was the result of (1) turning cows into cannibals and then (2) allowing farmers to save energy costs by giving their cattle food that hadn't been boiled long enough or at high enough temperatures to kill the deadly germs. But of course the Tory government of the day did not admit its complicity; nor did the farm lobby own up to its part. Instead, both parties pretended, for a long time, that the links between BSE and its crossover human variant, CJD [Creutzfeldt-Jakob Disease], were "unproven." And now here comes foot-and-mouth, and we discover that three years ago the present Labour government declined to outlaw the use of pigswill as feed (even though many of our European partners had done so) and failed, once again, to ensure that the swill was boiled long enough or at high enough temperatures to be safe. Once again, the decision was cash-driven: the farm lobby wanted to cut corners and save money, and the farm lobby got its way. Do we hear the government or the lobbyists admitting they were wrong? Of course not. "It wasn't us, it was this Chinese restaurant that imported illegal meat." So that's all right then. We can just blame the Chinese. We all know the kinds of things *they* eat.

Meanwhile, in India, the BJP-led government has contracted an acute case of snout-in-trough disease. The sting operation carried out by the excellent website tehelka.com—what a difference the Internet has made to press freedoms in India!—showed many of the country's leaders accepting bribes on videotape. There have been some resignations, but no admissions of guilt, and much talk, by the shamed leaders and other governing party figures, of a sinister "conspiracy" against the ruling coalition. The new BJP president has spoken of creating a new code of conduct for people in public life, but at the same time has refused to expel his corruption-tainted predecessor. Apparently, and in spite of the video evidence, it wasn't necessarily him.

And now, as the United States, the world's greatest contributor to global warming, repudiates the Kyoto treaty designed to reduce environmentally harmful emissions, President George W. Bush goes so far as to claim that the link between greenhouse gases and global warming has not been proven. ("It wasn't us.") This is what the cigarette companies used to say about cancer, and it's about as persuasive. But the president has a big megaphone, and if he goes on repeating his claims, he may even make them stick for a long, damaging time.

Just sometimes a song stumbles on a truth about the spirit of the age. The Shaggy-Rikrok hit is cheerfully unrepentant about its amoral little discovery. Deny your wrongs and you will right them. As Nancy Reagan might have put it, "Just say no." It's plainly an irresistible proposition. You hear it everywhere right now, hanging in the air like a mantra. All together now: "It wasn't me . . ."

MAY 2001: ABORTION IN INDIA

I have always believed myself fortunate to have come from a sprawling Indian family dominated by women. I have no brothers but plenty of sisters (three: believe me, that's plenty). My mother's sisters are a pair of aunts as formidable and irresistible as Bertie Wooster's Aunt Dahlia and Aunt Agatha. In my generation of cousins, girls outnumber boys by two to one. While I was growing up, the family's houses, in India and Pakistan, were full of the instructions, quarrels, laughter, and ambitions of these women, few of whom resemble the stereotype of the demure, self-effacing Indian woman. These are opinionated, voluble, smart, funny, arm-waving persons—lawyers, educators, radicals, movers, shakers, matriarchs—and to be heard in their company you must not only raise your voice but also have something interesting to say. If you aren't worth listening to, you will most certainly not be heard.

As a result, I feel, to this day, most at home in the company of women. Among my close friends the girls far outnumber the boys. In my writing, I have repeatedly sought to create female characters as rich and powerful as those I have known. The men in my books are rarely as flamboyant as the women. This is as it should be: or at least, in my experience, how it has been, more often than not.

It is therefore worrying, to say the least, that these women, or rather their potential successors in the Indian generation presently being conceived, are rapidly becoming an endangered species. In spite of the illegality of the practice—and under cover of spurious health checks— ultrasound tests to determine the gender of unborn children are increasingly being used all over India to identify, and then abort, obscene quantities of healthy female fetuses. The population is rapidly becoming lopsided, skewed toward male numerical dominance to a genuinely alarming degree.

Here's a tough nut for the pro-choice lobby on abortion, of which I've always been a fully paid-up member. What should be done when a woman uses her power over her own body to discriminate against female fetuses? Many Indian commentators say that if these sex-discriminatory abortions are to end, the refusals must come from Indian women. But Indian women want male children as much as their husbands do. In part this is because of the myriad pressures of a male-centered society, including the expenses of the dowry system. But fundamentally it's the result of modern technology being placed at the service of medieval social attitudes. Clearly not all Indian women are as emancipated as those among whom I was lucky enough to be raised. Traditional India still exists, and its values are still powerful. Women beware women: an old story, given a chilling new gynecological twist.

Ever since Indira and Sanjay Gandhi's attempt to introduce birth control by diktat during the forced-vasectomy excesses of the mid-seventies, it has been very hard to get the Indian masses to accept the idea of family planning. Mother Teresa's hard-line attack on contraception didn't help. Lately, Hindu nationalists have made things even harder by suggesting that the country's Muslims are breeding faster than Hindus, thus placing Hinduism "under threat." (This, even though the Hindu majority makes up a whopping 85 percent of the population.)

Abortion, along with contraception, has up to now been anathematized by Indian religious leaders. As a result India's population has soared past the one billion mark, and is projected to overtake China's within a decade or so. But now, suddenly, terminations of pregnancies have become acceptable to many Indians, for the most reprehensible of reasons; and the argument over the urgent issues of population control gets even murkier. There are those who claim that the new wave of abortions is actually beneficial, because the bias toward boys means that

Indian couples who have girl children will tend to go on having daughters until they have a son, thus contributing to overpopulation. Allowing them to make the choice, the argument continues, will not result in a scarcity of girl children but rather make sure there isn't a glut of them. The trouble with this theory is that the statistical evidence suggests that in a generation's time there will indeed be a girl shortage. Then what? Will girls become more valued than they are today, or will the masculinism of Indian society, reinforced by the weight of numbers, simply create more and more macho men, and increasingly downtrodden women?

Not all problems are capable of instant solution. Even though the nation imagines itself as a woman—Bharat-Mata, Mother India—and even though, in Hinduism, the dynamic principle of the godhead—shakti—is female, the scandal of the missing girls of India will end only when and if modern India succeeds in overturning centuries of prejudice against girl children.

This doesn't mean that nothing can be done. The government can and should crack down hard on the ultrasound clinics that are allowing people to defy the law. It should provide state benefits for families with girl children and perhaps even, for a time, impose tax penalties on families with boys. Politicians, educators, activist groups, even newspaper columnists can and should batter away at the ingrained prejudices that are at the heart of the trouble. In the end it all boils down to this: is today's India prepared to be seen as the country that gets rid of its daughters because it believes them inferior to men? The parents who are doing this may one day face questions from the children they allowed to live. "Where are my sisters?" What will they answer then?

JUNE 2001: REALITY TV

I've managed to miss out on reality TV until now. In spite of all the talk in Britain about nasty Nick and flighty Mel or, in America, about the fat, naked bastard Richard manipulating his way to desert-island victory, I have somehow preserved my purity. I wouldn't recognize Nick or Mel if I passed them in the street, or Richard if he were standing in front of me unclothed.

Ask me where the *Big Brother* house is, or how to reach Temptation

Island, and I have no answer. I do remember the American *Survivor* contestant who managed to fry his own hand so that the skin peeled away until his fingers looked like burst sausages, but that's because he got onto the main evening news. Otherwise, search me. Who won? Who lost? Who cares?

The subject of reality-TV shows, however, has been impossible to avoid. Their success is the media story of the (new) century, along with the ratings triumph of the big-money game shows like *Millionaire.* Success on this scale insists on being examined, because it tells us things about ourselves, or ought to.

And what tawdry narcissism is here revealed! The television set, once so idealistically thought of as our window on the world, has become a dime-store mirror instead. Who needs images of the world's rich otherness when you can watch these half-familiar avatars of yourself—these half-attractive half-persons—enacting ordinary life under weird conditions? Who needs talent when the unashamed self-display of the talentless is constantly on offer?

I've been watching [the British] *Big Brother 2,* which has achieved the improbable feat of taking over the tabloid front pages in the final stages of a general election campaign. This, according to the conventional wisdom, is because the show is more interesting than the election. The "reality" may be even stranger. It may be that *Big Brother* is so popular because it's even more boring than the election. Because it is the most boring, and therefore most "normal," way of becoming famous and, if you're lucky or smart, of getting rich as well.

"Famous" and "rich" are now the two most important concepts in Western society, and ethical questions are simply obliterated by the potency of their appeal. To be famous and rich, it's okay—it's actually "good"—to be devious. It's "good" to be exhibitionistic. It's "good" to be bad. And what dulls the moral edge is boredom. It's impossible to maintain a sense of outrage about people being so trivially self-serving for so long.

Oh, the dullness! Here are people becoming famous for being asleep, for keeping a fire alight, for letting a fire go out, for videotaping their clichéd thoughts, for flashing their breasts, for lounging around, for quarreling, for bitching, for being unpopular, and (this is too interesting to happen often) for kissing! Here, in short, are people becoming famous for doing nothing much at all, but doing it where everyone can see.

Add the contestants' exhibitionism to the viewers' voyeurism and you get a picture of a society sickly in thrall to what Saul Bellow called "event glamour." Such is the glamour of these banal but brilliantly spotlit events that anything resembling a real value—modesty, decency, intelligence, humor, selflessness, you can write your own list—is rendered redundant. In this inverted ethical universe, worse is better. The show presents "reality" as a prizefight, and suggests that in life, as on TV, anything goes, and the more deliciously contemptible it is, the more we'll like it. Winning isn't everything, as Charlie Brown once said, but losing isn't anything.

The problem with this kind of engineered realism is that, like all fads, it's likely to have a short shelf-life, unless it finds ways of renewing itself. The probability is that our voyeurism will become more demanding. It won't be enough to watch people being catty, or weeping when evicted from the house of hell, or "revealing everything" on subsequent talk shows, as if they had anything left to reveal.

What is gradually being reinvented is the gladiatorial combat. The TV set is the Colosseum, and the contestants are both gladiators and lions; their job is to eat one another until only one remains alive. But how long, in our jaded culture, before "real" lions, actual dangers, are introduced to these various forms of fantasy island, to feed our hunger for more action, more pain, more vicarious thrills? Here's a thought, prompted by the news that the redoubtable Gore Vidal has agreed to witness the execution by lethal injection of the Oklahoma City bomber Timothy McVeigh. The witnesses at an execution watch the macabre proceedings through a glass window: a screen. This, too, is a kind of reality TV, and—to make a modest proposal—it may represent the future of such programs. If we are willing to watch people stab one another in the back, might we not also be willing actually to watch them die?

In the world outside TV, our numbed senses already require increasing doses of titillation. One murder is barely enough; only the mass murderers make the front pages. You have to blow up a building full of people or machine-gun a whole royal family to get our attention. Soon, perhaps, you'll have to kill off a whole species of wildlife or unleash a virus that wipes out people by the thousands, or else you'll be small potatoes. You'll be on an inside page. And as in reality, so on "reality TV." How long until the first TV death? How long until the second?

By the end of Orwell's great novel *1984,* Winston Smith has been brainwashed. "He loved Big Brother." As, now, do we.

JULY 2001: THE RELEASE OF THE BULGER KILLERS

L ike a character in a Greek tragedy, a woman—Denise Fergus is her momentarily famous name—figuratively holds up the dead body of her murdered child, James Bulger, and howls for justice. The murderers have been released from jail, and the mother finds that unjust. "No matter where they are," she cries, "someone will be waiting. No stone will be left unturned." Then, descending from such classic blood-must-have-blood heights, and rather giving her game away, she adds, "For eight years I have kept my dignity. In the near future I will tell my side of the story." Let us hope that this doesn't mean that eye-for-an-eye calls for "justice" will soon be splashed all over a tabloid near you. Dignity doesn't rate the front page, after all. And if one or other of the released men is killed by vigilantes—or if innocent men, mistaken for the freed killers, are attacked by the same vigilantes—then so much the better for sales.

The case of the 1993 Merseyside murder of two-year-old James Bulger by the then ten-year-old Robert Thompson and Jon Venables raised big questions from the beginning. That the killers were themselves children, and that the killing was unusually brutal, made us ask ourselves about the nature of evil, a profound question inevitably rendered shallow by the media, for whom evil appeared to be some sort of video-nasty manifestation of the "demon seed" variety. It was indeed suggested that Venables and Thompson had been influenced by a video nasty which, as it turned out, they hadn't seen. But it wasn't the killers who thought in the clichéd stereotypes of horror fiction. It was the British press.

Because of the ugliness of the murder, lots of people clearly find it impossible to accept that Venables and Thompson could have been successfully rehabilitated. For many, their reported sorrow is just a devious ploy. In Evelyn Waugh's famous story "Mr. Loveday's Little Outing," a murderer who has been, for many years, the mildest, gentlest, sweetest-natured prisoner imaginable is finally paroled, and instantly kills again. This fear of re-offending is constantly voiced by opponents of Venables's and Thompson's release, and this is the spark of suspicion that British newspapers are trying so hard to fan into a fire.

Yet all the best-informed sources have been telling us that Venables and Thompson really have changed; that they are poster boys for the efficacy of rehabilitation. Mark Leech of the ex-offenders charity Unlock, for example, says that there is "no prospect that they will re-offend." So now we have to face this straightforward either/or decision. Either we believe that rehabilitation is possible, in which case we must accept the opinion of the experts that it has succeeded in these cases—or we reject that option, in which case, let's stop trying to rehabilitate people and decide that prison sentences should be society's revenge on criminals, who should be treated as lost causes and locked up for good in dreadful conditions. If people can't get better, if rotten eggs are rotten eggs and bad apples can't become good, then let's just throw them away.

The big questions just keep on coming. Repentance and forgiveness aren't as closely connected as people imagine. We sometimes forgive the unrepentant, and on other occasions condemn the genuinely re-morseful. So even if the Bulger killers really are different now, even if the eighteen-year-olds who are to be released on life licenses have been utterly transformed, they can be allowed to live the rest of their lives in anonymous peace only if a separate process—call it the growth of fairness—in the hearts of those most injured by their crime and, be-yond that, in society at large leads to their being forgiven.

It is because this is so complex and important a matter that the rabble-rousing behavior of much of the British press has seemed par-ticularly disgusting, and the old accusations about it being out of con-trol have seemed unusually apt. People, even lifetime free-speech stalwarts, have been saying that the behavior of the British tabloids makes the free-speech argument harder and harder to sustain—that a cherished democratic principle is being destruction-tested by yellow journalists. The feedback loop between events and their reporting is now so tight, so fast, that the media are major protagonists in the stories they report; and in this story they are working to subvert all civilized principles of justice and creating in their readers a lynch-mob mental-ity that may actually get people killed.

Something awful is happening here, some general degradation of public response caused by years of exposure to tabloid values. Spanish newspapers are reported to be prepared to pay big money for informa-tion about Venables's and Thompson's whereabouts—not because Spanish readers are particularly interested but because it's summer and Spain is full of Brits. The Internet, that brothel of irresponsibility, has already started providing this information, and more will no doubt flood out soon. Jon Venables and Robert Thompson can run but they probably can't hide, and in a Britain that's increasingly conducting itself like Dodge City or Tombstone at their wildest, these young men will be lucky not to end up in Boot Hill. We can only hope they don't, because on the run along with them is another idea of Britain, in which restraint is valued more highly than melodrama, compassion is better than revenge, and dignity is worth keeping for longer than eight years.

AUGUST 2001: ARUNDHATI ROY

Nargis, the Indian movie queen of the 1950s, who later had a career in politics, once denounced the great film director Satyajit Ray for making films that offered too negative an image of India. In her own movies, she said, she had always celebrated the positive. When asked for an example, she replied, "Dams."

Big Dams (defined as those over fifteen meters—41 feet—high) have long been an essential part of India's technological iconography, and their role in providing water and power to the nation was for a time unquestioned, even unquestionable. Lately, however, there has been "an increasingly confrontational debate about the role that large dams have played in development," to quote the chairman of the World Commission on Dams (WCD), South Africa's education minister, Professor Kader Asmal.

One of the biggest new dams under construction is the Sardar Sarovar Project on the Narmada River in the state of Gujarat, with a proposed final height of 136.5 meters (375 feet). Among its most vocal opponents is the novelist Arundhati Roy. "Big dams," she says, "have let this country down." She objects to the displacement of more than 200,000 people by rising waters, to the damage to the Narmada Valley's fragile ecosystem, and points, tellingly, to the failure of many big dams to deliver what they promised. (India's Bargi Dam, for example, irrigates only 5 percent of the area promised.) She argues further that while the rural poor are the ones who pay the price for a dam, it is the urban rich who benefit: "80 percent of rural households [still] have no electricity, 250 million people have no access to safe drinking water."

The recent report of the WCD largely supports Roy's arguments. The WCD was set up by the World Bank and the World Conservation Union and based its report on surveys of 125 large dams. (Mysteriously, permission to visit the Sardar Sarovar Project was refused by the Gujarat state government.) The report blames big dams for increased flooding, damage to farmland, the extinction of freshwater fishes. It agrees that the benefits of dams go largely to the rich, that many dams fall short of their targets, and that of the forty to eighty million people displaced by worldwide dam building, few have received the compensation they deserve. Arundhati Roy and the Narmada Valley campaigners have long argued that alternative methods are capable of meeting Gujarat's water needs; the WCD report echoes this view, stressing the need to focus on renewable energy, recycling, better irrigation, and reducing water losses.

The battle over the Narmada Dam has been long and bitter. However, there has been a surreal new twist. Arundhati Roy and two leading members of the protest movement, Medha Patkar and Prashant Bhushan, have been accused by five lawyers of having viciously attacked them during a December 13, 2000, protest, outside the Supreme Court in Delhi, against the Court's decision to allow work on the Sardar Sarovar Project to proceed. Roy and Patkar allegedly called on the crowd to kill the lawyers, and Bhushan grabbed one by the hair and also allegedly threatened him with death.

All this somehow happened under the unconcerned noses of a large detachment of policemen. Curiously, the affray also passed unrecorded by the filmmaker Sanjay Kak, who was covering the demonstration with a video camera. And it was later revealed that Mr. Bhushan had in fact been somewhere else entirely at the time.

In spite of the demonstrable absurdity of these charges, however, the Supreme Court decided to entertain the lawyers' petition and served the three activists with criminal-contempt notices. In doing so it ignored its own stipulated rules and procedures. The lawyers' petition was incorrectly filled out and did not receive, as it should have, the written support of the attorney general. Most important of all, the Supreme Court did not try to authenticate the claims in the petition, even though video and eyewitness evidence was readily available.

Summoned to court, Arundhati Roy delivered a characteristically trenchant affidavit in which she said that the Court's willingness to haul her and her colleagues up before it on such flimsy charges "indicates a disquieting inclination on the part of the court to silence criticism and muzzle dissent, to harass and intimidate those who disagree with it." The Supreme Court insisted that she withdraw this affidavit;

she refused, and the Court is now considering contempt-of-court charges that could send her to jail. She is, as she told a British journalist, "now deeper in the soup."

The Court should realize that by pursuing Arundhati Roy, Medha Patkar, and Prashant Bhushan in this fashion, it places itself before the court of world opinion. The U.S. Supreme Court has just disgraced itself internationally by carrying out the judicial coup that made George W. Bush "president." (Two authoritative new books, by Alan Dershowitz and Vincent Bugliosi, leave no doubt that the U.S. Supremes made a politically motivated judgment that already looks like very bad law.) Can it be that the Supreme Court of the "world's largest democracy" will emulate that of the world's most powerful country by revealing itself to be biased—in this case against free speech—and prepared to act as the "muscle" for a particular interest group—in this case the powerful coalition of political and financial interests behind the Narmada Dam?

Only by abandoning its pursuit of Arundhati Roy and the Narmada Valley campaigners can the Supreme Court escape this judgment. It should do so at once.*

SEPTEMBER 2001: TELLURIDE

I n the beginning were Butch Cassidy and the Sundance Kid, and the little town of Telluride, Colorado—originally To Hell You Ride, so named by the nineteenth-century silver miners who tobogganed down the mountains to what was then a wild place full of whorehouses—was the site of their first bank robbery. Then came the movie, and Robert Redford named his Sundance Institute after his most famous role. The Sundance Film Festival became a celebrated showcase for new, independent filmmakers. Telluride itself became the USA's other most famous festival for independent cinema, playing the role, you could say, of Butch to Sundance's Sundance.

---

* On March 6, 2002, Arundhati Roy was given a "symbolic" one-day jail sentence, and fined two thousand rupees (approximately fifty dollars), for contempt of court. The court said it wanted to show that it could be magnanimous and had taken into account that Arundhati Roy was "a woman."

I'm writing this in Telluride's thin air, amid spectacular mountain scenery, at the end of the town's twenty-eighth such film festival (to declare an interest, I was this year's guest director). Over the past four days, a feast of good movies has been reminding crowds of passionate moviegoers why they fell in love with the cinema in the days before the coming of the giant multiplexes and the domination of the first weekend's gross.

Anyone who's been going to the movies lately could be forgiven for thinking it might be more fun to stay home and stare at a wall. *Planet of the Apes* is, well, unkind to primates. A much-praised thriller, *The Score,* turns out to be a pedestrian, do-it-by-numbers heist movie. (The hackneyed figure of the old pro on his one last big job can also be seen in a somewhat better British film, *Sexy Beast.*) The Julia Roberts–Catherine Zeta-Jones "comedy," *America's Sweethearts,* is a movie-biz in-joke that nobody got. *Blow* sucks. The one genuine movie thrill on offer of late has been Coppola's *Apocalypse Now Redux,* and even this contains disappointments. The restored "French plantation sequence" is the biggest; it's too expository, not fabulist enough, for its place close to the heart of darkness. It's merely eccentric at a point in the film when insanity ought to rule. And Brando's performance as Kurtz hasn't improved with time (and a little re-editing). Still, given the high ambition of the filmmaking, and performances such as the great Robert Duvall's ("I love the smell of napalm in the morning"), and given, above all, the dross on offer elsewhere, it's easy to forgive its trespasses. *Apocalypse* is a Himalaya among anthills.

Listen to young filmmakers in L.A., and even the most talented of them will tell you that they have no choice, they have to bow down before the power of the marketplace and dilute their art to make their films commercially viable. There's an answer to this playing to packed houses in Telluride: the smash-hit French film *Amélie,* the story of an isolated girl who has always lived in her imagination until one day she starts trying to impose her startling inner reality upon the external world. The film bursts with visual inventiveness and a gently surreal cinematic wit, and its huge European success stands as a reproach to all those filmmakers who find compromise an easier option than originality.

The daring and radicalism of the feature films being financed by the cable-television channel HBO, a selection of which has been a highlight of the Telluride festival, stand as a further reproach to the pusillanimity of so much big studio fare. (Look out in particular for Agnieszka Holland's *Shot in the Heart,* an adaptation of Mikal Gilmore's brilliant book about his murderer brother Gary.) And some fine films from places not thought to be at the center of world cinema offer further proof that the center does not hold. I was particularly impressed by the style and grace of Danis Tanovic's first feature, *No Man's Land,* in which wounded Bosnian and Serb soldiers, caught in a trench between opposing front lines, become a vision in microcosm of their vicious, absurdist war. It's as if Beckett's Vladimir and Estragon were bleeding in a trench, and when Godot comes, he turns out to be wearing the impotent blue helmet of the UNPROFOR troops. ("Here come the Smurfs!" is the movie's funniest line.) It struck me that Hollywood would have insisted that the wounded soldiers should gradually befriend each other, their common humanity overcoming the craziness of their war; and one of the most tough-minded, as well as bitterly funny, virtues of Tanovic's movie is that he makes the opposite happen, leading to a bloody climax as blackly satirical as *Catch-22*—so "feel-bad" an ending that no L.A. producer would have tolerated it.

In Telluride, this year, we screened Andrei Tarkovsky's great movie *Solaris,* to honor a sci-fi masterpiece before the contemporary plague of remakes comes to obliterate it. This exploration of the unreliability of reality and the power of the human unconscious, this great examination of the limits of rationalism and the perverse power of even the most ill-fated love, needs to be seen as widely as possible before it's transformed by Steven Soderbergh and James Cameron into what they ludicrously threaten will be "*2001* meets *Last Tango in Paris.*" What, sex in space with floating butter? Tarkovsky must be turning in his grave.

Another success from the past was Satyajit Ray's enchanting film for children, *The Golden Fortress,* a film whose lack of international recognition always distressed its great director. Perhaps its huge impact here will finally earn this neglected film a release. Today Telluride, tomorrow the world?

There are two kinds of film festivals: there are the mega-hyped, hoopla-infested selling circuses like Cannes and even Sundance; and there is Telluride, where no prizes are given, and where, if people have come to buy and sell, they keep pretty quiet about it. It is extraordinarily exciting, in this age of the triumph of capitalism, to discover an event dedicated not to commerce but to love. And if that sounds old-fashioned and starry-eyed, so be it. The cinema was always in the business of gazing at the stars.

A POSTSCRIPT

To Hell You Ride, indeed. On September 11, 2001, just eight days after the end of the film festival, two terrorist-hijacked civilian aircraft brought down the twin towers of the World Trade Center in New York. A third smashed into the Pentagon. In Pennsylvania a fourth plane crashed short of its target, thanks to the selfless heroism of its passengers, who fought the terrorists and frustrated their designs. How idyllically innocent our Telluride days at once began to seem: as if we had been cast out of Eden, holding the fruit of the tree of knowledge of good and evil in our trembling hands.

OCTOBER 2001: THE ATTACKS ON AMERICA

In January 2000's column I wrote that "the defining struggle of the new age would be between Terrorism and Security," and fretted that to live by the security experts' worst-case scenarios might be to surrender too many of our liberties to the invisible shadow-warriors of the secret world. Democracy requires visibility, I argued, and in the struggle between security and freedom we must always err on the side of freedom. On Tuesday, September 11, however, the worst-case scenario came true.

They broke our city. I'm among the newest of New Yorkers, but even people who have never set foot in Manhattan have felt her wounds deeply, because New York in our time is the beating heart of the visible world, tough-talking, spirit-dazzling, Walt Whitman's "city of orgies, walks and joys," his "proud and passionate city— mettlesome, mad, extravagant city!" To this bright capital of the visible, the forces of invisibility have dealt a dreadful blow. No need to say how dreadful; we all saw it, are all changed by it, and must now ensure that the wound is not mortal, that the world of what is seen triumphs over what is cloaked, what is perceptible only through the effects of its awful deeds.

In making free societies safe—safer—from terrorism, our civil liberties will inevitably be compromised.* But in return for freedom's partial erosion, we have a right to expect that our cities, water, planes, and children really will be better protected than they have been. The West's response to the September 11 attacks will be judged in large measure by whether people begin to feel safe once again in their homes, their workplaces, their daily lives. This is the confidence we have lost and must regain.

Next: the question of the counterattack. Yes, we must send our shadow-warriors against theirs, and hope that ours prevail. But this secret war alone cannot bring victory. We will also need a public, political, and diplomatic offensive whose aim must be the early resolution of some of the world's thorniest problems: above all the battle between Israel and the Palestinian people for space, dignity, recognition, and survival. Better judgment will be required on all sides in future. No more Sudanese aspirin factories to be bombed, please. And now that wise American heads appear to have understood that it would be wrong to bomb the impoverished, oppressed Afghan people in retaliation for their tyrannous masters' misdeeds, they might apply that wisdom, retrospectively, to what was done to the impoverished, oppressed people of Iraq. It's time to stop making enemies and start making friends.

To say this is in no way to join in the savaging of America by sections of the Left that has been among the most unpleasant consequences of the terrorists' attacks on the United States. "The problem with Americans is . . ." "What America needs to understand . . ." There has been a lot of sanctimonious moral relativism around lately, usually prefaced by such phrases as these. A country that has just suffered the most devastating terrorist attack in history, a country in a state of deep mourning and horrible grief, is being told, heartlessly, that it is to blame for its own citizens' deaths. ("Did we deserve this, sir?" a bewildered worker at "ground zero" asked a visiting British journalist recently. I find the grave courtesy of that "sir" quite astonishing.)

Let's be clear about why this bien-pensant anti-American onslaught is such appalling rubbish. Terrorism is the murder of the innocent; this time, it was mass murder. To excuse such an atrocity by blaming U.S.

---

* When I wrote these words, I'd meant to say that we'd probably be subjected to more annoying, intrusive checks at airports. I failed to foresee the eagerness with which Messrs. Ashcroft, Ridge, et al. would set about creating the apparatus of a more authoritarian state.

government policies is to deny the basic idea of all morality: that individuals are responsible for their actions. Furthermore, terrorism is not the pursuit of legitimate complaints by illegitimate means. The terrorist wraps himself in the world's grievances to cloak his true motives. Whatever the killers were trying to achieve, it seems improbable that building a better world was part of it.

The fundamentalist seeks to bring down a great deal more than buildings. Such people are against, to offer just a brief list, freedom of speech, a multi-party political system, universal adult suffrage, accountable government, Jews, homosexuals, women's rights, pluralism, secularism, short skirts, dancing, beardlessness, evolution theory, sex. These are tyrants, not Muslims. (Islam is tough on suicides, who are doomed to repeat their deaths through all eternity. However, there needs to be a thorough examination, by Muslims everywhere, of why it is that the faith they love breeds so many violent mutant strains. If the West needs to understand its Unabombers and McVeighs, Islam needs to face up to its bin Ladens.)

United Nations Secretary-General Kofi Annan has said that we should now define ourselves not only by what we are for but by what we are against. I would reverse that proposition, because in the present instance what we are against is a no-brainer. Suicidist assassins ram wide-bodied aircraft into the World Trade Center and Pentagon and kill thousands of people: um, I'm against that. But what are we for? What will we risk our lives to defend? Can we unanimously concur that all the items in the preceding list—yes, even the short skirts and dancing—are worth dying for?

The fundamentalist believes that we believe in nothing. In his world-view, he has his absolute certainties, while we are sunk in sybaritic indulgences. To prove him wrong, we must first know that he is wrong. We must agree on what matters: kissing in public places, bacon sandwiches, disagreement, cutting-edge fashion, literature, generosity, water, a more equitable distribution of the world's resources, movies, music, freedom of thought, beauty, love. These will be our weapons. Not by making war but by the unafraid way we choose to live shall we defeat them.

How to defeat terrorism? Don't be terrorized. Don't let fear rule your life. Even if you are scared.

NOVEMBER 2001: NOT ABOUT ISLAM?

T his isn't about Islam." The world's leaders have been repeating this mantra for weeks, partly in the virtuous hope of deterring reprisal attacks on innocent Muslims living in the West, partly because if the United States is to maintain its coalition against terror it can't afford to allege that Islam and terrorism are in any way related.

The trouble with this necessary disclaimer is that it isn't true. If this isn't about Islam, why the worldwide Muslim demonstrations in support of Osama bin Laden and Al-Qaida? Why did those ten thousand men armed with swords and axes mass on the Pakistan-Afghanistan frontier, answering some mullah's call to jihad? Why are the war's first British casualties three Muslim men who died fighting on the Taliban side?

Why the routine anti-Semitism of the much-repeated Islamic slander that "the Jews" arranged the hits on the World Trade Center and Pentagon, with the oddly self-deprecating explanation offered by the Taliban leadership among others: that Muslims could not have the technological know-how or organizational sophistication to pull off such a feat? Why does Imran Khan, the Pakistani ex–sports star turned politician, demand to be shown the evidence of Al-Qaida's guilt while apparently turning a deaf ear to the self-incriminating statements of Al-Qaida's own spokesmen (there will be a rain of aircraft from the skies, Muslims in the West are warned not to live or work in tall buildings, et cetera)? Why all the talk about U.S. military infidels desecrating the sacred soil of Saudi Arabia, if some sort of definition of what is sacred is not at the heart of the present discontents?

Let's start calling a spade a spade. Of course this is "about Islam." The question is, what exactly does that mean? After all, most religious belief isn't very theological. Most Muslims are not profound Quranic analysts. For a vast number of "believing" Muslim men, "Islam" stands, in a jumbled, half-examined way, not only for the fear of God—the fear more than the love, one suspects—but also for a cluster of customs, opinions, and prejudices that include their dietary practices; the sequestration or near-sequestration of "their" women; the sermons delivered by their mullah of choice; a loathing of modern society in general, riddled as it is with music, godlessness, and sex; and a more

particularized loathing (and fear) of the prospect that their own imme-
diate surroundings could be taken over—"Westoxicated"—by the liberal Western-style way of life.

Highly motivated organizations of Muslim men (oh, for the voices
of Muslim women to be heard!) have been engaged, over the last thirty
years or so, on growing radical political movements out of this mulch
of "belief." These Islamists—we must get used to this word, "Islamists,"
meaning those who are engaged upon such political projects, and
learn to distinguish it from the more general and politically neutral
"Muslim"—include the Muslim Brotherhood in Egypt, the blood-
soaked combatants of the FIS and GIA in Algeria, the Shia revolution-
aries of Iran, and the Taliban. Poverty is their great helper, and the fruit
of their efforts is paranoia. This paranoid Islam, which blames outsiders, "infidels," for all the ills of Muslim societies, and whose proposed remedy is the closing of those societies to the rival project of
modernity, is presently the fastest-growing version of Islam in the
world.

This is not really to go along with Samuel Huntington's thesis about
the "clash of civilizations," for the simple reason that the Islamists'
project is turned not only against the West and "the Jews" but also
against their fellow-Islamists. Whatever the public rhetoric, there's little love lost between the Taliban and Iranian regimes. Dissensions between Muslim nations run at least as deep as, if not deeper than, those
nations' resentment of the West. Nevertheless, it would be absurd to
deny that this self-exculpatory, paranoiac Islam is an ideology with
widespread appeal.

Twenty years ago, when I was writing a novel about power struggles
in a fictionalized Pakistan, it was already de rigueur in the Muslim
world to blame all its troubles on the West and, in particular, the United
States. Then as now, some of these criticisms were well-founded; no
room here to rehearse the geopolitics of the Cold War, and America's
frequently damaging foreign policy "tilts," to use the Kissinger term,
toward (or away from) this or that temporarily useful (or disapproved-
of) nation-state, or America's role in the installation and deposition of
sundry unsavory leaders and regimes. But I wanted then to ask a question which is no less important now: suppose we say that the ills of our
societies are not primarily America's fault—that we are to blame for our
own failings? How would we understand them then? Might we not, by
accepting our own responsibility for our problems, begin to learn to
solve them for ourselves?

It is interesting that many Muslims, as well as secularist analysts with roots in the Muslim world, are beginning to ask such questions now. In recent weeks Muslim voices have everywhere been raised against the obscurantist "hijack" of their religion. Yesterday's hotheads (among them Yusuf Islam, a.k.a. Cat Stevens) are improbably repackaging themselves as today's pussycats. An Iraqi writer quotes an earlier Iraqi satirist: "The disease that is in us, is from us." A British Muslim writes that "Islam has become its own enemy." A Lebanese writer friend, returning from Beirut, tells me that, in the aftermath of September 11, public criticism of Islamism has become much more outspoken. Many commentators have spoken of the need for a Reformation in the Muslim world. I'm reminded of the way non-communist socialists used to distance themselves from the tyrannous "actually existing" socialism of the Soviets; nevertheless, the first stirrings of this counterproject are of great significance. If Islam is to be reconciled with modernity, these voices must be encouraged until they swell into a roar.

Many of them speak of another Islam, their personal, private faith, and the restoration of religion to the sphere of the personal, its depoliticization, is the nettle that all Muslim societies must grasp in order to become modern. The only aspect of modernity in which the terrorists are interested is technology, which they see as a weapon that can be turned against its makers. If terrorism is to be defeated, the world of Islam must take on board the secularist-humanist principles on which the modern is based, and without which their countries' freedom will remain a distant dream.

FEBRUARY 2002: ANTI-AMERICANISM

They told us it would be a long, ugly struggle, and so it is. America's war against terror has entered its second phase, a phase characterized by the storm over the condition, status, and human rights of the prisoners held at Camp X-Ray; by the frustrating failure of the United States to find Osama bin Laden and Mullah Omar; and by growing opposition to the continued bombing in Afghanistan. Additionally, if America now attacks other countries suspected of harboring terrorists, it will almost certainly do so alone, without the backing of the coalition that supported the action in Afghanistan. The reason is that America finds itself facing an ideological enemy that may turn out to be harder to defeat than militant Islam: that is to say, anti-Americanism, which is presently taking the world by storm.

The good news is that these post-Taliban days are bad times for Islamist fanatics. Dead or alive, bin Laden and Omar look like yesterday's men, unholy warriors who forced martyrdom on others while running for the hills themselves. Also, if the persistent rumors are to be believed, the fall of the terrorist axis in Afghanistan may well have prevented an Islamist coup against Musharraf in Pakistan, led by the more Taliban-like elements in the armed forces and intelligence services— people like the terrifying General Hamid Gul. And President Musharraf, no angel himself, has been pushed into arresting the leaders of the Kashmiri terrorist groups he used to encourage. (It's just two and a quarter years since he unleashed the same groups against India and engineered the last Kashmir crisis.)

Around the world, the lessons of the American action in Afghanistan are being learned. Jihad is no longer quite as cool an idea as it was last fall. States under suspicion of giving succor to terrorism have suddenly been trying to make nice, even going so far as to round up a few bad guys. Iran has accepted the legitimacy of the new Afghan government. Even Britain, a state that has been more tolerant of Islamist fanaticism than most, is beginning to see the difference between resisting "Islamophobia" and providing a safe haven for some of the worst people in the world.

America did, in Afghanistan, what had to be done, and did it well. The bad news, however, is that none of these successes have won friends for the United States. In fact, the effectiveness of the American campaign may paradoxically have made the world hate America more than it did before. Western critics of America's Afghan campaign are enraged because they have been shown to be not only spineless but wrong at every step: no, U.S. forces weren't humiliated the way the Russians had been; and yes, the air strikes did work; and no, the Northern Alliance didn't massacre people in Kabul; and yes, the Taliban did crumble away like the hated tyrants they were, even in their southern strongholds; and no, it wasn't that difficult to get the militants out of their cave fortresses; and yes, the various factions succeeded in putting together a new government that is surprising people by functioning pretty well.

Meanwhile, those elements in the Arab and Muslim world who blame America for their own feelings of political impotence are feeling more impotent than ever. As always, anti-U.S. radicalism feeds off the widespread anger over the plight of the Palestinians, and it remains true that nothing would undermine the fanatics' propaganda more comprehensively than an acceptable settlement in the Middle East. However, even if that settlement were arrived at tomorrow, anti-Americanism would probably not abate. It has become too useful a smoke screen for Muslim nations' many defects—their corruption, their incompetence, their oppression of their own citizens, their economic, scientific, and cultural stagnation. America-hating has become a badge of identity, making possible a chest-beating, flag-burning rhetoric of word and deed that makes men feel good. It contains a strong streak of hypocrisy, hating most what it desires most, and elements of self-loathing ("we hate America because it has made of itself what we cannot make of ourselves"). What America is accused of—closed-mindedness, stereotyping, ignorance—is also what its accusers would see if they looked into a mirror.

Anybody who has visited Britain and Europe, or followed the public conversation there during the past five months, will have been struck, even shocked, by the depth of anti-American feeling among large segments of the population, as well as the news media. Western anti-Americanism is an altogether more petulant phenomenon than its Islamic counterpart and, oddly, far more personalized. Muslim countries don't like America's power, its "arrogance," its success; in the non-American West, the main objection seems to be to American *people.* Night after night, I have found myself listening to Londoners' diatribes against the sheer weirdness of the American citizenry. The attacks on America are routinely discounted ("Americans care only about their own dead"). American patriotism, obesity, emotionality, self-centeredness: these are the crucial issues.

It would be easy for America, in the present climate of hostility, to fail to respond to constructive criticism. The treatment of the Camp X-Ray detainees is a case in point. Colin Powell's reported desire to grant these persons POW status and Geneva Convention rights was a statesmanlike response to global pressure; his apparent failure to persuade President Bush and Mr. Rumsfeld to accept his recommendations is a worrying sign. The Bush administration has come a long way from its treaty-canceling beginnings. It should not retreat from consensus-building now. Great power and great wealth are perhaps never popular. And yet, more than ever, we need the United States to exercise its power and economic might responsibly. This is not the time to ignore the rest of the world and decide to go it alone. To do so would be to risk losing after you've won.

MARCH 2002: GOD IN GUJARAT

The defining image of the week is of a small child's burned and blackened arm, its tiny fingers curled into a fist, protruding from the remains of a human bonfire in Ahmadabad, Gujarat. The murder of children is something of an Indian specialty. The routine daily killings of unwanted girl babies, the massacre of innocents in Nellie, Assam, in the 1980s, and of Sikh children in Delhi during the horrifying reprisal murders that followed Mrs. Gandhi's assassination bear witness to our particular gift, always most dazzlingly in evidence at times of religious unrest, for dousing our children in kerosene and setting them alight, or cutting their throats, or smothering them, or just clubbing them to death with a good strong length of wood. I say "our" because I write as an Indian man born and bred, who loves India deeply and knows that what one of us does today, any of us is potentially capable of doing tomorrow. If I take pride in India's strengths, then India's sins must be mine as well.

Do I sound angry? Good. Ashamed and disgusted? I certainly hope so. Because, as India undergoes its worst bout of Hindu-Muslim bloodletting in over a decade, many people have not been sounding anything like angry, ashamed, or disgusted enough. Police chiefs have been excusing their men's unwillingness to defend the citizens of India without regard to religion, by saying that these men have feelings too, and are subject to the same sentiments as the nation in general.

Meanwhile, India's political masters have been tut-tutting and offering the usual soothing lies about the situation being brought under control. (It has escaped nobody's notice that the ruling BJP—the Bharatiya Janata Party or Indian People's Party—and the Hindu extremists of the VHP—the Vishwa Hindu Parishad or World Hindu Council—are sister organizations, offshoots of the same parent body.) Even some international commentators, like Britain's *Independent* newspaper, urge us to "beware excess pessimism." The horrible truth about communal slaughter in India is that we're used to it. It happens every so often; then it dies down. That's how life is, folks. Most of the time, India is the world's largest secular democracy; and if, once in a while, it lets off a little crazy-religious steam, we mustn't let that distort the picture.

Of course there are political explanations. Ever since December 1992, when a VHP mob demolished a four-hundred-year-old Muslim mosque, the Babri Masjid in Ayodhya, which they claim was built on the sacred birthplace of the god Ram, Hindu fanatics have been looking for this fight. The pity of it is that some Muslims were ready to give it to them. The murderous attack on the trainload of VHP activists at Godhra (with its awful, atavistic echoes of the killings of Hindus and Muslims by the trainload during the Partition riots of 1947) played right into the Hindu extremists' hands.

The VHP has evidently tired of what it sees as the equivocations and insufficient radicalism of the BJP government. Prime Minister Vajpayee is more moderate than his party; he also heads a coalition government, and has been obliged to abandon much of the BJP's more extreme Hindu-nationalist rhetoric to hold the coalition together. But it isn't working anymore. In state elections across the country, the BJP is being trounced. This may have been the last straw for the VHP firebrands. Why put up with the government's betrayal of their fascistic agenda when that betrayal doesn't even result in electoral success?

The electoral failure of the BJP (used by the let's-not-get-carried-away gang to show that India is turning away from communalist politics) is thus, in all probability, the spark that lit the fire. The VHP is determined to build a Hindu temple on the site of the demolished Ayodhya mosque—that's where the Godhra dead were coming from—and there are, reprehensibly, idiotically, tragically, Muslims in India equally determined to resist them. Vajpayee has insisted that the notoriously slow Indian courts must decide the rights and wrongs of the Ayodhya issue. The VHP is no longer prepared to wait.

The distinguished Indian writer Mahasveta Devi, in a letter to the Indian president, K. R. Narayanan, blames the Gujarat government (led by a BJP hard-liner) as well as the central government for doing "too little too late," and pins the blame firmly on the "motivated, well-planned out and provocative actions" of the Hindu nationalists. However, another writer, the Nobel laureate V. S. Naipaul, speaking in India just a week before the violence erupted, denounced India's Muslims en masse and praised the nationalist movement. The murderers of Godhra must indeed be denounced, and Mahasveta Devi in her letter demands "stern legal action" against them. But the VHP and its other related organization, the equally sinister RSS (Rashtriya Swyamsevak Sangh, or Association of National Volunteers, from which both the BJP and the VHP take inspiration), are determined to destroy that secular democracy in which India takes such public pride and which it does so little to protect; and by supporting them, V. S. Naipaul makes himself a fellow-traveler of fascism and disgraces the Nobel award.

The political discourse matters, and explains a good deal. But there's something beneath it, something we don't want to look in the face: namely, that in India, as elsewhere in our darkening world, religion is the poison in the blood. Where religion intervenes, mere innocence is no excuse. Yet we go on skating around this issue, speaking of religion in the fashionable language of "respect." What is there to respect in any of this, or in any of the crimes now being committed almost daily around the world in religion's dreaded name? How well, with what fatal results, religion erects totems, and how willing we are to kill for them! And when we've done it often enough, the deadening of affect that results makes it easier to do it again.

So India's problem turns out to be the world's problem. What happened in India, happened in God's name. The problem's name is God.

PART IV

Step Across This Line

The Tanner Lectures

on Human Values,

Yale, 2002

Part One

───────

T he first frontier was the water's edge, and there was a first moment, because how could there not have been such a moment, when a living thing came up from the ocean, crossed that boundary, and found that it could breathe. Before that first creature drew that first breath there would have been other moments when other creatures made the same attempt and fell fainting back into the waves, or else suffocated, flopping fishily from side to side, on the same seashore and another, and another. There were perhaps millions of these unrecorded retreats, these anonymous deaths, before the first successful step across the waterline. As we imagine the scene of that triumphant crossing—our volcanic young planet, the smoky, sulfurous air, the hot sea, the red glow in the sky, the exhausted entity gasping on the unfamiliar, inhospitable shore—we can't help wondering about those proto-creatures. What motivated them? Why did the sea so thoroughly lose its appeal that they risked everything to migrate from the old into the new? What urge was born in them that overpowered even the survival instinct? How did they intuit that air could be breathed—and how, living underwater as they did, could they begin to grow the lungs that allowed them to breathe it?

But our extremely pre-human ancestors did not have "motives" in the sense that we understand the term, the scientist in the room protests. The sea neither appealed to them, nor did it disappoint. They had no intuitions, but were driven by the imperatives hidden in their uncracked genetic codes. There was no daring here, no heroism, no adventurous, transgressive spirit. These beach-crawlers did not travel from water to air because they were curious, or in search of jobs. They neither chose nor willed their deeds. Random mutation and natural selection were their mighty, impersonal driving forces. They were just fish who by chance learned how to crawl.

But so, in a way, are we. Our own births mirror that first crossing of the frontier between the elements. As we emerge from amniotic fluid, from the liquid universe of the womb, we, too, discover that we can breathe; we, too, leave behind a kind of waterworld to become denizens of earth and air. Unsurprisingly, then, imagination defies science and sees that first, ancient, successful half-and-halfer as our spiritual ancestor, ascribing to that strange metamorph the will to change its world. In its victorious transition we recognize and celebrate the prototype of our own literal, moral, and metaphorical frontier crossings, applauding the same drive that made Columbus's ships head for the edge of the world, or the pioneers take to their covered wagons. The image of Armstrong taking his first moonwalk echoes the first movements of life on earth. In our deepest natures, we are frontier-crossing beings. We know this by the stories we tell ourselves; for we are storytelling animals, too. There is a story about a mermaid, a half-and-half creature, who gave up her fishy half for the love of a man. Was that it, then, we allow ourselves to wonder. Was that the primal urge? Did we come questing out of the waters for love?

—

Once upon a time the birds held a conference. The great bird-god, the Simurgh, had sent a messenger, a hoopoe, to summon them to his legendary home far away atop the circular mountain of Qâf, which girdled the earth. The birds weren't particularly keen on the idea of this dangerous-sounding quest. They tried to make excuses—a previous engagement, urgent business elsewhere. Just thirty birds embarked on the pilgrimage. Leaving home, crossing the frontier of their land, stepping across that line, was in this story a religious act, their adventure a divine requirement rather than a response to an ornithological need. Love drove these birds as it drove the mermaid, but it was the love of God. On the road there were obstacles to overcome, dreadful mountains, fearsome chasms, allegories and challenges. In all quests the voyager is confronted by terrifying guardians of territory, an ogre here, a dragon there. So far and no farther, the guardian commands. But the voyager must refuse the other's definition of the boundary, must transgress against the limits of what fear prescribes. He steps across that line. The defeat of the ogre is an opening in the self, an increase in what it is possible for the voyager to be.

So it was with the thirty birds. At the end of the story, after all their vicissitudes and overcomings, they reached the summit of the mountain of Qâf, and discovered that they were alone. The Simurgh wasn't there. After all they had endured, this was a displeasing discovery. They made their feelings known to the hoopoe who had started the whole thing off, whereupon the hoopoe explained to them the punning etymology that revealed their journey's secret meaning. The name of the god broke down into two parts: "si," meaning "thirty," and "murgh," which is to say "birds." By crossing those frontiers, conquering those terrors and reaching their goal, they themselves were now what they were looking for. They had become the god they sought.

—

Once upon a time—"a long time ago," perhaps, "in a galaxy far, far away"—there was an advanced civilization, free, liberal, individualistic, on a planet whose ice caps began to grow. All the civilization in the world could not halt the march of the ice. The citizens of that ideal state built a mighty wall, which would resist the glaciers for a time but not forever. The time came when the ice, uncaring, implacable, stepped across their lines and crushed them. Their last act was to choose a group of men and women to travel across the ice sheet to the far side of the planet, to bring news of their civilization's death, and to preserve, in some small way, the meaning of what that civilization had been: to be its representatives. On their difficult journey across the ice cap, the group learned that, in order to survive, they would need to change. Their several individualisms had to be merged into a collectivity, and it was this collective entity—the Representative—that made it to the far side of the planet. What it represented, however, was not what it had set out to represent. The journey creates us. We become the frontiers we cross.

—

The first of these stories is medieval: the "Conference of the Birds" by the Sufi Muslim poet Fariduddin Attar. The second is an account of Doris Lessing's science-fiction novel *The Making of the Representative for*

Planet 8, itself inspired by the doomed journey toward the South Pole of Scott of the Antarctic and his companions—but also by Lessing's own long-standing interest in Sufi mysticism. The idea of overcoming, of breaking down the boundaries that hold us in and surpassing the limits of our own natures, is central to all the stories of the quest. The Grail is a chimera. The quest for the Grail is the Grail. Or, as C. P. Cavafy suggests in his poem "Ithaka," the point of an Odyssey is the Odyssey:

> Setting out on the voyage to Ithaka
> You must pray that the way be long,
> Full of adventures and experiences.
>
> . . .
>
> Be quite old when you anchor at the island,
> Rich with all you have gained on the way,
> Not expecting Ithaka to give you riches.
>
> Ithaka has given you your lovely journey.
> Without Ithaka you would not have set out.
> Ithaka has no more to give you now.
>
> Poor though you find it, Ithaka has not cheated you.
> Wise as you have become, with all your experience,
> You will have understood the meaning of an Ithaka.*

The frontier is an elusive line, visible and invisible, physical and metaphorical, amoral and moral. The wizard Merlin is responsible for the education of a boy called Arthur, who will one day draw a sword from a stone and become king of England. (The wizard, who is living backward through time, knows this, although the boy does not.) One day Merlin changes the boy into a bird, and as they fly over the countryside he asks Arthur what he sees. Arthur notices the usual things, but Merlin is talking about a thing that can't be seen, asking Arthur to see an absence: *From the air, there are no frontiers.*† Later, when Arthur has possessed Excalibur and his kingdom, he will learn that wizards are not always wise, and the view from the air isn't much

---

* Translated by John Mavrogordato in *Poems by C. P. Cavafy* (Chatto & Windus, 1951).
† From T. H. White, *The Sword in the Stone.*

use on earth. He will fight his share of frontier wars, and he will also find that there are frontiers which, being invisible, are more dangerous to cross than the physical kind.

When the king's best friend, the king's champion, falls in love with the king's wife, when Lancelot of the Lake trespasses on the territory of the king's happiness, a line has been crossed that will destroy the world. In fact the collection of tales known as the *Matter of Britain* have, at their heart, not one but two illicit, transgressive loves: that of Lancelot for Guinevere, and its occult mirror-image, the incestuous love of Arthur and Morgan le Fay. Against the power of these line-crossing lovers, the Round Table cannot stand. The quest for the Grail cannot cleanse the world. Not even Excalibur can prevent the return of darkness. And in the end the sword must be returned to water, and vanish beneath the waves. But wounded Arthur on his way to Avalon is crossing yet another line. He's being transformed, becoming one of the great sleepers who will return when the right moment comes. Barbarossa in his cave, Finn MacCool in the Irish hills, the Australian *wandjina* or ancestors in their subterranean resting places, and Arthur in Avalon: these are our once and future kings, and the final frontier they are fated to cross is not space but time.

To cross a frontier is to be transformed. Alice at the gates of Wonderland, the key to that miniature world in her grasp, cannot pass through the tiny door beyond which she can glimpse marvelous things until she has altered herself to fit into her new world. But the successful frontierswoman is also, inevitably, in the business of surpassing. She changes the rules of her newfound land: Alice in Wonderland, shape-shifting Alice, terrifies the locals by growing too big to be housed. She argues with Mad Hatters and talks back to Caterpillars and, in the end, loses her fear of an execution-hungry Queen when she, so to speak, grows up. *You're nothing but a house of cards*—Alice the migrant at last sees through the charade of power, is no longer impressed, calls Wonderland's bluff, and by unmaking it finds herself again. She wakes up.

The frontier is a wake-up call. At the frontier we can't avoid the truth; the comforting layers of the quotidian, which insulate us against the world's harsher realities, are stripped away and, wide-eyed in the harsh fluorescent light of the frontier's windowless halls, we see things as they are. The frontier is the physical proof of the human race's divided self, the proof that Merlin's utopian sky-vision is a lie. Here is the truth: this line, at which we must stand until we are allowed to walk across and give our papers to be examined by an officer who is entitled to ask us more or less anything. At the frontier our liberty is stripped away—we hope temporarily—and we enter the universe of control. Even the freest of free societies are unfree at the edge, where things and people go out and other people and things come in, where only the right things and people must go in and out. Here, at the edge, we submit to scrutiny, to inspection, to judgment. These people, guarding these lines, must tell us who we are. We must be passive, docile. To be otherwise is to be suspect, and at the frontier to come under suspicion is the worst of all possible crimes. We stand at what Graham Greene thought of as the dangerous edge of things. This is where we must present ourselves as simple, as obvious: I am coming home. I am on a business trip. I am visiting my girlfriend. In each case, what we mean when we reduce ourselves to these simple statements is, I'm not anything you need to bother about, really I'm not: not the fellow who voted against the government, not the woman who is looking forward to smoking a little dope with her friends tonight, not the person you fear, whose shoe may be about to explode. I am one-dimensional. Truly. I am simple. Let me pass.

Across the frontier the world's secret truths move unhindered every day. Inspectors doze or pocket dirty money, and the world's narcotics and armaments, its dangerous ideas, all the contrabandits of the age, the wanted ones, those who do have something to declare but do not declare it, slip by; while we, who have nothing much to declare, dress ourselves in nervous declarations of simplicity, openness, loyalty. The declarations of the innocent fill the air, while the others, who are not innocent, pass through the crowded, imperfect borders, or make their crossings where frontiers are hard to police, along deep ravines, down smugglers' trails, across undefended wastelands, waging their undeclared war. The wake-up call of the frontier is also a call to arms.

This is how we are thinking now, because these are fearful days. There is a photograph by Sebastião Salgado that shows the wall between the United States and Mexico snaking over the crests of hills, running away into the distance, as far as the eye can see, part Great Wall of China, part gulag. There is a kind of brutal beauty here, the beauty of starkness. At intervals along the wall there are watchtowers, and these so-called sky-towers are manned by armed men. In the photograph we can see the tiny, silhouetted figure of a running man, an illegal immigrant, being chased by other men in cars. The strange thing about the picture is that, although the running man is clearly on the American side, he is running toward the wall, not away from it. He has been spotted, and is more afraid of the men bearing down on him in cars than of the impoverished life he thought he had left behind. He's trying to get back, to unmake his bid for freedom. So freedom is now to be defended against those too poor to deserve its benefits by the edifices and procedures of totalitarianism. What kind of freedom is it, then, that we enjoy in the countries of the West—these exclusive, increasingly well-guarded enclaves of ours? That is the question the photograph asks, and before September 11, 2001, many of us—many more, I suspect, than today—would have been on the running man's side.

Even before the recent atrocities, however, the citizens of Douglas, Arizona, were happy to protect America from what they called "invaders." In October 2000 the British journalist Duncan Campbell met Roger Barnett, who runs a towing and propane business near Douglas but also organizes wetback hunting parties.* Tourists can sign up for a weekend hunting human beings. "Stop the invasion," the billboards in Douglas say. According to Campbell, Barnett is a legendary character in these parts. He thinks it would be a "hell of an idea" for the United States to invade Mexico in return. "There's a lot of mines and great beaches there, there's farming and resources. Think of what the United States could do there—gee whiz, they wouldn't have to come up here anymore."

Another citizen of Douglas, Larry Vance, Jr., thinks Mexicans are like the wildebeest of Africa: fair game for predators. "Where a native population has been diluted by invaders it runs into a bloodbath. We abhor violence but we realize that people have the God-given right to defend themselves." Perhaps the running man in Salgado's picture is being chased by Mr. Barnett's thrill-seekers, who are in no doubt that they are the defenders of the right, or by supporters of Mr. Vance's organization, the Cochise County Concerned Citizens—that's four *C*'s, not three *K*'s. The Mexican view of things is different, as Campbell reminds us:

> "We didn't cross the border, the border crossed us," is the much-used remark by Mexicans who have made it. To an extent this is true: the settlement of the Mexican-American war of 1846–48 meant that, for the sum of $18,250,000, the whole of California, most of Arizona and New Mexico and parts of Utah, Nevada, Colorado and Wyoming passed to the U.S.

*From an article in *The Guardian*.

But history, as they say, is made up of interviews with winners, and nobody's asking the wall-jumpers and wetbacks for their worldview right now. And if, in the aftermath of terrorist horror, many more of us are prepared to accept the need for a border gulag-world of sky-towers and manhunters; if, being afraid, we prefer to sacrifice some of what freedom means, then should we not worry about what we are becoming? Freedom is indivisible, we used to say. We are all thinking about dividing it now.

Think for a moment about this image of a running man, a man who has nothing, who is no danger to anyone, fleeing the land of the free. For Salgado, as for myself, the migrant, the man without frontiers, is the archetypal figure of our age. Salgado has spent many years among the world's displaced peoples, the uprooted and the re-rooted, chronicling their border crossings, their refugee camps, their desperations, their ingenuities: creating an extraordinary photographic record of this most important of contemporary phenomena. The pictures show that there has never been a period in the history of the world when its peoples were so jumbled up. We are so thoroughly shuffled together, clubs among diamonds, hearts among spades, jokers everywhere, that we're just going to have to live with it. In the United States, this is an old story. Elsewhere, it's a new one, and it doesn't always go down well. As a migrant myself, I have always tried to stress the creative aspects of such cultural commingling. The migrant, severed from his roots, often transplanted into a new language, always obliged to learn the ways of a new community, is forced to confront the great questions of change and adaptation; but many migrants, faced with the sheer existential difficulty of making such changes, and also, often, with the sheer alienness and defensive hostility of the peoples among whom they find themselves, retreat from such questions behind the walls of the old culture they have both brought along and left behind. The running man, rejected by those people who have built great walls to keep him out, leaps into a confining stockade of his own.

Here is the worst-case scenario of the frontier of the future: the Iron Curtain was designed to keep people in. Now we who live in the wealthiest and most desirable corners of the world are building walls to keep people out. As the economics Nobel laureate Professor Amartya Sen has said, the problem is not globalization. The problem is a fair distribution of resources in a globalized world. And as the gulf between the world's haves and have-nots increases (and it is increasing all the time) and as the supply even of essentials like clean drinking water becomes scarcer (and it is getting scarcer all the time), the pressure on the wall will build. Think of Lessing's ice, inexorably moving forward. So if we send representatives to tell the future who we were, what story will they have to tell? A story, perhaps, of a jeweled people, sitting tight on their treasure hoards, "wearing bracelets, and all those amethysts too, and all those rings on their fingers with splendid flashing emeralds, [and] carrying their precious walking sticks, with silver knobs and golden tops so wonderfully carved," and waiting for the barbarians, as Cavafy tells us—Cavafy again, that Borgesian mythomane who is also one of the great poets of miscegenation—

> Because the Barbarians will arrive today;
> Things of this sort dazzle the Barbarians.

At the frontier there has always been the threat, or, for a decadent culture, even the promise of the barbarians.

> What are we waiting for all crowded in the forum?
>   The Barbarians are to arrive today.
> Within the Senate-house where is there such inaction?
> The Senators making no laws what are they sitting there for?
>   Because the Barbarians arrive today.
>   What laws now should the Senators be making?
>   When the Barbarians come they'll make the laws.
>   . . .
> Why should this uneasiness begin all of a sudden,
> And confusion. How serious people's faces have become.
> Why are all the streets and squares emptying so quickly,
> And everybody turning home again so full of thought?
>   Because night has fallen and the barbarians have not come.
>   And some people have arrived from the frontier;
>   They said there are no Barbarians any more.

> And now what will become of us without Barbarians?—
> Those people were some sort of a solution.

"What will become of us without Barbarians?" J. M. Coetzee's novel also called *Waiting for the Barbarians* offers a dystopic gloss on the Cavafy poem. Those who spend their time on guard, waiting for the barbarians to arrive, in the end don't need any barbarians to come. In a dark variation on the ending of the "Conference of the Birds," they themselves become the barbarians whose coming they so feared. And then there are no solutions.

"Why should this uneasiness begin all of a sudden?" It's not so long since the American frontier was a location of freedom, not unease. Not so long since Sal Paradise took off into Mexico with his pal Dean Moriarty to begin that part of his life you could call his life on the road. To re-read *On the Road* now is to be struck, first of all, by how well it has lasted: its prose sprightly, leaner, and less prolix than expected, its intense vision still bright. It's a celebration of the open road, and of the open frontier as well. To cross into another language, another way of being, is to take a step toward beatitude, the worldly blessedness to which all dharma bums aspire.

I have always mentally paired *On the Road* with another classic modern fable of the U.S.-Mexican border, Orson Welles's great film *Touch of Evil*. The Welles picture is the dark flip-side of the Kerouac book. Like the novel, the film takes the openness of the frontier for granted: its story is made possible by the frontier's unpoliceability. However, the movie's bums are not of the dharma variety. Its characters are not blessed, or even seeking enlightenment. Welles's frontier is fluid, watchful, constantly shifting focus and attention: in a word, unstable. In the famous opening take, when minute after minute passes without a cut, the inhabitants of Welles's transit zone engage in a cryptic dance of death. The frontier's everyday life may look banal, meaningless, and above all continuous, but it begins with the planting of a bomb and ends with the radical discontinuity of an explosion. This frontier is anonymous, denaturing; it strips humanity bare. Life, death. Not much else matters, except, maybe, alcohol. Marlene Dietrich says it best when she delivers the flawed hero's epitaph as he floats facedown in a shallow canal: "He was some kind of a man. What does it matter what you say about people?"

Some kind of a man. This crooked policeman had some good in him somewhere. A whore loved him, sort of. So what, he's dead. A man steps across a line, he suffers the penalty. This man got away with it for a long time and then did not get away with it. What else is there to say? The frontier watches the come-and-go of life. It does not judge. Another man, the dead man's antagonist, a Mexican lawman, comes to this border town with an American blonde. He, too, has crossed a line: the frontier of the skin, of racial difference. The blonde is his transgression, his crime against the natural order, in which such women are off limits to such men. She is therefore also his weakness. He is an honest man, but when his wife is attacked—drugged, framed—he stops being a lawman, puts down his badge, and becomes merely a man fighting for his woman. The frontier has stripped him of the law, of civilization. This is normal. The frontier strips you down, and then you are what you are and you do what you do. This is how it is. What does it matter what you say about people?

The world-weariness—the *word*-weariness—of all this is profoundly at odds with the eager, voluble world of the Beats, and the related world of the rest of literature, in which there is nothing more important than what you say about people, except how you say it. Gravel-voiced, shoulder-shrugging Marlene Dietrich saying good-bye to dead Orson echoes and invokes an older American idea of the frontier, that laconic world where actions spoke louder than words, the Boot Hill, OK Corral, Hole-in-the-Wall, outlaw frontier of which we perhaps still think most often when we combine the words "American" and "frontier," the westward-moving front-line, first of Natty Bumppo and later of Davy Crockett—but also of John Ford and the monosyllabic John Wayne. The West as it has come down to us is a myth of a largely pre-literate, almost pre-verbal world, a world of "kids"—Sundance, Cisco—who barely even needed names, and of "Bills"—Wild, Buffalo—for whom an epithet was enough, and at least one Bill, or Billy, who managed to be a Kid as well. Yet these men's reputations were constructed by writers, whose names we have not remembered: fabulist Boswells to the Wild West's desperado Johnsons, print-the-legend glamorizers who called themselves reporters. What does it matter what you say about people? Plenty, it turns out, if you're in the legend business. The American frontier affected to despise words, but it was a landscape built of words. And it's gone now, but the words remain. Animals, as they pass through landscape, leave their tracks behind. Stories are the tracks we leave.

The actually existing American frontier was officially declared to have disappeared forever in 1890, when the superintendent of the census reported, "At present . . . there can hardly be said to be a frontier line. In the discussion of its extent, its westward movement, etc., it can not, therefore, any longer have a place in the census reports." Just three years after this somewhat dry funeral oration, the Frontier Thesis was born. At a meeting of the American Historical Association in Chicago on July 12, 1893, Frederick Jackson Turner, the thirty-two-year-old son of a journalist and local historian from Portage, Wisconsin, delivered his paper "The Significance of the Frontier in American History," which would later be called "the single most influential piece of writing in the history of American history," and suffered the traditional fate of the pioneer: that is to say, his ideas were completely ignored. Not for long, however. His star rose rapidly, and even though he never delivered the big books based on his ideas about the frontier—books for which he nevertheless signed contracts and accepted advances—he proved a skillful academic careerist and, after being courted by colleges from Berkeley to Chicago and Cambridge, he ended up on the faculty at, if I may mention the word, Harvard.

According to the Turner thesis,

> the existence of an area of free land, its continuous recession, and the advance of American settlement westward, explain American development . . . [which] has exhibited not merely advance along a single line, but a return to primitive conditions on a continually advancing frontier line, and a new development for that area. American social development has been continually beginning over again on the frontier. This perennial rebirth, this fluidity of American life, this expansion westward with its new opportunities, its continuous touch with the simplicity of primitive society, furnish the forces dominating American character.

Turner characterizes the frontier as "the meeting point between savagery and civilization," a formulation that will not endear him to a more culturally sensitive modern audience. Less contentiously and more interestingly, he says that "at first, the frontier was the Atlantic coast. It was the frontier of Europe in a very real sense. Moving westward, the frontier became more and more American. As successive terminal moraines result from successive glaciations, so each frontier leaves its traces behind it, and when it becomes a settled area the region still partakes of the frontier characteristics. Thus the advance of the frontier has meant a steady movement away from the influence of Europe, a steady growth of independence on American lines." The frontier, he proposes, is the physical expression of Americanness. "The universal disposition of Americans to emigrate to the western wilderness, in order to enlarge their dominion over inanimate nature, is the actual result of an expansive power which is inherent in them." The frontier is created by this inherent Americanness, but it also creates much of what we recognize as quintessentially American. "The frontier promoted the formation of a composite nationality for the American people." And: "The growth of nationalism and the evolution of American political institutions were dependent on the advance of the frontier. . . . Nothing works for nationalism like intercourse within the nation. Mobility of population is death to localism." And also: "The frontier is productive of individualism . . . [so that] the most important effect of the frontier has been in the promotion of democracy."

All this adds up to nothing less than the American character.

> To the frontier the American intellect owes its striking characteristics. That coarseness and strength combined with acuteness and inquisitiveness; that practical, inventive turn of mind, quick to find expedients; that masterful grasp of material things, lacking in the artistic but powerful to effect great ends; that restless, nervous energy; that dominant individualism, working for good and for evil, and withal that buoyancy and exuberance which comes with freedom—these are traits of the frontier. The people of the United States have taken their tone from the incessant expansion which has not only been open but has even been forced upon them. . . . Movement has been [America's] dominant fact, and, unless this training has no effect upon a people, the American energy will continually demand a wider field for its exercise.

The Frontier Thesis offers a triumphalist vision of America's coming-to-be with which it's easy to take issue, and since Turner first presented it, almost every single one of its ideas and assumptions has been contested. Most obviously, was there ever really such a thing as a frontier of free land, a virgin territory against which pioneer America measured itself? What, then, of the conquered and even annihilated Native American tribes—even before the coming of political correctness, I found it odd to speak, in the American context, of "Indians"— who were there long before the frontier's inexorable line began to step across their land?★ Turner concedes that what the settlers found

★ In the film *Little Big Man,* the old Cheyenne chief, who calls the Cheyenne "the Human Beings," which is apparently what "Cheyenne" means in Cheyenne, explains mournfully to the eponymous hero that there is no resisting the advance of the white man because, while there appears to be an inexhaustible supply of white men, there is a strictly limited number of Human Beings.

at the frontier was "not tabula rasa," but his evident contempt for the displaced "savages" colors, and damages, his argument, or rather gives it a darker meaning he did not intend. "The American energy will continually demand a wider field for its exercise." This optimistic formulation sounds almost imperialist now. If the original inhabitants of America were trampled over and brushed aside as the frontier snaked west, then should the rest of the world, that "wider field," now feel apprehensive of America's intentions?

Historians have further reasoned that the great differences between the East of the Puritans, the slavery-tainted South, and the West of gold rushes and railroads make it impossible to sustain any unified theory of frontier development—each of these is better understood as a discrete region, with its own historical dynamics. The frontier's supposed formative effect on the American self is also disputed. The land swallowed by the frontier was by no means handed out in democratically equal parcels to the early pioneers; and as regards the formation of the American character, it was a sense of community, not of rugged individualism, that enabled much of the West to thrive, and develop toward statehood. A contemporary account suggests that

> most migrant wagon trains, for example, were composed of extended kinship networks. Moreover, as the nineteenth century wore on, the role of the federal government and large corporations grew increasingly important. Corporate investors headquartered in New York laid the railroads; government troops defeated Indian nations who refused to get out of the way of manifest destiny; even the cowboys, enshrined in popular mythology as rugged loners, were generally low-level employees of sometimes foreign-owned cattle corporations. The West has not been the land of freedom and opportunity that both Turnerian history and popular mythology would have us believe. For many women, Asians, Mexicans who suddenly found themselves residents of the United States, and, of course, Indians, the West was no promised land.*

So it seems that poor old Turner was a dozen ways wrong. And yet he may, like Freud, have been wrong in the right way. Medievalist

---

* By Stephen Ives and Ken Burns, from their documentary *The West*; see www.pbs.org/weta/thewest.

historians, applying Turnerian frontier theory to the development of Europe in the Middle Ages, have found his ideas useful. The medieval European frontier, pushing outward from England into Wales and Ireland; and across central Europe; and clearing the great forests of Russia; and finally in the conflicts with Islam in the Crusader East and the Spanish Reconquista can be seen, to quote one specialist in the period, Professor C. J. Bishko of the University of Virginia, as being clearly "one frontier, a unity not in geographical contiguity but in its expression of the same deep forces of medieval dynamics and basic similarities of aims, techniques, and accomplishments.

"The frontier," Professor Bishko argues,

created for history not only new lands of European culture, but new peoples—the Portuguese, the Castilians, the Austrians, the Prussians, the Great Russians, peoples who move swiftly to dominate the modern history of their respective countries. It produced a frontier literature in . . . heroic works like the *Lay of Igor's Campaign* or the *Poema del Cid*. It created in abundance new types of medieval men and women the frontier noble, whether he be called bogatyr, caballero, lord marcher, or knight; it produced the Military Orders which were so prominent in frontier warfare and colonization; the frontier churchman, the colonizing bishop or abbot, the missionary, the priest of the lonely frontier parish; the frontier merchant and the frontier townsman; the land speculator and colonial promoter; above all, the frontier farmer, axe-swinging, plow-guiding, or stock-trailing. These are the frontiersmen who pushed forward the edges of medieval civilization, with or without the support of their rulers; these are the men whose warlike or peaceful dealings with non-Europeans first raise for medieval thinkers the great questions of the rights of native peoples and the legitimacy of just war against them—the beginning of the controversies that in the sixteenth century were enlarged to include the Indians of the New World and led medieval-minded Spanish theologians and jurists to lay the foundations of international law and the rights of non-European man. For many medieval men, who never saw the rising royal capitals, the bustling mercantile cities, the ancient feudal domains, or the new books and universities of the medieval renaissance, the medieval frontier represented the chief best hope of life, the call to robust adventure and to the risks and rewards of courage and enterprise. And like so many things medieval, the frontier did not end in 1453, or 1492, or 1500, but passed on into the making of modern civilization.★

It is one of the great characteristics of frontiers to be disputed. Give me a line drawn across the world and I'll give you an argument. We can concede the point of almost all of F. J. Turner's adversaries' criticisms— can agree that the frontier was differently formed and meant different things in different parts of America; that much of what went on in frontier society was more oligarchic than democratic; that the country into which it moved was "free" only in the sense that the white settlers refused to accept the previous inhabitants' rights over the land; and that community values, corporatism, and federalism were far more impor- tant than Turner allowed—in short, we can reduce great swathes of the thesis to ashes, and still, in the midst of the smoking ruins, some- thing substantial remains standing. The image persists of a line snak- ing westward across a continent, changing everything as it goes, mak- ing up a world. That line acts upon our imaginations as it acted upon the imaginations of those engaged in pushing it onward, and indeed the imaginations of those engaged in resisting its advance. In American literature from Twain to Bellow we recognize the workings of that frontier intellect whose characteristics Turner so eloquently set down, and in the dark side of modern America, in its government-hating mili- tias and Unabombers, we recognize that dominant individualism, work- ing for evil, whose existence he so perfectly understood. Take away the triumphalist note, and Turner's thesis seems to foreshadow much of American history since the closing of the frontier: a history of fluctua- tions, in which there are periods of energetic engagement with the world, a pushing out of frontiers, an expansion of America's sphere of influence, and then periods of retreat behind the fortress walls of a frontier that no longer possesses the power of movement.

The old imperial powers, such as the British, have found it hard to adapt to their new, diminished status in the post-colonial world. For the British, their empire was a kind of transcendence, a way not only of overwhelming nations, subsuming their frontiers within the larger frontier of the pax Britannica, but also of breaking out of the frontiers of the self, casting off the reticence of England and becoming an un-

★ "The Frontier in Medieval History," American Historical Association (1955).

buttoned, operatic people, hot and large, striding across the great stage of the world instead of the cramped boards of home. In empire's aftermath, they have been pushed back into their box, their frontier has closed in on them like a prison, and the new opening of political and financial borders in the European Union is still viewed by them with suspicion. America, the closest thing we have to a new imperial power, is experiencing this problem in reverse; as its influence spreads across the planet, America is still battling to understand its new, post-frontier self. Beneath the surface of the American century, with its many triumphs, we may discern something unsettled, a disquiet about identity, a recurring uncertainty about the role that America should play in the world, and how it should play it.

Time, perhaps, to propose a new thesis of the post-frontier: to assert that the emergence, in the age of mass migration, mass displacement, globalized finances and industries, of this new, permeable post-frontier is the distinguishing feature of our times, and, to use Turner's phrase, explains our development as nothing else can. For all their permeability, the borders snaking across the world have never been of greater importance. This is the dance of history in our age: slow, slow, quick, quick, slow, back and forth and from side to side, we step across these fixed and shifting lines.

Part Two

————————

Uncertainty is not only America's curse. All of us now face the future with varying degrees of foreboding. To a large degree, I want to suggest, this is because of the change in the nature of the frontier that has taken place in our globalized world. From the most intimate of frontiers, that of the home, to the largest, pan-global scale, the new permeability of the frontier has become the overriding issue. Terrorism is the most appalling consequence of the permeable frontier, but terrorism, after all, is only one of the forces in the modern world that expressly reject frontiers in the way of the empires of the last century and the century before. The twin worlds of business and finance do the same thing, and the concerns of many people about the consequences of the globalized economy don't need to be rehearsed here. Other groups—artists, scientists—have always scorned the limitations that frontiers represent, drawing freely from whatever wells they please, upholding the principle of the free exchange of knowledge. The open frontier, created by the bringing down of walls, has been and remains a symbol of other opennesses. But, if I may quote a passage I wrote a couple of years ago in an article about, of all things, rock and roll music,

> The music of freedom frightens people and unleashes all manner of
> conservative defense mechanisms. As long as Orpheus could raise his
> voice in song, the Maenads could not kill him. Then they screamed,

and their shrill cacophony drowned his music, and then their weapons found their mark, and he fell, and they tore him limb from limb.

Screaming against Orpheus, we too become capable of murder. The collapse of Communism, the destruction of the Iron Curtain and the Wall, was supposed to usher in a new era of liberty. Instead, the post–Cold War world, suddenly formless and full of possibility, scared many of us stiff. We retreated behind smaller iron curtains, built smaller stockades, imprisoned ourselves in narrower, ever more fanatical definitions of ourselves—religious, regional, ethnic—and readied ourselves for war.★

———

The most precious book I possess is my passport. Like most such bald assertions, this will come across as something of an overstatement. A passport, after all, is a commonplace object. You probably don't give a lot of thought to yours most of the time. Important travel document, try not to lose it, terrible photograph, expiry date coming up soonish: in general, a passport requires a relatively modest level of attention and concern. And when, at each end of a journey, you do have to produce it, you expect it to do its stuff without much trouble. *Yes, Officer, that's me, you're right, I do look a bit different with a beard, thank you, Officer, you have a nice day too.* A passport is no big deal. It's low-maintenance. It's just ID.

I've been a British citizen since I was seventeen, so my passport has indeed done its stuff efficiently and unobtrusively for a long time now, but I have never forgotten that all passports do not work in this way. My first—Indian—passport, for example, was a paltry thing. Instead of offering the bearer a general open-sesame to anywhere in the world, it stated in grouchy bureaucratic language that it was valid only for travel to a specified—and distressingly short—list of countries. On inspection, one quickly discovered that this list excluded almost any country to which one might actually want to go. Bulgaria? Romania? Uganda? North Korea? No problem. The USA? England? Italy? Japan? *Sorry, sahib. This document does not entitle you to pass those ports.* Permission to visit attractive countries had to be specially applied for and, it was made clear, would not easily be granted. Foreign exchange was one problem. India was chronically short of it, and reluctant to get any shorter. A

★ Q.v., "Columns," April 1999.

bigger problem was that many of the world's more attractive countries seemed unattracted by the idea of allowing us in. They had apparently formed the puzzling conviction that once we arrived we might not wish to leave. "Travel," in the happy-go-lucky, pleasure-seeking, interest-pursuing, vacationing Western sense, was a luxury we in India were not allowed. We could, if we were lucky, be granted permission to make trips that were absolutely necessary. Or, if unlucky, denied such permission, which was just our tough luck.

In *Among the Believers,* V. S. Naipaul's book about his travels in the Muslim world, a young man who has been driving the author around in Pakistan admits that he doesn't have a passport and, keen to go abroad and see the world, expresses a yearning for one. Naipaul reflects, more than a little caustically, that it's a shame that the only freedom in which this young fellow appears to be interested is the freedom to leave the country. When I first read this passage, years ago, I had a strong urge to defend that young man against the celebrated writer's celebrated contempt. In the first place, the desire to get out of Pakistan, even temporarily, is one with which many people will sympathize. In the second and more important place, the thing that the young man wants—freedom of movement across frontiers—is, after all, a thing that Naipaul himself takes for granted, the very thing, in fact, that enables him to write the book in which the criticism is made.

I once spent a day at the immigration barriers at London's Heathrow Airport, watching the treatment of arriving passengers by immigration personnel. It did not amaze me to discover that most of the passengers who had some trouble getting past the control point were not white but black or Arab-looking. What was surprising is that there was one factor that overrode blackness or Arab looks. That factor was the possession of an American passport. Produce an American passport, and immigration officers at once become color-blind and wave you quickly on your way, however suspiciously non-Caucasian your features. To those to whom the world is closed, such openness is greatly to be desired. Those who assume that openness to be theirs by right perhaps value it less. When you have enough air to breathe, you don't yearn for air. But when breathable air gets to be in short supply, you quickly start noticing how important it is. (Freedom's like that, too.)

The reason I needed that first Indian passport, limited as its abilities were, was that eight weeks after I was born a new frontier came into being, and my family was cut in half by it. Midnight, August 13–14,

1947: the partition of the Indian subcontinent, and the creation of the new state of Pakistan, took place exactly twenty-four hours before the independence of the rest of the former British colony. India's moment of freedom was delayed on the advice of astrologers, who told Jawaharlal Nehru that the earlier date was star-crossed, and the delay would allow the birth to take place under a more auspicious midnight sky. Astrology has its limitations, however, and the creation of the new frontier ensured that the birth of both nations was hard and bloody. My own Indian Muslim family was fortunate. None of us was injured or killed in the Partition Massacres. But all our lives were changed, even the life of a boy of eight weeks and his as-yet-unborn sisters and his extant and future cousins and all our children, too. None of us are who we would have been if that line had not stepped across our land.

One of my uncles, my mother's younger sister's husband, was a soldier. At the time of Independence he was serving as an aide-de-camp to Field Marshal Sir Claude Auchinleck, commanding officer of the outgoing British Army in India. Auchinleck, known as the Auk, was a brilliant soldier. He had been responsible for the reconstruction of the British Eighth Army in North Africa after its defeats by Erwin Rommel, rebuilding its morale and forging it into a formidable fighting force; but he and Winston Churchill had never liked each other, so Churchill removed him from his African command and packed him off to oversee the sunset of Empire in India, allowing his replacement, Field Marshal Montgomery, to reap the glory of all Auchinleck's work, by defeating Rommel at El Alamein. Auchinleck was a rarity among World War II field marshals in that he resisted the temptation of publishing his memoirs, so this is a story that came down to me from my uncle, his ADC, who later became a general in the Pakistani Army and for a time a minister in the Pakistani government as well.

My uncle the general told another story, too, which created a ripple of interest when he published his own memoirs late in life. The Auk, he said, had been convinced that he could stop the Partition Massacres if he were allowed to intervene, and had approached Britain's prime minister, Clement Attlee, to ask for permission to do so. Attlee, rightly or wrongly, took the view that the period of British rule in India was over, that Auchinleck was there only in a transitional, consultative capacity, and should therefore do nothing. British troops were not to get involved in this purely Indo-Pakistani crisis. This inaction was the final act of the British in India. What Nehru and Jinnah would have felt about a British offer of help is not recorded. It is possible they would not have agreed. It is probable they were never asked. As for the dead, nobody can even agree on how many there were. One hundred thousand? Half a million? We can't be sure. Nobody was keeping score.

During my childhood years my parents, sisters, and I would sometimes travel between India and Pakistan—between Bombay and Karachi—always by sea. The steamers plying that route were a pair of old rust-buckets, the *Sabarmati* and the *Sarasvati*. The journey was hot and slow, and for mysterious reasons the boats would always stop for hours off the coast of the Rann of Kutch, while unexplained cargoes were ferried on and off: smugglers' goods, I imagined eagerly, gold, or precious stones. (I was too innocent to think of drugs.) When we reached Karachi, however, we entered a world far stranger than the smugglers' marshy, ambiguous Rann. It was always a shock for us Bombay kids, accustomed as we were to the easy cultural openness and diversity of our cosmopolitan hometown, to breathe the barren, desert air of Karachi, with its far more closed, blinkered monoculture. Karachi was boring. (This, of course, was before it turned into the gun-law metropolis it has now become, in which the army and police, or those soldiers and policemen who have not been bought off, worry that the city's criminals may well be better armed than they are. It's still boring, there's still nowhere to go and nothing to do, but now it's frightening as well.) Bombay and Karachi were so close to each other geographically, and my father, like many of his contemporaries, had gone back and forth between them all his life. Then, all of a sudden, after Partition, each city became utterly alien to the other.

As I grew older the distance between the two cities increased, as if the borderline created by Partition had cut through the landmass of South Asia as a taut wire cuts through a cheese, literally slicing Pakistan away from India, so that it could slowly float away across the Arabian Sea, the way the Iberian Peninsula floats away from Europe in José Saramago's novel *The Stone Raft*. In my childhood the whole family used to gather, once or twice a year, at my maternal grandparents' home in Aligarh, in the northern Indian state of Uttar Pradesh. These family gatherings held us together; but then my grandparents moved to Pakistan, the Aligarh house was lost, the gatherings ended, and the Indian and Pakistani branches of the family began to drift apart. When I met my Pakistani cousins I found, more and more, how unlike one another we had become, how different our basic assumptions were. It became easy to disagree; easier, for the sake of family peace, to hold one's tongue.

As a writer I've always thought myself lucky that, because of the accidents of my family life, I've grown up knowing something of both India and Pakistan. I have frequently found myself explaining Pakistani attitudes to Indians and vice versa, arguing against the prejudices that have grown more deeply ingrained on both sides as Pakistan has drifted further and further away across the sea. I can't say that my efforts have been blessed with much success, or indeed that I have been an entirely impartial arbiter. I hate the way in which we, Indians and Pakistanis, have become each other's others, each seeing the other as it were through a glass, darkly, each ascribing to the other the worst motives and the sneakiest natures. I hate it, but in the last analysis I'm on the Indian side.

—

One of my aunts was living in Karachi, Pakistan, at the time of Partition. She was a close friend of the famous Urdu poet Faiz Ahmed Faiz (1911–1984). Faiz was the first great writer I ever met, and through his oeuvre and his conversation he provided me with a description of the writer's job that I accepted fully. Faiz was an exceptional lyric poet, and his many *ghazals,* set to music, earned him literally millions of admirers, even though these were, often, strangely unromantic, disabused serenades:

> Do not ask of me, my love,
> that love I once had for you . . .
> How lovely you are still, my love,
> but I am helpless too;
> for the world has other sorrows than love,
> and other pleasures, too.
> Do not ask of me, my love,
> that love I once had for you.

He loved his country, too, but one of his best poems about it took, with lyrical disenchantment, the point of view of the alienated exile. This poem, translated by Agha Shahid Ali, was put up on posters in the New York subway a couple of years ago, to the delight of all those who love Urdu poetry:

> You ask me about that country whose details now escape me,
> I don't remember its geography, nothing of its history.
> And should I visit it in memory,
> It would be as I would a past lover,
> After years, for a night, no longer restless with passion,
>   with no fear of regret.
> I have reached that age when one visits the heart merely
>   as a courtesy.

An uncompromising poet of both romantic and patriotic love, Faiz was also a political figure and a very public writer, taking on the central issues of his time both inside and outside his poetry. This double-sided conception of the writer's role, part-private and part-public, part-oblique and part-direct, would, thanks in large part to the influence of Faiz's example, become mine as well. I did not share his political convictions, in particular his fondness for the Soviet Union, which gave him the Lenin Peace Prize in 1963, but I did quite naturally share his vision of what the writer's job is, or should be.

But all this was many years later. Back in 1947, Faiz might not have survived the riots that followed Partition had it not been for my aunt.

Faiz was not only a Communist but an outspoken unbeliever as well. In the days following the birth of a Muslim state, these were dangerous things to be, even for a much-loved poet. Faiz came to my aunt's house knowing that an angry mob was looking for him and that if they should find him, things would not go well. Under the rug in the sitting room there was a trapdoor leading down into a cellar. My aunt had the rug rolled back, Faiz descended into the cellar, the trapdoor closed, the rug rolled back. And when the mob came for the poet, they did not find him. Faiz was safe, although he went on provoking the authorities and the faithful with his ideas and his poems—draw a line in the sand and Faiz would feel intellectually obliged to step across it—and, as a result, in the early 1950s he was obliged to spend four years in Pakistani jails, which are not the most comfortable prisons in the world. Many years later I used the memory of the incident at my aunt's house as the inspiration for a chapter in *Midnight's Children,* but it's the real-life story of the real-life poet, or at any rate the story in the form it reached me by the not entirely reliable route of family legend, that has left the deeper impression on me.

As a young boy, too young to know or love Faiz's work, I loved the man instead: the warmth of his personality, the grave seriousness with which he paid attention to children, the twisted smile on his kindly Grandpa Munster face. It seemed to me back then, and it seems to me still, that whatever endangered him, I would emphatically oppose. If the Partition that created Pakistan had sent that mob to get him, then I was against it. Later, when I was old enough to approach the poems, I found confirmation there. In his poem "The Morning of Freedom," written in those numinous midnight hours of mid-August 1947, Faiz began:

> This stained light, this night-bitten dawn
> This is not the dawn we yearned for.

The same poem ends with a warning and an exhortation:

> The time for the liberation of heart and mind
> Has not come as yet.
> Continue your arduous journey.
> Press on, the destination is still far away.

The last time I saw Faiz was at my sister's wedding, and my final, gleeful memory of him is of the moment when, to the gasping horror of the more orthodox—and therefore puritanically teetotal—believers in the room, he proposed a toast to the newlyweds while raising high a cheery glass brimming with twelve-year-old Scotch whiskey on the rocks. When I think about Faiz and remember that good-natured, but quite deliberately transgressive incident, he looks to my mind's eye like a bridge between the literal and metaphorical worlds, or like a Virgil, showing us poor Dantes the way through Hell. It's as important, he seems to be saying as he knocks back his blasphemous whiskey, to cross metaphorical lines as it is to cross actual ones: not to be contained or defined by anybody else's idea of where a line should be drawn.

———

The crossing of borders, of language, geography, and culture; the examination of the permeable frontier between the universe of things and deeds and the universe of the imagination; the lowering of the intolerable frontiers created by the world's many different kinds of Thought Policemen: these matters have been at the heart of the literary project that was given to me by the circumstances of my life, rather than chosen by me for intellectual or "artistic" reasons. Born into one language,

Urdu, I've made my life and work in another. Anyone who has crossed a language frontier will readily understand that such a journey involves a form of shape-shifting or self-translation. The change of language changes us. All languages permit slightly varying forms of thought, imagination, and play. I find my tongue doing slightly different things with Urdu than I do "with," to borrow the title of a story by Hanif Kureishi, "your tongue down my throat."

The greatest writer ever to make a successful journey across the language frontier, Vladimir Nabokov, enumerated, in his "Note on Translation," the "three grades of evil [that] can be discerned in the strange world of verbal transmigration."* He was talking about the translation of books and poems, but when as a young writer I was thinking about how to "translate" the great subject of India into English, how to allow India itself to perform the act of "verbal transmigration," the Nabokovian "grades of evil" seemed to apply.

"The first, and lesser one, comprises obvious errors due to ignorance or misguided knowledge," Nabokov wrote. "This is mere human frailty and thus excusable." Western works of art that dealt with India were riddled with such mistakes. To name just two: the scene in David Lean's film of *A Passage to India* in which he makes Dr. Aziz leap onto Fielding's bed and cross his legs *while keeping his shoes on,* a solecism that would make any Indian wince; and the even more unintentionally hilarious scene in which Alec Guinness, as Godbole, sits by the edge of the sacred tank in a Hindu temple *and dangles his feet in the water.*

"The next step to Hell," Nabokov says, "is taken by the translator who skips words or passages that he does not bother to understand or that might seem obscure or obscene to vaguely imagined readers." For a long time, or so I felt, almost the whole of the multifarious Indian reality was "skipped" in this way by writers who were uninterested in anything except Western experiences of India—English girls falling for maharajas, or being assaulted, or not being assaulted, by non-maharajas, in nocturnal gardens, or mysteriously echoing caves—written up in a coolly classical Western manner. But of course most experiences of India are Indian experiences of it, and if there is one thing India is not, it is cool and classical. India is hot and vulgar, I thought, and it needed a literary "translation" in keeping with its true nature.

* In *Lectures on Russian Literature,* 1981.

The third and worst crime of translation, in Nabokov's opinion, was that of the translator who sought to improve on the original, "vilely beautifying" it "in such a fashion as to conform to the notions and prejudices of a given public." The exoticization of India, its "vile beautification," is what Indians have disliked most. Now, at last, this kind of fake glamorizing is coming to an end, and the India of elephants, tigers, peacocks, emeralds, and dancing girls is being laid to rest. A generation of gifted Indian writers in English is bringing into English their many different versions of the Indian reality, and these many versions, taken together, are beginning to add up to something that one might call the truth.

In dreams begin responsibilities. The way we see the world affects the world we see. As our ideas of female beauty change, so we see different sorts of women as beautiful. As our ideas of healthy living change, so we begin to look at the things we eat differently. Our dreams of our own and our children's future shape the everyday judgments we make, about work, about people, about the world that either enables or obstructs those dreams. Daily life in the real world is also an imagined life. The creatures of our imagination crawl out from our heads, cross the frontier between dream and reality, between shadow and act, and become actual.

Imagination's monsters do the same thing. The attack on the World Trade Center was essentially a monstrous act of the imagination, intended to act upon all our imaginations, to shape our own imaginings of the future. It was an iconoclastic act, in which the defining icons of the modern, the world-shrinking airplanes and those soaring secular cathedrals, the tall buildings, were rammed into each other in order to send a message: that the modern world itself was the enemy, and would be destroyed. It may seem unimaginable to us, but to those who perpetrated this crime, the deaths of many thousands of innocent people were a side issue. Murder was not the point. The creation of a meaning was the point. The terrorists of September 11, and the planners of that day's events, behaved like perverted, but in another way brilliantly transgressive, performance artists: hideously innovative, shockingly successful, using a low-tech attack to strike at the very heart of our high-tech world. In dreams begin irresponsibilities, too.

I am trying to talk about literature and ideas, but you see that I keep being dragged back to catastrophe. Like every writer in the world, I am trying to find a way of writing after September 11, 2001, a day that has become something like a borderline. Not only because the attacks were a kind of invasion but because we all crossed a frontier that day, an invisible boundary between the imaginable and the unimaginable, and it turned out to be the unimaginable that was real. On the other side of that frontier, we find ourselves facing a moral problem: how should a civilized society—in which, as in all civilizations, there are limits, things we will not do, or allow to be done in our name, because we consider them beyond the pale, unacceptable—respond to an attack by people for whom there are no limits at all, people who will, quite literally, do anything—blow off their own feet, or tilt the wings of an airplane just before it hits a tower, so that it takes out the maximum number of floors?

———

> The evil that men do lives after them,
> the good is oft interrèd with their bones.

It is not surprising that the word "evil" has been used a great deal these past months; perhaps too often. The terrorists became "the evil-doers," their leader became "the evil one," and now comes the discovery of that unusual phenomenon, an "axis of evil," on which the president of the United States is threatening to make war. It's an oddly contradictory word, "evil," too freighted with absolute meaning to be an appropriate description of the messy relativity of actuality, too debased by over-use to mean as much as it should. Thus the comedy website SatireWire.com reveals that

> bitter after being snubbed for membership in the Axis of Evil, Libya, China, and Syria today announced that they had formed the Axis of Just as Evil, which they said would be way eviler than that stupid Iran–Iraq–North Korea axis. Cuba, Sudan, and Serbia said they had formed the Axis of Somewhat Evil, forcing Somalia to join with Uganda and Myanmar in the Axis of Occasionally Evil, while Bulgaria, Indonesia, and Russia established the Axis of Not So Much Evil Really as Just Generally Disagreeable. Sierra Leone, El Salvador, and Rwanda applied to be called the Axis of Countries That Aren't the Worst but Certainly Won't Be Asked to Host the Olympics; Canada, Mexico, and Australia formed the Axis of Nations That Are Actually Quite Nice but Secretly Have Nasty Thoughts About America, while

Spain, Scotland, and New Zealand established the Axis of Countries That Sometimes Ask Sheep to Wear Lipstick.

"That's not a threat, really, just something we like to do," said Scottish Executive First Minister Jack McConnell.

I wish, myself, that the president had not promised to "rid the world of evil"—that's a big project, a war he probably can't win. "Evil" is a term that can obscure as well as clarify. For me, the greatest difficulty with it is that it dehistoricizes these events, depoliticizes, and even depersonalizes them. If evil is the devil's work, and in this deeply religious administration one must assume that many people in high places think it is, then that, to my unbeliever's way of thinking, actually lets the terrorists off the hook. If evil is external to us, a force working upon us from outside ourselves, then our moral responsibility for its effects is diminished.

The most attractive thing about the Shakespearean attitude to evil is its emphasis on human, not divine, responsibility for it. "The evil *that men do,*" Mark Antony says, and that's the only kind that interests Shakespeare. The conspirators in *Julius Caesar* are obsessed with omens and auguries. "Never till now," says Casca,

> Did I go through a tempest dropping fire.
> Either there is a civil strife in heaven,
> Or else the world, too saucy with the gods,
> Incenses them to send destruction.

And that's not all.

> Men all in fire walk up and down the streets.
> And yesterday the bird of night did sit,
> Even at noon-day, upon the market-place,
> Hooting and shrieking. When these prodigies
> Do so conjointly meet, let not men say
> "These are their reasons, they are natural";
> For, I believe, they are portentous things
> Unto the climate that they point upon.

The conspirators talk themselves into believing that the omens and portents, the signs from the gods, justify, even necessitate, their crime.

To read the transcript of the so-called smoking-gun bin Laden video-tape, the notorious "giggling" video in which he laughs about his crimes and the deaths of his own men, is to be struck by the similarities between the mind-set of Al-Qaida and that of Caesar's murderers. The tape is full of talk about prophetic dreams and visions. Bin Laden himself says: "Abu al-Hasan al-Masri told me a year ago: 'I saw in a dream, we were playing a soccer game against the Americans. When our team showed up in the field, they were all pilots!' He said the game went on and we defeated them. So that was a good omen for us." Or, again: "This brother came close and told me that he saw, in a dream, a tall building in America. . . . I was worried that maybe the secret would be revealed if everyone starts seeing it in their dream." At this point, on the tape, another person's voice is heard recounting yet another dream about two planes hitting a big building.

Dreams and omens are murderers' exculpations. Shakespeare knew better. It is again Casca, portent-ridden Casca, who speaks: "The fault, dear Brutus, lies not in the stars, / but in ourselves, that we are underlings." He's talking about the need for a coup. But after the assassination, we forget the final clause; it is the first part of the couplet, the part about responsibility for one's own actions, whose truth we are made to feel. "The fault, dear Brutus, lies not in the stars, / but in ourselves." It is Shakespeare's genius to put in the mouth of an assassin the very thought that will damn him afterward. Shakespeare doesn't believe in the devil's work. In the last scene of *Othello,* when the Moor finally learns how he has been duped by Iago, he says, "I look down towards his feet; but that's a fable." No cloven hoofs protrude from the villain's hose. "If that thou be'st a devil, I cannot kill thee." The world is real. There are no demons. Men are demonic enough.

The evil that men do, in Shakespeare, is always a kind of excess. It has to do with the denial of limits, the willingness to cross any moral frontier. Goneril and Regan, Lady Macbeth, Iago: for them, the end justifies everything. *By any means necessary.* Whereas Hamlet is the opposite: a man so beset by moral qualms that it takes him an eternity to act. The great question of action and the frontiers of action—how far can we go? How far is too far, how far is not far enough?—is at the heart of Shakespeare's world; also, now, of ours.

The problem of limits is made awkward for artists and writers, including myself, by our own adherence to, and insistence upon, a no-limits position in our own work. The frontierlessness of art has been and remains our heady ideology. The concept of transgressive art is so widely accepted—"if it isn't transgressive, it isn't underground"—as to constitute, in the eyes of conservative critics, a new orthodoxy. Once the new was shocking not because it set out to shock but because it set out to be new. Now, all too often, the shock *is* the new; and shock, in our jaded culture, wears off easily. Like the children in the Disney movie *Monsters, Inc.,* we don't scare as easily as we used to. So the artist who seeks to shock must try harder and harder, go further and further, and this escalation may now have become the worst kind of artistic self-indulgence. And now, in the aftermath of horror, of the iconoclastically transgressive image-making of the terrorists, do artists and writers still have the right to insist on the supreme, unfettered freedoms of art? Is it time, instead of endlessly pushing the envelope, stepping into forbidden territory, and generally causing trouble, to start discovering what frontiers might be necessary to art, rather than an affront to it?

The British writer (and lawyer) Anthony Julius addresses such questions in a new book, *Transgressions: The Offences of Art.* Dealing mainly, but not only, with the visual arts, he valuably reminds us of the word's arrival in English in the sixteenth century, "freighted with negative scriptural overtones," and its rapid acquisition of other layers of meaning: "rule-breaking, including the violation of principles, conventions, pieties, or taboos; the giving of serious offence; and the exceeding, erasing or disordering of physical or conceptual boundaries." He examines the transgressive art of Edouard Manet in the 1860s; in *Olympia,* a picture of a whore to which Manet gave a name often used by the whores of the period, he visited the frontier between art and "pornography"— which literally means "whore-painting," and is another new word hailing from the same epoch—crossing the boundaries between the nude (an aesthetic, unerotic idea) and the naked woman, gazing out of the picture with frankly erotic intent. In *Dead Christ with Angels,* Manet questioned the resurrection, and the painting caused great offense. Even *Le Déjeuner sur l'herbe* was accused of "transgressing the laws both of perspective and morality." Now that time has installed Manet and his great contemporaries as the art world's blue-chip masterworkers, we have one answer to those who would reimpose limits on art: which is, that one age's pornography is another's masterpiece. In 1857, after all, *Madame Bovary* so outraged conventional, decent people that Flaubert was prosecuted for writing it. Guardians of the frontiers of public morality should always beware, lest history make them look like fools.

Julius rightly credits the twentieth-century French writer Georges Bataille with the formulation of much of our modern idea of the transgressive. It is interesting, however, that Bataille believed that the breaking of taboos was both a necessity and a "reinscription" of the violated border. "Transgressions suspend taboos without suppressing them." Julia Kristeva amplifies this: "The issue of ethics crops up wherever a code must be shattered in order to give way to the free play of negativity, need, desire, pleasure, and jouissance, before being put together again, although temporarily." Here, then, is a second possible answer to the would-be censors in our new, more timorous age: artworks, unlike terrorists, change nothing.

On the five defenses of art, Julius is excellent: the First Amendment defense; the "aesthetic alibi"—"art is a privileged zone in which the otherwise unsayable can be said"; the "estrangement defence" (it is the job of art . . . to alienate us from our preconceptions, by making the familiar strange and the unquestioned problematic); the "canonic defence" (works of art exist in a tradition of such works and must be judged and understood in relation to that tradition); and the "formalist defence" (that art has its own distinct mode of existence and is not to be confused with cognate but distinct works of the imagination, such as propaganda and polemic). As someone who has had some experience of transgression and its consequences, I have at different times employed all these defenses, as Julius is kind enough to note. He concludes, however, that "the aesthetic potential of the transgressive has been exhausted." In this I am not sure he is right.

Even before the attacks on America, I was concerned that, in Britain and Europe as well as America, the pressures on artistic and even intellectual freedoms were growing—that cautious, conservative political and institutional forces were gaining the upper hand, and that many social groups were deliberately fostering a new, short-fuse culture of easy offendedness, so that less and less was becoming sayable all the time, and more and more kinds of speech were being categorized as transgressive. Outside the Western world—across the Arab world, in many African countries, in Iran, China, North Korea, and elsewhere— writers and intellectuals are everywhere under attack, and more and more of them are being forced into exile. If it was important to resist this cultural closing-in before 9/11, it's twice as important now. The freedoms of art and the intellect are closely related to the general freedoms of society as a whole. The struggle for artistic freedom serves to crystallize the larger question that we were all asked when the planes hit the buildings: how should we live now? How uncivilized are we going to allow our own world to become in response to so barbaric an assault?

We are living, I believe, in a frontier time, one of the great hinge periods in human history, in which great changes are coming about at great speed. On the plus side, the end of the Cold War, the revolution in communications technology, great scientific achievements such as the completion of the Human Genome Project; in the minus column, a new kind of war against new kinds of enemies fighting with terrible new weapons. We will all be judged by how we handle ourselves in this time. What will be the spirit of this frontier? Will we give the enemy the satisfaction of changing ourselves into something like his hate-filled, illiberal mirror-image, or will we, as the guardians of the modern world, as the custodians of freedom and the occupants of the privileged lands of plenty, go on trying to increase freedom and decrease injustice? Will we become the suits of armor our fear makes us put on, or will we continue to be ourselves? The frontier both shapes our character and tests our mettle. I hope we pass the test.

February 2002

ACKNOWLEDGMENTS

In addition to those journals and institutions already acknowl-
edged during the course of this book, I must particularly thank
Gloria B. Anderson and her team at *The New York Times,* who syn-
dicated all the columns collected in Part III; and *The New Yorker,*
where nine of these pieces first appeared in print: "Out of Kansas"
(also published as a British Film Institute booklet, "The Wizard of
Oz"); "In Defense of the Novel, Yet Again"; "Reservoir Frogs";
"Heavy Threads"; "On Leavened Bread"; "Crash"; "The People's
Game"; "Damme, This Is the Oriental Scene for You!"; and "A
Dream of Glorious Return." "Step Across This Line" was written
for, and first delivered as, the 2002 Tanner Lectures on Human
Values at Yale. "In the Voodoo Lounge" originally appeared in
The Observer, and "U2" was first published in the *Sunday Times.*
"The Best of Young British Novelists" and "Beirut Blues" ap-
peared in *The Independent on Sunday.* "On Being Photographed"
appeared (in French translation) in *Egoïste.* Many thanks to
Richard Avedon and to Nicole Wisniak, publisher and editor of
Egoïste, for allowing the Avedon portrait of me to be reproduced in
this book. And to Article 19, especially Frances D'Souza and
Carmel Bedford, who led the Rushdie Defence Campaign; to all
those who participated in the Rushdie Defence Committees in
various countries, to all those writers, publishers, booksellers,
readers, politicians, diplomats, security officers, and well-wishers
who joined us in the struggle, I offer deeper gratitude than I have
words to express.

S.R.

INDEX

SALMAN RUSHDIE is the author of eight novels: *Grimus, Midnight's Children* (for which he won the Booker Prize and the "Booker of Bookers"), *Shame, The Satanic Verses, Haroun and the Sea of Stories, The Moor's Last Sigh, The Ground Beneath Her Feet,* and *Fury,* and one work of short stories, *East, West*. He has also published four works of nonfiction: *The Jaguar Smile, Imaginary Homelands, The Wizard of Oz,* and *Mirrorwork*.

ABOUT THE TYPE

This book was set in Bembo, a typeface based on an old-
style Roman face that was used for Cardinal Bembo's
tract *De Aetna* in 1495. Bembo was cut by Francisco
Griffo in the early sixteenth century. The Lanston
Monotype Company of Philadelphia brought the well-
proportioned letterforms of Bembo to the United
States in the 1930s.